Coercive Commerce

Coercive Commerce

Global Capital and Imperial Governance at the End of the Qing Empire

Stacie A. Kent

Hong Kong University Press
The University of Hong Kong
Pok Fu Lam Road
Hong Kong
https://hkupress.hku.hk

© 2025 Hong Kong University Press

ISBN 978-988-8876-75-4 (*Hardback*)

All rights reserved. No portion of this publication may be reproduced or transmitted in any form or by any means, electronic or mechanical, including photocopying, recording, or any information storage or retrieval system, without prior permission in writing from the publisher.

British Library Cataloguing-in-Publication Data
A catalogue record for this book is available from the British Library.

Digitally printed

For fellow travelers

Contents

List of Figures and Table	viii
Acknowledgments	ix
Note on Romanization, Translation, and Place Names	xi
Introduction	1
1. Calling Forth Governance: Treaties and Coercion on the China Coast	23
2. Institutional Structures for Capital Growth	55
3. Disorderly Order	87
4. Not All Commerce Is Capitalism	116
5. Boundary Struggles: Treaties, Taxation, and the Erasure of Difference	141
6. Experiments for the Future	180
Conclusion	216
Appendix	227
Bibliography	229
Index	253

Figures and Table

Figures

Figure 2.1: Imperial Maritime Customs Quarterly Revenue and Expenditure Form, issued May 1862	66
Figure 3.1: Ports with IMC operations, 1861	97
Figure 3.2: Ports with IMC operations, 1911	97
Figure 3.3: Footprint of foreign goods in Jiangxi Province, 1874	101
Figure 4.1: Regional specialization of sail shipping, early twentieth-century China	120
Figure 5.1: Map showing location of Jiujiang and shared borders for Anhui, Hubei, Jiangsu, Jiangxi, and Zhejiang provinces	157
Figure 5.2: Comparative table of barrier charges (*lijin*) and (treaty) transit duties	160
Figure 5.3: Table of *lijin* levies on imports and exports	161
Figure 6.1: Government borrowing, 1865–1912	200
Figure 6.2: Purpose of government borrowing, 1865–1912	200

Table

Table 1.1: Port charges levied in Guangzhou, ca. 1730	48

Acknowledgments

My work on this book began over a decade ago as research for my PhD dissertation at the University of Chicago. As such, it is the product of innumerable intellectual debts. Foremost among these are the formative conversations I had with James Hevia and Moishe Postone. I was fortunate enough to meet Jim as an undergraduate at the University of North Carolina, where our discussions about orientalism, imperialism, and China studies forever shifted how I think about history and the present. Our reunion at Chicago was both unanticipated and fortuitous. As a PhD student at Chicago, I benefited from Moishe's extraordinary commitment to teaching. My reading of Marx is deeply indebted to his graduate seminar on *Capital* as well as the many enlivening staff meetings he led of the "Self, Culture, and Society" Core in The College.

The world I inhabited at Chicago was intensely intellectual, often combative, and always sincere. To the participants of the Social Theory Workshop, East Asia Transregional History Workshop, and the short-lived Empires and Colonies Workshop as well as to cohorts of Harper-Schmidt Fellows, I offer my profound thanks for many pleasurable hours of learning and discussion. As a first-year student, Bill Sewell took me under his wing as a research assistant, and he remains today an inspirational and much appreciated interlocuter. Inside and outside the classroom, I benefited from the intellect and generosity of Jun-Hyung Chae, Paul Cheney, Bruce Cumings, Prasenjit Duara, Parker Everett, Larisa Jasarevic, Reha Kadakal, Kenneth Pomeranz, Song Nianshen, Robert Stern, Limin Teh, and Jake Werner. My special thanks to Mark Bradley for lessons in the importance of authorial voice, to Michael Rossi for questions about what a machine was in the nineteenth century, and to Judith Farquhar for taking seriously my thoughts about the emotional lives of Qing officials.

Material support for this project came from the University of Chicago Social Sciences Division and History Department. A Social Sciences Divisional Achievement Fellowship supported coursework and preliminary research. Eric Cochrane and Kunstadter travel grants from the Department of History funded research trips to London and Shanghai. Additional research funding was provided by the Nicholson Center for British Studies. The University of Chicago Center for East Asian Studies and the Doris Quinn Foundation generously funded the dissertation write-up. Anwen Tormey at the Chicago Center for Contemporary Theory provided a "room of one's own" when it was sorely needed. Last but not least, I should acknowledge the unintentional but still generous research funding provided by the dining publics of Citizen Bar, Sepia, Fred's, and Elate. Without you, this project would have remained only an idea.

Much of the material in this project was presented at seminars and conferences in the United States, Britain, Canada, France, Denmark, China, India, and Taiwan. For these opportunities, I would like to thank Robert Bickers at the University of Bristol, Matheus Duarte da Silva at the University of St. Andrews, Soren Ivarsson at the University of Copenhagen, Viren Murthy at the University of Wisconsin, Lukas Rieppel at Brown University, Tad Skotnicki at the University of North Carolina, Greensboro, and the University of Chicago Paris Center. These gatherings facilitated invaluable discussions. Over the years, I also benefited from conversations—sometimes casual, sometimes less so—with many researchers both in and far outside of the China field. Although it is impossible now for me to recall them all, I would like to acknowledge Alvaro Santana-Acuña, Tani Barlow, Pär Cassel, Meghna Chaudhuri, Douglas Howland, Macabe Keliher, and Peter Thilly. Pat Giersch provided helpful comments on a draft of Chapter 4 presented at the Harvard Global Capitalism Seminar, organized by Sven Beckert. Judit Bodnar, Jon Levy, and Andrew Sartori have provided timely interventions when they were greatly needed. I have also been fortunate to have supportive colleagues at Boston College. These include Julian Borg, Nicole Eaton, Devin Pendas, Prasannan Parthasarathi, Franziska Seraphim, and Conevery Valencius. I especially thank Angie Picone for her tireless friendship.

Over the years, my approach to the materials that make up this book has changed. Earlier versions were much more indebted to engagements with theories of imperialism and colonial modernity, the histories of political economy and free trade in England, the development of international law, Bruno Latour's work on "immutable mobiles," and Foucault's writings on governmentality. These engagements, while less visible here, are nonetheless part of the bedrock upon which I built this book. I would also like to acknowledge the generosity of James Vernon, who graciously allowed me to sit in on his graduate seminar at Berkeley when I was first considering a PhD project. It was in conversation with him that it first seemed possible and necessary to write a different history about British trade in China.

Finally, my thanks to Aaron Hill whose own intellectual engagements have helped sharpen mine and whose enthusiasm for stories about paperwork and taxes has, over the years, always been a pleasant surprise.

Note on Romanization, Translation, and Place Names

When British consular officers in China produced many of the archival documents used in this study, there was no standard system of romanization for the Chinese language. This book uses of a number of Qing government communications recorded, in translation, in the British Foreign Office archives. These are noted as such. In all cases, I attempted to find Chinese-language originals. When these were available, I have amended the Legation translation or provided my own based on the Chinese text. To minimize irregularity, wherever possible, I have updated the romanization to pinyin, except in the document titles where maintaining the original will aid in location.

Also wherever possible, I have used current-day place names for ports and towns in China. At times, it was impossible to correlate the nonstandard romanization used in archival documents with historical or current-day place names. In these cases, I have left the original name in quotation marks.

To aid readers who wish to pursue their own study of China's treaty ports using English or Chinese-language materials, the Appendix provides a table listing for each treaty port open in 1911 its historical English-language name, present-day romanized name, and Chinese-character name. Geolocation information is also provided.

There are a few irregularities introduced by my choice to use present-day place names. The treaty port of "Newchwang" was never actually located in present-day Niuzhuang (牛莊). Instead, foreign trade took place at the port of Yingkou (營口), which was more accessible to foreign ships. English-language use never marked this changed location, likely because it would have admitted trade was happening outside the explicitly designated location. I use Yingkou in the text and Niuzhuang or Newchwang when dealing with English-language primary sources.

Trade at the treaty port of "Chefoo," otherwise known as Yantai (煙台), was likewise originally designated for elsewhere—nearby Dengzhou (鄧州), today's Penglai (蓬萊). I use Yantai to refer to the port but keep "Chefoo Convention" to refer to the Sino-British treaty.

Introduction

In some ways, research for this book began with a single piece of paper that rests in the British Foreign Office archives at Kew. The paper is an imposing size (nearly 21 inches in height) and is covered in large Chinese characters.[1] But, it is not, as its residence might suggest, a diplomatic communication or a government proclamation issued in the name of the emperor of China. It is, rather, a more quotidian record—a customs receipt that accompanied import and export goods as they traveled the Qing Empire's waterways. Even more, one cannot say it is a singular record of an eventful moment. It is a form, retained by British officials in China because it represented many more like it. Most specifically, the form is a transit pass, a document with a limited purpose: to record duties paid to the Qing Imperial Maritime Customs, and to in turn free those duty-paid goods from further taxation. The simplicity of transit pass, further research uncovered, disguised a much more complicated history.

The transit pass is an entry point into two interconnected histories. One is a history of capital. The other is a history of Qing governance. For a time in the latter half of the nineteenth century, how capital circulated and expanded and how officials of the Qing Empire policed and taxed commerce intersected in destructive and regenerative ways. One purpose of this book is to reconstruct these interactions. Along the way, it has two central concerns. One is the historical significance of regulatory features that seem, at first glance, like the transit pass, commonsensical. The other is Qing policies and actions that seem, at first glance, obstructive. Last, this book is about how commerce and its governance looked different depending on whether their purpose was the circulation of useful things or the growth of value.

It is not much of an overstatement to say that the transit pass is the most infamous paperwork in the history of Sino-British relations. As one of several tools developed to implement treaty privileges granted to Euro-American merchants, transit passes generated decades of administrative confusion, mercantile ire, and diplomatic impasse. But the transit pass is historically significant for other reasons

---

1. FO 682/1168/1-3, The National Archives (hereafter TNA).

as well. It was among a handful of nineteenth-century technologies, including the steamship and telegraph, designed to speed up and cheapen global commodity circulation during an era of unprecedented expansion in world trade, built on the back of industrial production.[2]

Regulatory frameworks typically garner little attention from historians of global economic integration, but my purposes here are somewhat different. First, I am interested in better understanding how Qing governance changed under the framework of commercial treaties. An instrument like the transit pass marks a discontinuity between a concrete art of governance, which took measures to support the circulation of strategically important goods, to provide relief to suffering populations, or to not overburden those who lived on the margins and an art of governance that facilitated commercial circulation itself, which as a social good was largely abstracted from any particular use values or livelihoods.[3] This shift in governance is a key concern of this book. Second, I am interested in better understanding why commercial treaties and the regulatory apparatus built to implement them looked and functioned the way they did. In the following sections of this introduction, I will unpack some of the key assumptions in existing scholarship on the role of foreign commerce in Chinese history, on the Qing "treaty port era," and on the practice of Qing governance after 1842, and drawing from my critical engagement with them, I will indicate the ways in which this book takes a different approach.

Foreign Commerce in China: "A Fly on an Elephant"?

Commercial treaties with Euro-American states, which the Qing government signed in the dozens between 1842 and 1901, were a late chapter in imperial China's commercial history. When European maritime trading companies first arrived in

---

2. Recent histories of the nineteenth-century expansion of global trade include Jürgen Osterhammel, *The Transformation of the World: A Global History of the Nineteenth Century* (Princeton: Princeton University Press, 2014), chap. 14; Steven C. Topik and Allen Wells, "Commodity Chains in a Global Economy," in *A World Connecting, 1870–1945*, ed. Emily S. Rosenberg (Cambridge, MA: Harvard University Press, 2012), 593–812. Alternative perspectives offered by earlier scholarship include Immanuel Wallerstein's world systems theory and Eric Hobsbawm, *The Age of Capital, 1848–1875* (New York: Vintage, 1996). On East Asia's role in particular, see Giovanni Arrighi, Takeshi Hamashita, and Mark Selden, eds., *The Resurgence of East Asia: 500, 150, and 50 Year Perspectives* (New York: Routledge, 2003); Takeshi Hamashita, *China, East Asia and the Global Economy: Regional and Historical Perspectives*, ed. Linda Grove and Mark Selden (New York: Routledge, 2008).

3. On Qing customs operations, see Yuping Ni, *Customs Duties in the Qing Dynasty, ca. 1644–1911* (Leiden: Brill, 2017) and Qi Meiqin, 清代權關制度研究 [Research on the Qing customs system] (Hohot: Nei meng gu da xue, 2004). For examples of tax remissions during the Qianlong reign, see Helen Dunstan, *State or Merchant: Political Economy and the Political Process in 1740s China* (Cambridge, MA: Harvard University Press, 2006), 107, 396.

southern China in the sixteenth century, they anchored at the edge of a vast territory with well-developed internal and external commercial networks. For at least a millennia, Chinese producers and traders had been important participants in the creation and growth of merchant capital around the world. Between the sixteenth century and the advent of the "treaty era" (ca. 1842) that participation intensified. China became a "sink" for New World silver, brought by European traders seeking silk and tea. Qing emperors lifted a long-standing Ming-era ban on maritime trade, which allowed the "Nanyang" (southern sea) trade to swell with ever larger ships and more voyages.[4] Then, in the eighteenth century, increasingly large shipments of opium from India created a new pattern of global economic integration with China at its heart.[5]

Conditioning and reinforcing all this trade were two commercial and financial revolutions in China—the first in the eleventh century Song dynasty (960–1279) and then again in the sixteenth century during Ming rule (1368–1644). During these periods of intense market growth, the size and number of handicraft workshops grew, farmers sold more of their crops, and urban populations swelled, fed by long-distance domestic trade in grain, cloth, and salt as well as by a monetized economy that paid wages to artisans and urban service professions. From at least the mid-Ming dynasty onward, even peasants outside urban economies were often "at least partly dependent on the market for their household grain," and earned currency through the sale of surplus cloth woven within the household. Meanwhile, domestic capital networks, organized through familial or native place ties, provided banking and credit that facilitated interregional trade.[6] In one scholar's summation, apart from its connections with foreign trade, "late imperial China had its own large-scale economic networks, which created integrated macro regions larger than most countries."[7]

---

4. Gang Zhao, *The Qing Opening to the Ocean: Chinese Maritime Policies, 1684–1757* (Honolulu: University of Hawai'i Press, 2013); Ng Chin-Keong, *Trade and Society: The Amoy Network on the China Coast, 1683–1735* (Singapore: Singapore University Press, 1983).

5. Carl Trocki, *Opium, Empire, and the Global Political Economy: A Study of the Asian Opium Trade* (London: Routledge, 1999).

6. Dunstan, *State or Merchant*, 4; William Guanglin Liu, *The Chinese Market Economy, 1000–1500* (Albany: State University of New York Press, 2015); K. C. Liu, *China's Early Modernization and Reform Movement: Studies in Late Nineteenth-Century China and American-Chinese Relations* (Taipei: Institute of Modern History, Academia Sinica, 2009), 40; William Rowe, *Hankow: Commerce and Society in a Chinese City, 1796–1889* (Stanford: Stanford University Press, 1984), 52–62; Wu Chengming, Introduction to *Chinese Capitalism, 1522–1840*, ed. Xu Dixin and Wu Chengming, trans. Li Zhengde, Liang Miaoru, and Li Siping (New York: St. Martin's, 2000), 1–22; Zhaojin Ji, *A History of Modern Shanghai Banking: The Rise and Decline of China's Finance Capitalism* (Armonk: M. E. Sharpe, 2003).

7. Kenneth Pomeranz, *The Making of a Hinterland: State, Society, and Economy in Inland North China, 1853–1937* (Berkeley: University of California Press, 1993), 1, citing G. William Skinner, "Cities

This domestic commercial activity, about which a substantial and growing literature exists, provides critical context for foreign merchant activity in China. The tea sought by British traders in the eighteenth and nineteenth centuries had been a well-established cash crop since the eighth century, when an interregional market for it first developed in China.[8] At the treaty port of Hankou ("among the largest urban places in the world" after 1850), key exports to foreign markets, including hides, tung oil, hemp, iron ore, and coal, originated within "an intensely active marketing system spanning thousands of miles."[9] Even the unwanted opium trade depended on an opportunistic network of Fujianese brokers, who integrated opium into their existing transport business in rice, sugar, and cotton.[10] After treaties granted Euro-American merchants more trading privileges in China, most commerce through Chinese ports continued to service domestic markets.

The relative size and impact of Chinese commercial activity and Euro-American commercial activity in China has been an important point of conversation for historians in the China field. Some of the earliest field-defining scholarship of the Cold War era examined the Qing Empire's "response" to treaties, foreign merchants, and Western industry.[11] Early economic histories, in particular, focused almost exclusively on the Chinese littoral touched by the treaty regime and foreign capital.[12] The field's first engagements with questions of imperialism, likewise, focused on treaty ports, foreign actors, and unequal commercial privileges.[13] As a corrective, in the past forty years, "China-centered" research has both created distance between the study of China and the study of Euro-American presence

---

and the Hierarchy of Local Systems," in *The City in Late Imperial China*, ed. G. William Skinner (Stanford: Stanford University Press, 1977), 273–351. An important caveat to add is that although the absolute levels of commercial activity in Qing China were undeniably high, current scholarly consensus holds that commercial expansion alone was not capable of producing sustained real economic growth. For a recent summary of this position, see Christopher Isett, "China: The Start of the Great Divergence," in *The Cambridge Economic History of the Modern World*, ed. Stephen Broadberry and Kyoji Fukao (Cambridge: Cambridge University Press, 2021), 1:97–122.

8. Robert Gardella, *Harvesting Mountains: Fujian and the China Tea Trade, 1757–1937* (Berkeley: University of California Press, 1994), 23.
9. Rowe, *Hankow*, 1, 82–83.
10. Peter Thilly, *The Opium Business: A History of Crime and Capitalism in Maritime China* (Stanford: Stanford University Press, 2022), 24–26.
11. Paul A. Cohen, *Discovering History in China: American Historical Writing of the Recent Chinese Past* (New York: Columbia University Press, 1984), 9–12.
12. For example, Albert Feuerwerker, *The Chinese Economy, ca. 1870–1911* (Ann Arbor: Michigan Papers in Chinese Studies, 1969); Albert Feuerwerker, *China's Early Industrialization: Sheng Hsuan-Huai (1844–1916) and Mandarin Enterprise* (Cambridge, MA: Harvard University Press, 1970).
13. For a programmatic, if critical, survey of the scope of such inquiries, see Andrew Nathan, "Imperialism's Effects on China," *Bulletin of Concerned Asian Scholars* 4, no. 4 (1872): 3–8.

there and documented Chinese merchant operations of remarkable breadth and sophistication.[14]

Much of this more recent work has argued that in China's extensive nineteenth-century commercial world, the influence of foreign trade and traders was minimal. In his landmark social history of the Yangzi trading center Hankou, William Rowe concluded, "Not only were Western traders isolated from the greater portion of the production and marketing process, but Chinese parties to the trade were likewise isolated from both the personal influence of the foreigners and from any significant awareness that a shift to a foreign market may have occurred."[15] For Rowe, foreign trade was a derivative and peripheral economic activity, and even so, it was dominated by Chinese firms. Interestingly, although Rowe downplayed Hankou's status as a treaty port, his conclusion that foreign trade was not all that important echoed a conclusion offered by earlier scholarship intently focused on the treaty ports. Using a very different source base and with different goals in mind, Rhoads Murphey famously proposed treaty ports and foreign presence in China were "like a fly on an elephant"—an irritant—"but not enough to change the elephant's basic nature."[16]

Historiography of Treaty-Era Commerce

To be sure, we have little reason to think that the Euro-American import-export trade played anything more than the most minimal role in the daily existence of the majority of Qing subjects—if that. Yet, other veins of research have countered that despite its relative size, the fly did change the elephant's behavior. At the very least, treaty ports became spaces of novel economic, administrative, juridical, and cultural practices.[17] These included unexpected combinations of Chinese and non-Chinese

---

14. Representative works include Rowe, *Hankow*; Susan Mann Jones, *Local Merchants and the Chinese Bureaucracy, 1750–1950* (Stanford: Stanford University Press, 1987); Madeleine Zelin, *The Merchants of Zigong: Industrial Entrepreneurship in Early Modern China* (New York: Columbia University Press, 2005); Christopher Isett, *State, Peasant, and Merchant in Qing Manchuria, 1644–1862* (Stanford: Stanford University Press, 2007); George Qiao, "The Rise of Shanxi Merchants: Empire, Institutions, and Social Change in Qing China, 1688–1850" (PhD diss., Stanford University, 2017); C. Patterson Giersch, *Corporate Conquests: Business, the State and the Origins of Ethnic Inequality in Southwest China* (Stanford: Stanford University Press, 2020); Meng Zhang, *Timber and Forestry in Qing China: Sustaining the Market* (Seattle: University of Washington Press, 2021).
15. Rowe, *Hankow*, 83.
16. Rhoads Murphey, "The Treaty Ports and China's Modernization," in *The Chinese City between Two Worlds*, ed. G. William Skinner and Mark Elvin (Stanford: Stanford University Press, 1974), 18–71; quote on 39.
17. Representative texts include Leo Ou-fan Lee, *Shanghai Modern: The Flowering of a New Urban Culture in China, 1930–1945* (Cambridge, MA: Harvard University Press, 1999); Michael Tsin, *Nation, Governance, and Modernity in China: Canton, 1900–1927* (Stanford: Stanford University Press, 1999); Ruth Rogaski, *Hygienic Modernity: Meanings of Health and Disease in Treaty-Port*

capital—central to the story of this book—that morphed and expanded circuits of commercial circulation.[18] More broadly, evidence shows that treaty-era commercial reorientations intensified differences between the empire's littoral and hinterland regions, produced "realignment of the urban structure," and shifted imperial political economy away from long-standing concerns and practices.[19] Research for this book shows that for those tasked with governing China's "commercial revolution," significant segments of the commercial world became muddled, unstable, and disruptive. All this suggests that Murphey's fly-elephant metaphor perhaps missed the point. The fly brought with it a rash.

One reason it has been possible to discount the effects of foreign mercantile activity in China is that the regulatory framework that structured it has been, with the exception of studies of the Chinese Maritime Customs, relatively neglected since the early decades of the postwar era. This neglect means that in important respects John King Fairbank's work, in particular, *Trade and Diplomacy on the China Coast* (1953), remains paradigmatic. In this text, Fairbank examined what kind of trading conditions the British sought in China and why Qing leadership was so resistant to providing them. In the interpretative paradigm Fairbank advanced, which set a research agenda for at least a generation of Harvard-based scholarship. The "treaty order" was emblematic of all that was modern and progressive in the nineteenth century: a regime that recognized the importance of commerce and treated it with respect, which is to say, according to the rule of law. The treaty regime was a much-needed corrective, thought Fairbank, to the burdens and restrictions that arrogant,

---

China (Berkeley: University of California Press, 2004); Wen-Hsin Yeh, *Shanghai Splendor: Economic Sentiments and the Making of Modern China, 1843–1949* (Berkeley: University of California Press, 2008); Marie-Claire Bergère, *Shanghai: China's Gateway to Modernity* (Stanford: Stanford University Press, 2009); Samuel Y. Liang, *Mapping Modernity in Shanghai: Space, Gender, and Visual Culture in the Sojourners' City, 1853–98* (New York: Routledge, 2010); Isabella Jackson, *Shaping Modern Shanghai: Colonialism in China's Global City* (Cambridge: Cambridge University Press, 2019).

18. Yen-p'ing Hao, *The Commercial Revolution in Nineteenth-Century China: The Rise of Sino-Western Mercantile Capitalism* (Berkeley: University of California Press, 1985); Eiichi Motono, *Conflict and Cooperation in Sino-British Business, 1860–1911: The Impact of the Pro-British Commercial Network in Shanghai* (New York: St. Martin's, 2000); Ji, *A History of Modern Shanghai Banking*; Edward LeFevour, *Western Enterprise in Late Ch'ing China: A Selective Survey of Jardine, Matheson & Company's Operations, 1842–1895* (Cambridge, MA: Harvard University Asia Center, 1968); Susan Mann Jones, "Merchant Investment, Commercialization, and Social Change in the Ningpo Area," in *Reform in Nineteenth Century China*, ed. Paul A. Cohen and John E. Schrecker (Cambridge, MA: Harvard University East Asian Research Center, 1976): 41–48; Robert Gardella, "Reform and the Tea Industry and Trade in Late Ch-ing China: The Fukien Case," in *Reform in Nineteenth Century China*, ed. Paul A. Cohen and John E. Schrecker (Cambridge, MA: Harvard University East Asian Research Center, 1976), 71–79.

19. Mark Elvin, introduction to *The Chinese City between Two Worlds*, ed. Mark Elvin and G. William Skinner (Stanford: Stanford University Press, 1974), 1–16; quote on 8; Pomeranz, *Hinterland*.

anti-commercial Qing rulers had placed on trade. Namely, the treaty regime promised to free economic activity from the bonds of "traditional" Chinese culture and anti-modernization politics.[20] Although Fairbank's career continued for decades, his position on the fundamental challenge "modernization" posed to Qing China did not change.

There are at least three problems, though, with Fairbank's influential paradigm. One, initially pointed out by critics in the 1970s, is the way in which modernization, as Fairbank used it, functioned as apologetics for foreign intrusion and distortions in China's economic development that followed in its wake. The modernization paradigm banished coercion and colonialism from view.[21] Second, Fairbank's culturalist interpretation of the Chinese government, grounded in questionable theorization of Qing foreign relations, profoundly mischaracterized Qing official attitudes toward commerce and Euro-American states.[22] Finally, the paradigm fails to account for the historical specificity of the principles and practices that constituted the "treaty order." All three errors result from Fairbank's failure to see that the trade sought by British merchants and the reasons they sought it were not universal or natural. To be sure, Fairbank and those who followed him emphasized the treaty order's novelty in the *Chinese* context, but they bracketed any interrogation of why a "modern" administrative order would prize transparency, geographic uniformity, or the diminution of personalized forms of power, all of which were key characteristics of the treaty regime. This failure to adequately historicize the treaty regime generated an imbalance within the Fairbankian paradigm: the Chinese acted from within the constraints of "culture"; the British, who were nearly synonymous with the treaty order, had escaped such a world of culture-based illusions. They merely pursued what made good sense. The more critical attention to day-to-day treaty administration offered

---

20. John King Fairbank, *Trade and Diplomacy on the China Coast: The Opening of the Treaty Ports, 1842–1854* (Stanford: Stanford University Press, 1969), especially pithy statements of this position can be found on 5, 20–21, 31–33, 53, 83, and 468; John King Fairbank, "Synarchy under the Treaties," in *Chinese Thought and Institutions*, ed. John King Fairbank, with contributions by T'ung-tsu Ch'u (Chicago: University of Chicago Press, 1957), 204–31; Katherine F. Bruner, John K. Fairbank, and Richard J. Smith, eds., *Entering China's Service: Robert Hart's Journals, 1854–1863* (Cambridge, MA: Council on East Asian Studies, Harvard University, 1986), 1–12.
21. James Peck, "The Roots of Rhetoric: Professional Ideology of America's China Watchers," *Bulletin of Concerned Asian Scholars* 2, no. 1 (1969): 59–69; Joseph Esherick, "Harvard on China: The Apologetics of Imperialism," *Bulletin of Concerned Asian Scholars* 4, no. 4 (1972): 9–16. A new version of this argument appeared in the 1990s; see Tani E. Barlow, "Colonialism's Career in Postwar China Studies," in *Formations of Colonial Modernity in East Asia*, ed. Tani E. Barlow (Durham, NC: Duke University Press, 1997), 373–412.
22. For alternative accounts of Qing coastal trade management, see Paul A. Van Dyke, *The Canton Trade: Life and Enterprise on the China Coast, 1700–1845* (Hong Kong: Hong Kong University Press, 2005); Zhao, *The Qing Opening to the Ocean*. For critique of Fairbank on these grounds, see James L. Hevia, *Cherishing Men from Afar: Qing Guest Ritual and the Macartney Embassy of 1793* (Durham, NC: Duke University Press, 1995), 9–25.

here does not so much dislodge what we know now of Chinese and non-Chinese commerce in China as it disrupts the triumphal modernization narrative associated with the treaty-based regulatory order. To return to the metaphor proffered above, if foreign merchants and their places of trade were the empire's flies, the treaty-based regulatory regime was its rash.

Treaty Regime as Virus

The Qing Empire's treaty ports originated in the first Sino-British treaty, which itself originated in war. From 1839 to 1841, military forces of the Qing and British Empires fought a series of coastal battles in an altercation known as the Opium War.[23] Qing officials' seizure of British-owned opium cargos precipitated the war, but its deeper causes included long-injured British pride and speculative commercial ambitions. Since the end of the eighteenth century, the British government had struggled to station a diplomatic resident in Beijing and to persuade Qing authorities to allow British traders access to more Chinese ports. These particular frustrations mixed with a miasma of conjured orientalist truths about China—that it was a lawless place suffering under local despotism and arrogant imperial incompetence—as well as bourgeois fantasies about civilization, barbarism, and universal law.[24] The combination was explosive.

British victory in 1841 led to a "Treaty of Peace, Friendship, and Commerce" (Eng: Treaty of Nanjing, Ch: 江寧條約 *Jiangning tiaoyue*, 1842), which ceded Hong Kong to British control and gave British traders long-sought commercial privileges. Fifteen years into the new arrangements, a second round of hostilities erupted over Chinese policing of these privileges. The Treaty of Tianjin (Ch: 天津條約, *Tianjin tiaoyue* 1858), which concluded this war, was an even more an even more

---

23. Hsin-pao Chang, *Commissioner Lin and the Opium War* (Cambridge, MA: Harvard University Press, 1964); Maurice Collis, *Foreign Mud, Being an Account of the Opium Imbroglio at Canton in the 1830's & the Anglo-Chinese War That Followed*, 1st American ed. (New York: A. A. Knopf, 1947); Peter Ward Fay, *The Opium War, 1840–1842: Barbarians in the Celestial Empire in the Early Part of the Nineteenth Century and the War by Which They Forced Her Gates Ajar* (Chapel Hill: University of North Carolina Press, 1975); Glenn Melancon, *Britain's China Policy and the Opium Crisis: Balancing Drugs, Violence and National Honour, 1833–1840* (Burlington, VT: Ashgate, 2003); Michael Greenberg, *British Trade and the Opening of China, 1800–42* (Cambridge: Cambridge University Press, 1951).
24. Lydia Liu, *Clash of Empires: The Invention of China in Modern World Making* (Cambridge, MA: Harvard University Press, 2004), 31–691; Li Chen, *Chinese Law in Imperial Eyes: Sovereignty, Justice, and Transcultural Politics* (New York: Columbia University Press, 2016); Teemu Ruskola, *Legal Orientalism: China, the United States, and Modern Law* (Cambridge, MA: Harvard University Press, 2013).

transformative agreement to regulate China's foreign trade.[25] When the last Qing emperor abdicated in 1912, the government had officially designated fifty-one treaty ports where Euro-Americans could live, often under some form of self-rule, where their merchant and military vessels could call, and where their businesses could conduct affairs. These were also the places where steamships could load and unload cargo, whether flying a Chinese or non-Chinese flag.

Once the Treaty of Tianjin took effect, much of how the Qing Empire governed foreign trade and managed relations with Europe and the United States changed. The agreement allowed permanent embassies in Beijing and elaborated an alternative regulatory apparatus for Euro-American trade, often referred to as the "treaty port system." The treaty port system was, on paper, a regime of institutions and rules separate from those that governed Chinese merchant activity. But this nominal regulatory segregation did little to keep foreign capital from mingling with domestic commerce and governance. Recent work by Anne Reinhardt on steam transport networks has shown that although treaty ports were often conceptualized as "self-contained points of entry" into China, in practice they became nodes in "an emerging transport system whose complex social, economic, spatial, and temporal effects extended well beyond arenas of foreign activity and involvement."[26] Here, I examine how the circulation of imports and exports connected to global trade carried with them the coercive force of this alien regulatory regime.

A viral model of historical change, suggested by the rash metaphor, is helpful in this account in so far as it can accommodate gradual, site-specific change in which initial entry leads to processes of replication and spread. A virus begins as an event but becomes systemic through its colonization of cells. During this colonization it inserts its own DNA into the structure of the host cells, which then redirects the reproductive functions of the cell. Host cells, which had been busy reproducing their own components, now reproduce the viral components. Using this hermeneutic, we can rethink treaties as a set of regulatory prescriptions that entered through the treaty ports but did not remain there. Instead, as protocols and instruments that governed commercial circulation, they traveled wherever foreign goods and foreign capital did. During this movement, the treaty regime reshaped practices of local governance with which they came into contact.

The viral model is helpful in a second way as well. During the period of this study, British merchants remained chronically disappointed by their gains in China. According to one study of this sentiment, mercantile folklore held that "China was

---

25. J. Y. Wong, *Deadly Dreams: Opium and the Arrow War (1856–1860) in China* (Cambridge: Cambridge University Press, 1998). The Qing government signed four nearly identical treaties at Tianjin, with the governments of Great Britain, France, Russia, and the United States.
26. Anne Reinhardt, *Navigating Semi-colonialism: Shipping, Sovereignty, and Nation-Building in China, 1860–1937* (Cambridge, MA: Harvard University Asia Center, 2018), 101.

the Eldorado never fully explored, whose riches in concessions and customers were immeasurable."[27] Like a body that offers trillions of cellular opportunities for reproduction and growth, so too did China's millions of acres and hundreds of millions of persons provide incalculable opportunities for British capital's reproduction and growth. If only these people and places could be reached and at the right price. In this vein, the viral model also captures what theorists and historians alike have shown to be essential to capital's existence: as it grows, it endlessly appropriates ever more resources, commodities, and consumers and thereby reengineers landscapes, human needs, and human desires to its own ends. These three metaphorical registers work together as this book thinks about the treaty regulatory apparatus. On the surface, there are regulations, procedures, and paperwork. Beneath these manifestations of rule and order are desires and anxieties of the human actors who created and used them. Shaping these in their particular insatiable and abstract form was capital, in a specific sense of the term.[28]

Capital

"Capital," admittedly, can mean many things. In a classic proverb, six blind men, each of whom has touched one portion of an elephant, disagree about what an elephant is. "It is a wall," says the one who has touched its side. "It is a spear," says the one who has touched its tusk. "It is a giant cow," says the one who has touched its four legs. And so on.[29] The proverb gives an elementary lesson in how people with different perspectives arrive at different conclusions. As such, it also provides a helpful

---

27. Nathan Pelcovits, *Old China Hands and the Foreign Office* (New York: American Institute of Pacific Relations, 1948), 3.
28. The cast of British merchants, consuls, and diplomats in this story play the role of what Marx termed *traeger*—that is, the "conscious bearer" of capital (*Capital: A Critique of Political Economy*, vol. 1, trans. Ben Fowkes [New York: Vintage Books, 1977], 253–55). In taking this approach, I draw inspiration from studies that have traced how capitalist social relations shaped a new form of "common sense." An idiosyncratic bibliography of such work includes Theodor Adorno, "On the Fetish Character in Music and Regression of Listening," in *The Essential Frankfurt School Reader*, ed. Andrew Arato and Eike Gebhardt (New York: The Continuum Publishing Co., 1982 [1938]), 270–99; E. P. Thompson, *The Making of the English Working Class* (New York: Vintage Books, 1963); David Harvey, *The Condition of Postmodernity: An Enquiry into the Origins of Cultural Change* (Oxford: Blackwell, 1989); Mary Poovey, *A History of the Modern Fact: Problems of Knowledge in the Sciences of Wealth and Society* (Chicago: University of Chicago Press, 1998); Leslie Salzinger, *Genders in Production: Making Workers in Mexico's Global Factories* (Berkeley: University of California Press, 2003); Andrew Sartori, *Bengal in Global Concept History: Culturalism in the Age of Capital* (Chicago: University of Chicago Press, 2008); John Comaroff and Jean Comaroff, *Ethnicity, Inc.* (Chicago: University of Chicago Press, 2009); William H. Sewell Jr., *Capitalism and the Emergence of Civic Equality in Eighteenth Century France* (Chicago: University of Chicago Press, 2021).
29. For one retelling, see https://www.peacecorps.gov/educators/resources/story-blind-men-and-elephant/.

touchstone for thinking about the historiography of capitalism. By selecting different archives and examining different research sites, historians have produced varied histories of capitalism. But capital's different forms of appearance is not just the result of methodological choices by historians. Unlike the elephant in the metaphor, concrete forms of capital expansion have varied considerably depending on time and place. This historical variability has led to historiographical debates about what capitalism is or is not and what its origins are or are not. It has also led to analyses that reject the proposition capitalism "has [any] inherent nature [or] essential features."[30]

This study argues that capitalism does have an essence. This essence, however, is not identical with closely associated phenomenon such as free labor, industrial factories, and global commodity chains. Rather, I make use of a reading of Karl Marx's *Capital*, offered by Moishe Postone, that unpacks what Marx thought to be the structure of capital and its immanent historical dynamic.[31] Neither Postone nor Marx, in his mature critique of political economy, offer an account of how capital shaped historical change around the world, but they do offer a categorial analysis of capital that allows us to identify its historical forms of appearance.

Two aspects of capital are of particular importance in this study. The first is the unique form of wealth capital entails. Marx's theory of the commodity attempts to explain how, in addition to a mass of goods, capital entails a form of wealth that is not consumed but rather accumulated ad infinitum. This form of wealth Marx called value, and he theorized that in the capitalist formation value mediates socially foundational activities, such as what gets produced and who gets to consume it. The second aspect is the historically specific form of coercion capital produces. Marx's theory that social wealth in capitalist society is both material and nonmaterial also suggests that it is the social role played by the nonmaterial form of wealth that helps to explain key characteristics of capitalist society. Among these characteristics is the appearance of a form of coercion that appears otherwise, what Postone calls "abstract domination." Postone reads Marx's category of capital as a theory of social mediation, and he points out that when value is the dominant form of social wealth, social processes that had been mediated by custom, lineage, or overt forms of personal power come to be mediated by impersonal laws.[32] The upshot of this mediation for those living in a capitalist social formation, according to Postone, is that "social relations are social in a peculiar manner." "They exist," he writes, "not as overt

---

30. Gary Hamilton and Chang Wei-an, "The Importance of Commerce in the Organization of China's Late Imperial Economy," in *The Resurgence of East Asia: 500, 150, and 50 Year Perspectives*, edited by Giovanni Arrighi, Takeshi Hamashita, and Mark Selden (London: Routledge, 2003), 173–213, here 176.
31. Moishe Postone, *Time, Labor, and Social Domination* (Cambridge: Cambridge University Press, 1993).
32. Postone, *Time, Labor, and Social Domination*, 154.

interpersonal relations but as a quasi-independent structure that are opposed to individuals, a sphere of 'objective' necessity and 'objective dependence.'"[33] I find the concept of abstract domination helpful in thinking about Euro-American coercion in China. To be sure, gunboats were a tool used at moments of heightened tension to pursue commercial gains in China. But more routine, and so arguably more decisive, efforts to rewrite economic and political power in China employed less overt forms of coercion. These inhered in treaties and mechanisms of commercial administration deployed to grow circuits of capital.[34]

Up to this point, forms wealth and abstract domination have not been axes for studies of China's "history of capitalism." The robust "sprouts of capitalism" debate in China in the 1950s looked to metrics of industrial production as well as specialization in agriculture and commerce. These metrics remained central some decades later in the now classic study, *Chinese Capitalism, 1522–1840*, edited by Xu Dixin and Wu Chengming first published in China in 1985 as *Zhongguo zibenzhuyi fazhan shi* (中國資本主義發展史).[35] *Chinese Capitalism* was a self-consciously Marxist query into China's economic history and followed a traditional Marxist methodology, examining agricultural productivity, technological development in handicraft industries, and the socioeconomic role of commercial capital.[36] In the United States, Sucheta Mazumdar's monumental 1998 study *Sugar and Society in China* foregrounds the question of capitalist transformation by following the model of Marxist historian Robert Brenner, examining legal rights, noneconomic strategies of accumulation, and Chinese production for the world market.[37] "Can there be a China-centered history even as this history is being shaped in the crucible of

---

33. Postone, *Time, Labor, and Social Domination*, 125.
34. Earlier attempts to make sense of the peculiar nature of Euro-American coercion in China include Jürgen Osterhammel, "Semi-colonialism and Informal Empire in Twentieth Century China: Towards a Framework of Analysis," in *Imperialism and After: Continuities and Discontinuities*, ed. Wolfgang Mommsen and Jürgen Osterhammel (London: Allen & Unwin, 1986), 290–314. For a recent iteration of Osterhammel's framing of the problem, see Bryna Goodman and David S. G. Goodman, "Colonialism and China," in *Twentieth Century Colonialism and China: Localities, the Everyday, and the World* (London: Routledge, 2012), 1–22.
35. Arif Dirlik, "Chinese Historians and the Marxist Concept of Capitalism: A Critical Examination," *Modern China* 8, no. 1 (January 1982): 105–32. Important representative work includes 中國資本主義萌芽問題討論集 [Collected essays on the question of the sprouts of capitalism in China] (Beijing: Xinhua shudian, 1957); Jian Bozan (翦伯贊) 中國歷綱要 [Outline of Chinese history] (Beijing: Renmin chubanshe, 1962).
36. Xu Dixin and Wu Chengming, *Chinese Capitalism, 1522–1840*, trans. Li Zhengde, Liang Miaoru, and Li Siping (New York: St. Martin's, 2000).
37. Sucheta Mazumdar, *Sugar and Society: Peasants, Technology, and the World Market* (Cambridge, MA: Harvard University Asia Center, 1998); Robert Brenner, "The Agrarian Roots of European Capitalism," in *The Brenner Debate: Agrarian Class Structure and Economic Development in Pre-industrial Europe*, ed. T. H. Ashton and C. H. E. Philpin (Cambridge: Cambridge University Press, 1985), 213–328.

world capitalism?" she writes.[38] More commonly, though, studies of Chinese economic, social, and political change produced by US-based historians eschew explicit engagement with the question of capital even as they engage with closely associated phenomena, including industrialization, economic development, and sociocultural forms of "modernity." These conversations for the most part have little need for a rigorous theoretical specification of what it means for "capital" to be "in China." Their interest lies in locally specific factors of historical change. I, like Mazumdar, am less sure that *certain* local historical events and changes are comprehensible without considering how capital advances using, appropriating, and transforming what it finds at hand.[39]

My purpose in using a theory of capital to examine the Qing-era treaty regime is not to provide an origin story for capitalism in China, either in the sense of "modern economic growth" or in the sense of a commercially sophisticated society. Nor do I examine social transformations that in classic Marxist theory undergird a "transition to capitalism." The book offers, rather, an analysis of what Saskia Sassen has called "a tipping point," when one set of organizing logics that have governed the deployment of a state's "capabilities" takes over from another.[40] I argue that in the decades after 1860, capital was social form that "tipped" late-Qing governance a direction of novel logics and practices. Capital, which had long been present in Chinese merchants' pocketbooks, during the "treaty era" came to shape, if not govern, Chinese statecraft. In this capacity, it was both disruptive and generative.

Qing Governance

Another pillar of this book is an argument about Qing governance. There is no single story of what happened within Qing governance after 1842. For as much as the treaty regime posed problems, where and how these problems appeared depended on the extent and character of an area's participation in globally connected commercial life.[41] In addition, Qing "governance" was not a monolith. The textual tradition within which Qing officials trained was sufficiently diverse to generate hundreds

---

38. Mazumdar, *Sugar and Society*, 387.
39. On approaching capital as a process, see Jonathan Levy, "Capital as Process and the History of Capitalism," *Business History Review* 91 (2017): 483–510; Andrew Liu, "Production, Circulation, and Accumulation: The Historiographies of Capitalism in China and South Asia," *Journal of Asian Studies* 78, no. 4 (2019): 767–88; William H. Sewell Jr. "The Capitalist Epoch," *Social Science History* 38 (Spring 2014): 1–11.
40. Saskia Sassen, *Territory, Authority, Rights: From Medieval to Global Assemblages* (Princeton: Princeton University Press, 2006), 7–9.
41. On the littoral as a distinct space, see Paul A. Cohen, "The New Coastal Reformers," in *Reform in Nineteenth-Century China*, ed. Paul A. Cohen and John E. Schrecker (Cambridge, MA: Harvard University East Asian Research Center, 1976), 255–64.

of years of commentary and debates about government policy. Some officials of the treaty era, like Zeng Guofan, were deeply immersed in moral preoccupations typically attributed to Confucian learning. Others, like Li Hongzhang, were not. Officialdom, moreover, was composed of numerous offices, some more specialized than others. There is little evidence that the management of treaty affairs, handled by the *Zongli geguo shiwu yamen* (總理各國事務衙門) had bearing on the work of the Board of Rites (禮部), for instance. Outside of Beijing, a county magistrate and a provincial governor general were responsible for the overall well-being of the populace, which included attending to matters as different as crop cultivation, local hydraulics, and temple festivals. The treaty regime might interfere with one subset of responsibilities but leave others untouched. Finally, governance was not a monolith because the work of the sparse official bureaucracy was supplemented with the participation of local elites in matters such as tax collection, social welfare, security, and infrastructure.[42]

For the period after 1861, it is particularly difficult to argue that Qing governance was integrated around any single person or set of ideas. At the apex of the dynastic state was the emperorship, composed of the body of the emperor, who claimed authorization from Heaven, the rituals he performed, as well as the people around him and the work they did.[43] As an embodiment of the empire in all its domains, a Qing emperor was a "composite creation" formed through education that made him a "reservoir of ethico-political values," while his personal connection with Heaven endowed him with the "power to regulate cosmic forces."[44] However, from the death of the Xianfeng emperor in 1860 until the abdication of Puyi in 1912, Qing emperors were mostly children, and this important institution was a site of struggle and unorthodox leadership. Scholars have argued that the five decades of regency, headed by the Manchu empress dowager Cixi, was, if not corrupt, largely unable to deploy the kind of functional power that characterized the reigns of the Yongzheng (1722–1735) or Qianlong (r. 1736–1795) emperors. In an era of boy emperors, Cixi's anomalous, self-made role "created a political reality that was difficult to assimilate to orthodox rituals or morality."[45] In this context, researchers

---

42. Robert J. Antony and Jane Kate Leonard, eds., *Dragons, Tigers, and Dogs: Qing Crisis Management and the Boundaries of State Power in Late Imperial China* (Ithaca: Cornell East Asia Program, 2002); R. Kent Guy, *China's Political Economy in Modern Times: Changes and Economic Consequences, 1800–2000* (London: Routledge, 2012), 26.
43. Pamela Kyle Crossley, "The Rulerships of China," *American Historical Review* 79, no. 5 (1992): 1468–83.
44. Daniel Barish, *Learning to Rule: Court Education and the Remaking of the Qing State, 1861–1912* (New York: Columbia University Press, 2022), 33; Peter Zarrow, *After Empire: The Conceptual Transformation of the Chinese State, 1885–1924* (Stanford: Stanford University Press, 2012), 9, 12.
45. Barish, *Learning to Rule*, 6; John E. Schrecker, *The Chinese Revolution in Historical Perspective* (New York: Greenwood, 1991), 107–8; Zarrow, *After Empire*, 17.

argue, much of the momentum in governing shifted to governor-generals as well as to growing cohorts of gentry managers and private secretariats.⁴⁶

Treaties introduced an additional layer of authority into this multilayered institutional complex. Many local officials, including county magistrates, prefects and circuit intendents (*daotai* 道台) found that "treaties complicated [their] duties." As Jennifer Rudolph describes them, these officials (I would also include governor generals) maintained "their traditional responsibilities of maintenance of peace and stability and revenue collection," but carrying them out became more complex with the addition of "national and international ramifications."⁴⁷ My research finds that the operation of commercial treaties in particular posed a consistent set of problems involving the interpretation and application of regulations. In this archive patterns of responses emerge across various offices of the Qing government. How to interpret those responses is the next consideration I take up.

Historical Subjects

What Qing officials thought about Euro-American presence and how they acted in the context of it have been important questions in historians' research on the last decades of Qing rule. During the field-defining decades of the 1950s and 1960s, scholars like Mary Wright and Joseph Levenson engaged in teasing out what Confucianism meant for "China's response to the West." Levenson and Wright, like Fairbank, viewed China in primarily culturalist terms and cast Euro-American presence as an existential challenge to the imperial state that Confucian resources largely failed to meet. Several decades later, however, this approach and narrative, largely indebted to a tradition of intellectual history, largely fell out of favor. New social scientific methodologies brought attention to *longue durée* socioeconomic causes of imperial decline—namely, population growth, which researchers found, strained natural resources, social institutions, and administrative effectiveness. Imperial China, this research suggested, ended for reasons that were not exclusively political or cultural.

Out of this space, a strident counter to the earlier failure narrative appeared. Studies of Qing-era "reform" launched in the 1970s continued a tradition of intellectual history but excavated currents of Chinese thought that far from impeding

---

46. Raymond W. Chu and William G. Saywell, *Career Patterns in the Ch'ing Dynasty: The Office of Governor General* (Ann Arbor: University of Michigan Center for Chinese Studies, 1984), 6; Pamela Kyle Crossley, *Wobbling Pivot, China since 1800: An Interpretative History* (Oxford: Wiley Blackwell, 2010), 118; Frederic Wakeman Jr., *The Fall of Imperial China* (New York: Free Press, 1975), 163–72, 187–88, 193–95.
47. Jennifer M. Rudolph, *Negotiated Power in Late Imperial China: The Zongli Yamen and the Politics of Reform* (Ithaca: Cornell University East Asia Program, 2008), 171–72.

vigorous resistance to Western intrusion provided resources for it.[48] More recent work on the construction of Chinese political modernity takes an institutional turn. Research by Richard Horowitz, Stephen Halsey, Jennifer Rudolph, Philip Thai, and Hans van de Ven has argued that after the Treaty of Tianjin concluded the dynasty's second ignoble military defeat, the Qing state engaged in a series of directed and vigorous efforts to increase revenue, centralize control of foreign affairs, augment its military capacities and police its borders. Crucially, the case built by this "state strengthening" literature rejects the identification of government institutions with Confucian ideology and instead offers a narrative of pragmatic, problem-solving leadership in Beijing and the provinces. This leadership, these scholars argue, was not stymied by the moral preoccupations of the traditional scholar official, nor was it completely enthralled to Euro-American practices and norms. It did, however, accept the necessities of the moment.

I am skeptical that either the intellectual histories that emphasized "Confucian" failure or the more recent institutional alternatives to it are completely correct. As two poles of a debate, the positions track uncomfortably close to a problematic binary between culture and rationality in which an ideational concept of culture explains China's concrete historical differences and an ahistorical concept of modernity casts specific institutional changes as inevitable and reasonable.[49] As a third path, I take inspiration from recent work by Tong Lam, Andrea Janku, and Andrew Liu that grounds China's "modernity" in a universe of social relations and registers the conceptual and ontological shifts entailed in late-Qing problem-solving.

Lam's book on the emergence of social surveys in China, for instance, shows that as the Qing government and its successors deployed new administrative categories and enumerative practices to "correct" newly visible "factual deficiency," they also "reconceptualize(d) the demographic and territorial landscapes" of the empire. The 1909 census did more than count households, Lam argues; it also produced a changed relation between state and subject. "The transition from the so-called 'pre-modern' to the 'modern'" was not the invention of legibility, Lam explains, but rather a "shift from one form of legibility and governmental rationality to another."[50] Similarly, Janku's work on genres of late-Qing statecraft writing documents how solving problems of wealth and power central to state-building entailed reorganizing extant systems of knowledge to authorize a "fundamentally changed role of

---

48. For example, Paul A. Cohen and John E. Schrecker, eds., *Reform in Nineteenth-Century China* (Cambridge, MA: Harvard University East Asian Research Center, 1976).
49. Judith B. Farquhar and James L. Hevia, "Culture and Postwar American Historiography of China," *positions* 1, no. 2 (1993): 486–525.
50. Tong Lam, *A Passion for Facts: Social Surveys and the Construction of the Chinese Nation-State, 1900–1949* (Berkeley: University of California Press, 2011), 70, 73.

the state."⁵¹ Using grain policies as an example, Janku shows that "famine relief," a long-standing category of imperial statecraft, almost completely disappeared from statecraft essay collections published in the 1880s onward. In its place, publications included "the new science of political economy" that emphasized activist state involvement in a broader and more abstract "economy."⁵² Most recently, Andrew Liu's work on Chinese participation in the global tea trade presents findings similar to Janku's. For Liu, the 1890s were an important period in the development of Chinese political economy because "global competition compelled" a small number of Qing officials to shift their understanding of wealth. These thinkers turned away from policies centered on commercial circulation to a focus on human productivity and "infinite expansion."⁵³ In all three of these studies, key trappings of the modern state, including abstract categories, robust bureaucratic sightlines, and growth-oriented policy, are not merely instrumental choices but developed in tandem with social, conceptual and even ontological reconfigurations. This research suggests that as the nineteenth century ended, strategies and tactics of governance changed because the entities and possibilities that constituted the world to govern also changed.

Bringing conceptual and ontological orientations into the study of Qing governance means bringing historically constituted subjectivity back into the story of the late-Qing state. Such ideational concerns are largely jettisoned in the institutional approach used by recent histories of Qing state-building. Nor do ideological commitments garner much attention when researchers emphasize the practical considerations that animated late Qing state policy and action. In both mainland China and the United States, readings of statecraft thought (*jingshi* 經世), an important and innovative strain of late imperial politics, have cast it as a practical problem-solving strain of governance distanced from the moral and ethical concerns of the moribund Confucian state depicted in earlier culturalist approaches.⁵⁴ Statecraft thought, upon this reading, differed from "orthodox Neo-Confucianism" because unlike the latter, it privileged institutional solutions realized by collective coordination rather

---

51. Andrea Janku, "New Methods to Nourish the People: Late Qing Encyclopaedic Writings on Political Economy," in *Chinese Encyclopaedias of New Global Knowledge (1870–1930)*, ed. M. Dolezelov-Velingerova and R. G. Wagner (Berlin: Springer-Verlag, 2014), 329–65; quote on 344.
52. On this transition, see also Pierre-Etienne Will and R. Bin Wong, *Nourish the People: The State Civilian Granary System in China, 1650–1850* (Ann Arbor: University of Michigan Press, 1991), 7.
53. Andrew Liu, *Tea War: A History of Capitalism in China and India* (New Haven: Yale University Press, 2020), 154–56.
54. Hao Chang, "The Intellectual Context of Reform," in *Reform in Nineteenth Century China*, ed. Paul A. Cohen and John E. Schrecker (Cambridge, MA: Harvard University East Asian Research Center, 1976), 145–49. Zhou Jiming and Lei Ping, "*Qingdai jingshi sichao yanjiu shuping*" 清代經世思潮研究述評 [Critique of Studies on Qing Dynasty Jingshi Thought], *Hanxue yanjiu tongxun* 漢學研究通訊 25 (2006): 1–10.

than moral solutions internal to the individual.[55] Statecraft thinkers, which included many of the era's "state strengtheners," were pragmatic problem solvers, governing in the empire's littoral zones to build the modern state.

There are, however, empirical reasons to doubt that Qing officials abandoned moral and ethical training or the worldview it cultivated. In his recent study of late-Qing governance, Peter Zarrow suggests that the use of the term "statecraft thought" by Qing-era writers intended to differentiate an orientation toward governance that prioritized "practical" problems in contradistinction to "philosophical or textual questions." But although statecraft thinking prioritized a different set of problems from orthodox neo-Confucianism, focus on a different set of questions did not foreclose use of the same philosophical training to solve them. Zhang Zhidong, for example, who features prominently in historical studies of *jingshi*, advised that the first priority among *jingshi* topics was the fundamentals of morality as articulated in the Five Classics.[56] Statecraft thought more generally, according to Zarrow, drew substantially from the *Gongyang Commentary* (公羊傳), a commentary on the *Spring and Autumn Annals* (*Chunqiu* 春秋), which gave "practical thoughts about reviving the infrastructure and reforming the tax system, for example, a philosophical and even metaphysical base." Cosmological referents were not abandoned in the statecraft tradition, Zarrow suggests, but flexibly deployed as a set of resources leaders could use "to understand the trends of their time and act accordingly."[57]

In this study, to make sense of how Qing officials navigated the landscape of treaty-based regulations and collaborations, I keep in mind the subject formation, rooted in classical education, that shaped Qing officials. People act on the basis of the realities they perceive, and these perceptions are neither unrestrained nor unlimited. Rather, historical periods and cultural locales can be known through their "collectively produced constraints on the thinkable and the knowable."[58] Classical education, it is safe to assume, was one such collectively produced constraint that shaped the world officials recognized as well as the strategies they developed for ordering it. My purpose here is not to recuperate the "Confucian" official but rather to interpret historical records in light of the historically plausible subjects who wrote them.

---

55. Schrecker, *The Chinese Revolution*, 111.
56. Feng Tianyu, 張之洞評傳 [An annotated biography of Zhang Zhidong] (Nanjing: Nanjing daxue chubanshe, 1991), 292.
57. Zarrow, *After Empire*, 49.
58. Farquhar and Hevia, "Culture and Postwar American Historiography," 514.

Considerations in the Writing of This Historical Narrative

Framing Qing officials' exercise of their conceptual and ontological commitments was Euro-American power, visible in gunboats as well as treaty texts. If the treaty system was something more than modern rationality, as I argue it was, then the disruptions it caused and the changes it institutionalized were also something other than the creation of a modern economy and modern state. To narrate the treaty apparatus as a vector of historical change, I have found it helpful to think with the concepts of deterritorialization and reterritorialization. As terms originally developed by Gilles Deleuze and Félix Guattari to think about capital's historical dynamic as well as the nature of historical event, deterritorialization and reterritorialization conceptualize change as ontologically transformative as well as episodic. [59] To be deterritorialized or reterritorialized is not a permanent or totalized state but is conditioned on the presence of specific actors, institutions, and arrangements. It was possible for the Qing Empire to be deterritorialized by capital and simultaneously or subsequently to not be.

When James Hevia used the concepts deterritorialization and reterritorialization in his 2003 study of British imperialism in China, he offered a way to think about twinned processes that "proposed to teach the Qing elite and Chinese people in general through various means of coercion and enticement how to function properly in a world dominated militarily and economically by European-based empires."[60] In this formulation, China, after 1842, was a space in which Euro-American powers alternated between inflicting overt military violence and attempting to "reform" China so it could join the "family of nations." For Qing leaders, pursuit of peace, stability, and prosperity meant processing attempts alien powers

---

59. Gilles Deleuze and Félix Guattari, *Anti-Oedipus: Capitalism and Schizophrenia*, trans. Robert Hurley, Mark Seem, and Helen R. Lane (Minneapolis: University of Minnesota Press, 1983); Stuart Rockefeller, "Flow," *Current Anthropology* 52, no. 4 (August 2011): 557–78. In *Anti-Oedipus*, Deleuze and Guattari expand on the observation by Marx that at the center of capitalism are paired, synchronous phenomena—namely, a falling rate of profit alongside an increase in absolute amounts of surplus value (34–35). Examples of destructive transformation include "the transformation of the agrarian structures that constitute the old social body. . . . For the free worker: the deterritorialization of the soil through privatization; the decoding of the instruments of production through appropriation. . . . And for capital: the deterritorialization of wealth through monetary abstraction . . . the decoding of States through financial capital and public debts" (225). Processes of transformative reconstitution include "the Third World" which "is deterritorialized in relation to the center of capitalism but belongs to capitalism, being a pure peripheral territoriality of capitalism" (374). The episodic character of deterritorialization and reterritorialization is further clarified in *A Thousand Plateaus: Capitalism and Schizophrenia*, trans. Brian Massumi (Minneapolis: University of Minnesota Press, 1987).
60. James Hevia, *English Lessons: The Pedagogy of Imperialism in Nineteenth Century China* (Durham, NC: Duke University Press, 2003), 13.

to unmake and remake imperial sovereignty and government institutions. Hevia appropriated the terms to reopen a conversation about imperialism in China in comparative perspective with colonialism elsewhere. "Euroamerican empire building was both destructive and constructive," writes Hevia. "It eradicated old worlds and the ways of understanding those worlds, and made something new in their place."[61] Here, I combine Hevia's use of the terms as a way to conceptualize deconstructive and reconstructive processes with particular attention to the episodic and institutionally situated character of these events.

Each chapter in this book examines an episode of deterritorialization and reterritorialization. The ordering of the chapters is roughly chronological, beginning with Qing-British treaty negotiations in the 1840s and 1850s and ending with Qing tax reforms in the first decade of the twentieth century. In order, the chapters also roughly approximate the path that "infection" by capital took. The book begins with regulatory texts, moves into key institutions, and through those, out of the treaty ports and into the empire, more broadly. My goal in using the virus metaphor is not to argue that Euro-American presence made China sick but rather to offer a handle on the way in which capital was present in the Qing Empire. Although it is commonplace to talk about the "expansion" of global capital, local histories of capital caution against reading this expansion as an even, homogenous, or even primarily spatial, process. I find it most productive to think of capital as a virus, or perhaps even a vortex, that draws in and appropriates useful elements where it finds them. Even though these elements are located in space and place, they are not synonymous with it. Thus, it was possible for capital in the 1860s to deterritorialize and reterritorialize Chinese merchants but to not transform the geobody "China" into a capitalist society.

Chapter 1 charts how capital shaped the initial Qing-British treaties, signed in 1842 and 1858. I argue that treaties were an important mechanism through which nineteenth-century British capital sought a "spatial fix." At the same time, they were perhaps more fundamentally transformative because they institutionalized abstract domination. This alienated form of control reinscribed trade management as something other than what Qing officials understood it to be and interpellated officials as mere instruments of commodity circulation. Chapter 2 then examines the Imperial Maritime Customs (IMC), an institution Qing authorities innovated to administer treaty-based trade. Historians have argued that the IMC was, in many ways, the paradigmatic institution of the treaty era. Here, I argue its status as such should be attributed to how it institutionalized value growth as the basis for a new Qing political economy. After setting the regulatory and institutional landscape that took shape in the early 1860s, in Chapters 3 and 4 I look more closely at problems

---

61. Hevia, *English Lessons*, 20.

within treaty administration. Chapter 3 surveys what I call the "disorderly order" catalyzed by the creation of the treaty regime and the paths of deterritorialization it created. Chapter 4 reconstructs the debate in the 1860s between Qing and British officials over foreign participation in soybean transport. This reconstruction shows how not all commerce is synonymous with the kind of social reproduction that dominates in capitalist society. Chapters 5 and 6 move the story forward into the last three decades of Qing rule. Written as a pair, Chapter 5 uses foreign agitation against Qing taxes to unpack the full extent of the deterritorialization and reterritorialization immanent within the treaty apparatus. Chapter 6 subsequently shows how experiments in taxation, taken up by officials in Beijing and the provinces, went a considerable distance toward realizing the alternative forms of governance and territoriality pushed for decades by the foreign community.

Finally, a few words on why, despite the sophistication of commercial society and economic thought in China, my study begins with the assumption that Qing China was not a capitalist society. First, I argue that we should make a distinction between the existence of capital in a society and the existence of capital as a dominant social form. Experience with intense commercialization meant that long before Marx proposed his "general formula for capital," Chinese thinkers had already identified "capital" (*ben* 本) as a dynamic thing with capacity to grow and vulnerable to atrophy.[62] All the same, classic texts of Chinese "economic thought," which remained salient into the last decades of Qing rule, discussed problems of production, exchange, and taxation as political problems. "Economic thought" was not a self-constituting, self-contained realm of observation and prediction but rather political thought that recognized the centrality of the people's material circumstances to a ruler's wealth and power.[63] Stated somewhat differently, these texts suggest that capital was a resource that arts of governance could use in pursuit of political goals but nothing more.[64] Second, although wealth, within this intellectual tradition, was not synonymous with goods—money and coinage were also forms of wealth—the purpose of wealth, no matter its form, was the satisfaction of human

---

62. For example, *The Guanzi*, Sima Qian's "Biographies of Men of Enterprise," Su Shi in *Collections of Answers to the Emperor's Call*, cited in Hu Jichuang, *A Concise History of Chinese Economic Thought* (Beijing: Foreign Languages Press, 1988), 143, 250, 403; William Rowe, *Speaking of Profit: Bao Shichen and Reform in Nineteenth Century China* (Cambridge, MA: Harvard University East Asian Research Center, 2018), 91.
63. R. Bin Wong, "Coping with Poverty and Famine: Material Welfare, Public Goods, and Chinese Approaches to Governance," in *Public Goods Provision in the Early Modern Economy* (Berkeley: University of California Press, 2019), 130–46.
64. Yuri Pines, introduction to *Ideology of Power and Power of Ideology in Early China*, ed. Yuri Pines, Paul Goldin, and Martin Kern (Leiden: Brill, 2015), 1–29; cf. Diane Coyle, *GDP: A Brief but Affectionate History* (Princeton: Princeton University Press, 2014).

needs and desires—which is to say, consumption.[65] The materiality and utility of wealth shaped an engagement with market mechanisms that was foremost concerned with concrete goals: "protect the people from the change of the seasons, the climate, and the market, and to ensure their access to daily necessities at all times."[66] A central concern of this text is to show how the treaty regime, as an expression of capital, institutionalized a more abstract and dominating form of wealth that generated new realties to govern and new metrics by which to judge governance.

---

65. Isabella M. Weber, "China's Ancient Principles of Price Regulation through Market Participation: The *Guanzi* from a Comparative Perspective," in *European and Chinese Histories of Economic Thought: Theories and Images of Good Governance*, ed. Iwo Amelung and Bertram Schefold (London: Routledge, 2021), 246–58; Olga Borokh, "Rethinking Traditional Attitudes towards Consumption in the Process of Formation of Chinese Economics (Late Qing and Republican Periods)," in *European and Chinese Histories of Economic Thought: Theories and Images of Good Governance*, ed. Iwo Amelung and Bertram Schefold (London: Routledge, 2021), 233–45; Paul Goldin, "Economic Cycles and Price Theory in Early Chinese Texts," in *Between Command and Market: Economic Thought and Practice in Early China*, ed. Elisa Sabattini and Christian Schwermann (Leiden: Brill, 2022), 43–77.

66. Weber, "Price Regulation," 254.

1
Calling Forth Governance
Treaties and Coercion on the China Coast

And I have known the eyes already, known them all—
The eyes that fix you in a formulated phrase,
And when I am formulated, sprawling on a pin,
When I am pinned and wriggling on the wall,
Then how should I begin
To spit out all the butt-ends of my days and ways?
    And how should I presume?
        —"The Love Song of J. Alfred Prufrock," T. S. Eliot (1888–1965)

人人自有定盤針,
萬化根源總在心。
卻笑從前顛倒見,
枝枝葉葉外頭尋。
        —"詠良知四首:三",王陽明

Within each person a compass resides,
to the heart all worldly matters are traced.
Now I laugh at erstwhile delusions
of chasing after specious twigs.
        —"Ode to Innate Knowledge: Three," Wang Yangming (1472–1529)[1]

A Reprimand

Mistakes were made. The issue was why.

---

1. Translation by Tony Yingchong Li.

Late in the fall of 1868 two Qing officials, one who managed maritime trade at the treaty seaport of Ningbo and his colleague upriver at the treaty port of Hankou, received imperial reprimands for policing actions they had taken earlier that fall.[2] The affair began simply enough. In September, Ningbo officials arrested several Chinese dealers for failure to pay the local *lijin* (釐金) tax on recently imported cargo.[3] According to local investigators, the textile dealers colluded with two foreign firms to buy transit passes to exempt the textiles from *lijin* payments they otherwise owed. After arrest, the Chinese firms admitted wrongdoing and paid a fine. It appeared to be a straightforward case of revenue fraud but the matter did not end there and then in Ningbo. Rather, because transit passes were a treaty-granted privilege and the textiles were British manufactures, the British acting-consul in Ningbo protested the case's outcome to the higher offices of the regional superintendent of customs, stationed at Hankou. The consul argued that the Chinese merchants had done nothing wrong, given that treaties protected British-owned goods from *lijin*. The superintendent disagreed with the consul but felt he had no authority to enforce his view of the case. He turned to Beijing for assistance.

In Beijing, the case arrived at the offices of the *Zongli geguo shiwu yamen* (總理各國事務衙門; hereafter Zongli yamen), a seven-year-old agency established to manage treaty-related affairs. The Zongli yamen, led by imperial prince Yixin (王奕訢, 1833–1898) and senior Manchu statesman Wenxiang (文祥, 1818–1876) decided against local officials at Hankou and Ningbo. "The Superintendent has much misapprehended the sense of the treaty provisions," wrote the Zongli yamen officers. The reprimand explained that both the Treaty of Nanjing (1842) and the more recent Treaty of Tianjin (1858) both held force, "and when the Superintendent, on the ground that [the Nanjing treaty] is out-of-date, and the present circumstances differ, opines [that] the Treaty is being strained, he is all together wrong."[4] According to the Zongli yamen, local officials in Ningbo and Hankou had made two mistakes: first, they failed to understand that the treaty of 1858 built on the treaty of 1842. Second, they failed to understand the limits treaties placed on local taxation. "So great care having been taken regarding the levy of duties inland on foreign trade, when the treaty was framed, how can it be argued that the foreign merchant is to pay duties at every barrier he passes?" queried the Zongli yamen in its reprimand. The

---

2. The official in Ningbo was an imperially appointed intendant (*daotai* 道台), who supervised a transprefectural region. His colleague at Hankou was the superintendent of customs.
3. *Lijin* was a commercial tax that took various forms. I will discuss it extensively beginning in Chapter 2.
4. "Copy of a circular of instructions upon a report by the Superintendent of Customs at Ningbo of the punishment of the Ch'ien-ta and other dealers in foreign manufactures to the effect that treaty is not to be broken for the sake of likin," Legation translation, China: Miscellaneous Papers and Reports, Chinese Secretary's Office, Volume 11 Transit Duties and Likin, The National Archives, FO 233/83 (hereafter cited as Chinese Secretary's Office Volume 11).

central agency recommended the officials "carefully examine" several treaty articles and rules that clearly indicated Chinese merchants transporting foreign imports covered by transit passes did not need to pay *lijin*.

The root cause of the errors at Ningbo and Hankou, Zongli yamen officers surmised, was officials' failure to appreciate the new hierarchy of obligations framing action in trade-related matters. To complain that Chinese merchants carrying such goods evaded *lijin* was, wrote the Zongli yamen "[to argue according to] the text of the *lijin* regulations, and not according to the Treaty."

> The Superintendent, having the repairs of the sea-dykes before him, is not without a reason for his eagerness to collect the *lijin*, but in these questions affecting foreign interests, in which he is every day concerned, he has not read the Tariff rules and different regulations as forming parts of a whole. . . . He must act according to Treaty and he must not hold so tenaciously to his own view of the matter.[5]

No matter what a local official judged to be the local effect of treaty provisions, the Zongli yamen instructed, he could not set them aside. Local prerogatives and an official's sense of what was best came second to treaty obligations.

The Zongli yamen's reprimand was a not insignificant intervention by what was a very new central government agency. The Qing empire contained was both geographically and socio-economically diverse. So although its bureaucracy administered laws and implemented policies formulated in Beijing, political legitimacy entailed the creation and maintenance of a "flexible and pluralistic structure."[6] Local officials often interpreted and modified Beijing's instructions to best serve the particular needs of a locality or "to make adjustments to meet changing conditions" (*bian tong* 變通).[7] Attention to local conditions gave governance an overall tenor of "flexibility and accommodation to adapt to challenges and obstacles effectively."[8] The Zongli yamen's intervention pointed out, however, that officials in Ningbo and Hankou now managed at an intersection of local needs and obligations to foreign states. This convergence called on them to adapt to a new set of considerations—namely, that the writ of the many treaties, tariffs, and regulations produced after 1842 to govern Euro-American commercial activity in China had to be consulted as an integrated set of requirements and implemented to the word at all times.

---

5. "Treaty is not to be broken for the sake of likin," Legation translation, Chinese Secretary's Office Volume 11.
6. Wang Hui, "From Empire to State: Kang Youwei, Confucian Universalism, and Unity," in *Chinese Visions of World Order: Tianxia, Culture, and World Politics*, ed. and trans. Ban Wang (Durham, NC: Duke University Press, 2017), 49.
7. Thomas A. Metzger, *The Internal Organization of the Ch'ing Bureaucracy: Legal, Normative, and Communication Aspects* (Cambridge, MA: Harvard University Press, 1973), 53.
8. Jennifer M. Rudolph, *Negotiated Power in Late Imperial China: The Zongli Yamen and the Politics of Reform* (Ithaca: East Asia Program, Cornell University, 2008), 12.

Treaties as Global Governance

After the Opium War of 1839–1842, commercial governance in China became entangled with many, often overlapping, bilateral agreements. Between 1842 and 1901, the Qing government signed or issued over 313 treaties, agreements, protocols, and regulations to govern and regulate foreign trade and foreign settlements in the empire.[9] Prior to this period, the practice of treaty-making was, with one notable exception, not part of the Qing repertoire of managing relations with other political entities.[10] Treaties were, rather, a novel "interface of modernity" that projected into China a "naturalized hegemonic discourse" of international law and an emergent geopolitical hierarchy.[11] They were at once a reflection of Eurocentric confidence in its legal universality and a reflection of European judgments that China lacked the forms of law that defined civilization.[12]

During the nineteenth century, treaties were also a technology central to the global institutionalization of European capital circuits. In the 1790s, the number of treaties annually contracted around the world ranged from twenty to thirty. In the 1890s, the number reached 140–150 a year.[13] During this period, British commercial treaties included simple agreements to codify free or safe passage to merchants as well as more detailed arrangements that limited or eliminated the non-British signatory's state revenue perquisites.[14] In some cases, treaties eliminated, differences

---

9. Count drawn from Wang Tieya, ed., 中外舊約章彙編 [Collection of China's historical international treaties], vol. 1 (Beijing: Shenghuo, dushu, xinzhi sanlian shudian, 1982).
10. Peter C. Perdue, "Boundaries and Trade in the Early Modern World: Negotiations at Nerchinsk and Beijing," *Eighteenth Century Studies* 43, no. 3 (2010): 341–56.
11. Pär Kristoffer Cassel, "Extraterritoriality in China: What We Know and What We Don't Know," in *Treaty Ports in Modern China: Land, Law, and Power*, ed. Robert A. Bickers and Isabella Jackson (London: Routledge, 2016), 23–42; James L. Hevia, *Cherishing Men from Afar: Qing Guest Ritual and the Macartney Embassy of 1793* (Durham, NC: Duke University Press, 1995), 27.
12. Li Chen, *Chinese Law in Imperial Eyes: Sovereignty, Justice, and Transcultural Politics* (New York: Columbia University Press, 2016); Teemu Ruskola, *Legal Orientalism: China, the United States, and Modern Law* (Cambridge, MA: Harvard University Press, 2013); Eileen Scully, *Bargaining with the State from Afar: American Citizenship in Treaty Port China, 1844–1942* (New York: Columbia University Press, 2001).
13. Edward Keene, "The Treaty-Making Revolution of the Nineteenth Century," *International History Review* 34 no. 3 (2012): 475–500.
14. The following argument is based on a review of over eighty British treaties published in Clive Parry, ed., *The Consolidated Treaty Series* (Dobbs Ferry, NY: Oceana Publications, 1969–) and in Great Britain. Foreign Office, *British and Foreign State Papers* (London: James Ridgway & Sons, 1841–1977), hereafter *BFSP*. To place Qing-British treaties within a global context, the research group was defined according to the following criteria: treaties signed within a year of major Qing-British treaties (1842–1911) and treaties in force at the time of the first Qing-British treaty in 1842. Parties to treaties that limited or recalibrated internal taxation of the non-British party, included Turkey (1838), Shoa (1841), Buhawalpore (1843), Hanover (1844), Borneo (1847), Japan (1858), Bansda (1858), Acqua (1858), France (1873/74) Cambay (1885), and Ankole (1901).

between domestic capital and foreign capital. An 1842 treaty with Uruguay, for example, stipulated that any future increase in shop license fees would equalize the amount paid by Uruguayan-owned shops and British-owned shops.[15] What all of these commercial treaties shared was the codification of limits on the exercise of sovereignty in order to lower, eliminate, or regularize merchant costs generated in the transportation of goods from one location to another—what we can, in shorthand, call circulation costs.

From the 1830s to the 1870s, when Qing treaty-making first intensified, the empire participated in what was clearly a global trend. During this period, the annual rate of new agreements doubled from a low of 60 a year to a high of 140 a year, and the growth of treaty-making between European and non-European polities either kept track with intra-European treaty-making or exceeded it.[16]

The Qing-British treaties of 1842 and 1843 have previously been recognized as an important moment in Qing political history. They "constructed not merely a new framework of international relations into which the Qing was forcibly slotted, but a new language of sovereignty" patterned on the development of international law since the seventeenth century.[17] But these treaties were also always commercial, and in this respect, they also reshaped terms of commerce. Qing entry into this world of treaty-making drew from these precedents and contemporary practices but also departed from them. In broad outlines, British treaties with the Qing, like those negotiated elsewhere, stipulated conditions for the movement of British merchants and goods as well as regular limits on the costs of circulation. However, the level of procedural specification that appears in Qing treaties was anomalous.[18] Only in the 1880s did treaties between the United States and Europe begin to codify customs procedures in ways visible in China in the 1850s and 1860s. Why did this procedural specification occur (first) in China? What did these protocols mean for how Qing administrators fulfilled official obligations? This chapter considers the language and content of the first Qing-British treaties as a way to explore deterritorialization and

---

15. In addition to the Uruguay agreement, British treaties containing parity clauses include those with Austria (1838), Bolivia (1840), Brazil (1827), Buenos Aires (1825), Colombia (1825), Denmark (1824), Guatemala (1849), Hanover (1844), Mexico (1827), the Netherlands (1837), Prussia (1824), and Texas (1840). See Parry, *Consolidated Treaties*.
16. Keene, "Treaty-Making Revolution," 482, 491.
17. Peter Zarrow, *After Empire: The Conceptual Transformation of the Chinese State, 1885–1924* (Stanford: Stanford University Press, 2012), 93.
18. Only the 1841 Danish Sound Toll agreements paid comparable attention to institutional protocol. Foreign Office, "Treaty between Denmark, Hamburgh, and Lubeck, for Facilitating the Transit Trade through the Duchy of Holstein, 8 July 1840," *BFSP*; "Agreement between Great Britain and Denmark, relative to the Sound Duties, 13 August 1841," *BFSP*; "General Tariff of the Rates of Duty Levied at the Oresound and the 2 Belts; Regulations of the Danish Customs House; and Tables of Weights and Measures, 23 December 1841," *BFSP*.

reterritorialization that accompanied Eurocentric circuits of capital accumulation. Although treaties were a global phenomenon, in the Chinese context, they had peculiar effects on the emperorship as well as Qing officiating. These changes within governance were some of the first mechanisms to shape China into an expanded frontier for capital accumulation.

Treaties and Abstract Domination

Within the Euro-American tradition of international law, treaties hold an important place, albeit one that is relatively recent. Only during the nineteenth century did relations between European states became characterized by what one prominent legal historian has called "an intensive inclination towards contractual specification and codification."[19] According to this account, treaty making was part of a shift in the foundations of international law, away from the a priori authority of nature, God, or a globally supreme sovereign, to the demonstrated will and consent of states. Documents that testified to that will and consent accrued, new importance in the formation of the interstate order. Increasingly, only expressed will, objectified in written agreements such as treaties, determined what law was between sovereigns.[20]

The increasing importance of codification in the international arena reflected other recent and ongoing changes within European countries. In the political arena, sovereignty transferred from the embodied personal power of the sovereign to the divided legal power of the state with responsibilities to society. Constitutional governments institutionalized "rule of law" as the just basis for the conduct of society and deployed codification as a means to delineate and protect rights and obligations.[21] In the social and economic arenas, European societies were becoming collections of formally equal members, styled variously as citizen or commodity owners. In France, commercial capitalism helped give rise to discourse of civic equality.[22] In England, market forces supplanted the power of feudal lords to shape agricultural production.[23] Urban centers swelled with the buying and selling of goods and labor. In these nascent capitalist societies, forms of mediation central to social regulation in other places and at other times, including status, privilege, and overt coercion, became less functional or even illegitimate means of social regulation. Taking their place were

---

19. Wilhelm Georg Grewe, *Epochs of International Law* (New York: Walter de Gruyter, 2000), 504–6.
20. Grewe, *Epochs*, 512.
21. Grewe, *Epochs*, 483–86; see also Keene, "Treaty-Making Revolution," 496.
22. William H. Sewell Jr., *Capitalism and the Emergence of Civic Equality in Eighteenth Century France* (Chicago: University of Chicago Press, 2021).
23. Robert Brenner, "The Agrarian Roots of European Capitalism," in *The Brenner Debate: Agrarian Class Structure and Economic Development in Pre-industrial Europe*, ed. T. H. Ashton and C. H. E. Philpin (Cambridge: Cambridge University Press, 1985), 213–327.

value and law. On the one hand, societies of formally equal citizens developed and deployed legal systems defined by their objective and universal standards.[24] On the other hand, the value of goods and value of labor developed into an objective system of mediation for processes of production and distribution.[25] Commercial treaties combined these two projects, using a legal form predicated on formal equality to expand circuits of value production and circulation globally.

How we understand these novel systems of social regulation has bearing on how we understand treaty relations in China. For nearly a century after their appearance, treaty relations were praised as handmaidens of China's progress. Ostensibly, treaties liberated from meddling officials as well as oppressive regulations and reined in the excesses of a corrupt bureaucracy. Such praise rested on the assumption that law and a self-regulating market were realms of freedom. Later critiques that the treaties were unequal did not so much dislodge this assumption as use it as their grounds. I see reasons to set aside this assumption. Both law and self-regulating markets are uniquely characterized by what Moishe Postone has called "objective necessity" or "abstract domination." Whereas in all societies, some people overtly dominate other people (through violence, custom, etc.), according to Postone capitalist societies are historically specific because people's social practices also generate abstract social structures that dominate them.[26]

Precisely because capitalist social structures are abstract, it can be difficult to see the forms of domination they generate. Value's function, determining what social goods are produced and who has access to them, remains largely hidden behind commodities and market operations. In legal relations, domination takes the form what one critical legal scholar calls "an objective and impartial norm," independent of any particular individuals or set of individuals. In its ideal form, law mediates rights and claims only with reference to itself and in so doing provides an objective "mechanism of constraint" acting on all.[27] The difficulty recognizing either the law or the open market as a source domination partly explains how in the nineteenth century Europe's dominant geopolitical presence generated self-authorizing, valedictory narratives. Conversely, recognition of the domination that inheres in law and markets allows us to see that a core thrust of deterritorialization and reterritorialization in China was to create structures of abstract domination.

---

24. For an alternative to Grewe's account, see Evgeniĭ Pashukanis, *The General Theory of Law & Marxism* (New Brunswick, NJ: Transaction, 2002).
25. Moishe Postone, *Time, Labor, and Social Domination* (Cambridge: Cambridge University Press, 1993), chap. 4.
26. Postone, *Time, Labor, and Social Domination*, 29–31.
27. Pashukanis, *General Theory*, 17.

What a British Merchant Wants—What He Really, Really Wants

Constraint was exactly what the British commercial and political establishments were after in China.

The more familiar story, of course, is that the British were after markets. By the early decades of the nineteenth century, machinery in key British industries, namely textiles, had noticeably reduced the time and human labor required to produce yarn, cloth, and finished goods—the main legal articles of trade that British firms hoped to sell in China.[28] Because of the capitalist orientation within these industries, manufacturers followed the logic of potential capital accumulation, not current demand.[29] The result was monumental increases in material goods but a smaller pool of domestic wages to purchase them. In the words of economic historian Eric Hobsbawm, the first half of the nineteenth century was a period of "contrast between the enormous and rapidly growing productive potential of capitalist industrialization and its inability, as it were, to broaden its base." Industrial capital was growing dramatically, but such growth had not translated into sufficiently expanded markets, more profitable investment opportunities, or higher employment and wages.[30] This was equally true for capital goods, such as iron and machines, which by the 1840s suffered diminishing returns in the domestic market and "actively sought new outlets."[31]

By 1817 political economists in England recognized that mechanized production chronically shed workers—producing structural unemployment and with it the demise of the rapid consumption needed to keep up with rapid production.[32] Soon after, industrialists began eyeing other parts of the world, including China, as the solution to the newly emerged endemic gap between production and consumption at home. Whereas trade itself was a practice that predated the capitalist

---

28. Nicholas Crafts, *Forging Ahead, Falling Behind, and Fighting Back: British Economic Growth from the Industrial Revolution to the Financial Crisis* (Cambridge: Cambridge University Press, 2018), 15, 19–20; Joel Mokyr, "Accounting for the Industrial Revolution," in *The Cambridge Economic History of Modern Britain*, vol. 1, ed. Roderick Floud and Paul Johnson (Cambridge: Cambridge University Press, 2004), 1–27. Industrial labor productivity growth grew nearly tenfold between 1759 and 1851, with (labor-saving) technical innovation the main source of gains. Current consensus points to 1850 as a starting point for "indisputable economic expansion" (Moykr, "Accounting," 3). Opium was, of course, the most profitable trade for British agency houses in the region. It was an illegal trade until 1858.
29. David Harvey, *Limits to Capital*, rev. ed. (New York: Verso, 2006), 89–93.
30. Eric Hobsbawm, *The Age of Capital 1848–1875* (New York: Vintage, 1996), 33.
31. Giovanni Arrighi, *The Long Twentieth Century: Money, Power, and the Origins of Our Times* (New York: Verso, 1994), 160–61.
32. J. Barton, *Observations on the Circumstances which Influence the Condition of the Labouring Classes of Society* (London: n.p., 1817); E. S. Cayley, *On Commercial Economy in Six Essays* (London: J. Ridgway, 1830), 33, 56. Keith Tribe, "'Industrialisation' as a Historical Category," in *Genealogies of Capitalism* (Atlantic Highlands, NJ: Humanities Press, 1981), 101–20.

world economy in the decades when industrialization accelerated and augmented production of material wealth, "reshuffling goods in space and time" was critical to "the self-expansion of capital."[33] The Manchester Chamber of Commerce reported to Parliament in 1827, "We are now beginning to find our great capital and means of production of goods cramped for want of more extensive markets. The vast fields for commercial enterprise which the East Indies offer to us ... would assuredly make up for the falling away from all our former customers and give full employment to our redundant capital and dense population."[34] A place like China, where the population was soon to reach 450 million, became an attractive solution to the falling rate of profit in England.[35]

There was only one problem. At the same time industrialists' enthusiasm for potential markets in China grew, so did the commercial sector's complaints about the conditions under which existing trade took place. In part, these complaints targeted the Crown-granted monopoly to the East India Company, which was accused of undermining the potential growth of British trade in China.[36] Another strain of complaints targeted the Chinese government. Longtime Canton "resident" and opium trader William Jardine cautioned the British government, "Great Britain can never derive any important advantage from the opening of the trade to China while the present mode of levying duties and extorting money from [Chinese] merchants exists." Jardine, well respected in the commercial community, advised Parliament, "We must have a *commercial code* with these celestial barbarians before we can extend advantageously our commercial operations."[37]

The object of Jardine's critique was a regulatory framework in place since 1757, commonly known as the "Canton system." Most well known today for confining British trade to a single port and restricting Chinese participation in foreign trade to a group of licensed merchants, the Canton system was nonetheless an effective regulatory regime that oversaw sizable growth in foreign commerce.[38] Jardine's complaint, however, was not about these limits on trade so much as about how

---

33. Arrighi, *The Long Twentieth Century*, 177, 221–27; Karl Marx, *Capital: A Critique of Political Economy*, vol. 2, trans. David Fernbach (New York: Penguin, 1978), chap. 6.
34. "Proceedings of the Manchester Chamber of Commerce," quoted in Michael Greenberg, *British Trade and the Opening of China, 1800–42* (Cambridge: Cambridge University Press, 1951), 181.
35. The historical growth of the British economy and the overseas expansion of British investment and economic activity is a much more multifaceted story than the very condensed account given here.
36. On the end of the East India Company monopoly, see Anthony Webster, *The Twilight of the East India Company: The Evolution of Anglo-Asian Commerce and Politics, 1790–1860* (Martlesham, UK: Boydell & Brewer, 2013), 94–103; H. V. Bowen, *The Business of Empire: The East India Company and Imperial Britain, 1756–1833* (Cambridge: Cambridge University Press, 2006), 296–99.
37. William Jardine, Private Letter Book, quoted in Greenberg, *British Trade*, 179; emphasis added.
38. Paul Van Dyke, *The Canton Trade: Life and Enterprise on the China Coast, 1700–1845* (Hong Kong: Hong Kong University Press, 2007); Gang Zhao, *The Qing Opening to the Ocean: Chinese Maritime Policies, 1684–1757* (Honolulu: University of Hawai'i Press, 2013), 169–86.

officials executed the regulatory order. Decades of interaction had shown that conditions of trade in Guangzhou (廣州) could vary greatly according to who was in charge.[39] Local officials exercised latitude to set and reset key conditions of trade, and the judgments of these men varied. Indeed, according to historians, much of the Canton system's past success was due to the ability of administrators to negotiate the varied, time-sensitive needs of ships coming to trade. Even before 1757, foreign ships flocked to Guangzhou because they knew they could "do business" with local merchants and officials.

In the first decades of the nineteenth century, however, the "Canton" regime came under British fire precisely for its flexibility. A Parliamentary Select Committee convened in 1814 judged that British commerce in China was "'protected by no laws, but on the contrary subject to such regulations as are made so vague and undefined, as to admit of any interference or interpretation that a corrupt or despotic government may be disposed to given them."[40] The East India Company, well versed in Canton negotiations, warned that commerce at Guangzhou was "at all times and seasons, at the mercy of the caprice and rapacity of local authorities, and their subordinates." Such conditions, in light of the flurry of treaty-making that had recently commenced, were reinterpreted as anomalous. Sir J. B. Urmston, head of the EIC's factory in 1819–1820, reported back to London,

> neither our trade nor general intercourse with the Chinese is carried on under those established and reasonable regulations, as such usually attend our commerce in other parts of the world; but on the contrary, such laws and regulations as do exist (if the arbitrary system of the Chinese can be so termed), touching the foreign trade at Canton, are altogether vague and undefined.[41]

Industrialists and traders wanted more access to China, and they also wanted that access under different terms.

By the time the British government "opened" China to non–East India Company traders in 1833, a loud chorus proclaimed that under the current regime in Guangzhou, Qing officials had latitude to act "capriciously"; they levied "arbitrary dues" and changed tax rates at will.[42] A treaty with China, many thought, could do

---

39. Hosea Ballou Morse, *The Chronicles of the East India Company, Trading to China 1635–1834*, 5 vols. (Oxford: Clarendon Press, 1926–1929), 2:13–22, 2:347–56, 3:195–98, 4:144–60, 4:199–221, 4:278–92.
40. James Matheson, *Present Position and Prospects of the British Trade with China* (London: Smith, Elder, 1836), 25.
41. John Phipps, *A Practical Treatise on the China and Eastern Trade Comprising the Commerce of Great Britain and India Particularly Bengal and Singapore with China and the Eastern Islands* (London: William H. Allen, 1836), 16–20.
42. See also Peter Auber, *China. An Outline of Its Government, Laws, and Policy: And of the British and Foreign Embassies to, and Intercourse with, That Empire* (London: Parbury, Allen, 1834), esp. 255–56.

much to secure better facilities for trade by bringing a "code" and "principles of international law" to bear.[43] In addition, as trader Walter Stevenson Davidson warned Parliament, it was equally important this code limit the ability of Qing officials to act on their own accord. What was wanted in China, Davidson claimed, was a treaty "wherein the duties of the foreigners who visit China shall be clearly and distinctly defined, wherein their rights in return shall be acknowledged, and the whole connexion [sic] proceeded upon the sanction of such laws and regulations."[44]

* * *

In 1842, after decades of smuggling opium against the wishes of the Chinese government and fighting a war to defend their commercial interests in China, the British got their treaty. For contemporaries, this was a triumphal moment. "Eldorado" had been opened and the advance of international law signaled "the commencement of a new era" in which the Chinese people would "rise from their real degradation, and take their proper rank among the other kingdoms and empires of this world."[45] With foreign presence and law now guaranteed, "new forces" would work on China.

In recent decades, historians have been more critical of the treaties, pointing out that these agreements did not construct relations of "perfect equality" but were instead rather unequal. Terms granted unreciprocated privileges to British subjects and impinged on the Qing government's ability to exercise the very forms of sovereignty international law purportedly fashioned for it.[46] But there are other grounds as well from which to push back against Eurocentric legal triumphalism. These become evident when we look more closely at what the legal form of the treaties and their lexical particularities did to the content of Qing governance, both in terms of the emperorship and in terms of the more quotidian work of local administrators.

---

43. Lord Napier to Viscount Palmerston, 14 August 1834, *Correspondence Relating to China*, [223] [224] [230] [234] (1840), 13.
44. Great Britain, *First Report from the Select Committee on the Affairs of the East India Company: China Trade* (1830), 207.
45. "Eldorado" is Nathan Pelcovits's term; see *Old China Hands and the Foreign Office* (New York: American Institute of Pacific Relations, 1948); "ART. I. Present Condition of the Chinese Empire, Considered with regard Both to Its Domestic and Foreign Relations, Especially as Affected by the Late War and Treaty," *Chinese Repository* 12, no. 1 (January 1843): 1–8.
46. Dong Wang, *China's Unequal Treaties: Narrating National History* (Lanham, MD: Lexington Books, 2005); Sun Zuji, 不平等條約討論大綱 [Discussion of the unequal treaties] (Beijing: Beijing zhongxian tuofang keji fazhan youxian gongsi, 2012).

Qing Language of Commercial Administration

British traders and politicians were not the only ones displeased with the state of trade at Guangzhou. Foreign trade was critical to the people's livelihoods in land-poor Guangdong, and the port's trade directly contributed to the imperial household's purse. Yet British seamen were also disruptive to local order. They brawled with residents and had been responsible for a number of deaths. British ships, moreover, consistently engaged in opium smuggling and showed little inclination to respect Qing law. With no possibility of restricting opium imports, when Qing negotiators considered what China would want from a commercial treaty, they turned their attention to managing British traders.

I have already briefly noted that personalities, dispositions, and embodied capacities were fulcrums of order within the Canton system. When considering how to better arrange commercial relations with Great Britain, imperial officials likewise looked to the subjective dimensions of the persons involved, including themselves. So, while both the British and Chinese persons involved with trade at Guangzhou pointed to problems caused by the behaviors of *other* persons, it was only for Qing officials that the orientations and dispositions of persons also pointed to solutions.

As an example, for high provincial official and anti-opium crusader Lin Zexu (林則徐, 1785–1850), one root of the intractable opium trade was what lay in the hearts and minds (*xin* 心) of British traders.[47] In his reports on the opium trade, Lin routinely attended to these. He excoriated the foreigners who arrived on ships from Bombay for being dominated by thoughts of greed (奸夷 利欲 薰心) and in particular for the "greed and cunning" (貪狡之心) that had perverted the more noble purposes of trade. He despaired as well that profits were so great that these men refused to "lose heart" even in the face of government prohibitions.[48]

The heart and mind were also equally important to Lin as a fulcrum for restoring order. He intended the punishments he meted out to work on the *xin* of traders. He also invoked the *xin* of the emperor and the English queen as paired sources of political order. In a letter to Queen Victoria, Lin wrote that the emperor, whose heart was the heart of heaven and earth (蓋以 天地之心為心也), by allowing the British to trade, had set in motion a relationship, which Lin now called on the queen

---

47. *Xin* is variously translated as heart and mind. I further explore this connection below.
48. Lin Zexu, "附奏東西各洋越竄夷船嚴行懲辦" [Addendum on the strict disciplinary action against unlawful activity by foreign ships on the coast], in *Wanqing wenxuan* [Selected writings from the late Qing], ed. Zheng Zhenduo, Zhongguo zhexue dianzihua jihua [Chinese Philosophical Text Digitization Project], https://ctext.org; Lin Zexu, "覆奏曾望顏條陳封關禁海事宜疏" [Reply to Zeng Wangyan's report on the closure of the customs and the prohibition of maritime affairs], in *Wanqing wenxuan*.

to correct. Despite persistent opium smuggling by her subjects, the queen's heart, Lin presumed, was inclined toward the transformative power vested in the Qing empire, so surely she could order her subjects to obey the laws of China.[49] It is clear from Lin's letter to the Queen and other correspondence that as much as British traders felt officials in Guangzhou did not show proper respect for law, so Qing officials felt the same way about the British coming to trade. But despite the shared ground of discontent, the Qing official Lin Zexu and the British merchant community represented by men like William Jardine offered different solutions. Whereas British merchants in China focused on codification of rights and obligations, Lin called forth embodied subjectivity to help create order on earth.

However historically singular Lin Zexu's letter to Queen Victoria, it partook in a common language spoken by other Chinese officials also charged with managing commercial relations with Euro-American merchants. In addition to *xin*, most accurately translated as "heart-mind" (more on this to come), managing these relations involved attention to *xing* (性 original nature), *qing* (情 nature and mind), and *shi* (勢 the disposition of things). Lin's correspondence invoked all three. So, too, did a key memorial written by two imperial clansmen, Qiying (耆英, 1787–1858) and Yi-li-bu (伊里布, 1772–1843), who held important positions within the central government and were appointed treaty negotiators after the first Opium War.[50] While working on the Treaty of Nanjing, (江寧條約), these senior statesmen, who had little practical experience with day-to-day port business, frankly assessed the difficulties involved in managing Euro-American trade on the China coast. They were particularly concerned that opening additional ports to British ships would ramify a difficulty that had emerged in Canton—namely, that the increasing volume

---

49. Lin Zexu, "拟谕英吉利国王檄" [Proposed edict to the English monarch], in *Wanqing wenxuan*. Chinese original: "谅贵国王向化倾心，定能谕令众夷，兢兢奉法." My gloss departs from standard interpretations in order to emphasize the charismatic position of the world-ordering emperor invoked by Lin as well as expectations of reciprocity from Great Britain as a past recipient of imperial grace, which were set up in the opening paragraph of the letter. More on imperial grace below. Compare with "the sovereign of your honorable nation, on pouring out your heart [*xin*] before the altar of eternal justice, cannot but command all foreigners with the deepest respect to reverence our laws!"; "Art. I Letter to the Queen of England from the High Commissioner Lin, and His Colleagues," *Chinese Repository* 8, no. 10 (February 1840): 497–503. A more modern version: "We presume that the ruler of your honorable country, who takes delight in our culture and whose disposition is inclined towards us, must be able to instruct the various barbarians to observe the law with care." From Ssuyu Teng and John Fairbank, *China's Response to the West* (Cambridge, MA: Harvard University Press, 1954), reprinted in Mark A. Kishlansky, ed., *Sources of World History*, vol. 2 (New York: HarperCollins, 1995), 266–69.

50. Qiying (耆英, 1787–1858) was a third-generation civil appointee who had served as first president of key central government boards: the Board of Rites, the Board of Works, and the Board of Civil Appointments. I-li-bu (伊里布, 1772–1843), had distinguished himself in a series of military expeditions in imperial borderlands. See Arthur Hummel, ed., *Eminent Chinese of the Ch'ing Period* (Washington, DC: Government Publishing Office, 1943–1944), 130–34, 387–89.

of foreign imports required increasingly long port stays to arrange sales and return cargo. During these longer stays, the task of maintaining order became more difficult. The negotiators went on,

> In our humble opinion, the reason foreign merchantmen have been so difficult to regulate truly is because they swiftly move back and forth in a gigantic wave. Morning in the east, evening in the west, in a flash, a thousand miles. Thus, they suffer from being far away. If [we allow them] places to work and store their goods and wives to tie up their heartminds [*xin*], then they will be pressed between their attachment to their capital [*zi* 資] and the family they bring with them. This will greatly nourish [*zi* 滋] their attention to attachments and love [*lian* 戀]. To control [*kongzhi* 控制] them will be easier. The English attach greater importance to women than men. Husbands are regulated [*zhi* 制] by their wives. [Such a strategy] caters to [*fu* 俯] and follows [*shun* 順] their internal state [*qing* 情], namely the concealed soft spot in their nature [*xing* 性]. It seems possible that [so doing] will we no longer need to be on guard when an issue arises.[51]

Several features of this analysis warrant comment. First, a slow pace of trade was as much as a problem from the point of view of Qiying and I-li-bu as it was for British merchants who complained about delays imposed by customs authorities. But although for British merchants sluggish trade was a problem for how it affected their capital, for these Qing authorities, it was a problem for how it affected merchants' mental and affective states. These traders lived a transitory existence, constantly and rapidly moving between Europe and China. They were far from home and family. This state of being in motion without stabilizing love attachments, the memorialists implied, was a source of their difficult behavior. To change policy and allow these men to reside on land and bring their wives (as the British requested during treaty negotiations) would nourish their *lian*—a term indexing affection-based attachment—making them more manageable. Subsequently, the memorialists further attended to the occupation of English heart-minds (*xin*), to where their constant original nature (*xing*) showed signs of yielding, and to what tactics would make use of what the English actively manifest as their nature and mind (*qing*).

A governing strategy that identifies states of *xin*, *xing*, and *qing* as levers for generating a peaceable trading environment places the management of English trade squarely amid neo-Confucian discussions of the nature of the human and sources of action. Or stated somewhat differently, such neo-Confucian discussions appear here to have offered a framework for thinking through strategies and tactics for managing foreign trade. Although I cannot say definitively why Qiying, I-li-bu, and the other memorialists chose to use a neo-Confucian lexicon in these discussions,

---

51. *Chouban yiwu shimo* 籌辦夷務始末 [A complete record of foreign affairs] (digital), Daoguang 22, juan 59, 41.1–41.2.

neo-Confucian learning was at the time still central to education at court and for imperial examinations. It is worth considering this framework in more detail if we want to understand how it was possible to think that the affections of British merchants were the key to improved commercial and interstate relations.

Neo-Confucian Ontological Foundations for Governance

Up until the last years of the dynasty, the typical education of a learned person in China used a curriculum based in the *Four Books* and *Five Classics*, compilations of philosophical and poetic texts and dialogues. These texts, closely but not exclusively associated with Confucius (c. 551–c. 479 BCE), concerned among other things the nature of man and the inner source of human action as well as principles of conduct both in general and specific circumstances.[52] As the cornerstone of classical education, the texts educated the reader in a process of self-cultivation and linked that process to a well-ordered society and specific functions of government.[53] In the words of Benjamin Elman, within the framework of orthodox classical learning, "political, social, and cultural harmony depended on the moral rigor of each individual."[54] Imperial education not only trained students to understand how the world was formed by dynamic energy (e.g., *qi* 氣) but provided a curriculum of instruction, including bodily practices such as calligraphy, to cultivate the ability to actualize inherent potential (*shi*).[55] In preparation for imperial exams, officials at all levels would have read that the good official's ability to govern was an embodied one, personal to his moral cultivation and mobilized through emotional states, such as earnestness.[56]

---

52. For an introduction to the *Four Books* and *Five Classics* and their role in imperial education, see Daniel K. Gardner, *The Four Books: The Basic Teachings of the Later Confucian Tradition* (Indianapolis: Hackett, 2007) and Michael Nylan, *The Five "Confucian" Classics* (New Haven: Yale University Press, 2001).
53. The *Five Classics* were compiled 1000 BCE–200 BCE. The Qing exam format 1793–1898 drew primarily from these texts. See Benjamin Elman, *A Cultural History of Civil Examinations in Late Imperial China* (Berkeley: University of California Press, 2000), 737.
54. Benjamin Elman, *Civil Examinations and Meritocracy in Late Imperial China* (Cambridge: Cambridge University Press, 2013), 75.
55. François Jullien, *The Propensity of Things: Toward a History of Efficacy in China*, trans. Janet Lloyd (New York: Zone Books, 1995), 75–79. On calligraphy, see Jonathan Hay, "The Kangxi Emperor's Brush Traces: Calligraphy, Writing, and the Art of Imperial Authority," in *Body and Face in Chinese Visual Culture*, ed. Wu Hung and Katherine R. Tsiang (Cambridge, MA: Harvard University Asia Center, 2005), 311–34.
56. William Rowe, *Saving the World: Chen Hongmou and Elite Consciousness in Eighteenth-Century China* (Stanford: Stanford University Press, 2001). An alternative route to office involved purchase, but there is little evidence that office purchasers were uneducated. See Lawrence Zhang, *Power for a Price: The Purchase of Official Appointments in Qing China* (Cambridge, MA: Harvard University Press, 2022).

Within these texts, *xin*, *qing*, and *xing*—the levers invoked by Qiying and I-li-bu for gaining better control of English trade—are interacting entities that form the nature of living things, human and nonhuman. *Xing* referred to an inborn, constant, original, structural nature. *Qing*, by contrast, was a nature that was active, dynamic, and expressive. It inhered in expansive collective phenomena (e.g., 軍情 *junqing*, armed troops *qing*) and was also, in a sense closer to the English term "emotion," an internal state (e.g., 人情 *renqing*, the *qing* of humanity).[57] Recent work on *qing* explains it as a genuine yet unfixed state of existence, a term that refers to a "dynamic pattern of emergence, generation, and manifestation of things and events, and our direct and engaged understanding of them."[58] Unlike *xing*, *qing* was in motion, accessible to the outside observer and therefore could be the target of governance.[59]

What this excursion into the Chinese classical lexicon tells us is that in 1842, as the Treaty of Nanjing was drafted, a classically educated official saw a world populated by internal, dynamic embodied states, which were the source of events and, as such, provided a fulcrum for constructive intervention. By catering to (*fu*) and following (*shun*) the *qing* of the English, authorities could neutralize the English propensity to generate and escalate disagreements. These propositions suggest to the historian that successful governance, according to canonical criteria, entailed first assessing what was active in the nature of those you sought to govern and then adopting tactics that worked with it to produce your desired situation.[60] Which is to say, good governance entailed exactly what Lin Zexu was up to.

Attention to how *xin* figured in Qiying's and I-li-bu's recommendations further reinforces the sense that governing trade entailed discerning and manipulating psychophysical entities. It is notable that although the memorialists see that market mechanisms are a source of problems—too many goods slows sales—they eschew the market as the point of intervention. Rather, their solution targets *xin*—an entity to be redirected toward familial attachment. Interpretations of *xin* as it appears

---

57. Bongrae Seok, *Embodied Moral Psychology and Confucian Philosophy* (Lanham, MD: Lexington Books, 2013), esp. 123–37.
58. Seok, *Embodied Moral Psychology*, 130; see also Attilio Andreini, "The Meaning of *Qing* in Texts from Guodian Tomb No. 1," in *Love, Hatred, and Other Passions: Questions and Themes on Emotions in Chinese Civilization*, ed. Paolo Santangelo and Donatella Guida (Leiden: Brill, 2006), 149–65.
59. Seok, *Embodied Moral Psychology*, 96–137. Seok glosses three explanations of *qing* in Chinese philosophical texts: "a) ontologically as the true nature of the world and human being; b) epistemologically as the way the mind (not as a distant observer but as a close resonator) understands the world; c) axiomatically as the positive sense of harmony or commitment to higher moral values" (123). In my reading, the memorialist's *qing* most closely resonates with (a) and (b). Trade-related memorials from the 1830s and 1840s recorded in *Chouban yiwu shimo* 籌辦義務始末 [A complete record of foreign affairs] show that English *xing* and *qing* were often the target of official scrutiny and assessment by Qing officials.
60. This reading of governing strategy resonates with recent analysis of strategic thinking in the Confucian tradition more generally; see Jullien, *Propensity of Things*.

within the neo-Confucian corpus have variously identified it as "fecund matter" out of which moral character and action sprout, the "seat of one's emotional and cognitive faculties," and the foremost means "to participate consciously and conscientiously in the creative and productive process of Heaven-and-earth."[61] Whereas the English language discriminates between heart and mind, *xin* is a concept that combines the emotional and the epistemological. The basic activity of the heart-mind is to discriminate and distinguish, and it applies these energies to speech and action.[62] When Qing officials targeted the heart-mind in their discussions of troubled commercial relations, they placed internal intellectual/emotional disposition at the center of event-making and called on themselves to devise strategies to effect it.

At this point, it is necessary to point out that *xin* was also important in governance because of the role it played generating the disposition of the official. In one well-established view, still current after 1850, government was men acting on other men. For one example, we can look to imperial prince Yixin, who was deeply educated in the classics and headed the Zongli yamen. Later in his life, he wrote an extensive set of reflections on governance in which he argued that the obligations of government arise from "norms of ethical human relationships" and that "the aim of government is to so move the hearts of men by setting an example of virtue." Governance, for Yixin and others like him, carried out ethical norms. The potential for actions serve the public good in part depended on the state of an actor's *xin*.[63]

The foundation for this view can be traced to key tenets within classical education, which taught aspiring officials that physical reality was not created by an external agent (as in the Judeo-Christian world) but rather was a "spontaneously generating life process" characterized by "continuity, wholeness, and dynamism."[64] Within such

---

61. Antonio S. Cua, "*Xin* (Mind/Heart) and Moral Failure: Notes on an Aspect of Mencius's Moral Psychology," in *Human Nature, Ritual and History: Studies in Xunzi and Chinese Philosophy* (Washington, DC: Catholic University of America Press, 2005), 348–70; Andrew Plaks, "*Xin* as the Seat of the Emotions in Confucian Self-Cultivation," in *Love, Hatred, and Other Passions: Questions and Themes on Emotions in Chinese Civilization*, ed. Paolo Santangelo and Donatella Guida (Leiden: Brill, 2006), 113–25; Wm. Theodore de Bary, *The Message of the Mind in Neo-Confucianism* (New York: Columbia University Press, 1989), 6.
62. Jane Geaney, *On the Epistemology of the Senses in Early Chinese Thought* (Honolulu: University of Hawai'i Press, 2002), 84–85.
63. Jason H. Parker, "The Rise and Decline of I-Hsin, Prince Kung, 1858–1865: A Study of the Interaction of Politics and Ideology in Late Imperial China" (PhD diss., Princeton University, 1979), 282–83, 303, citing Yixin's *Collected Essays of the Ledao Studio*.
64. Tu Wei-ming, *Confucian Thought: Selfhood as Creative Transformation* (Albany: State University of New York Press, 1985), 37–40; Frederick Mote, *Intellectual Foundations of China*, 2nd ed. (New York: McGraw Hill, 1989), 12–16. Zeng Guofan is one exemplar of this approach to governance; see Hao Chang, "The Intellectual Context of Reform," in *Reform in Nineteenth Century China*, ed. Paul A. Cohen and John E. Schrecker (Cambridge, MA: Harvard University East Asian Research Center, 1976), 145–49.

a reality, order and well-being were not the product of strictly implementing regulations (e.g., commandments) but rather the result of constant interplay between a judgment-making subject and other forces.[65] In light of his role in actualizing the potential for order and prosperity, it was important for the neo-Confucian official to tend to his heart-mind.[66] In the nineteenth century, this tending would have begun at the onset of classical education, when the first texts the student engaged were those designed to cultivate understanding of the self and when the student recorded their engagements with these texts to practice of self-criticism and self-cultivation, using textual passages to acknowledge and resolve perceived inner weaknesses.[67] Attention to one's own inner life could be expected to carry through an official's career. In communication with the emperor about foreign trade and treaty negotiations, officials signaled attention to their *xin* with terms such as *cheng* (誠 sincere), *renzhen* (認真 earnest), *xixin* (悉心 with great care), *zhenxin* (真心 heartfelt), and *liuxin* (留心 pay attention to).[68]

Following the work of anthropologist Catherine Lutz, it is possible to say that such communications not only positioned speakers relative to a symbolic cultural milieu but were also generative acts that negotiated and created social reality. These terms named, justified, and persuaded the emperor of the work field officials performed. Stated somewhat differently, as they voiced an internal state, the terms also acted interpersonally and—in this specific context—politically as well. "The sense of emotion words for those who use them is as much to be found in how they work in social life as in any necessary resonance with a preverbal emotional experience," writes Lutz. "[Emotion words are] coalescences of complex ethnotheoretical ideas about the nature of the self and social interaction."[69] This suggests the language of emotion can be read as more than mere show. When officials invoked actions of the *xin* as part of discerning, judging, deciding, and moving, even if they did so by convention, they performed the centrality of heart-mind and the thinking/feeling subject within the political field.

---

65. Mote, *Intellectual Foundations*, 39–46. Rowe's study of Chen Hongmou offers examples of such an orientation; see Rowe, *Saving the World*, 90–91, 96. Rowe describes Chen's views as "orthodox and ordinary" (86).
66. Plaks, "Xin," esp. 116, 120–21.
67. Barry C. Keenan, *Neo-Confucian Self-Cultivation* (Honolulu: University of Hawai'i Press, 2011), 90, 105–6. One way to express what a student had "taken away" from a text was "*xin de*" 心得, literally to "obtain by the heart/mind."
68. Terms appear in memorials from high officials involved in managing British affairs, including Governor-Generals Lin Zexu and Deng Tingzhen (鄧廷楨, 1776–1846), Imperial Commissioner and treaty negotiator He Guiqing (何桂清, 1816–1862), and one-time Shanghai *daotai* Xue Huan (薛煥, 1815–1880), as published in *Chouban yiwu shimo* 籌辦夷務始末 [A complete record of foreign affairs].
69. Catherine A. Lutz, *Unnatural Emotions: Everyday Sentiments on a Micronesian Atoll and Their Challenge to Western Theory* (Chicago: University of Chicago Press, 1988), 9–10.

Charismatic Emperorship in Treaty Relations

We should not be surprised, then, to find in the Chinese-language versions of the Treaty of Nanjing and 1843 Supplementary Treaty of Hoomun Chai (五口通商附粘善後條款) language that indexes internal states and intersubjective relationships. Although the Chinese and English versions of these agreements generally correspond in phrasing and meaning, affective language is largely absent from the English-language versions. Such moments of non-correspondence allow us to see what differed in the Qing approach to commercial governance at the highest levels of government.

Perhaps the most revealing term in this respect is *en* (恩), often glossed as "imperial grace" or "imperial kindness."[70] *En* was a hierarchical but also intersubjective relationship constructed between the Qing emperor and other parties. It indexed what some have identified as the emperorship's charismatic kingship in which the emperor was a "communal enunciator" channeling divine favors and actively regulating change.[71] A supreme lord gave *en* to a loyal inferior, initiating an ordering process, and it was important as well as expected that the loyal inferior would recognize the receipt of *en* and thereby complete the process.[72] As Peter Zarrow explains, "Whether Mongol prince, Manchu servant, or Han official, one ritually acknowledged the imperial grace, a favor literally beyond the recipient's capacity to ever repay, though one should devote one's life to the effort to be deserving."[73] *En*, then, should be read as a crucial marker of both the higher lord–lesser lord relationship typically constituted by the emperorship as well as of the ongoing dialogue at the center of this relationship.[74]

In the Chinese-language versions of the 1842 and 1843 treaties, *en* constructed an ongoing intersubjective relationship between the emperor and British merchants.[75] In a first use, imperial grace granted permission to British subjects and their

---

70. According to Pär Kristoffer Cassel, the first treaties between Qing and "the West" were concluded in Manchu, not Chinese; see Pär Kristoffer Cassel, *Grounds of Judgement: Extraterritoriality and Imperial Power in Nineteenth-Century China and Japan* (Oxford: Oxford University Press, 2012), 205. The Manchu text seldom appears in scholarship, and it is the Chinese-language version that appears in the Imperial Maritime Customs' (IMC's) treaty collection as well as Wang's compilation. Here, I treat the Chinese version as indicative of Qing performance of their role as the ruling government of China.
71. Pamela Crossley, "The Rulerships of China," *American Historical Review* 97, no. 5 (1992): 1480; Peter Zarrow, *After Empire: The Conceptual Transformation of the Chinese State, 1885–1924* (Stanford: Stanford University Press, 2012), 9–12.
72. Hevia, *Cherishing Men*, chap. 5.
73. Zarrow, *After Empire*, 14.
74. Hevia, *Cherishing Men*, 125.
75. It is unlikely that the Daoguang emperor directly participated in the drafting of this text. The use of *en*, rather, indexes what Qing negotiators (primarily Qi-ying) felt was an appropriate mechanism for bringing order to commerce.

families to reside in the five ports opened to foreign trade.[76] Later, *en* performed the work of creating what is known in English as "most favored nation status." The emperor bestowed imperial grace on all foreign merchants from the Western Ocean as a "single body" and pledged that should he bestow imperial grace upon any other country, the English would receive it as well as a show of "fairness and justness."[77] Both uses of *en* approximated the reciprocity imperial grace typically generated and laid out British obligations that followed its bestowal. In return for residence, the emperor expected the English queen to appoint to each of the five ports a consul to communicate with local officials and order (令 *ling*) British adherence to treaty provisions.[78] In the "most favored nation" clause, receipt of *en* obligated recipients to tend to their emotional states and not "wantonly and rashly" request new privileges.[79]

The British government had long resisted any sign that relations between Great Britain and China were anything other than "perfectly" equal. Yet *en*, buried as it was in practical provisions for residence and trade, did manage to assert something of the Qing version of sovereignty and governance. In this version, the emperor performed his power to actively order the world by setting in motion an ongoing hierarchical relationship between himself, the English queen, and British traders.[80] The language of persons (emperor, queen, merchant) and interpersonal actions (bestowal, request) as well as emotional states and their consequences (wanton, reckless) oriented thinking, feeling entities toward each other, and within this orienting framework, the parties were called upon to cooperate in the ongoing constitution of a beneficial commercial order.

Disabling Emperorship

An English-language equivalent of *en* is entirely missing from the English texts of the treaties signed in 1842 and 1843. These instead offered their own lexical particularities—namely, nonhuman entities such as "rights," "privileges," and "immunities," which compelled certain humans to act in certain ways. Likewise, English-language counterparts to *qing*, *xing*, and *xin* were also largely absent from the Anglophone discussion of how to best arrange British trade in China. In their place were calls

---

76. Treaty of Nanjing, Article 2. This discussion uses the multilingual treaty texts reproduced in China. Imperial Maritime Customs, *Treaties, Conventions, Etc. between China and Foreign States*, 2 vols., vol. 1, 2nd ed., Miscellaneous Series No. 30 (Shanghai: Inspector General of Customs, 1917). Here, 1:352. Chinese text has been cross-referenced with Wang's treaty compilation. Translations from the Chinese are my own.
77. Treaty of Hoomun Chai, Article 8, IMC, *Treaties*, 1:393.
78. IMC, *Treaties*, 1:352.
79. IMC, *Treaties*, 1:393.
80. On these aspects of emperorship, see Zarrow, *After Empire*, 12; Hevia, *Cherishing Men*, 125.

for codes, laws, and constraints on actions of individuals. As discussed above, one of the emergent social functions of legal codification was to create public order without depending on or referring to subjective orientations. The English-language treaty texts achieved this by offering a discourse that reoriented Qing governance toward static objectifications of imperial will.

Take, for example, the English text of the "most favored nation" clause in the Supplementary Treaty, which differs in several ways from the Chinese text discussed above. In the English text, the Qing emperor, in lieu of imperial grace, grants English merchants "the same terms" for trade as merchants from other countries. The article then stipulates that "should the Emperor hereafter, from any cause whatever, be pleased to grant additional *privileges* or *immunities* to any of the subjects or Citizens of such Foreign Countries, the same privileges and immunities will be extended to and enjoyed by British subjects."[81] In the English text, as in its Chinese counterpart, the emperor still grants and the merchants still receive, but is being given privileges and immunities, not imperial grace. The former are not, as *en* is, an ongoing reciprocal intersubjective relationship, but rather, they are intangible objectifications of the emperor's will. Legal historians use the term "express will" to capture the sense that a written document, such as a treaty, generates an enduring expression of a signatory's will. But what is particularly important here is that this expression of will has endowed a recipient with grounds to make claims on future action by the giver. Where Chinese texts inscribed a process of managing interacting, emotional persons, the English text expressed, alienated, and bound the emperor's will.

The semantic implications of these differences become clearer in light of lexical substitutions in Qing treaties signed with France and the United States the following year. These treaties, unlike the Qing agreement with Great Britain, were not peace treaties but exclusively commercial agreements, modeled on the 1842 and 1843 British agreements. In their French and English versions, the treaties elaborated the message that trade by non-Chinese persons in Qing territory was no longer produced out of the emperor's benevolence or world-ordering activities. Article 6 of the Chinese text of the Treaty of Whampoa (黃埔條約), for instance, states the French "people" (*ren* 人) would henceforth "export and import at five ports according to tariff and regulations decided on by the two countries." The French version however removed the reference to *ren* and put in its place "*les droits*" or "rights" of import and export. It also added a renunciation by the Qing government of "its faculty" to enact new restrictions or to modify the tariff "except after" the "full and entire consent" of the French government.[82] The key difference here between the two texts is that the French text does not allow Qing leaders to address themselves to French persons, as

---

81. IMC, *Treaties*, 1:393.
82. IMC, *Treaties*, 1:774.

the Chinese text envisioned. Instead, the subject Qing governance addresses is an abstract objectification possessed and exercised by French persons. This abstraction (*les droits*), although it originated in an act of the emperor's will and capacity, took on a corporeal-like existence apart from the emperor. Critically, according to the French text, this alienated imperial bequest now objectified into a French possession bound future imperial action.

A parallel procedure occurred in Article 2 in the US treaty (of Wang-Hea). Qing drafters retained a language in which the empire actively "granted" Americans an equal share of other benefits so to clearly "manifest" its fairness and justness. The US version alternatively reads, "And if additional advantages or privileges of whatever description be *conceded* hereafter by China to another nation, the United States and its citizens thereof shall be *entitled* thereupon to a complete, equal, and impartial participation in the same."[83] The Americans, lacking the politesse of the French (though possessing a similar discourse of rights) and the British affinity for royal prerogative, plainly stated that as it made new commercial arrangements, the Qing Empire surrendered things it had possessed and took on a codified obligation. The US version captured none of the affective positioning used in the Chinese-language version and relied instead on language that made the treaty clause itself grounds from which the Americans could make future claims.

It is possible, following the work of Lydia Liu, to see in these lexical differences what she called "hetero-cultural legacy of sovereign thinking."[84] Translation, which Liu calls "a trope of epistemological crossing," relies on the pretense of universally shared meaning—general agreement about what exists in the world. Noncommensurate moments in the treaties, conversely, flash signs of a power struggle between worldviews.[85] Where treaty language differed, sovereign thinking was ultimately incommensurable. Chinese texts invoked the role of the emperor as the charismatic source of power, whose authority rested neither in tradition nor law and whose work creating order was ongoing, contingent, and provisional, particularly when other centers of power were involved. The non-Chinese texts eliminated this function. In the latter, the "expressed will" of the Qing sovereign took on a life of its own and generated binding obligations on him and his delegates.

In this struggle between world-constituting emperorship and legal constraint, the 1842 and 1843 Qing-British treaties marked an impasse. Although Chinese and British translators had engaged in what, by key accounts, was an earnest iterative drafting process, at the end of it each side possessed a version of the agreements

---

83. IMC, *Treaties*, 1:677–78; emphases added.
84. Lydia He Liu, *Clash of Empires: The Invention of China in Modern World Making* (Cambridge, MA: Harvard University Press, 2004), 2.
85. Lydia He Liu, *Translingual Practice: Literature, National Culture, and Translated Modernity—China, 1900–1937* (Stanford: Stanford University Press, 1997), 1.

that more or less agreed with their vision of sovereignty and order.[86] A little over a decade later, however, the British won a semantic victory when Article 50 of the Treaty of Tianjin, signed in 1858 after a second military conflict, set English as the authoritative language of Qing-British official relations and treaty interpretation.[87] The article, which restricted Qing use of their own version of the commercial ordering project, was a key moment of teaching Qing political leaders "how to function properly in a world dominated militarily and economically by European-based empires."[88] Although the Chinese text of the Tianjin Treaty continued to provide specific modalities for constituting relations between centers of power and cooperatively engaging thinking/feeling persons to constitute a mutually beneficial commercial order, the British were able to ignore such propositions and insist that commercial governance was, properly, the diligent maintenance of a structure of rights and obligations.

Officiating in the New Regime

To fully appreciate why it mattered that Qing trade administration centered the management of human relations and English treaty texts recentered that work on the administration of things, it is helpful to look at how treaties created a commercial world different from what had prospered under unilateral Qing management. Institutions became more impersonal, terms of trade became more fixed, and the work of the administrator became more rote and less grounded in his self-cultivation and powers of perception. While it is quite clear that many of these changes were designed to cheapen circulation costs and expand the presence of British capital networks, it is equally important that they did so through a project of interpellation—that is, the calling forth of a certain subject to take the reins of governance.

Across the board, treaty provisions depersonalized port operations, placing them under new bureaucratic supervision and temporally conditioned scripts. A key change in this respect was the elimination of Chinese security merchants. The pre-treaty regulatory regime had used security merchants as a linchpin of commercial order. A limited number of firms, licensed by the Guangdong government, were responsible for all commercial and noncommercial aspects of a foreign ship's time in port—its duty payments, cargo sales and purchases, as well as the behavior and provisioning of its crew. Any offenses, criminal or customs, committed by the foreign ship and crew were transferable to the security merchant. This personal

---

86. John King Fairbank, *Trade and Diplomacy on the China Coast: The Opening of the Treaty Ports, 1842–1854* (Stanford: Stanford University Press, 1969), 119.
87. Liu, *Clash of Empires*, 32–33.
88. James L. Hevia, *English Lessons: The Pedagogy of Imperialism in Nineteenth-Century China* (Durham, NC: Duke University Press 2003), 13.

responsibility incentivized a close working relationship between ship captains and their security merchants and merged the conduct of business with the regulation of it.[89] When the Treaty of Nanjing eliminated the Guangdong government's licensing scheme, it did so on the grounds that to advance their trade, British subjects should be free to "carry on their mercantile transactions with whatever persons they please."[90] This new freedom of choice also separated administrative responsibilities from business dealings between foreign and Chinese firms. Whereas the Canton system relied on a "pyramidal type of hierarchical administration" with security merchants, linguists, pilots, and compradors all contributing to the system's governing function as they pursued their livelihoods, under the treaty regime, commerce was cleaved from governance. Supervisory and enforcement functions previously performed by security merchants transferred to British consuls, whose loyalties lay with English treaty text and their own nationals' pecuniary interests.

A second local functionary refigured by the Treaty of Nanjing was the linguist. Chinese linguists, hired by the ships, worked directly with the customs office, preparing paperwork, communications, and tracking duties and fees. They were both translators and cultural go-betweens who mediated interactions between foreigners and local officials. In the eighteenth century, a linguist was valued on the basis of his personality and ability to cultivate personal relationships. One English-language travelogue and guidebook from the period advised,[91]

> Nor can I recommend any but, Phtlits, and him, more fore his Ignorance than Honesty; For being naturally a Maudlin Sot, sweet Words and Sack will pump of him all the Intriegues his Colleague is concern'd in, to your Prejudice, within his Knowledge; nay, his own Designs he cannot so well hide; but you may be prepared to prevent them. 'Tis no great matter what other Linguist you hire with him, for the rest are all Sharpers; yet since 'tis usual to have two, get some-body who was lately there, to tell which is the honest Fellow, if he can.[92]

If we take the author at his word, he describes a world in which government licensed go-betweens were swindlers, intrigues abounded, and a successful merchant knew how to turn others' drunkenness to his own advantage. And yet, it was also a world in which profit could be and was made—by looking out for qualities of temperament and mind and assessing the extent of personal networks.

---

89. Paul A. Van Dyke, *Merchants of Canton and Macao: Success and Failure in Eighteenth-Century Chinese Trade* (Hong Kong: Hong Kong University Press, 2012).
90. Treaty of Nanjing, IMC, *Treaties*, 1:353.
91. Paul A. Van Dyke, *The Canton Trade: Life and Enterprise on the China Coast, 1700–1845* (Hong Kong: Hong Kong University Press, 2005), chap. 5.
92. Charles Lockyer, *An Account of the Trade in India* (London: Samuel Crouch, 1711), 102–3.

After 1842, the linguists who mediated British business with the customs house were hired by local consuls on behalf of a ship, and I am not able to say what qualities they sought in their employees. After 1858, an alternative, impersonal institutional interface between merchants and duty payments developed, centered in the written protocols of the English-speaking Imperial Maritime Customs. In 1863 when the fifth edition of S. Wells Williams's *The Chinese Commercial Guide* appeared to publicize post-Tianjin regulatory changes, linguists of the previous era had transferred their skills to other branches of trade, and useful knowledge to the trader was this protocol:

> I. Master must deposit their ship's papers and manifest with their consul within 48 hours after entering the port. II. The import manifest must contain a true account of the nature of the cargo on board, and must be handed to the Customs, before any application to break bulk can be attended to. III. The import manifest having been received and the ship's papers duly lodged with the consul or Customs, permits to land goods will be granted, on receipt of applications specifying the number of packages, with their marks, weight, quantity, and such like particulars.[93]

And so on. These dull invocations to dutiful fulfillment of protocol signal that in lieu of persons, the successful trader needed know temporal frameworks and orders of operation.

Depersonalizing commercial administration had other fronts. Alongside changes in how ships paid duties, new fee structures depersonalized duties. Fees paid in the conduct of unloading and loading cargos at Guangzhou prior to 1842 included a measuring fee, discounts and charges on this fee, and the "emperor's present" levied to fund the imperial household. Additional fees included peculage duty (distributed among customs staff); charges to transport money to Beijing; fees to pilots, linguists, and compradors; contributions to a fund collected by the security merchants to defray operating costs; contributions to an orphan hospital and the grain superintendent; charges for differences in scales; and unloading fees paid to the customs superintendent, secretaries, writers, linguists, weighers, and attending officers.[94]

What we can glean from this catalog of duties and fees is that merchants coming into Guangzhou directly bore the cost of each step the Qing government took to manage and tax trade. Payments were made to particular persons, offices, or groups,

---

93. S. Wells Williams, *The Chinese Commercial Guide*, 5th ed. (Hong Kong: A. Shortrede, 1863), 163.
94. Alexander Dalrymple, *Oriental Repertory* (London: W. Ballintine, 1808), 2:325–32; Phipps, *A Practical Treatise*, 142–44.

Table 1.1: Port charges levied in Guangzhou, ca. 1730

Measuring fee (calculated from size of ship)
20% emperor's discount on measuring fee
10% customs superintendent's charge on measuring fee
7% charge on measuring fee to compensate for difference in silver alloy content
2% charge on measuring fee for customs superintendent's office expenses
Emperor's present

Source: Paul A. Van Dyke, *The Canton Trade: Life and Enterprise on the China Coast, 1700–1845* (Hong Kong: Hong Kong University Press, 2005), 27.

all of whom, guides and resident traders warned, would arbitrarily augment their impositions and accept bribes. The catalog also tells us that some payments were structured as reciprocal gifts. For the emperor to give a discount and demand a present, as indicated by Van Dyke's schedule of port charges, was a bit of irrational accounting. But as gestures of giving, they signaled the emperor's care for the trade and the merchant's obligation to acknowledge that grant.

By contrast, the Treaty of Nanjing and the General Regulations of Trade issued in 1843 abolished the existing structure of fees and allowed only a set tonnage due (i.e., measuring fee) and import and export duties. Writing a treaty to rationalize costs and fees in this way institutionalized a clear shift away from the close association between money payments and functions performed by persons. The change internalized the costs of the state's customs administration, converting what had been direct levies on capital into government expenditures, which now needed to improvise mechanisms to fund customs operations and pay staff. Put another way, the change to the duty structure did not necessarily lower charges to commerce but did make the levies more impersonal. In lieu of a payment to a person, ships paid duties to the state.

A third area of change limited and conditioned official action. A key figure in the Canton system, as at many ports, was the pilot who guided oceangoing ships from open sea into anchorage. In places like the Pearl River delta, local knowledge of what lay under the water's surface (rocks, shoals, depth) was key to the safe arrival and departure of global cargoes. Under the Canton system, officials in the delta controlled the rate at which they released licensed pilots in order to pace the arrival and departure of ships. This pacing, in turn, affected the volume of goods in the market. By controlling the bodies of pilots, officials shaped market conditions in Guangzhou. This system of control abruptly ended in 1843 when new pilotage regulations issued as part of the treaty settlement required customs authorities to allow pilots to bring ships "immediately" into port and depart "without any stoppage and delay."[95] The new regulation simultaneously sped up the circulation of goods and eliminated a tool administrative decision-makers used to shape markets and behaviors. While on the surface, the change appeared to resolve long-standing British complaints that Chinese officials interfered with trade, it was less the case that the new regulation separated politics and markets and more the case that politics became institutionalized through regulations for non-interference in markets.

Other treaty articles enjoined government officers to follow new scripts. One type of script was to act within a set time frame. Whereas in 1787, the *Queen Charlotte*, at the custom's prerogative, waited fifteen days to be measured and to commence unloading, after 1861 a ship could expect to receive permission to discharge goods within forty-eight hours of arrival.[96] At best such stipulations expedited the movement of goods and at the very least formally subordinated administrative temporalities to the project of circulation. Other scripts were procedural, such as Article 9 in the Treaty of Tianjin, which set terms for British travel into the newly opened interior for the purpose of trade. This article, like others in the treaty, commanded a series of actions in the imperative mood ("will," "shall," "must") that told the official what to do under specific conditions. Such phrasing communicated that henceforth the official was to implement, not to improvise.

Other articles in the Tianjin treaty intended to prescribe what came into the official's field of vision. For example, the treaty's provision for the reexport goods scripted a series of interactions: "British merchants . . . shall be entitled to make application to the Superintendent of Customs, who, in order to prevent fraud on the revenue, shall cause examination to be made by suitable officers." During this examination, the scripts also stipulated what would be seen: "To see that the duties paid on such goods, as entered in the Custom-house books, correspond with the representation made, and that the goods remain with their original marks unchanged." Only then could the official "make a memorandum on the port clearance of the goods and

---

95. "General Regulations under which the British Trade Is to Be Conducted at the Five Ports of Canton, Amoy, Fuchow, Ningpo, and Shanghai (1843)," IMC, *Treaties*, 1:383. Van Dyke notes earlier economic consequences of changes to pilotage: "When foreigners began to use steamships in the 1830s, they gained the ability to traverse the river [to Canton] without the aid of pilots. This freedom took away the Hoppo's [superintendent of customs'] power to decide who came and left China, and with that loss came an undermining of the credit structures that supported the trade" (*Canton Trade*, 36).
96. George Dixon, *A Voyage round the World* (London: George Goulding, 1789), 293–96; Treaty of Tianjin Article 37, IMC, *Treaties*, 1:415. Morse records that in 1776, a breach of protocol during measurement of the East India Company's *Royal Henry* and an ensuing dispute with the customs superintendent resulted in a sixty-five-day delay before the ship could unload goods; see *East India Company*, 2:17–22.

of the amount of duties paid, and deliver the same to the merchant; and shall also certify the facts to the officers of Customs of the other ports."[97]

The actions the officer is tasked to do—direct, examine, record, and communicate—are not particularly notable in themselves and would have been routine clerks' business in any of the many offices of the Qing government. Yet, there they were, stipulated in an instrument of international law. And this was the point. The officer was directed in these responsibilities by an instrument of international law that generated a binding and enforceable obligation to fulfill them. Similar language in the treaty set protocols for fixing tares, adjudicating market values, deputing customs escorts, as well as issuing permission to discharge goods and port clearance.

Whether or not customs officers may have acted in a similar fashion in absence of the treaty article is somewhat beside the point here. What is important is that the treaty stipulated that they would always in every case act in this way. As in the story told at the start of this chapter in which Beijing rebuked officials in Ningbo and Hankou who insisted on collecting local taxes from Chinese merchants possessing transit passes, treaty language called for a mode of commercial governance that did not accommodate an official's assessment of local needs and conditions at a given moment in time. Order crafted by treaties was not shaped by dispositions and interactions, nor contingency, nor a studied assessment by authorities of whom they dealt with and what indirect mechanisms might produce the best results. Treaties, rather, stipulated a static order, reproduced in each port by scripted action. Not only were situationally fluid assessments of nature and heart-mind bracketed from commercial administration, so too were cultivated capacities to assess, discriminate, and actualize sidelined in the execution of office.

Spatial Fix and Interpellation

The Qing-British treaties of the mid-nineteenth century are part of a broader history of capital accumulation and the expansion of the global economy. Agitation in Great Britain to gain greater access to Chinese markets roughly coincided with a series of economic contractions and financial crises there—in 1836–1837 and again in 1839–1842, the same years as the Opium War in China. The Qing-British Arrow War of 1856–1860 took place amid high interest rates and an acute financial crisis in London.[98] One historian describes the entire decade of the 1840s, a period when commerce in China boomed with an influx of opium capital, as a "gloomy

---

97. Treaty of Tianjin, Article 45, IMC, *Treaties*, 1:417.
98. Nicholas Dimsdale and Ryland Thomas, *UK Business and Financial Cycles since 1660, Volume 1: A Narrative Overview* (London: Palgrave Macmillan, 2019), 127–45. See also Anthony Howe, "Britain and the World Economy," in *A Companion to Nineteenth-Century Britain*, ed. Chris Williams (Malden, MA: Blackwell, 2004), 7–33.

and uncertain era of capitalist development" in the United Kingdom.[99] Yet, at the same time, vast amounts of capital—by one estimate around sixty million pounds a year—sought some sort of profitable outlet. The British economy alone "simply did not provide scope for industrial investment on this scale."[100]

The second half of the century, however, and in particular its middle decades (roughly 1850–1870) were a boom time for global trade and British export growth. During these years, British exports of railroad iron and steel tripled, first to Europe, then to the United States, and later to India. British machinery exports increased ninefold. Together, the "transportation revolution" (which also included the application of steam technology to shipping) and the increased export of capital goods out of British ports stimulated production elsewhere in the world, both of primary products and of manufactured goods. All these investments made it possible for British (and non-British) firms to ship goods farther, to source materials from more-distant locales, and to engage in a wider range of investment activities. The result, according to historians, was a global network that enlarged "the geographical size of the capitalist economy" and increased "the intensity of its business transactions."[101] In these decades of the middle nineteenth century, capital found, through the globalization of investments, steam power, and industrial manufacturing, what some have termed a "spatial fix" for capital's endemic tendency toward crisis.[102]

---

99. Hobsbawm, *Age of Capital*, 30. During the 1840s in Great Britain, rural poverty was persistent, standards of living for much of the recently urbanized population were worse than they had been in previous decades, trading conditions were difficult for textile producers (a leading sector of economic growth), and demand for labor did not keep track with population growth, leading to stagnating wages. See essays by Jane Humphries, Hans-Joachim Voth, and T. M. Devine in Roderick Floud and Paul Johnson, eds., *The Cambridge Economic History of Modern Britain, Volume I: Industrialization, 1700–1860* (Cambridge: Cambridge University Press, 2004). Meanwhile, historian Peter Thilly describes the period of 1840–1850 in China as one when a boom in opium imports fed the growth of "legal commerce and commercial capital in the treaty ports." See Peter Thilly, *The Opium Business: A History of Crime and Capitalism in Maritime China* (Stanford: Stanford University Press, 2022), 59.
100. Eric Hobsbawm, *Industry and Empire: The Birth of the Industrial Revolution* (New York: New Press, 1999), 90.
101. Hobsbawm, *Age of Capital*, 33–34; Ronald Findlay and Kevin H. O'Rourke, *Power and Plenty: Trade, War and the World Economy in the Second Millennium* (Princeton: Princeton University Press, 2007), 325–26; C. Knick Harley, "British and European Industrialization," in *The Cambridge History of Capitalism*, vol. 1, *The Rise of Capitalism: From Ancient Origins to 1848*, ed. Larry Neal and Jeffrey G. Williamson (Cambridge: Cambridge University Press, 2014), 491–532, here 507–8; C. Knick Harley, "Trade: Discovery, Mercantilism, and Technology," in *The Cambridge Economic History of Britain*, ed. Roderick Floud and Paul Johnson (Cambridge: Cambridge University Press, 2004), 175–203, here 187; Findlay and O'Rourke, *Power and Plenty*, chaps. 6 and 7; Arrighi refers to "system-wide speed-up in the rate at which money capital was converted into commodities" (*Long Twentieth Century*, 160–61, 224). See also Hobsbawm, *Industry and Empire*, 119.
102. Harvey, *Limits to Capital*, 415–19.

By the metric of heavy industry and railways, China appears as a late field of action in capital's search for a spatial fix. A mere 195 miles of railroad track were laid prior to 1895.[103] Industrial manufacturing, mining, and resource exploitation likewise remained modest prior to the twentieth century.[104] But this is not how China appeared to contemporaries, particularly to those familiar with it. For these men, who yearned to expand Great Britain's industry and profits, China was a first field of action because of its *commercial* potential. In the words of one member of Parliament, China offered "a vast field which would be opened to the enterprise and the industry of the Manufacturing and Producing Classes in this Country" should there be a "free and unrestricted intercourse of British Subjects" with its "ingenious and industrious Population."[105] Supporters of an energetic push into China envisioned, first and foremost, more of what British traders had already established: more ships sailing to China laden with British textiles, more agency houses moving more cargo through additional ports, enlarged markets and new opportunities for capital investments in commodity trades. This was not a vision—yet—of industrial development. That would come somewhat later. All the same, the goal pursued in the 1830s and 1840s was identical to that achieved by plantations and railways and factories elsewhere—to turn territory and peoples outside of Great Britain into factors of British capital growth.

Initially China did not become a frontier for capital's "spatial fix" in the classic terms of industrializing production, railways, and telegraphs. Rather, because Chinese society was highly commercialized and China and England already engaged in a robust trade, and because British leaders preferred to obtain greater access to the Qing Empire's land, people, and resources without territorial acquisition, treaties were the first tool used to make Qing territory more amenable to the growth of foreign capital.[106] Treaties did so on two fronts. First, they created new facilities for commerce: access to additional ports, exemption from local transit taxes, customs

---

103. Elizabeth Koll, *Railroads and the Transformation of China* (Cambridge, MA: Harvard University Press, 2019); Ralph Huenemann, *The Dragon and the Iron Horse: The Economics of Railroads in China, 1876–1937* (Cambridge, MA: Council on East Asian Studies, Harvard University, 1984).
104. Albert Feuerwerker, *The Chinese Economy, ca. 1870–1911* (Ann Arbor: Center for Chinese Studies, University of Michigan, 1969); Loren Brandt, "Reflections on China's Late 19th and Early 20th Century Economy," *China Quarterly* 150 (1997): 282–308. Recent research pushes the start date of such efforts back several decades; see Peter B. Lavelle, *The Profits of Nature: Colonial Development and the Quest for Resources in Nineteenth-Century China* (New York: Columbia University Press, 2020); Shellen Xiao Wu, *Empires of Coal: Fueling China's Entry into the Modern World Order, 1860–1920* (Stanford: Stanford University Press, 2015).
105. China trade. Resolutions to be proposed by Sir George Staunton, on Tuesday, the 16th April 1833, 1833, No. 27, Parliamentary Papers online, 1.
106. On British China policy, see Pelcovits, *Old China Hands*; Britten Dean, *China and Great Britain: The Diplomacy of Commercial Relations, 1860–1864* (Cambridge, MA: East Asian Research Center, Harvard University, 1974).

protocols to minimize less time in port and transport, and permission to contract at will with Chinese counterparts. The intended effects of these new facilities were visible to all: to widen the field of possibilities for capital growth, to cheapen circulation costs and to reduce circulation time. On a second front, the treaties called forth a new kind of official and style of officiating. This second front was critical to success on the first. As a petition by British firms in Hong Kong put it in 1857, "many facilities afforded to foreign trade are dependent on the manner in which the provisions of the tariff are interpreted and administered."[107]

For Qing officials like Lin Zexu, Qi-ying, and I-li-bu, levers for better order included adjusting the intersubjective orientations of merchants and administrators. But for British agitators, these relationships were obstacles to eradicate. For them, routine scripted action was the best basis for the future capital growth the British establishment envisioned.

Conclusion: Denaturalizing Treaties

Some of the earliest work on Qing-British treaties by John King Fairbank found, as I have here, that Qing negotiators approached these agreements with priorities and worldviews quite different from their British counterparts. For Fairbank, this difference was an omission. "Versed neither in economics nor Western law, the Manchu administration hardly realized what it gave away,"[108] he wrote. Today, this view still circulates among historians today.[109] Qing negotiators, Fairbank thought, used far more nebulous and nefarious reasoning. Qiying, he concluded, wanted to "capture" British friendship and "bring them into a kind of psychological subjection. This was the traditional Chinese technique towards barbarians."[110]

The error here was not archival. Fairbank deserves his reputation as one of the first first-rate researchers in the field. Yet his analysis was shot through with orientalism and Eurocentric confidence. To the point here, the Eurocentric economic-legal order was so naturalized for Fairbank as the proper standpoint for governing commerce that any departure from it had to be irrational. Which is too bad because Fairbank did seem to pick up on something I have elaborated here—that for Qing officials, the proper management of international commerce entailed the proper management of relationships between persons.

---

107. No. 50, Earl of Elgin to the Earl of Clarendon, 23 November 1857, Inclosure 2, *Correspondence relative to the Earl of Elgin's Special Missions to China and Japan, 1857–1859* (1859) No. 2571, Parliamentary Papers online, 70.
108. Fairbank, *Trade and Diplomacy*, 113.
109. Wang, *China's Unequal Treaties*, 10–11.
110. Fairbank, *Trade and Diplomacy*, 112.

Taking the Qing approach to be historically specific and reasonable in its own terms, we are in a better position to see how treaties were not a neutral political technology but rather a legal instrument that deterritorialized and reterritorialized Qing China in two respects. First, they disabled key mechanisms of order-making, including the charismatic emperorship, personalized obligations, and flexible officiating. Second, they created a new object realm for governance and techniques appropriate to it. These included crystallized and alienated sovereign will, procedural scripts, and a new kind of Qing official—one who would set aside his personal discernment of a situation and look to the writ of the treaties.

The extent to which the writ of treaty regularized and limited Qing officiating gives tangible, historical expression to Immanuel Wallerstein's suggestion that "the smooth operation of a [global] integrated division of labor cannot operate without certain guarantees about the possibility of regular flows of commodities, money, and persons across frontiers."[111] As one former employee of the East India Company testified to Parliament in 1830, exports to China were much smaller than those to India because "we do not possess the same power over the Chinese as we do over the Indian empire."[112] Treaties were the British move to possess power. They offered a mechanism of control, erected a framework of rules around commodity flows and provided means of enforcement. In the years that followed, the treaty regime became a taproot of further inversions in commercial governance, which in the following chapters examine: system-wide consistency and static order gained precedence over locally specific conditions and responsive flux, impersonal engagement replaced emotionally attuned assessment, regulations supplanted the mind as the source of action, and finally, officials were directed to perform actions rather than produce effects. Order, under the treaty framework, was not the product of persons but the product of documents. As treaty administrators, Qing officials were asked to step away from whatever processes of cultivation had shaped them into capable imperial authorities and whatever processes of discernment centered their activities as such.

---

111. Immanuel Wallerstein, *The Modern World System III: The Second Era of the Great Expansion of the Capitalist World Economy, 1730–1840s* (London: Academic Press, 1989), 179.
112. Quoted in Wallerstein, *World System III*, 150.

2
Institutional Structures for Capital Growth

> It is unnecessary to enter into criticisms upon the establishment in question or upon its modus operandi. They will suggest themselves in endless number and with painful force to every western mind.
>
> —Edward B. Drew, Jiujiang Customs Commissioner (1870), on the operation of the "old" Qing Customs House[1]

> "Reason," for a long period meant the activity of understanding and assimilating the eternal ideas which were to function as goals for men. Today, on the contrary, it is not only the business but the essential work of reason to find means for the goals one adopts at any given time.
>
> —Max Horkheimer, *Critique of Instrumental Reason*

Neither guest ritual, nor tribute trade, nor existing practices of trade management provided adequate precedent for the kind of order called for by Qing-British commercial treaties and the others that followed in their wake. At the Qing court, Prince Yixin (王奕訢), a key adviser to the "restoration" regime of the young Tongzhi emperor (同治 r. 1861–1875), felt it was wise to create an entirely new institution to coordinate the conduct of treaty relations.[2] Treaties forced centralized management of foreign relations, and the permanent presence of foreign embassies in the imperial capital signaled a novel routinization of diplomatic interaction. Whereas guest rituals involved the body of the emperor performing gestures of incorporation within specific built environments, new relays of diplomatic communications called

---

1. IMC, "Appendix No. III to Report on Trade for Kiukiang, 1869," *Trade Report for 1869*, 144.
2. Jennifer Rudolph, *Negotiated Power in Late Imperial China: The Zongli Yamen and the Politics of Reform* (Ithaca: East Asia Program, Cornell University, 2008), 56–61, 77–91.

for by treaty required a standing deliberative body and cohort of capable clerks.[3] Also driving institutional innovation in Beijing was the mandate, encoded in the Treaty of Tianjin, that all customs operations at treaty ports operate according to a "uniform system." Uniformity meant not only that foreign nationals' privileges and rights would be universally observed but that all ports would levy the same duties, follow the same protocols, and issue the same paperwork. The Zongli yamen, which Prince Yixin formed to conduct foreign relations in Beijing, delegated these latter tasks to a new maritime customs agency, the Imperial Maritime Customs (IMC).[4]

With these new institutions at the helm, the treaty regime quickly expanded. To oversee foreign affairs, the Zongli yamen developed a network of circuit intendents and customs superintendents, who now diversified their responsibilities to include matters of foreign trade and treaty interpretation.[5] Meanwhile, treaty obligations meant protocols were needed to ensure uniformity at all treaty ports, and even more rules, duty structures, and concerns about revenue security quickly emerged in response to merchant activities unanticipated by treaty negotiators. It was this combination of treaties, explicitly designated ports, Qing-issued regulations, and a network of coordinated customs houses that the popular phrase "treaty port system"—innovated in the first decades of the twentieth century—captured.[6] Circuits of capital accumulation ran through the system, expanding into and out of treaty ports in enterprises that were simultaneously speculative and seeking security against uncertainty. The regulatory regime attempted to manage this movement so as to keep it within bounds and grow it as much as possible. As it did so, the new regime of commercial regulation and the IMC, which coordinated it, engineered a space of value circulation and capital accumulation unlike any that had previously existed in the Qing Empire.

---

3. On built environments and foreign relations, see Ruth W. Dunnell, Mark C. Elliot, Phillippe Foret, and James A. Millward, *New Qing Imperial History: The Making of Inner Asian Empire at Qing Chengde* (Abingdon, UK: Taylor & Francis, 2004).
4. The origin of the IMC can be traced back to ad hoc innovations by the British consul at Shanghai during a period of political instability, 1853–1854; see John King Fairbank, *Trade and Diplomacy on the China Coast: The Opening of the Treaty Ports, 1842–1854* (Stanford: Stanford University Press, 1964), 393–461.
5. On the role of circuit intendents, see Yuen-sang Leung, *The Shanghai Taotai: Linkage Man in a Changing Society* (Honolulu: University of Hawai'i Press, 1990). Rudolph, *Negotiated Power*, provides the best study of the institutional features of the new foreign affairs administration centered in the Zongli yamen. For more of the diplomatic history, see Masataka Banno, *China and the West, 1858–1861: The Origins of the Tsungli Yamen* (Cambridge, MA: Harvard University Press, 1964).
6. I was not able to find any record of the phrase in print prior to 1900, and it may have been first published widely in Sheridan P. Read, "The Chinese as Business Men," *The Century Illustrated Monthly Magazine*, n.s., 38 (May–October 1900): 864–68. Read was a former American consul in China. The phrase gained currency quickly, and the "treaty port system" was soon an object of summary review; see Chu Chin, "The Tariff Problem in China," *Studies in History, Economics and Public Law* 72, no. 2 (New York: Columbia University, 1916).

The Imperial Maritime Customs

The IMC, which served as a customs collection agency in China from 1861 to 1949, became for Chinese and non-Chinese alike perhaps *the* paradigmatic treaty port institution. During its existence, it was lauded as "one of the most remarkable organizations in the country," an agency that "stands out in bold relief against every other Chinese institution."[7] Historian John King Fairbank, who for decades applied his energies toward documenting the work of the IMC's British inspector general, denominated the IMC "the institution most thoroughly representative of the whole [treaty-era] period."[8] The earliest accounts of its institutional history, penned by former IMC commissioner Stanley Wright, likewise placed the "cosmopolitan" agency at the center of era's commerce, diplomacy, and "road to international understanding and cooperation" in China.[9] Even in recent decades, when researchers have turned a more skeptical eye to Euro-American presence in China, historians have not hesitated to call the IMC "the single most important institutional innovation of the treaty port era" and an "innovation [that] had no parallels in late imperial Chinese administrative practice."[10]

As the ostensible paradigmatic institution of an era when foreign commercial ambitions in China mingled with more and less coercive geopolitics, the IMC raises a number of questions about its relationship to British imperialism (its longtime inspector general was awarded numerous British honors for his "service to the Crown"), and more recently, about the institution's role in China's integration into global modernity.[11] For historians working on the latter, *who* ran the IMC has been less important than *what* it did. This included mapping Chinese ports and hinterlands, compiling trade statistics, designing a lighthouse network, and providing security for Chinese government loans issued in Europe. Recent historians of the IMC have identified the IMC as "a conduit" for "bureaucratic and technocratic modernity" as well as an attempt "to construct a quintessentially British bureaucratic

---

7. Alexis Krausse, *China in Decay: The Story of a Disappearing Empire* (London: G. Bell, 1900), 231.
8. Fairbank, *Trade and Diplomacy*, 463.
9. Stanley Wright, *Hart and the Chinese Customs* (Belfast: W. Mullan, 1950), 8. Earlier, Wright authored a detailed regulatory history of the treaty system: *China's Struggle for Tariff Autonomy, 1843–1938* (Shanghai: Kelly & Walsh, 1938).
10. Robert Bickers, "'Good Work for China in Every Possible Direction': The Foreign Inspectorate of the Chinese Maritime Customs, 1854–1950," in *Twentieth-Century Colonialism and China: Localities, the Everyday, and the World*, ed. Bryna Goodman and David Goodman (London: Routledge, 2021), 25–36; Richard S. Horowitz, "Politics, Power, and the Chinese Maritime Customs: The Qing Restoration and the Ascent of Robert Hart," *Modern Asian Studies* 40, no. 3 (2006): 549–81.
11. Donna Brunero, *Britain's Imperial Cornerstone in China: The Chinese Maritime Customs Service, 1854–1949* (London: Routledge, 2006); Hans van de Ven, *Breaking with the Past: The Maritime Customs Service and the Global Origins of Modernity in China* (New York: Columbia University Press, 2014).

apparatus within the Chinese government."[12] Hans van de Ven has more cautiously stressed the "improvisational" character of the institution and the "patchwork" of modernity surrounding it. For Van de Ven, the IMC was distinct among institutions of Qing governance, "with its own structure, methods, esprit de corps, traditions, policies, rules, and regulations," but still, he demonstrates, it worked within a context strongly shaped by its host.[13]

Implicitly and explicitly, the recent "integrationist" interpretation of the IMC, which stresses its ties to global geopolitics and emergent "modern" technologies of governance, draws from earlier work by James Hevia, who argued that a China-centric analysis of the IMC needed to be integrated with a wider view of Euro-American imperialism. The IMC, Hevia argued, was like colonial institutions elsewhere that surveyed, recorded, and decoded to produce an object legible to foreign powers. For example, the IMC's statistical reports, which Felix Boecking argues changed the way Chinese scholars perceived the economy, were, in Hevia's words, part of an "investigative modality" that "helped to integrate Chinese into the global capitalist economy" by making visible in concrete, numerical terms the scale of specific commercial opportunities in China. The reports, published only in English for their first two decades of existence and eventually sold around the world, made it possible for "capitalists to plan for further penetration of the China market."[14] This kind of knowledge production and dissemination project, which the IMC developed and systematically elaborated, was anomalous within the context of Qing governance and rigorously pursued across decades of political and economic turbulence. It also looked a lot like colonial knowledge production elsewhere within the British empire and in global commercial centers. Likewise, other projects centered in the IMC—harbor infrastructure development, new communication facilities, and the elaboration of a "bureaucratic panopticon"—were also markers, worldwide, of the new, modern, and often imperial, state.

What Hevia pointed to, but which is not yet fully understood, is the extent to which the IMC shaped and institutionalized China's participation in global capitalism. To be sure, harbors and communications were essential infrastructure for commerce. It is also incredibly important, as previous studies have shown, that the

---

12. Felix Boecking, *No Great Wall: Trade, Tariffs, and Nationalism in Republican China, 1927–1945* (Cambridge, MA: Harvard University Asia Center, 2017), 92–93; Catherine Ladds, *Empire Careers: Working for the Chinese Customs Service, 1854–1949* (Manchester: Manchester University Press, 2013). For an account that stresses Chinese characteristics of the IMC, see Chihyun Chang, *Government, Imperialism, and Nationalism in China: The Maritime Customs Service and Its Chinese Staff* (London: Routledge, 2013).
13. Van de Ven, *Breaking with the Past*, 4.
14. James L. Hevia, *English Lessons: The Pedagogy of Imperialism in Nineteenth-Century China* (Durham, NC: Duke University Press, 2003), 123, 142–43. The IMC began publishing Chinese-language trade reports after 1889.

IMC facilitated China's integration into circuits of global financial capital, and faithfully administered the treaty tariff, critiqued in the twentieth century for hamstringing China's economic development.[15] But what we've so far missed, and what this chapter examines is how many of the features that made the IMC's organization and operation innovative in China were common among colonial institutions, and like these reterritorialized ports and inland regions into material conducive for the spread of capital accumulation, irrespective of whether it was foreign capital or Chinese. As such, the IMC was not merely an interface for China's participation in the global economy, but an alien body growing within the government apparatus, redirecting the work that parts of that apparatus would do. Later chapters will examine some of the IMC's institutional growth. Here I attend to the structure and function of the alien body itself, which was oriented towards growth and limitless circulation.

A Productive Apparatus

For more than forty years a single man helmed the IMC as its Inspector General (總稅務司). His name was Robert Hart (Ch: 赫德); he was from Ulster, and in the words of Hans van de Ven, he was an "autocrat."[16] Hart had a clear vision, as autocrats often do, of what he wanted to accomplish. From his first day "on the job," Hart worked to make the IMC a more productive apparatus.

One of the earliest records we have of Hart's vision for the new customs agency is a memorandum he wrote for the British Foreign Office soliciting its support. In this memo Hart placed customs management at the center of British troubles in China. The central government, he argued, suffered from "ignorance of the real value of maritime revenues," neglected potential revenue yields generated by goods flowing to its shores, and "seldom attempted to make any of the customs offices more productive."[17] In the absence of an ethic to maximize revenues, a system of administrative "laxity" had produced high profits for individual trading firms and customs officials. Overall, however, "the thoroughly rotten condition of the native Revenue Administration," Hart argued, threatened future commercial growth. The IMC, Hart explained to officials in London, existed to fix these strategic errors. It would *correctly* tie together the growth of commerce and the growth of state revenue. The inspector general boasted that the IMC "secured for the state funds from a hitherto underappreciated source and that, too, to an extent never dreamt of before" and that the agency operated to "develop sources from which, and remove whatever obstructs

---

15. On loans, see Van de Ven, *Breaking with the Past*, chaps. 4 and 5; on the treaty tariff, see Boecking, *No Great Wall* and Philip Thai, *China's War on Smuggling: Law, Economic Life, and the Making of the Modern State, 1842–1965* (New York: Columbia University Press, 2018).
16. Van de Ven, *Breaking with the Past*, 5.
17. Great Britain, *China No. 1* (1865), Foreign Customs Establishment in China [3509], 2.

streams by which, those duties come."[18] The "new" customs, offered a better system of commercial governance, Hart argued, because it recognized a more productive customs was also a tool to grow commerce.

It is unclear what sources, other than dominant Anglophone discourse, Hart used to develop his assessment of the Qing customs. His memorandum to London is replete with orientalist language about Qing "rapacity" and "manipulations" that echoed critiques first issued by the East India Company and merchants such as James Matheson (see Chapter 1). But he was right about one thing: customs revenues were not something the Qing government had tried to grow. In 1849, commerce generated around 20 percent of the state's revenue.[19] The Qianlong emperor, records show, understood customs duties as a subtraction from the welfare of merchants and the people, and chastised officials for devising ways to increase customs revenue.[20] There is little evidence his successors held a different opinion. Customs revenue quotas were relatively stable and set at absolute amounts. This frugal approach corresponded to a strain of model kingship and political economy that privileged "storing wealth with the people" (*cangfu yumin* 藏富於民).[21] Even during the period of High Qing prosperity, when some scholars argued in favor of elite spending to enhance general prosperity, there is little evidence to suggest that Qing leaders translated policies to improve livelihoods into calculations for the paired growth of commerce and revenue in the sense that Hart articulated in 1864.[22]

While the Qing state had collected revenues, Hart introduced a different project—he set about to engineer revenues through institutional design.

The strategy Hart favored in pursuit of growth and good governance was rigorous attention to "costs of collection" and to what he called "mechanical correctness." The former he invoked in his critique of Qing customs authored for the British Foreign Office. The latter first appeared in instructions he issued to customs commissioners that same year. In these Hart explained to his staff that he sought "an office routine that ought to make the transaction of business a matter of mechanical correctness." He aspired to "provide a rule for every business transaction and specify a punishment for every act committed in contravention of the course

---

18. Great Britain, *China No. 1*, 11, 13.
19. Richard von Glahn, *The Economic History of China: From Antiquity to the Nineteenth Century* (Cambridge: Cambridge University Press, 2016), table 9.7.
20. Yuping Ni, *Customs Duties in the Qing Dynasty, ca. 1644–1911* (Leiden: Brill, 2017), 18–19.
21. For example, William Rowe, *Saving the World: Chen Hongmou and Elite Consciousness in Eighteenth-Century China* (Stanford: Stanford University Press, 2001), chap. 8.
22. Margherita Zanasi, *Economic Thought in Modern China: Market and Consumption, c. 1500–1937* (Cambridge: Cambridge University Press, 2020), chap. 2; Helen Dunstan, *Conflicting Counsels to Confuse the Age: A Documentary Study of Political Economy in Qing China, 1644–1840* (Ann Arbor: Center for Chinese Studies, University of Michigan), 109–12, 128–33.

prescribed."[23] That is, Hart wanted the IMC to produce regulated patterns of administrative activity through rule-bound operations.

Whereas his colleagues in the Qing government, had they known of the intent, might have found it ill-conceived, there was a contemporary who would have fully empathized with Hart's aspirations: a British engineer. In the mid-nineteenth century when industrialization evoked "both eulogy and resistance, and above all, ambivalence," the British engineer helmed a critical social project.[24] Steam engines, with its unprecedented ability to produce material goods as well as social change, mesmerized natural philosophers, moralists, political economists, and scientists who debated whether mechanized production was a boon or a Trojan Horse. For those who supported the industrial project, the engine was an "organizing metaphor for a progressive society,"[25] and the engineer was responsible for advancing social progress through technical know-how and improvement. As an innovator whose work greatly aided the growth of industrial capital and whose failures imperiled social gains, the mid-nineteenth-century engineer labored over were problems of input and output ratios which, in the parlance of engineering, problems of work and waste.

"Improvement," for early nineteenth-century engineers and social statisticians, "meant turning unproductive waste into productive work."[26] It is in this sense that Hart, too, was an engineer. Although Hart's book orders from London give no reason to think he was a student of engineering, his designs for the IMC shared with the field a fascination with efficient use of resources and technical solutions to problems of waste.[27] An engineer, such as one W. M. Buchanan, employed by

---

23. China, Imperial Maritime Customs, *Inspector General's Circulars, First Series: 1861–1875*, Service Series No. 7 (Shanghai: Statistical Department of the Inspectorate General, 1879), no. 8, 21 June 1864, 55; no. 5, 17 January 1865, 73. Hereafter, *Circulars First*, followed by number, date, and page number.
24. Maxine Berg, *The Machinery Question and the Making of Political Economy, 1815–1848* (Cambridge: Cambridge University Press, 1980), 2. My account of nineteenth-century engineering science draws from a three-part series of articles by science historians Norton M. Wise and Crosbie Smith in which they demonstrate how early nineteenth-century political economy, machine science, and thermodynamics shared conceptual resources; see Norton Wise and Crosbie Smith, "Work and Waste: Political Economy and Natural Philosophy in Nineteenth Century Britain (1)," *History of Science* 27, no. 3 (1989): 263–301; "Work and Waste: Political Economy and Natural Philosophy in Nineteenth Century Britain (2)," *History of Science* 27, no. 4 (1989): 391–449; "Work and Waste: Political Economy and Natural Philosophy in Nineteenth Century Britain (3)," *History of Science* 28, no. 3 (1990): 221–61.
25. Wise and Smith, "Work and Waste 2," 393.
26. Wise and Smith, "Work and Waste 3," 231.
27. Hart came from a "modest middle-class" background and attended Queen's College in Belfast. He received his early education from a year at an English boarding school and studies at a Methodist primary school in Ireland; see Richard O'Leary, "Robert Hart in China: The Significance of His

a Glasgow shipbuilding yard, might worry about how much force was lost when a waterwheel turned.[28] In China, the IMC's inspector general worried about how much customs revenue was consumed by collection. For both men, waste produced losses that imperiled future progress. Further still, properly designed, an engine and a customs office could both be "an active purposeful agent which applies energies in a controlled, predictable fashion."[29] Buchanan attributed waste to "obvious sources of friction and to improperly shaped orifices."[30] The Chinese customs wheel, according to Hart, was full of leaky buckets due to improper protocols and insufficient attention to institutional design. The parallels between Buchanan's and Hart's efforts point to porous boundaries between problems of state wealth and industrial production as well as engineering and institutional design. In Great Britain, problems of capitalist political economy, namely growth and productivity, traveled into science and industry where they were translated into problems of machine engineering. Hart's numerous circulars to customs commissioners show how building the IMC into a rule-bound, mechanistic government agency translated the engineer's solutions for "efficiency" into a new mechanistic model of depersonalized governance.

Hart was not the only one contemplating improved bureaucratic procedure. Throughout the nineteenth century, states in Europe and elsewhere (Japan being the paradigmatic non-European example) took measures to create impersonal, government administrations. These measures were similar to those at the IMC: a finer division of labor, centrally directed exam-based hiring practices, codified pay grades, and the systematic collection of information to enable rational planning for future operations.[31] Both Hart and his contemporary Charles Trevelyan, who headed tax

---

Irish Roots," *Modern Asian Studies* 40, no. 3 (July 2006): 583–604. He was a prolific reader, but of the many book orders he placed with his London agent, few concerned science or engineering. See John King Fairbank et al., eds., *The I. G. in Peking: Letters of Robert Hart Chinese Maritime Customs, 1868–1907* (Cambridge, MA: Belknap Press, 1975), 1:84, 1:163–66, 1:185–86, 1:200–201. An order placed in 1880 for "Science Primers . . . All that have been published" were most likely for the customs college (351).

28. Wise and Smith attribute to Buchanan the era's "most penetrating investigation of efficiency"; see "Work and Waste 3," 229–31.
29. Wise and Smith, "Work and Waste 2," 411–12.
30. Wise and Smith, "Work and Waste 2," 229.
31. Much of this history is located in literature on the development of modern bureaucracies. For a classic overview, see G. E. Aylmer, "Bureaucracy," in *Companion Volume to the New Cambridge Modern History*, vol. 13, ed. Peter Burke (Cambridge: Cambridge University Press, 1979). For more recent summary, see Jürgen Osterhammel, *The Transformation of the World: A Global History of the Nineteenth Century* (Princeton: Princeton University Press, 2014), 605–16. Although Osterhammel cites efficiency as a goal for nineteenth-century bureaucratic reform, his discussion focuses more on the impersonal characteristics of bureaucracy thought to generate such efficiency. On British civil service reform where concerns about costs are explicitly discussed, see Emmeline Cohen, *The Growth of the British Civil Service, 1780–1939* (Hamden, CT: Archon Books, 1965). Concern with

reform efforts in India and civil service reform efforts in London, rejected systems of administration that left room for the pursuit of personal interests. Both focused their attention on problems of waste and efficiency and imagined a "machinery" of comprehensive, centralized accounting.[32]

For much of the nineteenth and twentieth centuries, "efficiency" and "productivity" became watchwords of good governance around the world. Attention in this chapter to how these yardsticks were concurrently preoccupations in machine engineering clarifies how much the making of modern bureaucracy was analogous to engineering industrial capital growth.[33]

Step One: Costs of Collection

The first steps Hart took to improve the productivity of Qing revenue collection were investigation and calculation. Like colonial administrators elsewhere and like many of his British countrymen in China, Hart wanted to know the concrete particulars that he, as the government's newest customs collector, was dealing with.[34] Although Hart's agency had a limited writ to administer treaty-based trade, he instructed each of the newly appointed IMC commissioners to compile a comprehensive accounting of the empire's trade and customs operations at his port. The scope of the revenue and expenditure return called for by Hart included not only IMC office expenses and the tax revenues generated by the import-export trade under foreign flags, but also levels of domestic trade and the expenses of other commercial revenue agencies in the empire, namely the *changguan* ("ordinary customs" 常關) under the management of the Board of Revenue and Board of Works, and the *lijin* bureaus run by the provinces.[35]

It is clear from the requested content of the return that Hart intended to generate a comprehensive accounting of the revenue generated by all trade and the total cost of collecting that revenue. "Costs of collection" was something Hart faulted the previous customs regime for neglecting. He calculated that at each step in the

---

"uniform system or principle" central to civil service reform also informed military organization in Europe, Great Britain, and India; see James L. Hevia, *The Imperial Security State: British Colonial Knowledge and Empire-Building in Asia* (Cambridge: Cambridge University Press, 2012).

32. Edward Hughes and H. O'Brien, "Sir Charles Trevelyan and Civil Service Reform, 1853–5," *English Historical Review* 64, no. 250 (January 1949): 53–88; Jennifer Hart, "Sir Charles Trevelyan at the Treasury," *English Historical Review* 70, no. 294 (January 1960): 92–110.
33. For a standard institutional history of the developments covered here, see Wright, *Hart and the Chinese Customs*, esp. 258–90; on paperwork protocols, see also Van de Ven, *Breaking with the Past*, 75–82.
34. On other such "decoding" efforts in China and their similarity to colonial deterritorialization and reterritorialization, see Hevia, *English Lessons*, 123–44.
35. IMC, *Circulars First*, no. 6, 4 July 1861, 7.

process of examining cargo, submitting paperwork, and recording duties, examiners and clerks underreported and pocketed sums such that a cargo owing 1,000 taels of duty ultimately rendered to Beijing's accounts only 500 taels.[36] Hart considered these local retentions of tariff duties a form of institutionalized corruption that crippled the central government and stymied the growth of trade. His effort to decode the entirety of existing Qing commercial revenue operations was a first step to lay bare where in those operations waste could be cut.

There was only one problem in Hart's intelligence-gathering operation: He did not have the bureaucratic standing to obtain the information he sought. As one of several institutions managing and taxing trade, the IMC did not occupy a position to command in the generation or dissemination of knowledge about customs revenue or its costs of collection. One key metric Hart sought was "the sum expended in the transaction of customs business in the yamen and inner office of Superintendent of Customs." But superintendents did not answer to Hart.[37] Furthermore, many customs superintendents held dual appointments that mixed customs business with territorial administration, creating difficulties for precise auditing Hart sought.[38] His return assumed the existence of a discrete set of activities called "revenue collection," but, as far as the superintendent's office was concerned, there was no practical way to separate the costs spent in "the collection of maritime revenue" from that spent in managing foreign affairs more generally or in supervising of several layers of local territorial administrators busy with a wide range of responsibilities.

Evidence indicates that Hart's Chinese colleagues were not particularly eager to participate in his audit. In Ningbo, the *daotai* charged with treaty affairs (including customs) refused to supply the salaries and expenses of his office, writing, "I find that the expenses of my office are not settled by the [treaty] regulations, therefore

---

36. Great Britain, *China No. 1* (1865), 3.
37. Van de Ven, *Breaking with the Past*, 72.
38. Across the empire, Qing customhouse leadership varied. Duties were commonly executed by a range of officials, including officers of the Board of Revenue (*hubu* 戶部) or Imperial Household Department (*neiwufu* 內務府), governor-generals (*zongdu* 總督), circuit intendants (*daotai* 道台), prefects (*fuzhi* 府知), and magistrates (*zhixian* 知縣). The supervisory role was often styled *jiandu* (監督), which at the time was translated into superintendent of customs. See Qi Meiqin, 清代権關制度研究 [Research on the Qing customs system] (Huhehaote Shi: Nei Menggu da xue chu ban she, 2004); Preston M. Torbert, *The Ch'ing Imperial Household Department: A Study of Its Organization and Principal Functions, 1662–1796* (Cambridge, MA: Harvard University Council on East Asian Studies, 1977). After the Treaty of Tianjin and the creation of the Zongli yamen, responsibility for customs matters in treaty ports was standardized: treaty ports became *daotai* seats and these *daotai* were often assigned customs responsibilities, eventually becoming a distinct branch of administration. See Leung, *Shanghai Taotai*, 5–12; Rudolph, *Negotiated Power*, 107–11.

there is no occasion for me to send this account."[39] He also denied Hart's request for information on provincial transit duties, explaining that it would be "presumptuous" to forward this information to the IMC given tax collection and reporting arrangements within the territorial administration.[40] As further evidence of widespread noncompliance, in his next annual accounting, Hart was compelled to allow commissioners to leave blank the line for "Expenditures in the Superintendent's Yamen" in the event, he wrote, "of unwillingness on the part of the Chinese Superintendent to furnish the requisite information."[41] Even more elusive were the data Hart sought on tax revenues, generated either by inland transit duties or by Chinese boats passing through non-IMC custom houses. It would be decades before Hart could calculate a sizable portion of the latter, and he never would find out—in his nearly four-decade-long career at the IMC—the former.

The liminal position of the IMC within the Qing government did not, however, foreclose Hart's rigorous accounting of what went on in his own offices. Subsequent to the initial organization of the new customs offices, returns of office personnel as well as reports of income and operational costs routinely measured the overall work and efficiency of the service. "Collection and Expenditure Reports" became a quarterly occurrence, and took cognizance of how much trade was present in Qing ports and how much revenue this trade produced through the collection of various duties. The reports measured this revenue yield against revenue expended in office operations, calculating a ratio of input to output, or in a slightly different parlance, the net profit of each customs office. This information was relayed in English as well as in Chinese to the Zongli yamen and Board of Revenue, although the Chinese-language report did not include information about volumes of trade or the source of collection costs.[42]

---

39. Ningbo Daotai to IMC Commissioner Hughes, no. 5, ND 1862. Maritime Customs Service Archive, Second Historical Archives of China, Nanjing, China, published as Robert Bickers and and Hans J. van de Ven, eds., *China and the West the Maritime Customs Service Archive from the Second Historical Archives of China, Nanjing* (Reading, UK: Primary Source Microfilm, 2004), reel 174; hereafter CMC microfilm, reel 174. From Hughes's records, it appears the *daotai* never did send the account. See Hughes to Daotai, no. 120, ND 1862, CMC microfilm, reel 174.
40. Hughes to Daotai, no. 44, 26 July 1861, CMC microfilm, reel 174; Daotai to Hughes, no. 87, 27 July 1861, CMC microfilm, reel 174.
41. IMC, *Circulars First*, no. 1, 12 May 1862, 18.
42. IMC, *Circulars First*, no. 1, 30 June 1861; no. 1, 12 May 1862, 17–18; no. 9, 16 February 1863, 32–35. It bears mentioning that Hart was ordered by the Zongli yamen to produce a quarterly report of expenses and revenue collected. What that report looked like appears to have been of Hart's own design.

OFFICE OF MARITIME CUSTOMS..

RETURNS FOR THE QUARTER ENDING........................... 1862.

A.—DUTIES COLLECTED: INDEMNITY: EXPENDITURE.

	Tls	m.	c.	c.

1. ....Foreign Vessels ....Tons: Entered during Quarter,.......................
   Import Duties, (exclusive of Opium),.............................
   Export   „
   Coast Trade Duties,..............................
   Tonnage Dues,..............................
2. ....Chests Opium ....Peculs, amount of Duty Tls........................
   Prepared
3. Duties collected by Commissioners on Merchandise laden in Chinese Bottoms:
   Import Tls..............., Export Tls..............
4. Total sum paid to English and French on account of Indemnity,..............................
5. Total sum paid to United States on account of Indemnity,..............................
6. Expenditure in Commissioner's Office,..............................
7.   „   „ Superintendent's Yamên,..............................

B.—CONFISCATION FUND.

1. Balance from previous Quarter,..............................
2. Proceeds of Goods Confiscated,..............................
3. Amount of Fines,..............................
4. Sums paid to Spies,..............................
5. Gratuities,..............................
6. Sums expended in purchase of Sundries,..............................
7. Sums handed to Superintendent,..............................
8. Balance in Commissioner's hands,..............................

C.—DETAILED ACCOUNT OF OFFICE EXPENDITURE.

1. Salaries of ( ) Commissioners, ( ) Deputy Commissioners, ( ) Assistants,........
2.   „   „ Foreign Tide-waiters,..............................
3.   „   „ Chinese Linguists,..............................
4.   „   „ Shupan and ( ) Writers,..............................
5.   „   „ Examiners, Weighers, Watchers,..............................
6. Wages of ( ) Office Boys, Runners, Buntiaen, &c.,..............................
7. Office Expenditure: Stationery, &c.,..............................
8. Miscellaneous Expenditure,..............................
9. Extraordinary   „
10. Preventive Service Expenditure; Guard Boats, &c.,..............................
11. Rent of Buildings, Chops, &c.,..............................

Total,..............................

(signature)

....
Commissioner of Customs.

N.B.—*Return A No. 7 may be left Blank in the event of unwillingness on the part of Chinese Superintendent to furnish the requisite information.*

Errors in these Returns must be most carefully guarded against.

Figure 2.1: Imperial Maritime Customs Quarterly Revenue and Expenditure Form, issued May 1862. Source: China, Imperial Maritime Customs, *Inspector General's Circulars. First Series 1861–1875*, Service Series No. 7 (Shanghai: Statistical Department of the Inspectorate General, 1879).

Step Two: "Efficient" Operations

To make Qing customs more productive, Hart offered to create "efficiency," which became an enduring byword for his ideal customs administration. Admonitions to "efficiency" regularly percolated through the inspector general's instructions to commissioners. Hart contextualized instructions to commissioners with explanations such as, "The Inspector General aims at making service efficient" and that he wanted "office work to go on smoothly and to be performed efficiently."[43] He instructed IMC employees to minimize the amount of bureaucratic procedure necessary to process a cargo, collect its duties, and send it on its way. "It is when trade flourishes," Hart wrote, "that the coffers of the revenue are most rapidly filled, and for trade to flourish, its operations should be as much facilitated and as little as fettered as possible." This could be achieved, Hart felt, by making rules and regulations "of the least cumbrous and most intelligible kind," by training a staff of individuals "thoroughly acquainted with the work of his own department," and by making it clear to merchants "to whom and in what way to apply for the transaction of their business."[44] Efficiency, for Hart, was closely connected to regularity in bureaucratic process—"a rule for every business transaction"—and simplified bureaucratic process, in turn, was an engine for capital accumulation. What Hart queried his employees were "the best means of simplifying the Customs' practice ... to diminish the work of the offices, and give increased facilities to merchants"?[45] Each commissioner, Hart instructed, "is to exert himself to make his office a model for correctness and dispatch in the transaction of business, and for facilities and encouragement given to trade."[46]

Issued as a directive to commissioners, "efficiency" was an invocation to improvement. But as an objective for institutional design, "efficiency" was something much more precise. Within the "costs of collection" framework institutionalized in quarterly returns of income and expenses, the customs existed to generate money; as an institution and employer, it was also inevitably a consumer of money. "Costs of collection" measured what was necessary in monetary terms to produce revenue and reproduce the actions of the customs apparatus. A low cost of collection meant most of the revenue assessed by the IMC passed through to government accounts. A high cost suggested a bloated or poorly working collection apparatus. Efficiency, for the IMC's IG, meant minimizing how much it cost to produce revenues. Work by science historians Norton Wise and Crosbie Smith allows us to place Hart's work in China in the company of a generation of British engineers, such as William Whewell, for whom "conservation v. waste of mechanical power in the production of economic

---

43. IMC, *Circulars First*, no. 8, 21 June 1864, 57; no. 25, 1 November 1869, 231.
44. IMC, *Circulars First*, no. 8, 21 June 1864, 57.
45. IMC, *Circulars First*, no. 5, 17 January 1865, 73.
46. IMC, *Circulars First*, no. 25, 1 November 1869, 231.

value was the central concern." Whewell, author of *Mechanics of Engineering* (1841, the standard textbook in use at Cambridge University), developed the field's distinction between "useful" and "impeding" resistances. One preserved force and turned it into an economic equivalent, value; the other wasted both. "Waste," Whewell thought, "threatened the profitability of manufacturing at every stage: waste of materials, waste of time, waste of power, waste of skill and waste (wear) of machines."[47] Hart wished to expunge from the IMC the bureaucratic form of waste: rules or protocols that did not "facilitate as much as possible the general transaction of business."[48]

During the first half of the nineteenth century in Great Britain, scientific progress, industrial development, the wealth of the nation, and questions of moral order converged around a shared problematic: how, in a world of limited resources, to maximize production and thus the social good. Engines, money, land, and people were all potential forces of production that "if set in motion, they yielded profits, rents, and wages; if idle they were wasted. Even worse, they might suffer depreciation, devastation, destitution, dissipation."[49] It was a Manichean world: activity and growth or stasis and decay. Hart's efforts to create administrative arrangements and align protocols that would work to maximize customs collections brought this particular project of "improvement" to the China coast. Improving governance in China through institutional design paralleled the creation of better industrial machines. Both would, when properly arranged, create a future more amply supplied with commerce, wealth, and growth.

The Work of the Customs

Like any industrial machine, what Hart's bureaucratic machine came to look like had much to do with its work. This work, in turn, had much to do with the duty structures it was responsible for upholding. Before examining Hart's bureaucratic engineering, then, it is necessary to take a look at these structures.

---

47. Wise and Smith, "Work and Waste 2," 418–21. Quotes pp. 420, 421.
48. IMC, *Circulars First*, no. 4, 20 February 1866, 85; no. 19, 15 June 1868, 155.
49. Wise and Smith, "Work and Waste 3," 231. Trevelyan also participated in this worldview when he complained the Exchequer was "an obsolete machinery" characterized by "loss of time, and labor, and money" and advised that reducing the number of civil servants would increase efficiency by "forcing people to work and substituting habits of activity for an idle, listless state of half employment" (quoted in Hughes and O'Brien, "Trevelyan," 54, and Hart, "Trevelyan," 107).

Exemptions

Written into the British Treaty of Tianjin were two limits on what we can call "costs of circulation." One pertained to goods moving inland from a port or outbound from a growing region, a period referred to as "transit." These foreign imports or exports were allowed to pay to the IMC a "transit duty" (*ban shui* 半税) that freed them from any other instance of transit taxation, which was otherwise a frequent occurrence owing to the institution of *lijin* during the Taiping Rebellion. The other limit pertained to foreign goods imported into a treaty port and subsequently exported to another treaty port. These were allowed to leave the first port and reenter a second or third treaty port without paying export duty or any additional import duty.[50] The IMC was responsible for assessing the taxes and issue corresponding paperwork, either a transit pass (*san lian dan* 三聯單) or an exemption certificate (*mian shui dan* 免税單). Both duties recoded people and territory of the Qing Empire to better serve market expansion and capital accumulation. They were designed to widen the sphere of circulation for British commodity capital, the first by cheapening goods for consumers farther inland and the second by allowing merchants to "try" multiple markets in search of ideal prices.[51] The duties consequently created a different scale of circulation costs for treaty-based trade. Non-treaty trade taking place in Chinese boats in the hands of Chinese merchants typically had to pay tax at each customs station or transit tax bureau they passed.

Prior to the treaty era, the Qing Empire maintained dozens of customhouses (*changguan*), dispersed along the empire's frontiers and major waterways and charged with collecting an annual quota of revenue due to the imperial government in Beijing. Each customs house was run by a superintendent who reported either the Board of Revenue or Board of Works, and in a busy port, the customs could employ several hundred people as clerks and river watchers.[52] The customs superintendent was personally responsible for funding the office as well as any revenue shortfalls. To deliver its quota, which reflected Beijing's conclusions about the customary level of agricultural and commercial activity in the area, each *changguan* office administered its own tariff and fees, and each tended to apply its tariff according to criteria such as the type of goods, the size of a vessel or caravan, and whether any anomalous social, political, or economic conditions prevailed in the surrounding area.[53]

---

50. Treaty of Tianjin, Articles 28 and 45, Imperial Maritime Customs, *Treaties, Conventions, Etc. between China and Foreign States*, 2 vols., vol. 1, 2nd ed., Miscellaneous Series No. 30 (Shanghai: Inspector General of Customs, 1917), 1:412–13, 1:417.
51. There seems to have been some precedent for exempting traders, who switched destinations, from double taxation; see Gang Zhao, *The Qing Opening to the Ocean: Chinese Maritime Policies, 1684–1757* (Honolulu: University of Hawai'i Press, 2013), 129.
52. IMC, "Appendix No. III to Report on Trade for Kiukiang, 1869," *Trade Report for 1869*, 142.
53. The Board of Revenue set rates of duty at each customs, but in practice, customs officials often

The *changguan* duty and fee structure reflected what we might think of as a concrete arts of governance. Fees reflected the physiological, staffing, and pecuniary needs of the customs office: food allowance (*fanshi* 飯食), warehouse safeguarding (*kan cang gui fei* 看藏規費), rulers' gifts (*gui li* 規禮).[54] Quotas reflected natural resources and productive activities in the area. The customs station at Jiujiang, for instance, collected duty from only four items: salt, tea, bamboo, and wood.[55] Tariff rates and exemptions were calibrated to livelihoods as well as the use value of goods. Customs stations in the vicinity of Nanjing, for example, offered tax exemptions for foodstuffs, sandals, and belts because these goods were sources of income for the poor. Commercially central Jiujiang customs on the Yangzi River exempted timber delivered to Beijing as well as tax silver, grain, and coal sent for the assistance of the army.[56]

Exemptions managed by the IMC did different work. Most important, their issuance was completely unrelated to concrete or temporally finite goals, such as securing supplies of rice or accommodating a drought. Rather, IMC exemption certificates facilitated movement, a goal that was both infinite and constantly postponed. Perhaps the most striking expression of the work done by the *mian shui dan* (exemption certificate) was the rise of Shanghai, which became the center of a hub-and-spoke model of commercial circulation, owing to the exemption and how the IMC administered it. The rise of Shanghai as a commercial center is well documented.[57] I need only mention here that for the period 1865–1925, 60 percent of foreign imports into Shanghai were reexported to other treaty ports.[58] In 1881, a year unmarked by global economic crisis or local political crisis, of the 43.8 million taels' worth of China-made goods that arrived in Shanghai, 80 percent were designated reexports to either other Chinese ports or ports in the region.[59]

---

increased these rates. Fees were typically surcharges to pay for working expenses and monetary obligations to other parts of the bureaucracy. See Madeline Zelin, *The Magistrate's Tael: Rationalizing Fiscal Reform in Eighteenth Century Ch'ing China* (Berkeley: University of California Press, 1984), 58–62.

54. Qi, [Research on the Qing customs system], 230.
55. IMC, "Appendix No. III to Report on Trade for Kiukiang, 1869," *Trade Report for 1869*, 142.
56. Ni, *Customs Duties*, 25–28, 49. On early Qing maritime customs operations (pre-"Canton system"), see Zhao, *The Qing Opening to the Ocean*.
57. Marie-Claire Bergère, *Shanghai: China's Gateway to Modernity* (Stanford: Stanford University Press, 2009); Linda Cooke Johnson, *Shanghai: From Market Town to Treaty Port, 1074–1858* (Stanford: Stanford University Press, 1995); Meng Yue, *Shanghai and the Edges of Empire* (Minneapolis: University of Minnesota Press, 2006).
58. Wolfgang Keller, Ben Li, and Carol Shuie, "Shanghai's Trade, China's Growth: Continuity, Recovery, and Change since the Opium War," NBER Working Paper Series 17754, National Bureau of Economic Research, Cambridge, MA, January 2012, 20–21, 57–58, http://www.nber.org/papers/w17754.pdf.
59. IMC, "Shanghai," *Trade Report for 1881*.

Hart viewed the exemption certificate as a tool to grow circulation, and he issued guidance to his commissioners to use a "liberal interpretation" of reexport rules that would "facilitate, and not fetter, commerce." [60] For Hart, this meant "that it is not necessary ... that the merchandise should be re-exported by the original importer" and that exemptions could be issued for goods that had changed ownership. Most immediately, this interpretation of the rule made it possible to market foreign imports at Shanghai to Chinese firms, which then distributed them elsewhere in the empire without paying additional taxes. More fundamentally, how Hart put the exemption certificate into practice recoded a treaty right granted to foreign persons into a facility available to goods. This switch, motivated by Hart's designs to grow commerce, drew Chinese persons under the treaty regulatory umbrella and out of the reach of other institutions that taxed trade. To the extent that treaty port commerce subsequently entailed foreign importers selling goods to Chinese merchants who further circulated them within China, this pattern of multinational capital accumulation was undoubtably facilitated by the reexport exemption.

Exemption certificates also recoded ports. Whereas *changguan* operated independent of one another and with little day-to-day imperial oversight, an exemption certificate entailed direction from above to create coordinated action across ports. For exemption certificate to work, when officials in Shanghai taxed the goods and issued the certificate, officials at any other port had to recognize and honor the paperwork. Consequently, bureaucratic action was conditioned by commodity circulation.

How any given customs office acted on any given cargo depended on where that office sat along the cargo's path of circulation. In the words of Prince Yixin at the Zongli yamen, "Up to now, inland [*neidi* 內地] merchants transporting goods paid tax at each customs they passed," but since the treaty, circumstances had changed. "Now, all the ports are connected."[61] In this sense, Qing ports were reterritorialized into a "treaty port system."

The reterritorialization of ports into connected nodes in a path of capital circulation reverberated through the Qing fiscal system. Almost as soon as exemptions were initially issued, they began to destabilize state revenue. When it granted the exemption facility to foreign merchants, the Zongli yamen expected occasional use of the certificates. After all, the government had opened additional ports to foreign ships, and the yamen reasonably expected foreign merchants would proceed directly to these ports.[62] Instead, ports farther north, like Tianjin (天津), unexpectedly

---

60. IMC, *Circulars First*, no. 5, 6 February 1863, 28.
61. *Chouban yiwu shimo* 籌辦夷務始末 [A complete record of foreign affairs] (digital), XF, juan 79, 31.1–31.2.
62. *CBYWSM* (digital), XF, juan 79, 37.2.

began to collect more exemption certificates than revenue. Reports received by the Zongli yamen in 1861 showed that Tianjin received exemption certificates worth more than 100,000 taels, 98 percent of which were issued by Shanghai authorities.[63] Within two years of the system's operation, revenue at the port declined 36 percent.[64] This abrupt fall in local collections alarmed officials in Tianjin because it portended shortfalls in funds for local administrative expenses. It also alarmed officials in Beijing because the losses imperiled funds for official salaries and the emperor's household expenses.[65] As is well known, the Qing court did not use a centralized budgeting process but earmarked specific revenue sources for specific expenses.[66] In Guangdong, for example, eight different authorities remitted independent lines of funds for specific uses in Beijing. In Shanghai, the single customs commissioner was responsible for six discrete remittances.[67] Authorities in Tianjin argued that cargo arriving in Tianjin needed to pay taxes in Tianjin, and yamen officials concurred that exemption certificates portended long-term systemic losses and abuses (*ri jiu bu wu liubi* 日久不無流弊).[68]

We should not be surprised that none of this bothered British authorities in China, who in the 1860s clearly did not see or care how the empire was put together administratively. From the viewpoint of British merchants, exemptions existed to save them from a complete or partial loss of capital invested in goods and their transit. So long as taxation remained within treaty-stipulated limits, "it is perfectly indifferent to me whether the duty be paid at Shanghai or at the port at which the

---

63. *CBYWSM* (print), TZ, juan 3, 11.2, 2–4. This discussion records that at the same time, the northern port of Yingkou, received 2,000 taels from tariff duties on foreign goods and exemption certificates worth 20,000 taels, again the majority issued from Shanghai.
64. Author's calculation using IMC trade report for 1865. The density of trade between Tianjin and Shanghai continued to intensify, growing 358 percent between 1876 and 1899. On the whole, Tianjin was a recipient of imports. See Hajime Kose, "Chinese Merchants and Chinese Inter-port Trade," in *Japanese Industrialization and the Asian Economy*, ed. A. J. H. Lathan and Heita Kawakatsu (London: Routledge, 1994), 133, fig. 6.2.
65. *CBYWSM* (digital), XF, juan 79, XF11 5M, 25.2; 三口通商大臣至天海關稅務司札文選編 [Selected correspondence between the imperial commissioner of trade at the three ports and the Tianjin customs commissioner] (Tianjin: Tianjinshi danganguan, 1989), 50, 75.
66. Ch'üan-shih Li, *Central and Local Finance in China: A Study of the Fiscal Relations between the Central, the Provincial, and the Local Governments* (New York: Columbia University, 1922); R. Bin Wong, "Taxation and Good Governance in China, 1500–1914," in *The Global Rise of Fiscal States: A Global History, 1500–1914*, ed. Bartolomé Yun-Casalilla and Patrick K. O'Brien, with Francisco Comin Comin (Cambridge: Cambridge University Press, 2012), 353–77; Takeshi Hamashita, "Despotism and Decentralization in Chinese Governance: Taxation, Tribute, and Emigration," in *China, East Asia, and the Global Economy*, ed. Linda Grove and Mark Selden (London: Routledge, 2008), 28; He Wenkai, *Paths toward the Modern Fiscal State: England, Japan, and China* (Cambridge, MA: Harvard University Press, 2013), 156.
67. Li, *Central and Local Finance*, 58–59.
68. *CBYWSM* (print), TZ, juan 3, 11.1, 6–7.

articles are entered for consumption," British minister Bruce wrote to Prince Yixin.[69] For Bruce, the salient geofiscal unit was "China." This was the unit for which the exemption had been created by treaty: cargoes paid tax once in China.

Where revenue accumulated within China did, however, matter to Qing officials, who in the face of exemption certificates rushed to create revised accounting procedures and duty regulations.[70] Qing fiscal administration, as institutionalized in Beijing, operated in terms of ports and their hinterlands; something as large and undifferentiated as "China" was not the salient administrative unit. The Board of Revenue calculated government expenditure in terms of spatially specific needs and assigned those needs to particular sources of wealth.[71] In response to the panic at Tianjin, the Zongli yamen in coordination with the Board of Revenue took steps to shore up correspondence between an area's commercial activity and its revenue accounts, despite changed patterns of commercial circulation.

It should be said, tax exemptions were not in themselves a problem for the government. In 1876, for example, the Tianjin *changguan* exempted 465 ships from 20 percent of their import duties and fully exempted vessels departing for Jiangsu and Zhejiang.[72] But the treaty exemption did something more than just save merchants money; it also generated new patterns of commercial circulation within China. With increased use of the exemption, trade and revenue clustered at Shanghai, unexpectedly rendering anachronistic the government's existing system of revenue allocation. Coupling geographically specific revenue sources to specific expenditures was well suited to practices of direct trade and local tax collection. Interport shipping under exemptions decoupled trade activity from revenue collection, except at a larger scale geofiscal unit (e.g., China). Some of the initial work of the IMC was to create, though mechanisms of interport coordination, this larger scale geofiscal unit.

A second kind of exemption bears mentioning at this point, though its history is sufficiently rich and complex that I deal with it separately in Chapter 5. This is the transit pass. Although issued by the IMC after an additional duty payment at the time of import or export, in practice transit passes operated as an exemption from provincial transit taxes. Their use was even more problematic than exemptions but for different reasons. Like the *mian shui dan*, transit passes recoded Qing territory to service to expansive capital accumulation by limiting the ability of political authorities to add to costs of circulation. In this case, however, it was not merely

---

69. Beijing Legation to Zongli Yamen, draft, 5 April 1862, TNA, FO 228/911.
70. CBYWSM (digital), XF, juan 79, 25.2; CBYWSM (print), TZ, juan 3, 12.1–12.2; IMC, *Circulars First*, no. 12, 16 February 1863, 38, and no. 19, 20 August 1863; *San kou tongshang dachen*, 53–55.
71. He, *Paths towards the Modern Fiscal State*, 160.
72. Li Hongzhang, "天津道同治十三年分海税徵收摺" [Report on the sea tax collection for Tianjin Province, 1876], *Li Hongzhang Quanji* (Hefei shi: Anhui jiu yu chu ban she, 2008), G1-04-024, 6:292–93.

ports that found their administrative and fiscal position on paths of capital circulation altered, but vast swaths of the empire's interior—wherever foreign imports or foreign exports traveled. These regions, which in the first instance were under the supervision of various territorial administrations, each with their own transit tax structures, were also, per treaty terms reterritorialized as a singular "China." Transit half-duty, paid at one locale, in substance erased all other tax jurisdictions. Also like the exemption certificate, the transit pass had the potential to reterritorialize Chinese merchants as bearers of foreign capital and thereby exempt from nontreaty commercial regulation. Crucially, though, unlike exemption certificates, which were exclusively managed by the IMC, the successful implementation of transit passes required the cooperation of local officials and *lijin* collectorates. These offices, unlike Hart's customs offices, had priorities other than growing circulation and were not in all instances easily turned into collaborators with the treaty regime.

Drawbacks

A third instrument reterritorializing circuits of Qing commerce and revenue was the drawback. Initially offered by authorities at Shanghai in the 1840s for the unfortunate merchant who brought foreign goods to sell but found he could not, drawbacks became a more general facility as the Qing government attempted to prevent revenue fraud and "settle on regulations so to avoid a situation in which one [customs port] gets little while another gets a lot."[73] Similar to the exemption certificate, the drawback lowered costs of circulation and integrated Chinese ports. Drawbacks allowed the Qing government to collect duties the moment goods entered or exited a port but then refund those duties if the forward circulation of the goods took certain paths.

Scenarios where the IMC issued drawbacks included foreign textiles imported into Xiamen and from there sent to Hong Kong. The goods, having never entered the local market for sale, were owed a refund of import duties. Domestic produce exported from treaty port A that passed through treaty port B on its way to treaty port C claimed a drawback on the domestic transit duties it paid at port B after it (re)paid them to port C. And on the Yangzi River, any domestic produce (namely tea) shipped from Hankou or Jiujiang to Shanghai and from thence exported abroad could also claim a drawback on domestic transit duties it was required to pay.[74]

For the Qing government, the instrument was an unwieldy prophylactic against smuggling and disordered revenue accounts. Authorities' preferred strategy was to inspect goods and tax them at multiple locations during transit, particularly

---

73. *CBYWSM* (digital), XF, juan 79, 21.1, 31.1–31.2; Wright, *China's Struggle*, 222.
74. IMC, *Circulars First*, no. 20, 20 August 1863, 43.

along the Yangzi River, which from a security viewpoint was no better than a leaky sieve.[75] The British Legation, however, insisted that the "spirit" of the treaties called for minimal interference in trade and limited their merchants' tax obligations to one import/export duty and one transit duty.[76] The drawback was a solution that allowed the state to collect its due before the cargo entered circulation and thereby became a possible vector of smuggling, while the refund kept taxation within limits acceptable to the British.

Notably, drawbacks were not claims for cash. Rather, they were presented as payments for taxes owed on other cargoes. This function had the consequence of recoding a tax payment as a capital investment. Taxes paid on cotton duties, for instance, could become a portion of taxes paid on opium. The institutionalization of this abstract equivalence between the exchange value of A and the exchange value of B was a boon for firms that did not specialize in a single line of trade. So long as authorities properly recognized the instruments, capital paid toward cotton duties in Xiamen remained a reliable investment, even if the cotton could not be successfully marketed there, and opium became the next best opportunity.[77]

That the drawback functioned for British merchants as a capital reserve is perhaps best attested to by complaints in the treaty port press against them. In the main, merchants resented the drawback for how it tied up their capital in unproductive ways. "Why should a man desirous to do a small and legitimate business here have to hand over to the Imperial Customs a sum of, say, according to circumstances, Tis. 4000 to Tls, 7000. How well could his money be employed! How fair an income could he make from good investment of this money!" complained Hankou-based tea traders.[78] For such men, the drawback amounted to a conspiracy between the Chinese government and Chinese merchants. One letter-writer to the *North China Herald* charged that advance duty payments, such as those paid in the tea trade, provided Chinese banks with interest free "floating capital," which the banks unproductively diverted to pay official bribes.[79]

Forced to live with the drawback, British merchants sought to make it more adequate to their processes of capital accumulation. They wanted, for instance, drawbacks paid in cash instead of an IOU redeemable only at a specific port. The restriction, the Shanghai Chamber of Commerce groused, forced holders of drawbacks

---

75. *CBYWSM* (digital), XF, juan 79, 20.2–23.1, 36.1, 37.2–38.1; *CBYWSM* (print), TZ, juan 2, 6.1, 7–8.
76. Wright, *China's Struggle*, 198.
77. Entry Book of Letters from Yamen, TNA, FO 230/76; Great Britain, Inclosure 2 in No. 105, *China No. 3 (1864) Papers relating to the Affairs of China*, 148–49. In this case, authorities disputed the attempt "to use one item to pay for another."
78. Duty Payers, "Hankow Customs," NCH, 16 May 1863.
79. E pluribus unum, "Customs Exactions," NCH, 19 December 1863.

to make purchases of goods, which for "any person engaged in intermittent trading operations" exposed them to market risks, including inconsistent demand for "fancy goods" and "frequent rebellions." There was always a risk that an attempt to redeem a drawback through a future purchase would result in "stocks of unsalable goods."[80] The chamber not only wanted the drawback period extended but drawbacks paid in cash, full convertibility being the only security against being driven into less profitable business ventures.

Even more than convertibility, those who complained about the drawback wanted time. Initial regulations issued at the end of 1862 stated that merchants could only receive a drawback if their goods were exported abroad within three months. Merchant hands turned these three months into a time frame for gauging, betting, and waiting out the markets. Consequently, merchants felt the time limit was both inadequate and arbitrary, in case "circumstances of market, namely dullness, expectation of a rise &c. prevent their selling until the three months have expired."[81] British merchants pressed to extend the drawback's time horizon to ease pressure on them to sell at a disadvantage. As the editors of the *North-China Herald* put it in 1863, "[three months] for re-exportation was all together too limited to admit full advantage of being taken of the markets."[82] British merchants lobbied for and received an extension of the term to twelve months, but eventually this, too, was seen as inadequate. A decade later, the Shanghai Chamber of Commerce thought thirty months a practical number.[83] This steady extension in the desired time horizon for reexport seems curious against the overall speed-up in both transportation and communication times but was in fact a way to solve problems of commodity capital reproduction. Extending the time horizon of the government's obligation to refund duty eased pressure on the merchant to sell at a disadvantage.

Paperwork

Actualizing the limits on costs of circulation offered by exemptions, transit passes, and drawbacks all depended on the office work of the IMC. The use of paperwork as a tool to manage commerce was, of course, not unprecedented, but after 1861 its end goal was, at the very least, novel. During the eighteenth century, the customs station at Guangzhou, the *Yuehaiguan* (粵海關) employed several different forms of paperwork to supervise the arrival and departure of ships in the Pearl River delta. A pilot, engaged at Macao, reported to a local office the name of the foreign captain

---

80. "Memorial of the Shanghai General," NCHMR, 9 November 1867.
81. Duty Payers, "Hankow Customs."
82. "Yang-Tsze Regulations," NCH, 18 July 1863.
83. F. B. Johnson, "Drawbacks and Transit Passes. The Chamber of Commerce to Mr. Low," NCHSCCG, 29 June 1872.

who hired him, the country whose flag the ship sailed under, the ship's armaments, size of crew, and trading goods. The office at Macao forwarded this information to the *Yuehaiguan*. As the ship proceeded to Guangzhou, the same information was checked and recorded at the Bocca Tigris (Ch: Humen 虎門) customs station, located in the narrow strait where the Pearl River met the South China Sea. The check at Bocca Tigris appears, following Paul Van Dyke's account, to have paid little attention to cargo. It focused instead on the ship's armaments and number of persons on board, verifying the correctness of the information reported at Macao. The Bocca Tigris station then sent a separate report with this information to the head officer of the *Yuehaiguan*, the Guangzhou customs superintendent (*hoppo*), an appointee in the Imperial Household Department.[84] The two reports from Macao and Bocca Tigris allowed the superintendent to discriminate between authorized and unauthorized ships as well as check that all ships used licensed pilots, the number of which was limited to control the volume of trade into and out of the port.[85] Other paperwork tracked the fees owed by the ships and enabled government agents to monitor against smuggling. All foreign ships docked at Whampoa (Ch: Huangpu 黃埔), just outside of Guangzhou, and from there, small, locally owned cargo boats unloaded and loaded. These boats, on the journey to and from Whampoa, stopped at three tollhouses where permits and cargo were checked. To curb smuggling, the *Yuehaiguan* limited the number of small cargo boats that could work on a given day, and the passes granted to these boats were chopped at each tollhouse and then surrendered either in Guangzhou or Whampoa, depending on the direction of the trip.[86] Intermediate checks between Whampoa and Guangzhou facilitated prompt detection of unauthorized loading and unloading of cargo. By collecting all the cargo boat passes, the *Yuehaiguan* also kept a running total of the fees owed by each ship and which Chinese merchants were the guarantors of those charges.[87]

In short, the *Yuehaiguan* issued, viséd, and collected paperwork to monitor the arrival of ships and prevent smuggling, an activity that carried over to the post-treaty regulatory apparatus. A great deal of the novelty surrounding the drawback and the exemption was the extent of the bureaucratic coordination required for them to work. For one, the instruments enlarged the geographical scale of coordination. In the tea trade where the drawback was commonly employed, tea that shipped outward from a river port (e.g., Hankou) simultaneously paid two departure taxes—an export tax and coast trade duty. Upon exiting the river 600 miles later at Shanghai, if the tea was declared for export and all its packaging found intact, Shanghai customs issued

---

84. Paul A. Van Dyke, *The Canton Trade: Life and Enterprise on the China Coast, 1700–1845* (Hong Kong: Hong Kong University Press, 2005), 21.
85. Van Dyke, *Canton Trade*, 37–38.
86. Van Dyke, *Canton Trade*, 23, 96.
87. Van Dyke, *Canton Trade*, 25.

a reexport certificate. The shipper could then return to the original port (Hankou in this example) and exchange this certificate for another. This second piece of paper, issued by the original port, was the drawback for the value of the coast trade duty. In addition, the drawback grafted onto policing practices, facilities for capital. The shipper kept the drawback until he elected to present it, sometime in the future, in lieu of cash for duties owed.[88] In the meantime, the drawback functioned as a capital reserve.

The success of this bureaucratic relay depended on the quality of the inscriptions. Properly produced, inscriptions eased the flow of goods and reproduction of capital. Improper paperwork, however, generated wasteful friction in the system. Consider, for example, a cargo of ginseng that arrived in Ningbo from Shanghai with a cargo manifest that did not match its exemption certificate.[89] The Ningbo customs had questions: What had produced the discrepancy? Was the paperwork changed en route, or did the customs office that issued the exemption certificate take part in an attempt to defraud the revenue? To settle the matter, the IMC (at the merchant's request) sent the ginseng back to Shanghai, where it was discovered that an erroneous translation in the creation of the cargo certificate was the source of the discrepancy. Settling the matter took eleven days, during which, according to the ginseng importer, prices fell and he suffered a loss of market valued at nearly $500. The merchant claimed an indemnity against the IMC, which the agency refused. After many rounds of correspondence between the British consul and the customs commissioner, the consul referred the matter to Beijing, charging the customs with an increasing disposition to act in ways "unjust and prejudicial" to the foreign merchant. At the British Legation, what had been a case of suspected revenue fraud became an investigation into whether the customs and consul had followed the proper order of operations.

The ginseng case attests to how friction could occur at many points within the treaty port system, both inside and outside the IMC. Each pass or certificate issued at one port needed to be checked or acted on at the next port of call without exception. To do otherwise raised the specter of capricious behavior and fostered distrust among the institutions of the treaty apparatus. Hart recognized this. With treaty-based trade taking place at multiple ports, "it became absolutely requisite to have a custom system under which . . . records [were] correctly kept, office work thoroughly understood and efficiently produced."[90] Questionable documents caused delay and mistrust all around, so the ability to produce secure and reliable

---

88. IMC, *Circulars First*, no. 2. 5 December, 1862, 21; no. 20, 20 August 1863, 43.
89. Following account taken from Consul Fittock to Minister Alcock, No. 16, 8 August 1869, TNA, FO 228/469.
90. Great Britain, *China No. 1*, 11.

customs documents was key to whether operations within and between offices took place with little interruption, irregularity, or ambiguity. Paperwork was the linchpin of whether the customs would be an efficient, productive apparatus and encourage the growth of trade. "A document officially issued at one Custom house cannot be dishonored at another," Hart instructed.[91]

Engines and Trains of Mechanism

The mediation paperwork provided for interport shipping put office protocol and interoffice coordination at the center of IMC operations. Three tactics became central to Hart's efforts to make these operations an engine for the growth of trade and revenue: division of labor, standardized office paperwork, and detailed work protocols, including temporal guidelines for work processes. All three were critical parts of an efficient office and were needed to coordinate an unimpeded flow of commodity capital.

Division of Labor

In the 1820s and 1830s, engine science concluded that complex, integrated machine operations in mines and factories achieved optimal ratios of work and waste when they were planned from above. Such planning took into account both the function of each individual machine and the "trains of mechanism" that connected them.[92] In China, given an "unchecked position" to design the IMC's operations, Hart reached similar conclusions.[93] Although asked by the Zongli yamen to produce certain revenues and reports, he created for himself a much more ambitious project to engineer new offices as well as moving pieces to drive coordination between them.[94]

The inspector general began with the division of labor. Just days after taking office, asked his commissioners to provide a list of all customs personnel whose work was not "indispensable" to the conduct of business.[95] Hart later explained, "The efficiency of public servants may be greatly increased by a more complete application of the idea of a departmental division of labor."[96] In this case, the re(division) of customs labor commenced with determining the minimal staff needed to operate the customs. Subsequently, Hart assigned to each IMC office a definite geographic

---

91. IMC, *Circulars First*, no. 2, 4 July 1861, 4; see also no. 25, 1 November 1869, 240.
92. Wise and Smith, "Work and Waste 2," 412.
93. Horowitz, "Politics, Power," 551.
94. Great Britain, *China No. 1* (1865), 12. Hart sensed that the design of the IMC had to respond to the interconnected nature of the ports.
95. IMC, *Circulars First*, no. 6, 4 July 1861, 7.
96. Great Britain, *China No. 1* (1865), 12.

jurisdiction and a staff allocation based on levels of commercial activity.[97] A second division of labor took place within each office, which the inspector general subdivided into a "General Office" for "foreign rigged ships and steamers" moving to and from foreign ports or treaty ports, a second "River Steamer Office" for steamers plying the Yangzi River, and a third "Junk Office" for Chinese rigged boats flying foreign flags.[98] A third division segregated operations into "indoor" work, performed by nine classes of clerks who processed applications, calculated duties, and issued passes, and "outdoor" work done by nine classes of staff who supervised docking, unlading, and lading and also examined cargoes. The overall division of labor, which Hart considered a "useful idea" the IMC had introduced into China, corresponded to a scale of salaries that facilitated strict accounting for office expenses.[99]

Through control of personnel allocations, salaries, and office expenditures, Hart set bounds on the bureaucratic consumption of revenue, which he argued consequently "secured for the State funds . . . to an extent never dreamt of before." The maximal growth of revenue resulted, he argued, from the substitution of "honest and effective revenue administration" for "underhand arrangements" and "corrupt, dishonest, and inefficient offices."[100] Like engines, which had "governors" that regulated the consumption of fuel, the IMC had personnel allocations and salaries that bound the bureaucracy's consumption of revenue.[101] Salaries were a particularly visible change that earned Hart much contemporary praise for running an "honest" service, though it is also unclear whether Hart or his fans understood the fee structures of Qing offices.[102] Viewed more critically, salaries were another front on which the treaty apparatus depersonalized commercial governance. Whereas *changguan* levied direct fees in support of their staff (creating the conditions of possibility for much of

---

97. IMC, *Circulars First*, no. 8, 21 June 1864, 58.
98. *Regulations of the Chinese Maritime Customs, Compiled by Thomas Dick, Office of Maritime Customs, Shanghai* (Shanghai: A. H. De Carvalhao, 1864), 41–42; hereafter *CMC Regulations 1864*. The office division appears to have mapped to the particular anchorage needs of the different vessels and streamlined policing operations that still depended on visual sighting of vessels. Each office needed to keep an eye out for only one kind of ship.
99. Great Britain, *China No. 1* (1865), 12; IMC, *Circulars First*, no. 25, 1 November 1869, 234–41.
100. Great Britain, *China No. 1* (1865), 11.
101. Wise and Smith, "Work and Waste 2," 412.
102. For example, staffing in a county magistrate's yamen routinely and openly exceeded centrally stipulated limits. Staff were unsalaried and took ad hoc customary fees that varied by locality. Magistrates also employed personal servants and private secretaries who assisted with official government business. Servants earned cash from customary fees; secretaries, used at all levels of provincial government, received a salary from the official employing them. It is not clear that anyone involved in these operations, even those who paid the fees, considered any of this activity "corrupt," except when it exceeded established conventions. See T'ung-Tsu Ch'u, *Local Government in China under the Ch'ing* (Cambridge, MA: Cambridge University Press, 1962), 38–39, 44–49, 74–88, 93–106, 112–13. On Qing-era "anti-corruption" campaigns, see Zelin, *The Magistrate's Tael*.

the "corruption" Hart decried), the IMC was funded from a percentage of tonnage dues, which were held in a general account and redistributed through a centralized budget. Although the funding source for both customs regimes was trade, under the treaty apparatus, charges were depersonalized and regularized, which Hart argued freed trade from "risks, temptations, and uncertainties."[103]

Work Protocols and Time

Bureaucratic hierarchy itself was in no way new to the Qing Empire, but how the IMC mobilized this structure and to what ends were specific to Hart's pursuit of growth and efficiency. In addition to using personnel allocations and budgets to govern customs operations, Hart also took measures to establish common rates of work. He divided indoor business into specific functions that matched discrete stages in the import and export of cargoes and issued rules for how the bilingual staff would perform their duties. In the General Office, business was divided between five desks. Two desks handled inbound and outbound permitting, another registered and translated receipts for duty paid at the Chinese customs bank, a fourth generated documents that facilitated tax exemptions, and a fifth issued departure clearances. Clerks trained in the work of a particular desk and routinely applied a subset of customs regulations and protocols. In the engineering parlance of the era, these measures set skill and labor in action in "controlled, predictable fashion".[104]

Creating structures for the regular application of bureaucratic labor power created the possibility to temporally condition work. Time mattered in two registers. First, there was the simple issue of inconvenience to trade: ships, cargoes, captains, and consignees waiting around on account of bureaucratic processes. More consequential, from an administrative point of view, was how time could shape and misshape extended commodity flows. As in other machine systems, each task performed by a clerk in an IMC office produced raw material for the next. A slowdown or delay at one point would stop the movement of cargo, waste time, lead to market losses, and discourage trade. The IMC, pace complaints against it, did not want to be the cause of any missed profits. Thus, problems of office efficiency were never too far from problems of time and merchant profit. How to use as little time as possible to generate the largest possible volume and velocity of commercial circulation?

The IMC's solutions to the problems of friction and time were prescribed forms and standardized turnaround time. Early on, IMC notices admonished merchants to stop submitting scraps of paper to conduct business with the customs.[105] Landing

---

103. Great Britain, *China No. 1* (1865), 11.
104. *CMC Regulations* 1864, 41–42; Wise and Smith, "Work and Waste 2," 411–12.
105. *CMC Regulations* 1864, 42.

a cargo, according to regulation, instead required the shipmaster to present to the Import Permit Desk a letter-paper-sized "inward manifest" listing "the marks, numbers, and contents entailed of every package on board." After the shipper submitted the manifest, the consignees of the cargo submitted "Applications to Land," which also listed marks, numbers, and contents as well as weight, quantity, and to whom the cargo was to be delivered. Within twenty-four hours of this application, the Customs Memo Desk had to match the application with the tariff and issue a calculation of duties payable. The merchant then had another twenty-four hours to return to the IMC office with proof of duties paid and to register this proof with the Memo Desk using a specially designed "chit book."[106]

These protocols and others like them generated work processes that conditioned clerks, merchants, and commissioners to conform to specified temporal rhythms, apply general rules to a specific instance, and master prescribed formats for presenting and recording information. Instructions to IMC commissioners regarding the production and use of exemption certificates, for instance, detailed specific conditions that needed to be met for the certificate to be issued. These included who could receive a certificate, when the office could and could not issue one, and when the office could and could not receive one. As stated in the inspector general's circular to commissioners,

> You will note that these documents are never to be issued, except for goods shipped on board vessels clearing for Treaty ports, and that they are to be issued either before or simultaneously with shipment of the goods; in no case will you entertain applications that may be made for them subsequent to the departure of the vessels concerned. In like manner, such documents should never be received by the Customs, save when handed in before the landing of the goods covered by them.[107]

As seen here and elsewhere throughout IMC regulations, time and form governed office work, tuning the trains of mechanisms that moved cargoes and customs inscriptions through the Qing Empire. Just as a waterwheel spinning too quickly or slowly would fail to collect the optimum amount of water, timing inscriptions synchronized commodity movements and customs surveillance so trade and revenue could grow.

---

106. *CMC Regulations* 1864, 39–42.
107. IMC, *Circulars First*, no. 8, 4 November 1861, 9.

Work Done

Through precise guidelines for office divisions of labor, examination protocols, and inscription practices, the IMC called forth a transprovincial administrative infrastructure coordinated through daily operations. The customs, accordingly, also provided an appropriate institutional home for the kind of rote, alienated officiating prescribed by treaties. "Carrying out regulations, a Commissioner can act safely," Hart advised his staff. "Setting them aside, he will get into endless difficulties."[108] Stated somewhat differently, IMC employees were, to borrow a phrase from the industrial context, "appropriated by the process."[109] In a machine system, one dedicated student of large-scale industry observed, "the total [production] process is examined objectively, viewed in and for itself, and analyzed into its constitutive phases."[110] Such objective analysis divides the laboring process into a series of narrow specialized tasks and consequently reshapes the worker into an instrument for the apparatus. Rather than the worker appropriating a box of possible tools to accomplish ends he himself identifies, the machine tells him when, at what rate, and how to do its work.[111] Similarly, Hart's systematic redesign of Qing customs operations as a productive apparatus centered the creation of rule-bound bureaucrats, whose correct work never exceeded the proper application of those rules.

It is clear from how Hart talked about his work that his institutional design used prescribed forms and temporally conditioned activity with the intent to smooth transitions between discrete acts of receiving, processing, and permitting and to reduce the amount of time goods spent in transit. Under this regime merchants would benefit from shortened time distances and less risk of loss of market. But alienated work and temporal compression did more than aid the ongoing circulation and reproduction of capital; they also reconditioned bureaucratic practice into an expression of capital's imperative to move swiftly and ceaselessly. Institutional commitment to regularity, uniformity, and alienated work animated a doctrine of noninterference that placed governance in the position of serving capital—its needs set the limits of what officials should and could do.

In his own words, the mechanical correctness Hart sought to achieve was a means of bringing customs administration in line with "the requirements of trade," which he argued had to be consulted to devise "efficient" operations that "meet the

---

108. IMC, *Circulars First*, no. 24, 18 December 1873, 490.
109. Karl Marx, *Capital: A Critique of Political Economy*, vol. 1, trans. Ben Fowkes (New York: Vintage Books, 1977), 501.
110. Marx, *Capital*, I:501.
111. Marx, *Capital*, I: chap. 15; Karl Marx, "The Grundrisse," in Robert C. Tucker, ed., *The Marx-Engels Reader*, 2nd ed. (New York: Norton, 1978), 278–81.

claims of the public."[112] What he thought trade required, Hart never programmatically stated. He did state that whereas the traditional Qing customs establishment undermined commercial progress, the treaties signed since 1842 appreciated "what the development of trade required externally."[113] We can reasonably surmise, then, that these requirements included transparent regulations, fixed fees, lowered costs of circulation, and uniform administration. The IMC's design further suggests that requirements of trade included the predictable and controlled application of energy to a limited range of tasks.

There would seem to be something of a paradox in constructing a static, regulatory infrastructure for ever-shifting commodity flows, except that Hart seems to have recognized in the sphere of commerce the operation of abstract, lawlike compulsions. For scientists and engineers, physical laws dictated what was possible in machine science, and discovery of these laws was part of the practical project of solving the problem of waste. Hart also thought in terms of inevitable causality. In his initial assessment of the failures of Qing customs administration, he posited a merchant who was not so much a free agent and independent moral decision-maker as a dependent actor, determined at subjective and practical levels by forces outside him and led down better and worse paths according to the administrative structure in which he found himself. He possessed "interests," and in pursuit of these he became demanding, demoralized, or dishonest, depending on the circumstances he encountered.[114] In a position to create these circumstances, Hart instructed customs commissioners to eliminate "unnecessary" or "vexatious" procedures and rules; governance needed to interfere as little as possible with merchant operations and convenience.[115]

Conclusion: Signs of Infection

It must be kept in mind that during the first decade of the IMC's existence, as much as Hart was the central architect of the IMC, day-to-day operations involved other parts of the Qing territorial administration. These partners, the Chinese superintendents of customs foremost among them, were crucial for the immediate exercise

---

112. Great Britain, *China No. 1*, 11; see also 7, 12.
113. Great Britain, *China No. 1*, 11.
114. On the naturalization of "interests" as a lawlike pursuit of material, economic advantage, see Albert O. Hirschman, *The Passions and the Interests: Political Arguments for Capitalism before Its Triumph* (Princeton: Princeton University Press, 1997). Among the many voices Hirschman features is John Millar, who in the eighteenth century wrote that the interests and actions of mercantile people proceed "'with the uniformity of a machine'" (93).
115. For example, IMC, *Circulars First*, no. 1, 2 January 1869, 201; no. 8, 21 June 1864, 57; "Customs Notification No. 8", 20 October 1863 in *CMC Regulations* 1864, 42.

of the new customs' authority.[116] The authority of the superintendent at Ningbo, for instance, was needed for the new IMC office to issue passes and certificates and inspect cargoes.[117] At the same time, these officials were also not readily assimilated into the IMC's new regime of rules and protocols. The Ningbo superintendent diverted customs revenues due to Beijing to supply funds for defense needs and he appropriated IMC personnel to help manage affairs at the local *changguan*.[118] He suspended treaty provisions and regulations to solve local commodity shortages and, contra Hart's insistence on bureaucratic professionalism, saw no need to keep local gentry and merchants from assisting with local customs investigations.[119] As much as the superintendent was an important part of the IMC's early years, this work by the superintendent also had little to do with Hart's program of growth and, at times, worked at cross-purposes with it.

Institutionalizing an alternative program of growth and order predicated on administrative uniformity, homogeneity, and routinized patterns of action broke with tenets of Qing governance that privileged the creative response of an official to particular conditions at a place in time. This, of course, was much of the point. "The Inspectorate will be for a time," Hart predicted in 1864, "and while it exists [it will be] a more and more efficient, though extraneous, public servant; it will have finished its work when it shall have produced a native administration, as honest and as efficient, to replace it."[120] Hart offered the IMC as more than a better way to collect revenue. It also offered a new model for what constituted good governance: Well-run institutions routinely reproduced static regulatory order; good administrators solved problems by applying rules. They did not improvise; they did not deviate. Instrumental reason flourished where moral reason was not needed. This was not a model of good governance Qing officials would have encountered in their studies for official exams. But it did echo the world of the engineer-scientist, who discovered eternal physical laws and used them to design machines that could reliably produce more and more of the same outcome hour after hour, day after day.

---

116. Van de Ven, *Breaking with the Past*, 72–75.
117. Daotai to Hughes no. 46, 13 July 1861, CMC microfilm, reel 174; Daotai to Hughes no. 88, 23 August 1861, CMC microfilm, reel 174; Hughes to Daotai no. 19, ND 1862, CMC microfilm, reel 174; Hughes to Daotai no. 20, ND 1862, CMC microfilm, reel 174; Hughes to Daotai no. 176, ND 1862, CMC microfilm, reel 174.
118. Daotai to Hughes no. 6, 11 June 1862, CMC microfilm, reel 174; Daotai to Hughes no. 19, 27 June 1862, CMC microfilm, reel 174; Daotai to Hughes no. 22, 30 June 1862, CMC microfilm, reel 174; Hughes to Daotai no. 25, ND 1862, CMC microfilm, reel 174.
119. Daotai to Hughes no. 129, 15 October 1861, CMC microfilm, reel 174; Daotai to Hughes no. 130, 18 October 1861, CMC microfilm, reel 174; Hughes to Daotai no. 9, ND, 1862, CMC microfilm, reel 174; Hughes to Daotai no. 14, ND 1862, CMC microfilm, reel 174.
120. Great Britain, *China No. 1*, 13.

Ultimately, there was more going on in creation of the IMC than just the institutionalization of a program of growth. The mutually constitutive relationship between the IMC's rule-bound order and the flow of trade between treaty ports suggests that administrative practice was also a response to a new object of governance. Qing customs operations had previously focused their energies on keeping an eye on who participated in trade, catching smuggled cargoes, and taxing the arrival and departure of goods in a specific port. Each port operated independently of one another, and occasionally ports competed to attract ships.[121] IMC operations, by contrast, executed paperwork processes to grow the movement of goods between points of production and points of sale. This is not to say the IMC did not police trade and assess duties—it did—but that alongside this work, its more novel function, the one that reterritorialized merchants, ports, and trade itself, was to govern the limitless movement of goods within China and between China and the rest of the world. Furthermore, close examination of these operations reveals the extent to which "efficiency" and the ethic of constant, regular application of systemic rules were a response to this particular objective. In other words, capital circulation and efficient, "rational" administration coconstituted each other.

---

121. Zhao, *The Qing Opening to the Ocean*, 179–81.

3
Disorderly Order

The Imperial Maritime Customs (IMC), designed as a machine to grow capital, was one of the most important vectors through which capital became part of Qing governance. The agency institutionalized capital circulation in China as an object of governance and in the name of Qing revenues self-consciously ministered to its growth. The work of commercial governance, however, was not confined to these specialized offices. One of the great ironies of the treaty era is that after fighting for treaties to grow international trade between Great Britain and China, under their framework, British mercantile energies shifted to circuits of domestic commodity circulation, either as buyers and sellers of Chinese produce, or as shippers, bankers, and insurers for Chinese merchants.[1] Consequently, although the treaty regime created specific terms for Euro-American trade and Euro-American capital, it actually became much more difficult to disentangle Chinese and non-Chinese forms of capital and trade.

Sino-foreign capital was an ambiguous object for the regulatory gaze, which had been trained to recognize Chinese and non-Chinese commercial activity. Combinations of Euro-American and Chinese resources such as ships, cargos, and money, blurred the boundaries of treaty jurisdiction and implicated territorial officials, including local magistrates and regional governors-general, in treaty-related affairs. These officials, who exercised jurisdiction over Chinese commerce, were often called on by the foreign establishment to govern in keeping with the expansive

---

1. Yen-p'ing Hao, *The Commercial Revolution in Nineteenth-Century China: The Rise of Sino-Western Mercantile Capitalism* (Berkeley: University of California Press, 1985); Zhaojin Ji, *A History of Modern Shanghai Banking: The Rise and Decline of China's Financial Capitalism* (Armonk: M. E. Sharpe, 2003); Edward LeFevour, *Western Enterprise in Late Ch'ing China: A Selective Survey of Jardine, Matheson & Company's Operations, 1842–1895* (Cambridge, MA: Harvard University Asia Center, 1968).

"spirit" treaty regime, not only with respect to foreign bodies and property but with respect to Chinese ones as well. As foreign capital expanded into Chinese domestic commodity circulation, Chinese bodies, space, and property became key to the program of Euro-American capital accumulation; whether this program's expansion into the empire's inland regions obligated or mustered change in local governance was the high-stakes question of the day.

During the 1860s, global capital moved through China a framework of regulatory ambiguity and contested treaty interpretation. In his book on smuggling in China, Philip Thai notes that the "new economy" that "pulled China into the ambit of the emergent global capitalist world order" also "placed complex restrictions on domestic authority." Among the restrictions that Thai cites were legal protections for foreign nationals, suspension of Qing tariff sovereignty and codified limits on the government's ability to protect domestic production and trade from foreign competition.[2] Thai argues, persuasively, that these restrictions and regulations, especially extraterritoriality, complicated Qing efforts to police trade. What this account misses, however, is that in the early years of the treaty regime, smuggling itself was an unstable object. By creating a parallel network of rules and offices for trade, treaty regulations unintentionally roused the specter of smuggling and bred disagreements as to what, exactly, counted as revenue fraud. In this framework, growing trade and commerce in China spread and intensified disorder, whether real or imagined.

At the center of administrative disorder was the interplay of extraterritoriality and processes of capital accumulation. Extraterritoriality as practiced in China was, as one recent history puts it, a form of "legal imperialism," "a kind of colonialism without colonies."[3] Extraterritorial jurisdiction was both an outcome of overt political coercion and an institution often capriciously invoked by foreign agents to further the political and economic interests of Euroamerican actors and states.[4] Typically thought of as a privilege with bearing on business disputes and criminal prosecution extraterritoriality also interfered with commercial governance. Extraterritoriality's two wards—personhood and property—also became conduits for circumventing and challenging Qing regulations pertaining to trade and taxation. In treaty ports, legal protections based in personhood enabled British traders to offer a commercial "protection racket" to Chinese counterparts. Chinese merchants in Guangzhou (廣州) and elsewhere "were able to 'rent' British nationality from willing foreigners, using it as protection to evade internal taxes."[5] Property, meanwhile, was coded

---

2. Philip Thai, *China's War on Smuggling: Law, Economic Life, and the Making of the Modern State, 1842–1965* (New York: Columbia University Press, 2018), 26.
3. Teemu Ruskola, *Legal Orientalism: China, the United States, and Modern Law* (Cambridge, MA: Harvard University Press, 2013), 28.
4. Ruskola, *Legal Orientalism*, 174.
5. Eileen Scully, *Bargaining with the State from Afar: American Citizenship in Treaty Port China,*

within international law as something so inviolate as to offer just grounds for war and retribution.[6] Treaties placed British property under explicit protections the sovereign Qing government was contractually obligated to uphold in order to maintain the peace.

Capital made upholding treaty obligations a much more complicated affair. To be clear, opportunistic profit seeking, such as smuggling and fraud, was as old as the hills. The Qing government had its ways of combating these. What became problematic, especially after 1861, was the peculiar set of claims advanced by British merchants and British consuls that their capital changed the regulatory status of Chinese persons, places, and produce. This chapter examines how British personhood and property, tied as they were to projects of capital accumulation, became vectors of deterritorialization and reterritorialization that rescripted interactions between the Qing government and its subjects. This dynamic, unprecedented in the long history of China's trade with the rest of the world, expressed a specific moment in the development of global capital. Sovereign boundaries that had long determined conditions under which capital traveled in China became, during the second half of the nineteenth century, a threat to a globally extended process of ceaseless accumulation. While treaties secured for British trade some protection from perceived threats, the pursuit of maximal capital growth quickly spawned efforts to expand these protections to Chinese bearers of British capital.

Localizing Global Capital

The European traders that gathered in Guangzhou from the seventeenth century onward ran global operations. Those that traveled the longest distances were the British East India Company and the Dutch Vereenigde Oost-Indische Compagnie, both of which operated across coastal Africa, the Arabian Sea, and South, Southeast, and East Asia, remitting goods and currency back to London and Amsterdam. The trading companies came for spices, silk, and tea; they built global empires. But even more irregular European arrivals, such as the *King George* and *Queen Charlotte* in 1787, funded with investments from rural England and laden with cargo from the Pacific northeast, forged globe-spanning circuits of capital accumulation.[7] The locals with whom these Europeans and (later) Americans traded were no less globally oriented. Houqua (Wu Bingjian 伍秉鑑, 1769–1843), one of the most prosperous merchants in Guangzhou, was both a contracted provider of teas to the East India

---

   1844–1942 (New York: Columbia University Press, 2001), 23, 43.
6. Li Chen, *Chinese Law in Imperial Eyes: Sovereignty, Justice, and Transcultural Politics* (New York: Columbia University Press, 2016), 215.
7. George Dixon, *A Voyage round the World* (London: George Goulding, 1789).

Company and a speculator in American tea markets.[8] In the 1760s, his colleague Monqua (Cai Wenguan 蔡文觀) borrowed Swedish capital to finance commercial voyages to Southeast Asia.[9] Guangzhou, Paul Van Dyke has shown, was where capital from the regional junk trade and international trade mingled. The persons and capital invested in voyages to Siam, Singapore, and Batavia were often the persons and capital invested in trade with Europe.[10]

Given the global character of the trading world that converged in Guangzhou before 1842, one of the curiosities of the treaty era is the decidedly domestic character of the circuits of capital accumulation that sprung up within the treaties' regulatory framework. For decades, British firms' calls to access to additional ports in China were driven by ambitions to expand international shipments of goods. What emerged in the 1860s after two rounds of treaties were many more opportunities to make money without ever leaving China's coast. One of the most visible signs of this shift was the growth of British shipping between Shanghai and other treaty ports, which absorbed 70 percent of British-flagged voyages by 1863.[11] British firms also commenced brisk business as commission agents for Chinese merchants trading commodities within China and the East Asia region.[12] While over the next two decades the value of China's foreign trade stagnated, British commodity exchange firms morphed into what one classic study called "managing agencies concerned more with the 'external economies' of trade," including insurance, shipping, and banking.[13] Economic growth in China, post-1842, had more to do with "the development of port facilities, steamships, and banking and insurance services to facilitate intra-Asian trade," rather than East-West trade.[14]

Although China's international trade failed to substantially expand during the first decades of the treaty era, it would be a mistake to conclude that British

---

8. John D. Wong, *Global Trade in the Nineteenth Century: The House of Houqua and the Canton System* (Cambridge: Cambridge University Press, 2016).
9. Paul A. Van Dyke, *The Merchants of Canton and Macao: Success and Failure in Eighteenth-Century Chinese Trade* (Hong Kong: Hong Kong University Press, 2016), 44.
10. Paul A. Van Dyke, *The Canton Trade: Life and Enterprise on the China Coast, 1700–1845* (Hong Kong: Hong Kong University Press, 2007), chap. 8.
11. Britten Dean, *China and Great Britain: The Diplomacy of Commercial Relations, 1860–1864* (Cambridge, MA: East Asian Research Center, Harvard University, 1974), 49.
12. Kazuko Furuta, "Kobe as Seen as Part of the Shanghai Trading Network: The Role of Chinese Merchants in the Re-export of Cotton Manufactures to Japan," in *Japan, China, and the Growth of the Asian International Economy, 1850–1949*, ed. Kaoru Sugihara (Oxford: Oxford University Press, 2005), 23–48; LeFevour, *Western Enterprise*, 53.
13. Wolfgang Keller, Ben Li, and Carol Shiue, "The Evolution of Domestic Trade Flows When Foreign Trade Is Liberalized: Evidence from the CMCS," in *Institutions and Comparative Economic Development*, ed. Masahiko Aoki, Timur Kuran, and Gerard Roland (New York: Palgrave Macmillan, 2012), 152–72; LeFevour, *Western* Enterprise, 48.
14. Richard von Glahn, *The Economic History of China: From Antiquity to the Nineteenth Century* (Cambridge: Cambridge University Press, 2016), 376.

capital failed to advance into China. Where and how it did advance was through participation in circuits of domestic and regional commodity circulation and through partnerships with Chinese counterparts.[15] This course of events, however, was largely unanticipated by the men who negotiated Qing commercial treaties, and the treaties, which codified distinctions between Chinese trade and foreign trade, provided a poor framework for taxing and policing this activity. Consequently, the Qing Empire authorized foreign capital to circulate through circuits of domestic commerce, effectively deterritorializing Chinese produce trades. At the same time, British merchants and consuls wielded treaty-granted privileges and rights as tools to reterritorialize Chinese merchants as factors in circuits of foreign capital accumulation. In these processes, the force undermining Qing sovereignty was not treaty articles per se but the advance of capital under the bifurcated and asymmetrical regulatory framework they created.

Three particular features of the treaty regime produced much of the commercial-administrative disorder experienced in and around treaty ports. The first was regulatory plurality which followed from codified distinctions between Chinese and foreign trade. The second was the anomalous privilege granted to foreign merchants to ship domestic produce between ports in China.[16] The third was extraterritoriality, which compounded the effects of the other two features. Working within the framework provided by these features, by the mid-1860s, it was possible for British merchants to buy tea leaves direct from growers, replacing the work of Chinese teamen and brokers. It was also possible for a Chinese merchant to consign his soy cargo to a British-flagged steamship to deliver his cargo ahead of slower Chinese-flagged junks. Such mixtures defied the assumption, codified in treaties, that it would remain possible to clearly identify foreign trade and Chinese trade. Instead, as foreign capital dispersed outside the confines of treaty ports, its collaboration with Chinese persons and capital meant boundaries between "Chinese trade" and "foreign trade" became porous and muddled.

It is possible that order could have been maintained, even with regulatory plurality, if Qing authorities and Euro-American authorities either could have agreed on what activities fell under treaty jurisdiction or under Qing law, or if one party held the ultimate right to decide. But neither was the case. Extraterritoriality and consular mediation demanded collaborative investigation between provincial officials, IMC officers, and foreign consuls, and new norms of diplomatic relations institutionalized routine meetings in Beijing to discuss commercial disputes. These parties,

---

15. The classic study is Hao, *Commercial Revolution*.
16. Britten Dean writes, "It has generally been recognized in international law that inland navigation and coasting trade are reserved for vessels of nationals, unless otherwise stipulated by treaty" (*China and Great Britain*, 47–48).

meanwhile held widely differing views on what happened when British capital and Chinese persons or capital combined. The next section will outline what regulatory plurality looked like in institutional terms. The following two sections will examine disorderly order as it erupted in key ports of trade. These ports were selected on the basis of available archival materials.

Regulatory Plurality

After 1861, the Qing Empire's commercial-regulatory landscape had three main parts: an original network of Qing customhouses (*changguan* 常關), treaty ports with offices of the IMC, and provincial *lijin* (釐金) regimes, an emergency measure initiated in response to the Taiping Rebellion.[17] Although on paper each institutional complex exercised jurisdiction over a specific segment of commercial activity, Chinese and British capital proved to be highly mobile across the regulatory landscape. It moved between institutions or circumvented them all together, creating institutional competition for commercial tax revenue and threatening the empire's fiscal stability.

Changguan

The *changguan* (常關) network discussed in the last chapter was the primary institution that taxed and policed the many thousands of Chinese ships sailing Qing waters ("junks" in the parlance of the day). Each office reported to either the Board of Works or Board of Revenue in Beijing, to whom *changguan* customs duties belonged. Informally, though, duties often provided funds for provincial yamen expenses.[18] Historically, *changguan* were a reliable source of state revenue, fed by well-established trade routes. Up until the treaty regulatory regime commenced, in most years most ports fulfilled their annual quota, which was set according to what Beijing understood to be customary levels of trade in the area. When a *changguan* fell short, it was typically due to flood, drought, or a temporary disturbance, either political or in nearby markets. After the designation of treaty ports, however, important commercial routes shifted, causing effected *changguan* stations to suffer severe, at times irreversible, declines in their revenues.

---

17. Number of treaty ports: 1842 = 5, 1861 = 14, 1877 = 18, 1897 = 27, 1911 = 49. On the gradual separation of customs operations for treaty-based trade, see John King Fairbank, *Trade and Diplomacy on the China Coast: The Opening of Treaty Ports, 1842–1854* (Cambridge, MA: Harvard University Press, 1964) and Stanley Wright, *China's Struggle for Tariff Autonomy, 1843–1938* (Shanghai: Kelly & Walsh, 1938).
18. Madeline Zelin, *The Magistrate's Tael: Rationalizing Fiscal Reform in Eighteenth Century Ch'ing China* (Berkeley: University of California Press, 1984), 58.

Effected localities included Ganzhou (贛州), once a main stopping point for silk and tea shipments to Guangzhou. The riparian city less than 300 miles from the coast became a marginal port of call as steam shipping through Shanghai (上海) and Jiujiang (九江) became available. Wenzhou (溫州), a once-bustling tea export market, was proximate enough to the treaty port of Ningbo (寧波) that it became a commercial hinterland. It could only attract the most limited steam connections and thereby lost its wholesale import-export businesses. On the Grand Canal, Huai'an (淮安) and Yangzhou (揚州) customs reported diminished levels of commerce after Zhejiang became a treaty port.[19] In Jiangxi province, where Ganzhou was located, and in Zhejiang province, home to Wenzhou, Governors-General Shen Baozhen (沈葆楨, 1820–1879) and Zuo Zongtang (左宗, 1812–1885) reported that IMC stations had "invaded and occupied" the regular customs collections.[20] *Changguan* stations could not collect when the boats did not call. In all of these instances, Chinese merchants, for whom the treaty regime was not designed, had either legally or illegally changed some aspect of their purchasing and/or transport operations so as to fall under IMC jurisdiction. Trade that had been a domestic affair governed by Qing rules was becoming an international affair governed by treaty.

Lijin

Even more problematic than *changguan* revenue losses was the competition that evolved between treaty port facilities and the provincially administered institution commonly known as *lijin*. Throughout the eighteenth century, *changguan* generated a mostly stable stream of revenue for the Qing state. Then, in 1851, as the Taiping Rebellion swept through the Yangzi valley area, revenue plummeted at many of the government's most lucrative customs stations. Customs stations in Yangzi valley and along the Grand Canal, in particular, either shut down operations or managed a fraction of their ordinary trade.[21] Recent research suggests the state

---

19. David Pong, "The Income and Military Expenditure of Kiangsi Province in the Last Years (1860–1864) of the Taiping Rebellion," *Journal of Asian Studies* 26, no. 1 (November 1966): 49–66, here 55–56; IMC, *Decennial Report of 1891*, 387–406; Yuping Ni, *Customs Duties in the Qing Dynasty, ca. 1644–1911* (Leiden: Brill, 2017), 79–81; Qi Meiqin, *Qingdai queguan zhidu yanjiu* 清代榷關制度研究 [Research on the Qing customs system] (Hohot: Neimenggu daxue chubanshe, 2004), 328.
20. "左宗棠奏" [Memorial from Zuo Zongtang], *Chouban yiwu shimo buyi* 籌辦夷務始末補遺 [Complete record of foreign affairs addendum] (CBYWSMBY) (digital), TZ3 6M 23D; "沈葆楨奏" [Memorial from Shen Baozhen], *CBYWSHBY* (digital), TZ3 12M 11D. In his memorial, Shen cites actual traffic levels, which is important. The Taiping Rebellion had devastated commerce along the river, so by pointing to actual levels of activity, Shen could more clearly attribute the shortfalls to the new administrative arrangements rather than the general disorder.
21. For tax revenue data for each station, see Ni, *Custom Duties*, 54–99.

lost two-thirds of its customs revenue during the rebellion.[22] During this period, the court authorized provinces to organize their own taxes on commercial activity. *Lijin* funds initially supported provincial armies and local reconstruction projects, which in the eighteenth century had been funded by allocations from Beijing. Like customs operations and local government finance earlier in the dynasty, *lijin* bureaus operated quasi-autonomously, each setting its own rates and modes of collection. Some *lijin* operations looked a lot like customs—taxing a wide number of goods in transit. Others looked more like guild fees—payments levied by groups of traders on their members. *Lijin* grew to be a considerable source of revenue for both provincial governments and Beijing.[23]

Treaty relations soon threatened this crucial revenue source by creating a *lijin* exemption (touched on in the previous chapter) for foreign nationals at the same time they received permission to travel up the Yangzi River valley and into other inland regions. By the Treaty of Tianjin, Euro-American traders gained access to three ports on the Yangzi River, the empire's busiest commercial thoroughfare. These included Zhenjiang (鎮江), where the river intersected with the Grand Canal; Jiujiang near the mouth of Poyang Lake (鄱陽湖); and Hankou (漢口), one of the empire's largest commercial centers. All three ports were significant regional distribution centers, where commodities such as tea and rice, grown in the surrounding countryside, found their way into circuits of more distant circulation.

In this geographic context, it was significant that the 1858 treaty also granted signatories access, for pleasure or trade, to "all parts of the interior, under passports" up to a distance of 100 *li* [roughly, 35 miles] from the nearest treaty port and for up to five days. Consequently, ports became important not only for their river access but also as jumping-off points to growing areas and smaller market towns further inland. In these hypothetical travels, Euro-American merchants had the option to clear their imports and exports of all transit duties (i.e. *lijin*) by payment of what became known as the "transit duty" or *ban shui* (半稅 half tax). Although nominally designed as a substitute charge for provincial *lijin*, in practice the transit duty funneled funds into accounts controlled in Beijing. The levy also created an enviable distinction between the tax payments due from Euro-American merchants and those due from Chinese merchants, both of whom could now travel some of the same roads and do business in more of the same places. In response to the distinction, Chinese firms both sought out foreign partnerships and falsely claimed foreign protection, creating one of the most intractable policing problems Qing administrators faced.

---

22. Ni, *Custom Duties*, 99.
23. The authoritative work on *lijin* remains Luo Yudong, 中國釐金史 [History of *lijin* in China], 2 vols. (Shanghai: Shangwu yinshuguan, 1936).

Imperial Maritime Customs

The final and most novel institution charged with policing and taxing trade was the IMC, also known as the "foreign customs" (*yangguan* 洋關) or "new customs," discussed extensively in Chapter 2. Initially, the IMC served non-Chinese, or more accurately, non-Qing subjects, who conducted their trade under the flags of treaty signatories. Here, it is important to recall that prior to the IMC, the Qing court maintained a number of different coastal customs offices (*haiguan* 海關) for maritime trade. Euro-American trade at Guangzhou was managed by one of these, the *yangguan* customs station known as *Yuehaiguan* (粵海關). These maritime customs stations reported directly to the imperial court and contributed funds for the emperor's household expenses.[24] Similar arrangements governed the IMC, which answered directly to the Zongli yamen and generated monies for Beijing's use.

Like the *Yuehaiguan*, the IMC monitored, taxed, and policed Euro-American bodies, the ships they claimed, and commodities they carried. But because internal trade between Chinese treaty ports increasingly involved Euro-American firms, capital, and steamships, the IMC, unlike its predecessor, became an important part of domestic commercial governance.[25] At the same time, the IMC offered new options for circulation times and circulation costs within China. Tax exemptions the IMC administered (Chapter 2) created variances between the circulation costs for foreign-flagged and those for Chinese-flagged shipping, making them partly responsible for the substantial growth in British-flagged transport between treaty ports. Finally, the Qing government purposely limited steam shipping to treaty ports and allocated its governance to the IMC.[26] Chinese merchants seeking to use the cutting-edge technology had to work through the "foreign" customs.

* * *

Between them, *changguan*, the IMC, and *lijin* collectorates collectively taxed and governed the empire's commercial circulation. On paper, each handled distinct segments of trade. But in practice, the different tax rates and regulations administered by each collectively shaped commercial circulation. In particular, incentives sprouted for domestic commerce to masquerade as foreign. It became common, for

---

24. Preston M. Torbert, *The Ch'ing Imperial Household Department: A Study of Its Organization and Principal Functions, 1662–1796* (Cambridge, MA: Harvard University Council on East Asian Studies, 1977); Gang Zhao, *The Qing Opening to the Ocean: Chinese Maritime Policies, 1684–1757* (Honolulu: University of Hawai'i Press, 2013).
25. Wolfgang Keller, Javier Santiago, and Carol Shiue, "China's Domestic Trade during the Treaty Era," *Explorations in Economic History* 63 (2017): 26–43. Data from the IMC show that the majority of exports (by value) passing through key IMC customhouses was Chinese produce.
26. Anne Reinhardt, *Navigating Semi-colonialism: Shipping, Sovereignty, and Nation-Building in China, 1860–1937* (Cambridge, MA: Harvard University Asia Center, 2018).

instance, for domestic produce, such as sugar, to pass through the British colony of Hong Kong so it could travel to other treaty ports under tax exemptions for foreign imports. Another practice popular with Chinese merchants was investment in foreign-flagged steamships so as to avoid *lijin* charges.[27] Chinese merchants in the silk filatures trade avoided *lijin* by partnering with foreign firms.[28] Less respectable activities catalyzed by regulatory plurality included sales by foreign traders of their flags, of their tax exemption certificates, or even of their body or name to allow Chinese firms to escape the reach of their government.

In light of these practices, provincial authorities became deeply suspicious of any Chinese merchant carrying foreign-origin goods and any Euro-American merchant transporting China-made goods. Indeed, much of what we know about problematic combinations of Chinese and foreign mercantile resources comes from the reports generated when provincial officials attempted to police these combinations. In Beijing, Prince Yixin (王奕訢, 1833–1898) as well as senior Manchu statesmen Guiliang (桂良, 1785–1862) and Wenxiang (文祥 1818–1876) were determined that the government, through the work of the newly created Zongli yamen, would strictly enforce the treaties to keep foreign activity within its prescribed limits.[29] But what was foreign activity and what were its prescribed limits? The multiple authorities with jurisdiction in China held decidedly different positions.

Geographic Dispersion

Throughout the 1850s, foreign firms routinely engaged in domestic commodity circulation between the Qing Empire's coastal ports, even though such activity was neither explicitly sanctioned or in keeping with international norms. After the Treaty of Tianjin (1858) sanctioned foreign trade at ports on the Yangzi River as well as at ports important in the north-south soy trade, officials in Beijing and the provinces worried about what could happen as foreign shipping expanded into more places. Officers of the newly established Zongli yamen took note of potential revenue losses for *changguan* as well as future business losses for Chinese firms, whose profits could be "surreptitiously snatched away" by Euro-American firms conducting business outside the strict limits of foreign import-export trade.[30] Officials managing affairs in Yangzi River valley provinces concurred that revenue fraud was likely to increase.

---

27. Anne Reinhardt, "Treaty Ports as Shipping Infrastructure," in *Treaty Ports in Modern China: Land, Law, and Power*, ed. Robert Bickers and Isabella Jackson (London: Routledge, 2016), 101–20.
28. Eiichi Motono, *Conflict and Cooperation in Sino-British Business, 1860–1911: The Impact of the Pro-British Commercial Network in Shanghai* (New York: St. Martin's, 2000), chap. 5.
29. Jennifer M. Rudolph, *Negotiated Power in Late Imperial China: The Zongli Yamen and the Politics of Reform* (Ithaca: East Asia Program, Cornell University, 2008), 55.
30. *CBYWSM* (digital), TZ, juan 2, 19.2. Memorial authored by Prince Yixin.

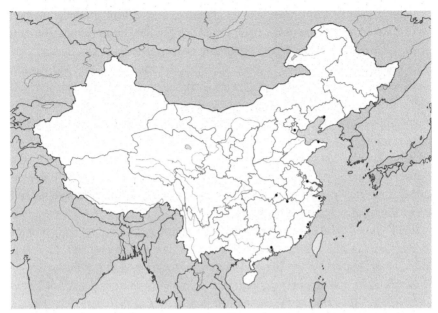

Figure 3.1: Ports with IMC operations, 1861. Background map of present-day China created by Milenioscuro under Creative Commons Attribution-Share Alike 3.0 Unported license.

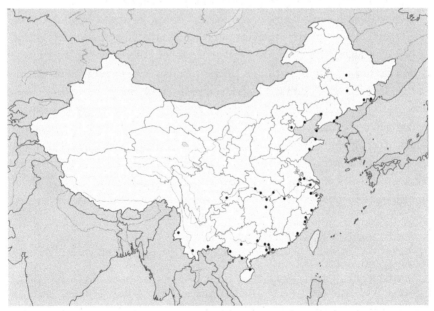

Figure 3.2: Ports with IMC operations, 1911. Locations drawn from Imperial Maritime Customs, *Decennial Report on Trade at the Treaty Ports of China, 1902–1911*, Statistical Series No. 6, 2 vols. (Shanghai: Statistical Department of the Inspectorate General of Customs, 1913). Background map of present-day China created by Milenioscuro under Creative Commons Attribution-Share Alike 3.0 Unported license.

Routine cargo inspections were bound to become more difficult as foreign-flagged boats traveled up and down the river. Could any possible measures confine their exchanges with Chinese traders to designated treaty ports? "How can foreign trade be carried out and there not be more and more evasion, smuggling, and wanton intercourse with inland merchants?" worried Hunan governor Mao Hongbin (毛鴻賓, 1806–1868).[31] The newly granted allowance for foreign firms to do business outside of ports meant "mountains, countryside, towns, and villages all become ports of trade."[32] Other officials in the region pointed out that Euro-American access to inland waters also meant it was possible for "crafty inland merchants [to] fly the British flag, [and] on the basis of this appearance engage in smuggling," particularly in strategically important goods, such as rice, lumber, iron, steel, copper, and lead.[33] Though the government had been forced to concede carriage of these goods to foreign firms, it did not countenance the same for Qing subjects. Permission for foreign firms to hire Chinese employees further muddied the waters. "Presently, interior merchants travel to places in Hunan and Hubei where they grow tea to purchase tea leaves and other goods," reported Guan Wen, governor-general of Hubei and Hunan. "They frequently *say* that they are the hired partners of the foreign merchants and resist without end the payment of lijin. In a situation like this, every crafty inland merchant can call themselves hired partners of foreign merchants, and all quantities of inland goods can be said to be purchased for foreign merchants."[34]

Qing officials sensed a clear and material threat generated by the potential dispersion of Euro-American merchants further into the empire's commercial landscapes and networks. Notably, the harm anticipated by officials in the Yangzi valley region did not actually require Euro-American bodies to be present; mere referents of their investments—contracted labor and boats flying their national flags—were enough to jeopardize fiscal and regulatory affairs. Stated somewhat differently, a potentially vast project of decoding and recoding trade was about to commence, which may or may not have been illicit, and the boundaries of which were unclear to those charged with maintaining order. Hunan governor Mao Hongbin described the situation as a metaphysical problem: the "vitality and momentum" (*qishi*/氣勢) of foreign trade, he wrote, threatened to overwhelm governance.[35] What was needed,

---

31. *CBYWSM* (digital), TZ, juan 4, 30.1.
32. *CBYWSM* (digital), TZ, juan 2, 6.1. Memorial authored by Hugang Governor General Guan Wen (官文, 1798–1871).
33. *CBYWSM* (digital), TZ, juan 2, 5.1. These were all goods interdicted to Chinese transport but permitted to foreign shipping with permit. Memorial authored by Hugang Governor General Guan Wen (官文, 1798–1871).
34. *CBYWSM* (digital), TZ, juan 2, 6.1–6.2, emphasis added.
35. *Qi* translates as both material and energy, a context-dependent volatile infinitesimal thing endlessly circulating and "coalescing in particular configurations to constitute particular things in the cosmos." See Jane Geaney, *On the Epistemology of the Senses in Early Chinese Thought* (Honolulu:

Mao thought, was the active intervention of a capable administrator to bring things back into balance. In Mao's words: to "make manifest in the world balance between the phenomenal (*shi* 事) and the noumenal (*li* 理)."[36]

In the uncertain and dynamic world Mao governed, the rules, regulations, and procedures prescribed by treaties and the new IMC were not sufficient to ensure order. Indeed, they had introduced slippage between what was and what should be, a disorder to which officials now needed to creatively adapt. The episodes that follow show how the disorder that confronted Mao and his colleagues was composed of a cohort of British firms and consuls determined to prove that the institutional organization of Chinese produce movements was no longer an exclusively Chinese affair and that treaty-based rules for foreign trade had absorbed Chinese merchants, Chinese produce, and Chinese officials. The new regulatory order set up the potential for a chaotic deterritorialization of Chinese commerce. How Qing officials attempted to manage that potential clarifies what was at stake.

Extraterritoriality and Commodity Circulation

A first question that arose as Euro-American firms dispersed into the Qing countryside to buy and sell Chinese and foreign goods was whether the foreign merchant and his cargo came under the jurisdiction of provincial commercial regulations. The extraterritorial provisions written into the Treaty of Tianjin placed "criminal act[s]" committed by British subjects under the jurisdiction of British authorities, but said nothing about other kinds of acts determined illegal by Chinese authorities. Other treaty provisions, however, created obligations for Chinese authorities to protect British property and provided for consular mediation in cases when a foreign national objected to his treatment by Qing authorities. Within this framework, it was not uncommon for British subjects to disregard local trade rules and then use the office of the consul to press for exemptions to those rules or indemnity for losses of property and market that followed from their enforcement.

What becomes clear reading through cases of consular mediation is the extent to which it was British *property*, not British *persons* that did the most to attenuate Qing regulatory reach. In one early victory against local regulatory power, for example,

---

University of Hawai'i Press, 2002), 9–10, 22–25; Daniel K. Gardner, *Confucianism: A Very Short Introduction* (Oxford: Oxford University Press, 2014), 73–77. *Shi* most fully translates as "the propensity of things," an ontological concept with implications for strategies and tactics of governance. *Shi* called for generals, calligraphers, poets, painters, politicians, and emperors to work through forces, tensions, and tendencies put forth by a situational configuration. Working with *shi*, constant adaption is necessary in "organizing circumstances in such a way as to derive profit from them." See François Jullien, *The Propensity of Things: Toward a History of Efficacy in China*, trans. Janet Lloyd (New York: Zone Books, 1995), 32.

36. *CBYWSM* (digital), TZ, juan 4, 31.1.

the British consul at Hankou in 1861 successfully blocked an arrest by the Hanyang (漢陽) magistrate Liu Qiyu (劉齊御) of a Chinese merchant who sold iron and oil to a British merchant. Although local rules prohibited the export of both commodities, British and Qing authorities in Beijing agreed the magistrate acted in violation of the tariff treaty, which explicitly authorized British subjects to export and import iron and oil.[37] The sale by the Chinese merchant, so went official reasoning, could not be illegal given that the British merchant was engaged in legal commerce.

The Hanyang ruling suggested early on that in matters of regulatory jurisdiction, the relevant question for local authorities was not exclusively *who* regulations covered, but also *what* they covered. This principle remained in force nearly two decades later when a British firm Bradley & Co. tried to buy and sell iron pans in the province of Guangdong. Either ignorant of local regulations or willing to break them, the firm bought iron pans (used in firing tea leaves) in the northeast of the province and attempted to transport them for sale in Chaozhou (潮州), an important center in the tea trade. Outside of Chaozhou, a local tax office detained and denied passage to the pans on the grounds that provincial regulations, intended to preserve local markets for local foundries, limited the sale of iron goods to their district of manufacture. For two years, Bradley & Co. fought for exemption to the provincial regulation. Ultimately, however, the firm's commodity lacked the protection of the treaty tariff, and it was left with no other choice but to sell the pans at a loss and sign a pledge to never again engage in the trade.[38] Bradley & Co. could only claim exemption from local regulatory power to the same extent its commodities could.

The centrality of commodities to decisions as to whether treaty signatories could be held culpable for infringing on local regulations introduces a new dimension to our consideration of "legal imperialism" as it was practiced in China. While extraterritoriality was a practice that extricated persons from the "cruel" Chinese legal system, the interpretation of other treaty privileges and rights could perform similar work for goods, defining for the regulatory gaze the status of their bearer and extricating them from forms of territorial authority that otherwise limited their circulation and sale. Significant for our purposes here, this interpretative practice provides a concrete form of Marx's observation about the "Traeger" relationship: the commodity is the subject, the human personifies its "consciousness and will."[39]

---

37. No. 8 Hankou Consul Gingell to Frederick Bruce, 13 May 1861, TNA, FO 228/313.
38. Chinese Secretary, Beijing Legation, No. 37, October 25, 1879. Swatow. Bradley & Co.'s Iron Pans. TNA, FO 233/64.
39. Karl Marx, *Capital: A Critique of Political Economy*, vol. 1, trans. Ben Fowkes [New York: Vintage Books, 1977], 254.

Disorderly Order 101

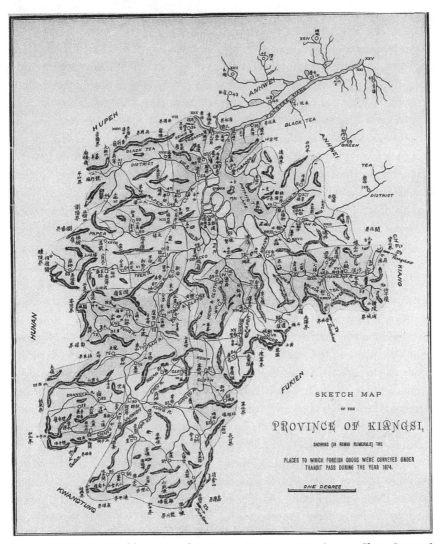

Figure 3.3: Footprint of foreign goods in Jiangxi Province, 1874. Source: China, Imperial Maritime Customs, *Decennial Report on Trade at the Treaty Ports of China, 1881–1891* (Shanghai: Statistical Department of the Inspectorate General, 1892).

Contagion

The iron and oil ruling in Hanyang suggests that using the commodity to decide regulatory jurisdiction meant that questions over the scope of treaty privileges and obligations quickly encompassed Chinese merchants as well. Once again, actions taken by the Hanyang magistrate Liu Qiyu are instructive.[40] When Hankou became a treaty port, Magistrate Liu attempted to bring British merchants under the rule of local *lijin* regulations, and he issued an official notice that British firms in the area needed to pay *lijin* tax on all the goods they sold to or bought from Chinese counterparts. The British consul in Hankou, Raymond Gingell, resisted. Gingell, like many in the China consular establishment, interpreted the treaties to mean that his consent was necessary for any local rule to apply to British merchants, and he refused to endorse the magistrate's order on grounds the transit pass privilege exempted British traders from the payment of *lijin*.

Deterred by Gingell from directly taking *lijin* from foreign firms, the magistrate modified his approach. If he could not levy the tax when goods passed into or out of British hands, he would require all items of trade to register at the local tax office, which would then collect what was due from Chinese sellers or buyers. To monitor the arrangements, Magistrate Liu issued regulations that ordered foreign firms to report the name of the vessel carrying their goods, provide a description of the goods, and to enter the names of all the Chinese firms that bought or bartered for the goods. Yet, even these regulations, which did not directly take *lijin* tax from foreign merchants but merely required them to participate in a system for taxing Chinese merchants, were also rejected by the British consul. Foreign merchants, Gingell reiterated in his correspondence, could not be called on to pay the *lijin* tax, even indirectly. In response, Magistrate Liu insisted that "the *lijin* toll must be collected not from the British merchant but from the native," and he called for a centralized depot to collect "every description of Foreign and native produce ... and that all sales and purchases between Foreign and native merchants were to be effected therein." The depot, not the British merchants, would pay the *lijin* tax. "I returned the document," Gingell reported to his superiors in Beijing, "saying I felt quite sure her Majesty's Minister would on no account recognize such an Establishment. Since then, I have heard nothing further on the subject."

Central to the exchange between Gingell and Liu was a struggle to define the boundary between rights and privileges that inhered in the bodies of foreign nationals and those that inhered in goods moving through import-export circuits. Liu engaged in a kind of quarantine operation: if he could take British persons out

---

40. All events in this paragraph and next detailed in No. 8 Hankou Consul Gingell to Frederick Bruce, 13 May 1861, TNA, FO 228/313.

of the picture, he could take actions on items of the import-export trade. Gingell, however, refused to countenance such a boundary. Gingell's position on the issue of *lijin* rested on the unstated assertion that the exchange of money and commodities between Chinese and British merchants recoded Chinese merchants and regulatory institutions as elements within circuits of privileged and protected British trade and brought the force of treaties to bear on the regulation of Chinese merchant activities. Such an assertion, if true, threatened more than just Qing control over foreign trade. It also challenged the authority of Qing officials to regulate and make claims on the activities of the Chinese commercial population. If Gingell's reading stood, treaty obligations in the name of global commodity circulation encompassed local governance of local commercial activities and institutions.

The extent of such recoding was on display in Ningbo several years later. In 1866–1867, hundreds of regional small craft, known as the "horse-mouth sampan" swarmed anchorages and damaged the river near the foreign customs. These small boats transshipped cargoes from large vessels to jetties and, according to local authorities, were an unruly bunch, driven by an aggressive entrepreneurial spirit. They were often associated with robberies and "constantly involved in doubtful transactions." The Boat Inspection Guild at Ningbo wanted to send them away, but there was one obstacle in doing so. Although local injunctions prohibited the sampans from carrying foreign-owned goods, foreign firms still employed them to "surreptitiously" bring goods into private warehouses. And precisely because the boats were commonly used by foreigners, the magistrate's river police found it "difficult to subject them to official inspection" unless they first received the British consul's consent, which was requested but not given.[41]

In both Hankou and Ningbo, Qing authorities experienced the abstract coercion treaties were designed to inflict. Local officials in those treaty ports found they had to curtail their actions because those actions either had to fall in line with treaty rules and/or because their actions were subjected to a novel, additional layer of alien supervision. To what extent was it possible to bring *shi* and *li* back into alignment (as suggested by Mao Hongbin) when confronted with an inflexible dominating code energetically enforced? In the case of the sampans, on what grounds did local officials discern the need to acquire British consent to police Chinese boat operators? No one claimed the sampans were British property, but under the shadow of treaty regulations and British appetite for enforcing them to the fullest possible extent even the most temporary integration of Chinese persons and property into processes of

---

41. Bi Zhixian to Acting Consul Forrest, 14 February 1866, Consular translation, TNA, FO 670/97; Bi Zhixian to Acting Consul Forrest, No. 40, 22 March 1867, Consular translation, TNA, FO 670/100; Acting Consul Forrest to Bi Zhixian, No. 27, 25 March 1867, TNA, FO 670/100.

British capital reproduction had the capacity to deterritorialize them and thereby inoculate them against Qing regulatory force.

Quarantine

It is not surprising that local Qing officials vigorously contested alien limits on their authority, particularly in places like Hankou, which as a center of domestic and international trading activity was a place where Euro-American goods and capital mixed with their Chinese counterparts. A number of foreign firms arrived in Hankou in 1861, shortly after the port was declared open to foreign trade. These included the prominent British trading companies Dent & Co., Gibb Livingston & Co., and the American firm Russell & Co., as well as smaller houses Lindsay & Co. and Fletcher & Co.[42] All came to the port because of its role as a tea entrepot, and it was in the tea trade that local officials worked with Chinese merchants to enact strong quarantine measures against the spread of deterritorialization.

Consistent with what we have seen so far of British commercial activity in China, when the foreign tea trading houses entered Hankou, they carried with them the potential to recode Chinese commercial activity and to geographically expand the reach of treaty rule. In this instance, although treaties limited foreign merchants' travel to a 100-*li* radius around each treaty port, in Hankou at least some of the British and American traders chose to ignore that limit. Instead, representatives of foreign firms reportedly traveled several hundred *li* upriver from Hankou to places near Jingzhou (荊州), where they planned to buy leaves directly from growers.[43] Sometimes the firms sent foreign employees; other times they sent Chinese representatives to whom they had advanced cash or signed a contract for later payment and to whom the firms typically transferred transit certificates, which coded the tea as foreign property and exempted them from *lijin* payments.

This "up-country" work by Chinese merchants was nothing new in the 1860s, but the transit certificates transferred to them placed the activity within a new regulatory category. Qing authorities strongly disapproved of certificate transfer, which meant foreign ownership of goods and foreign tax exemptions began much earlier in the commodity production and circulation process—at the places where tea leaves were grown, rather than at a port where it was sold in packed chests of fired leaves. Whereas tea growers and Chinese teamen transporting leaves to places like Hankou for processing and sale routinely paid local taxes on the raw product,

---

42. Consul Gingell to Minister Bruce, No. 21, July 3, 1861, TNA, FO 225/313. William Rowe also discusses the entrance of foreign firms into Hankou and the Xie Xing Gong; see *Hankow: Commerce and Society in a Chinese City* (Stanford: Stanford University Press, 1984), 125–36.

43. Zhang Daotai to Consul Gingell, No. 22, 2 August 1861, TNA, FO 228/313, Legation translation. Chinese original follows immediately after.

foreign firms deployed transit certificates to claim tax exemptions on raw leaves. They also attempted to use the passes to interdict taxes typically collected when tea leaves were fired and packed. For local administrators the transfer of transit certificates from foreign hands to Chinese ones had the potential to completely dry up the revenue collected on the empire's most significant article of foreign trade. The circuit intendent appointed to handle trade-related matters in Hankou protested to Consul Gingell, "These certificates solely relate to Foreign Merchants who *must go in person* with these certificates to conform to the article of Treaty.... [They] are not allowed to simply hire persons to go into the interior for them."[44]

Amid the flurry of foreign activity around Hankou, a group of Chinese merchants active in the area tried to inoculate tea supplies from the treaty protections afforded to British merchants. The group established a tea brokerage under the name Xie Xing Gong (協興公; Engl: Black Tea Hong), and under the terms of an imperial license to collect *lijin* taxes on tea, stipulated that all teas coming through Hankou had to pass through its doors. In the words of the proclamation authorizing the brokerage, the Xie Xing Gong proposed to "reduce all [merchants] to one rule": all tea leaves passing through the Hankou market would enter the Hong, which would collect a 3 percent charge and divide it between *lijin*, its own operations, and agents of foreign firms "for their trouble."[45] The arrangements were designed as a prophylactic against revenue fraud by Chinese merchants masquerading as employees of foreign firms and to eliminate the incentive for tea exporters to travel into the countryside around Hankou. Transit passes issued to British persons would find no purpose within a system of taxation engineered around goods.

As recounted by William Rowe, the British Consul immediately rejected the arrangements on the grounds that treaties prohibited any kind of monopoly, which he took the Black Tea Hong to be. The consul, according to Rowe, could not properly distinguish between a tea dealer granted a monopoly and the kind of brokerage work the Xie Xing Gong proposed to do, which did not interfere in actual sales.[46] Gingell did, however, grasp the implied limits treaty language and consular jurisdiction placed on local regulatory action. Until he received instructions from the British Minister resident in Beijing, Gingell pledged he would "continue to deny the right of any toll or tax further than the transit duties provided by Treaty." He also grasped that although regional authorities argued that the design of the Xie Xing Gong did not target foreign merchants, whatever arrangements Hankou authorities made for an article of trade with London most assuredly effected the British subjects he was bound to protect.

---

44. Zhang Daotai to Consul Gingell, No. 22, 2 August 1861, consular translation, TNA, FO 228/313.
45. Enclosures 1 and 2, Consul Gingell to Minister Bruce, No. 21, 3 July 1861, TNA, FO 228/313.
46. Rowe, *Hankow*, 127–30.

But did the Black Tea Hong actually implicate British merchants in *lijin* collection? It depends. According to the Qing officials involved, no. In their correspondence with Gingell, the foreign trade *daotai* Zhang (漢總辦通商事務道張) and Hanyang authorities explained that the rule to submit leaves to the Xie Xing Gong applied to the itinerant sellers of tea leaves—Qing subjects.[47] Zhang, in fact, refused to mediate Gingell's disagreement with local officials on the grounds that the brokerage proposal had nothing to do with foreign trade. In his opinion, it was perfectly within the jurisdiction of Hanyang authorities to issue the order without the consul's involvement.[48] In his best efforts to settle the matter with Gingell amicably, Zhang offered to remark the boundary between Chinese trade and foreign trade. The Xie Xing Gong, Zhang assured the consul, would not muddy the waters by taking leaves or payments from foreign firms. In return, Zhang suggested, foreign firms should not "meddle" (*ganyu* 干預) in Hankou commerce, by which he meant operate pack houses, send representatives to purchase leaves directly from growers, or otherwise try to determine the shape of the Chinese end of the trade.[49] From Zhang's point of view, participation by foreign capital in the tea trade did not accord foreign merchants say in the organization and administration of a Chinese produce trade. Commercial exchange contingently involved foreign firms' money, but British purchasers were not part of the Hankou trading community. If they did not like how the Chinese merchants arranged their business practices, they did not have to participate.

But perhaps the situation was not as clear as *Daotai* Zhang would have liked it to be? To what extent were foreign merchants meddling in Hankou mercantile affairs when they went there to purchase and process tea? If we take the viewpoint of capital reproduction and growth, Zhang's language of meddling was nonsense. British funds and markets were a long-standing feature of the tea trade. Surely, Zhang knew this. Moreover, as Gingell implied, actions taken to regulate Chinese persons had bearing on British ledgers, which if the arrangement stood would need balance brokerage charges of 1 percent, commission charges of 2.5 percent, and tea inspection charges of 0.5 percent.[50] From this more abstract view of the problem, as owners of capital, British persons were indeed targeted by the proclamation. The Xie Xing Gong proposal also raised the issue of "native agents." Gingell clearly felt

---

47. Zhang to Gingell, No. 20, 14 July 1861, consular translation, TNA, FO 228/313, folio 10–11. Chinese original follows, folio 12–14.
48. Zhang to Gingell, No. 37, 31 August 1861, as Enclosure 2 in Gingell to Bruce, No. 31, September 2, 1861, consular translation, TNA, FO 228/313.
49. Zhang to Gingell, No. 20, 14 July 1861, consular translation, TNA, FO 228/313, folio 10–11. Chinese original follows, folio 12–14.
50. Edward Townend, *Tables Shewing the Cost of Tea, with All Charges, as Bought in Hankow by the Pecul of 133 1/3 Pounds Avoirdupois for Taels of Sycee, and Sold in London by the Pound Avoirdupois, at the Several Exchanges* (London: Smith Elder, 1863).

that Chinese agents were mere employees, alienated labor if you will, completely subject to the will and direction of their "masters" who supplied the capital for their activities. "The Chinese employed in [a British] hong [are] mere servants to do his business," he assured British merchants in the area.[51] Claims put forward by British firms involved in the tea trade articulated just such a capital-wage labor relationship when they protested that their investment in tea leaves rendered the objects British property, even if a Chinese person was the visible and immediate possessor of the objects.

Treaty language might have arbitrated the dispute Hankou except that it contained ambiguous implications for the status of Chinese participants in British capital circulation. In laying out British exemptions from inland taxation, Article XXVIII of the Treaty of Tianjin read, "It shall be the option of any British subject, desiring to convey produce purchased inland to a port . . . to clear *his goods* of all transit duties, by payment of a single charge." The object most immediately touched by the transit pass—"his goods"—fell short of a British person in the embodied sense of the word even as it invoked a vaguely defined form of possession. So instead of resolving the problem of when transit passes were licitly or illicitly used, treaty language raised a more fundamental question: when did goods begin and cease being British goods? For British merchants and their consuls, capital was the thing that mattered. Consuls in the treaty ports routinely supported claims by British firms that their "agents" were exempt from the forms of taxation otherwise due from Chinese merchants to local governments. The consul at Jiujiang further extended the logic to operations that packed tea for export, arguing that revenue claims against these facilities were in fact claims against foreign commerce. In a pessimistic report to the Beijing Legation on transit pass use in the area, he wrote, "the teas undergoing preparation in these warehouses are all either actually foreign property upon which advances has been made by the foreign merchant, or they are intended for the foreign market."[52] These warehouses, although superintended by Chinese "agents" or owned by Chinese persons, were from the consul's perspective not an autonomous, territorialized branch of tea production so much as a temporary stop in a globe-spanning circulation of capital, which crucially ended in London tea markets and the ledgers of British firms.

Qing officials, on the other hand, tended to discriminate between foreign nationals who were granted privileges and "native agents," who as Qing subjects bore obligations to the empire. In one possible reading of the treaties favored by *Daotai* Zhang in Hankou and Zongli yamen officials in Beijing, neither of the agreements signed at Nanjing or Tianjin actually authorized Euro-American firms to employ persons to purchase produce in the interior or to prepare it exclusively on their

---

51. Enclosure 3 in Gingell to Bruce, No. 21, 3 July 1861, TNA, FO 228/313.
52. Jiujiang consulate, "Reports on Transit Pass Use," February 1, 1864, FO 228/371.

account and bring it to port. Reading the English-language treaty, this interpretation does not hold up well. The English-language version of Article XIII in the Treaty of Tianjin expressly stipulates, "The Chinese Government will place no restriction whatever upon the employment, by British subjects, of Chinese subjects, in any lawful capacity." The Chinese-language version, however, is a bit more ambiguous. It conveys the sense that officials would not in any way limit or prohibit English persons from seeking Chinese persons to help carry out arts and crafts (in the sense of industry).[53] At the time of the treaty's formulation, the English term "employment" held a definite valence of alienated work and subordination of the employed to the employer. This was the meaning that authorized consular officials' interpretation of treaty tax privileges. The Chinese-language version of Article XIII, however, connoted a search for certain talents or crafts and did not signal the subordination created by the capital–wage labor relationship. Qing officials likewise maintained that British capital invested in monies paid to a Chinese person or in the goods a Chinese person carried did not transform the Chinese person into something other than an autonomous, fully taxable Qing subject.

Multinational Capital and Reterritorialization

Regulatory plurality and jurisdictional ambiguity provided the substrate in which deterritorialization and reterritorialization grew apace decisions about the scope and application of regulatory powers. Often, these decisions targeted goods or persons, but ship builds and flags also provided a basis for deciding jurisdiction. Chinese and European sailing ships were of sufficiently different appearance that customs personnel could identify them at a distance. (Steamships were another matter, but both fell under IMC jurisdiction.) Flags, meanwhile, were the conventional marker of a ship's ownership and provenance in ports around the world. Yet in practice, in the Qing Empire's treaty ports it became quite difficult to be sure that a ship of Chinese appearance was also a Chinese-owned ship or that a ship flying a foreign flag actually carried foreign-owned goods. Any one of the elements that composed the appearance of commodity transport visible to the regulatory gaze (person, good, ship, flag) could veil a different nature, particularly when these elements combined to form what I will call "multinational capital."[54] By creating compound units that were both

---

53. IMC, *Treaties, Conventions, Etc. between China and Foreign States*, 2 vols., vol. 1, 2nd ed., Miscellaneous Series No. 30 (Shanghai: Inspector General of Customs, 1917), 1:409. Chinese original: "英民任便覓致諸色華庶勷執分內工藝中國官毫無限制禁阻."
54. Previous scholarship employs language of "compradors" and "joint" account trade. I use "multinational capital" to emphasize the effect, from the viewpoint of commercial administration, of joining Chinese and foreign mercantile resources.

Chinese and foreign, merchant practice crippled the operation of regulatory categories ill-equipped to police and tax such combinations.

A World of Multiple Signifiers

Sometimes the difficulty for administrators inhered in the signifier-signified relationship. Was the person or business really who they said they were? Take, for instance, the case of "Wong Hon Tae," who applied to ship a cargo of rice from Ningbo in 1861. At the time, residents of Ningbo suffered food shortages, and local authorities had placed an embargo on rice exports. This restriction, however, did not apply to Euro-American merchants, who possessed a treaty right to carry it between Qing ports. When Wong applied to ship his rice, it was common enough for non-Chinese firms to employ Chinese names that the *daotai* inquired with the IMC commissioner whether Wong was or was not Chinese. In his answer, the IMC commissioner side-stepped the question, preferring to bring other elements and signifiers into conversation. Put more bluntly, the IMC commissioner ignored the *daotai*'s question about Wong. Instead, he informed the *daotai* that he had already issued a permit to ship based on the nationality of the ship carrying the rice—a Spanish-flagged vessel. Wong, local intelligence soon revealed, was indeed Chinese, but his appropriation of a foreign signifier, combined with the lack of a standard criteria for deciding the regulatory jurisdiction, removed him from the reach of rules that indeed applied to him.[55]

The facility with which a merchant such as Wong appropriated a foreign signifier deeply concerned Qing authorities, but they could not unilaterally solve the problem. For example, late in 1861, Liangjiang governor-general Zeng Guofan reported to the Zongli yamen that a Chinese-run tea dealership (*cha hao* 茶號) set up in Qimen (祁門) county under the sign of Dent & Co. (寶順行) refused to pay local taxes to the county magistrate on the grounds that the shop was opened by a foreign merchant. After deliberation, Yamen officials were of two minds. On one hand, Qimen was more than several hundred *li* away from the nearest treaty port of Jiujiang. Given that foreign merchants were restricted to a radius of 100 *li* around a treaty port, it seemed possible that the Chinese proprietor falsely claimed foreign ownership.[56] On the other hand, the Zongli yamen had received reports that

---

55. Ningbo Daotai to Customs Commissioner, No. 53, 24 July 1861 in *China and the West: the Maritime Customs Service Archive from the Second Historical Archives of China, Nanjing*, ed. Robert Bickers and Hans van de Ven (Reading, UK: Primary Source Microfilm, 2004), microfilm reel 174 (hereafter, CMC microfilm); Ningbo Daotai to Customs Commissioner, No. 58, 28 July 1861, CMC microfilm, reel 174; Ningbo Daotai to Customs Commissioner, No. 61, 31 July 1861, CMC microfilm, reel 174.
56. *CBYWSM* (digital), TZ, juan 3, 40.1.

Euro-American firms were setting up warehouses inland to process their purchases, and Qimen was a key tea-growing area. Unable to conclude which was the case based on their information alone, the Zongli yamen called on the British Legation to help augment the information available to local officials. Per treaty, British consuls were supposed to know which of their nation's firms were doing business in a given port area. The Zongli yamen asked that this obligation be expanded to require merchants to inform the nearest consul of their intent to set up a warehouse and to require the consul to inform the superintendent of customs, who could depute local officials to inspect the arrangements. Yamen officials did not want local officials to police foreign activities, but they did want sufficient British policing of their own subjects in order to create conditions in which, "traitorous inland merchants will not be likely to falsely claim a foreign name."[57] Faced with expansive foreign commercial activity and multinational capital, Qing authorities had no choice but to recruit British assistance to secure against widespread sign-signifier slippage.

A Clash of Classificatory Schemas

The thornier problem presented by multinational capital was classificatory: Was a Chinese-style ship purchased with British capital Chinese or British? Were goods purchased with Chinese capital transported in a British-flagged ship protected by treaty? In the first instance such questions concerned the proper application of rules and regulations. But to properly classify something also meant making a claim about what it was, and capital complicated this operation. As an investment, capital shifts its forms of appearance. Chinese tea leaves, Chinese junks, or even Chinese persons could be animated by British capital. The questions officials wrestled with were the regulatory consequences of these combinations. What was the proper standpoint for governance: the concrete Chinese form or the abstract British capital invested in it?

Take, for example, what happened at the end of March 1865 near the treaty port of Jiujiang. A Chinese-styled vessel owned by the British firm Dent & Co. was traveling the Poyang Lake (鄱陽湖) when it was seized by a group of "militant" Chinese men, whose organization and authority (if any) were unclear to the vessel's crew. The vessel flew the company house flag with the words "Dent & Co. No. 2" written on both sides, and it carried a cargo of rice, an article foreign merchants could legally buy and sell between Chinese ports with the requisite permit. Chinese merchants could not do the same. Although Jiujiang was a treaty port with an IMC office, the Dent junk cleared the port through the *changguan* customhouse, which issued it a

---

57. *CBYWSM* (digital), TZ, juan 3, 40.2–41.1.

pass for travel across the lake. The Dent junk then proceeded to "Wooching" on the southwest corner of Poyang Lake, where it was seized.

The company complained of the seizure to the superintendent of trade at Hankou, who was not sympathetic. He responded that if the vessel was indeed British, it was liable to confiscation because it had traveled into an area off-limits to foreign firms, and if it was Chinese, it was liable to imprisonment for carrying a contraband good.[58] The British Legation, called in by the local consul to defend British property, complained in response that an "irregular" system of administration had recently evolved at Jiujiang. Dent, the British minister claimed, was "driven" to use the *changguan* because local officials, wanting to block foreign participation in the transit of Chinese produce, refused to acknowledge their transit pass privileges. The British Legation took the position that junks, sailed by British firms and carrying goods bought with British capital, were British property and, like British persons, were subject only to treaty and the jurisdiction of consular officials. The Legation further argued that even if a junk voluntarily subjected itself to the Chinese customs akin to Chinese property, it did not actually make the British property or persons subject to Chinese law.[59]

The incident at Jiujiang, the resolution of which is not part of the consular archive from which this case is taken, illustrates how routine questions about commercial governance entailed more fundamental questions about the historical and social role of capital. The British legation and consul attributed to capital transformative powers: Chinese things, animated by British capital, became British things. Chinese authorities were more ambivalent. When *changguan* officials passed the junk flying non-Chinese flags, they asserted domestic customs jurisdiction over a Chinese-built craft, most likely manned by a Chinese crew. A boat built with materials and craft local to China, carrying Chinese produce, and sailed by Chinese persons was, in many respects, a Chinese *thing* despite who owned it. From this viewpoint, which privileged the concrete Chinese forms of appearance, there was no transformative power inhering in capital. Moreover, even if British capital was involved, it was in this instance subordinated to Qing political power. That is to say, when the Dent & Co. ship voluntarily passed through the *changguan*, it engaged in an act of political submission. In either case, as superintendent of trade concluded, the ship fell under Qing law.

A kindred disagreement at Ningbo helps to elaborate the clash of classificatory schemas that routinely erupted in day-to-day administration. There, in 1862, the IMC commissioner observed that Portuguese merchants commonly sold their ships, a European-Chinese hybrid called a "*lorcha*," to Chinese firms that wanted to

---

58. Draft No. 64, 25 October 1865, TNA, FO 228/921.
59. Draft No. 64, 25 October 1865, TNA, FO 228/921.

pass goods of foreign provenance through the *changguan*. Treaty regulations held that foreign imports and exports passed through the IMC, but in this case, local regulations still channeled Chinese-flagged vessels through the local *changguan*. The commissioner thought the boat sales were improper given extant regulations, and he brought the Portuguese *lorcha* issue to the attention of his Qing colleague, the Ningbo *daotai*. The commissioner asked the *daotai* for a proclamation that "foreign goods imported by Chinese vessels, and saltpeter and sugar and tea and silk exported by them" pay duty of the IMC even though "the *Lorcha* were under the Chinese Flag." Such a rule would have accepted the novel boat sales and rechanneled Chinese merchant activity from the *changguan* to the IMC. The *daotai* took a different view of the situation: "*Lorcha* are Foreign Vessels and accordingly ought not to change their colors into the Chinese flag.... Foreign built [ships] should not be allowed to use the Chinese Flag."[60] This rule, by contrast, would have rejected the new practice in the name of shoring up long-standing sign-signifier relationships. Although both the *daotai* and the commissioner agreed that the Portuguese-Chinese hybrid vessel did not properly fall under *changguan* jurisdiction, the two colleagues also spoke past each other. The commissioner saw foreign commodities or commodities intended for foreign markets that fell under the treaty tariff; the *daotai* saw ships of foreign origin and refused to integrate them into the field of things Chinese or subject to Chinese law. As the British consul did at Jiujiang, the IMC commissioner argued that when Chinese things became imbricated with global commodity circulation, they too could be drawn into the globally oriented regulatory apparatus represented by the treaty tariff. Nationality aside, the commissioner suggested, there was a basic equivalence between what the Chinese-flagged lorcha did and what foreign ships did, and therefore they should receive the same treatment. For the Ningbo *daotai*, on the other hand, who sailed the ship and brought the cargo to shore was more important than the vessel's/cargo's functional equivalence within global commodity circulation.

Administrative difficulties at Jiujiang and Ningbo both traced to the presence of multinational capital, which prevailing regulatory frameworks were ill-equipped to govern. At both ports, an excess of ambiguous signifiers created the possibility for clashes over the application of regulatory categories. British officials and merchants advanced arguments that put capital at the center of regulatory decision-making with the implication that under the treaty regime governance had to subordinate political subjecthood to the function of those subjects within global trade. Practically speaking, the argument recoded foreign capital and Chinese participation in global commerce as limiting forces on Qing sovereignty, removing Chinese goods, ships,

---

60. IMC Commissioner to Ningbo Daotai, No. 103, 1862, CMC microfilm, reel 174; IMC Commissioner to Ningbo Daotai, No. 160, 1862, CMC microfilm, reel 174.

and persons from the reach of Qing law and Qing revenue collection. The converse, because of extraterritoriality and consular jurisdiction, was not possible. British goods, ships, and persons could never be made Chinese. Qing officials both clearly recognized these threats to their sovereign authority and countered with them claims of stable historical, territorial, and political boundaries between Chinese and foreign entities. The person, the goods he conveyed, the mode of conveyance, Qing authorities insisted, were stable, enduring elements particular to a discrete polity. The participation of Chinese things in global capital accumulation was a momentary conjuncture, not a transformative subsumption.

Conclusion: Virus versus Antibodies

The early 1860s was a difficult time for Qing authorities. For more than a decade until 1865, rebels of the Taiping Heavenly Kingdom controlled large amounts of territory in the empire's economic heartlands. In 1860, British and French military forces destroyed the emperor's residence (*Yuanming yuan* 圓明園) and marched on Beijing. Foreign-flagged ships, meanwhile, stanched the flow of customary domestic customs revenues, and a newly codified tax exemption (i.e. the transit pass) threatened to dry up provincial revenue crucial to fighting the rebellion. In 1861, the Xianfeng emperor (r. 1850–1861) died, triggering a palace coup that placed the child emperor Tongzhi (b. 1856, r. 1861–1875) on the throne. Although Tongzhi's reign would come to be known as a period of "restoration," under the direction of Empress Dowager Cixi, it was several years before the outlines of the dynasty's self-strengthening program became manifest.

During this period of political turbulence and fiscal uncertainty, treaties set in motion another set of destabilizing forces. These forces were primarily felt in ports and commercial centers, where a tripartite structure of commercial regulation quickly proved incapable of effectively policing new mixtures of Chinese and foreign capital. One of the most problematic aspects of the new commercial activity was its relative lack of geographic constraint. Euro-American merchants and their agents traveled between ports, up the Yangzi River and beyond, and as they did, they carried the treaty regulatory apparatus with them. Even at the level of county magistrate, Qing officials contended with how treaties and their interpretation by Euro-American counterparts destabilized local revenue collection and jurisdictional claims over Qing subjects. As British merchants claimed treaty-based treatment not only for themselves but also for their property—namely, ships and goods invested with their capital—they pulled Chinese produce, merchants, employees, and contractors toward the gravitational well of the treaty regime and out of the reach of territorial authorities. To be sure, much of this pull was aspirational at the time. As a one-man campaign in Hankou, Consul Gingell did not stop the creation of the Black

Tea Hong, but the interpretation he offered regarding the globe-spanning circulation of capital and its power to reterritorialize local people, goods, and businesses was not his alone and, as we will see in Chapter 5, became an enduring part of the British campaign to further transform Qing governance.

The disorderly order generated by and in spite of Qing commercial treaties tells us several things about the spatial expansion of capital and its interactions with Qing commercial governance. To begin, capital's expansion was not orderly, nor did it follow the playbook created by diplomats. Notably, it never took the form of a substantial growth in British woolen imports, and by most economic measures, treaties did not lead to foreign commercial dominance in China. Contemporaries observed that Euro-American linguistic skills were, by and large, too insufficient to navigate the world of inland producers.[61] At the same time, Chinese merchant networks were in general too robust and nimble to be displaced. Foreign firms found it both necessary and convenient to couple their efforts with Chinese intermediaries.[62] Recent research instead suggests that British capital and Chinese capital fed each other's mutual growth. Steamship lines, funded with multinational capital, prospered from the import-export trade as well was the domestic circulation of staple goods, both of which involved foreign and Chinese firms.[63] Compradors opened so-called native banks (*qianzhuang* 錢莊) to "funnel financing from foreign firms to domestic clients."[64] Foreign capital, to give just one example, became central to Chinese purchases of foreign-made cotton yarn.[65] As employers, contractors, partners, and creditors, British firms integrated Chinese persons, firms, farmers, and fixed capital into circuits of their own capital reproduction and vice versa.[66]

Out of the interaction between regulatory plurality and multinational capital a foundational dynamic of the treaty port era unfolded. Concrete combinations of Chinese and foreign capital erupted out of incentives and ambiguities created by the treaty regime, and they routinely slipped around or directly confronted boundaries that structured the tripartite system of commercial governance. The resulting regulatory disorder was not ancillary to the contemporaneous growth of capital at either the regional or global scale. We have seen with the case of Wong Hon Tae that the reterritorialization of Chinese persons as elements of foreign trade contributed directly to the growth of capital circuits. By combining his commodity capital (rice)

---

61. "H.E. the Taotai to H.B.M. Consul," 17 January 1867, NCDN, 9 February 1867.
62. "Mr. Consul Winchester to the Chairman of the Shanghai General Chamber of Commerce, 29 January 1867," NCDN, 9 February 1867; "The Compradore System," NCDN, 28 January 1867.
63. Reinhardt, *Navigating Semi-colonialism*, 65–77.
64. Von Glahn, *Economic History*, 386.
65. Kathy Le Mons Walker, *Chinese Modernity and the Peasant Path: Semicolonialism in the Northern Yangzi Delta* (Stanford: Stanford University Press, 1999), 92–94.
66. For helpful measures of these combinations, see Hao, *Commercial Revolution*, tables 7, 12, and 18.

with Spanish fixed capital (a ship), Wong effectively circumvented implications of his personhood, which would have kept the rice in Ningbo.[67] Instead, his activity, coded by the Ningbo IMC commissioner as foreign trade, provided revenue to the Spanish ship carrying Wong's rice cargo; this cargo, in turn, entered into regional commodity circulation and upon its sale (ideally) augmented Wong's own capital. How much of the growing interport trade and regional export trade was facilitated by maneuvers such as Wong's is impossible to know, but successful recoding of the sort that took place in Ningbo shows how regulatory plurality and jurisdictional ambiguity could engineer additional circuits of capital growth.

On the flip side, in these moments, capital's spatial expansion challenged Qing sovereignty over its subjects. As Chinese bodies circulated global commodities, they were both Qing subjects and bearers of Euro-American capital. The British commercial-diplomatic establishment aggressively pushed for this latter role to take precedence over the former. In twinned processes, extraterritoriality placed British property outside the reach of Qing law at the same time capital investments mobilized claims that Qing subjects, as participants in British capital accumulation, shed meanings or obligations associated with political subjecthood. Stated somewhat differently, as commodity circulation deterritorialized and reterritorialized, it offered a mechanism for the subsumption of Qing governance to capital. Chinese participation in British projects of capital accumulation would reset terms of the relationship between the empire and its subjects.

Finally, the administrative skirmishes of the 1860s also established a pattern of antagonistic interactions between the parties charged with cooperating to implement the treaties, which included British consuls and Qing territorial administrators in the treaty ports as well as the British Legation and Zongli yamen in Beijing. While authorities in Beijing conceded the participation of Euro-American merchants in domestic shipping, neither the Zongli yamen nor territorial administrators easily swallowed the reterritorialization process. They saw clearly that British claims were based on expansive interpretations of treaty provisions, and they were less than persuaded by arguments that persons, places, and things that were clearly Chinese to the eyes were actually otherwise. Officials at all levels countered reterritorialization with claims that reasserted boundaries between Chinese trade and Euro-American trade rooted in concrete features and political community. No strangers to capital as a resource critical to commerce, when they could Qing territorial administrators nonetheless resisted capital as a transformative social form that limited sovereignty and political autonomy. Economic integration was not the issue; the political and regulatory framework in which it took place was.

---

67. Ningbo Daotai to Customs Commissioner, No. 53, 24 July 1861, CMC microfilm, reel 174; Ningbo Daotai to Customs Commissioner, No. 58, 28 July 1861, CMC microfilm, reel 174; Ningbo Daotai to Customs Commissioner, No. 61, 31 July 1861, CMC microfilm, reel 174.

4
Not All Commerce Is Capitalism

The consular impossibility of saying where [merchants] wish to go is, in itself, very much of an answer to the demand to go everywhere: it means, in fact, nowhere.

—Robert Hart, June 13, 1868[1]

If we only consider the interests of foreign businessmen, then political sovereignty is no longer intact.

—Li Hongzhang, Guangxu 2, 4M[2]

In some ways, the Qing Empire and Great Britain were not all that dissimilar. Both were commercialized societies with governments that acknowledged the important role merchants and commercial circulation played in the production of social well-being. Accordingly, political leaders in both took measures to support, or at least not impede their operations. Yet, the modes by which they sought to support this activity differed substantively. Commenting on these differences in 1867, an ambitious and accomplished officer of the Qing government, Li Hongzhang (李鴻章 1823–1901), complained that of all the many difficulties the government had in recent years endlessly discussed with British officials, one of the most galling was the failure of British consuls to rein in the excessive desires of their commercial community. They not only gave into their merchants, Li complained, but were even led by them. Then, Li pointed out, when "[English] demands fail to materialize,

---

1. "Mr. Hart to Sir R. Alcock, 13 June 1868," Inclosure No. 2 in No. 73 Sir R. Alcock to Lord Stanley, TNA, Foreign Office Confidential (Numerical Series), FO 881/1655.
2. Li Hongzhang, "復總署 儀復赫德條陳" [Reply to Hart's proposals], *Li Hongzhang quan ji* [The collected works of Li Hongzhang], ed. Tinglong Gu and Yi Dai (Hefei shi: Anhui jiao yu chu ban she, 2008), 31:386–87. Written in Guangxu 2 (1876).

they increase the intimidation; as a matter of course, this is their normal behavior."[3] Poor governance by British officials in China meant violence was always a possibility. Amongst the British community resident in China, on the other hand, conventional wisdom coalesced around the conclusion that the Qing regime was hopelessly wedded to its own deeply misguided past. As the Hong Kong–based Scottish banker Charles Addis (1861–1945) put it in 1902, after foreign troops marched through Beijing, desecrated the imperial throne, and dictated new terms for how the dynasty would manage its affairs, "there is a vast amount of good advice running to waste in China just now. . . . For my part I do not see much good to be gained by offering advice to a country which shows so little disposition to act upon it."[4]

This chapter offers to explain how Li and Addis, who shared a deep interest in wealth and the power that follows from it, could each be so critical of how the other arranged commercial governance. The immediate topic of this chapter is soybean transport. The circulation of soy and soy products (pulse, bean cake) between northern China and southern China became the subject of intense diplomatic exchange in the early 1860s. In treaty negotiations with Great Britain in 1858, Qing officials had preserved the trade, which was closely tied to state-sponsored grain transport, for Chinese merchants. British merchants in China, however, soon found they needed the cargo to turn any kind of profit trading at the newly opened northern ports. Assured by the British minister that foreign participation in the trade would be minimal, the Zongli yamen lifted the restriction, only to see foreign carriage all but eliminate Chinese carriage of soybeans. Consequently, officials in Beijing and Shanghai moved to once again ban foreign participation in the trade, and a powerful coalition of merchants in Shanghai successfully boycotted sales of foreign-shipped soy in that most important of treaty ports.

The struggle over the soy trade, actualized as merchant competition and extended diplomatic debate, sheds light on how Qing and British strategies of commercial governance supported different modalities of social reproduction. In recent work on the China tea trade, historian Andrew Liu characterizes the distance between capitalist political economy (as it developed under conditions of capitalist industry) and Qing political economy (as it developed under conditions of merchant capital) as a difference between the "embrace [of] the endless pursuit of wealth as an end in itself" and the promotion of "wealth as something that could be physically

---

3. Li Hongzhang, "籌議修約事宜折" [Treaty negotiations], *Li Hongzhang quan ji* [The collected works of Li Hongzhang], ed. Tinglong Gu and Yi Dai (Hefei shi: Anhui jiao yu chu ban she, 2008), 3:166. Written in Tongzhi 6 (1867).
4. Charles Addis, "Leaves from a Diary" (January 8, 1902), PP MS 14/163, School of Oriental and African Studies (SOAS) Archives, University of London.

lifted from the ground."[5] For Liu, the key difference between the two modalities of political economy was the former's emphasis on productivity as the basis of wealth and power. Here, I develop another aspect of the differences. Whereas the Qing regime was deeply focused on the circulation of use values and the fate of specialized groups that circulated those utilities, the British mercantile-diplomatic establishment argued for the socially general benefits of *accelerated* commerce itself. In other words, Qing authorities and British authorities each worked with a different answer to the unstated question "What is the purpose of commercial circulation?" It is these different answers that help to explain why the British could advocate for the pursuit of wealth as an end in itself and why Qing officials thought first in terms of use values and concrete forms of capital. The gap between these two orientations provides a better framework to understand the frustration expressed by both Li Hongzhang and Charles Addis at either end of the Qing treaty port era.

Circulation and Social Reproduction: The Case of Soy

Our journey into soy begins with a bit of theory. This excursion is necessary to make plain how this chapter's story of the plight of the soy merchants of Shanghai differs from earlier accounts.[6] Rather than focus purely on the competition between foreign and Chinese shipping, I approach the episode through the lens of the distinction between value and use value as well as the structural relationship between production and circulation. The latter is helpful when thinking about indigenous forms of capitalism in China because it allows for an important distinction between firm-level activity and how that activity fits into or contributes to the reproduction of the social whole. Merchant capital, such as the Shanghai *sha chuan* (沙船, sand boat) owners, who pursued profit by moving useful goods from where they were readily available to where they were not, was a feature of the regional specialization that made the Qing Empire one of the most commercialized societies in the world. But in itself, merchant capital does not necessarily index the existence of a capitalist mode of social reproduction wherein the valorization of value (i.e., capital) takes a commanding role mediating social relations.[7] In a society where the capitalist

---

5. Andrew Liu, *Tea War: A History of Capitalism in China and India* (New Haven: Yale University Press, 2020), 162.
6. Britten Dean, *China and Great Britain: The Diplomacy of Commercial Relations, 1860–1864* (Cambridge, MA: Harvard University East Asian Research Center, 1974), chap. 4; Yi Li, *Chinese Bureaucratic Culture and Its Influence on the 19th Century Steamship Operation, 1864–1885* (Lewiston, NY: Edwin Mellen, 2001), 66–67.
7. This is not to say use values do not matter at all in capitalism, but as crises of overaccumulation and waste attest, the production and circulation of useful things becomes in the capitalist mode of production subordinate to the production of value. On the ecological angle of this dynamic, see John Bellamy Foster, Brett Clark, and Richard York, *The Ecological Rift: Capitalism's War on the Earth*

mode of production predominates, the production and circulation of any concrete, useful good is mediated by its more abstract and quantitative value dimension.[8] In the Qing Empire in the 1860s, we have substantial evidence that something else was going on. First, commercial circulation was mediated in important ways by state security projects. Second, whereas the capitalist mode of production creates a formal equivalence between all forms of use values in its pursuit of value, Qing governance prioritized circuits of specific use values. The possibility of expansive commercial circulation was less appealing than the preservation of existing resources and communities. What happened to the soy trade in China between 1861 and 1868 shows how commerce structured by the capitalist mode of production deterritorialized and reterritorialized already existing circuits of merchant capital.

In the nineteenth century, soy was an important article of interregional trade within China. The legume grew primarily in the Liao River valley of the empire's northeast (Qing Manchuria), but it was an important factor of production in southeastern (Jiangnan) commercial agriculture, where it was used to fertilize lands growing cotton, rice, sugar, and mulberry trees. Soy-derived bean cake was higher in nitrogen content than traditional manure and had been a popular fertilizer since the late Ming. It was critical to sustaining double-cropping in the heavily populated Jiangnan region. Each year during the winter months, carts laden with beans traveled from the growing fields to the Liao River and its tributaries where the beans waited for the spring thaw, when they traveled downriver by boat to the port of Yingkou (營口) for sale.[9] From there, the beans traveled south to Shanghai, Shantou, Fuzhou, and Xiamen where they were marketed for further distribution.

The boats that performed this transport came from Shandong, Fujian, Guangxi, Tianjin, and Shanghai, and estimates put their number around two thousand in the mid-nineteenth century. Among the participants in this trade were wealthy Shanghai merchants, who operated fleets of *sha chuan*, built especially for the sailing conditions to the north along the Shandong coast.[10] Commodity specialization was common in late imperial shipping, and the cargo carried by *sha chuan* was mainly bean cake, bean oil, and some wheat, worth more than ten million silver dollars,

---

(New York: New York University Press, 2010). My argument here is similar to that developed by Xu Dixin and Wu Chengming in *Chinese Capitalism, 1522–1840*, trans. Li Zhengde, Liang Miaoru, and Li Siping (New York: St. Martin's, 2000), but the line of reasoning differs.

8. This is why, for example, in the United States there are endemic shortages of important, generic drugs. Yuki Noguchi, "The Hospital Ran Out of Her Child's Cancer Drug. Now She's Fighting to End Shortages," National Public Radio, October 23, 2023, https://www.npr.org/sections/health-shots/2023/10/23/1204856094/hospital-ran-out-child-cancer-drug-shortage.
9. Richard Evan Wells, "The Manchurian Bean: How the Soybean Shaped the Modern History of China's Northeast, 1862–1945" (PhD diss., University of Wisconsin–Madison, 2018).
10. Xu and Wu, *Chinese Capitalism*, 364, 371.

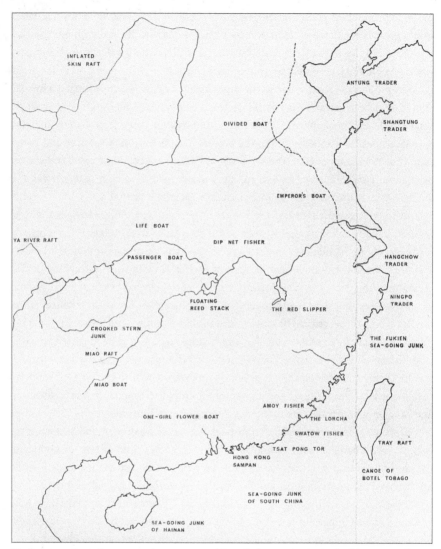

Figure 4.1: Into the twentieth century, sail-based shipping was marked by regional specialization. This map indicates regions where specific kinds of ships sailed. Source: G. R. G. Worcester, *Sail and Sweep in China: The History and Development of the Chinese Junk as Illustrated by the Collection of Junk Models in the Science Museum* (London: Her Majesty's Stationery Office, 1966).

annually.[11] In the early 1840s, prior to Shanghai's takeoff as a treaty port, one could find a stone tablet erected by the Shanghai Bean Cake Association: "As a transportation hub, Shanghai benefits mostly from beans. The beans were transported from Liaodong Peninsula and Shandong by *sha chuan*."[12]

A few features of this trade as it stood at mid-century deserve further notice.[13] The first was that the masses of beans flowing south were not matched by an equivalent flow of goods moving north. Grain (a category that includes legumes) was one of the few items of large-scale circulation in the Qing Empire (the others were cotton cloth and salt); soy was a commodity grown for the purposes of sale, and in this case, it was also a necessary factor in other commodity production (namely, cotton, silk, sugar, and some rice; see below). Ships headed north to transport bean products south often did so in ballast or carried a small quantity of cloth, tea, and sugar. A key reason for the lopsided trade was the relatively rural character of the area around the port of Yingkou, which was the entry point to the major soy growing region. Lacking a major urban center with populations that could purchase a diversity of goods, Yingkou was mostly an export distribution center for inland agricultural products. A second feature of the trade important for our purposes here was the social division of capital between shipowners and merchants. While *sha chuan* owners did historically carry goods on their own account, shipowners also signed carry contracts with other merchants. Shipowners, in turn, made much of their money from freight charges, tacking their charges to levels of merchant profits—charging higher rates when the volume of trade was higher and lowering rates when the goods available in northern markets were scarcer.[14] Scholarship has estimated that freight rates may have been as high as 23–28 percent of cargo value, which made many shipowners very rich, even after they paid taxes, seaman wages, and reinvested in ship maintenance.[15]

A final feature of this trade to note here was its imbrication with both global markets and state-managed political-economy. Soybeans were an integral factor in the Qing Empire's commodity production, including export-oriented production.

---

11. Xu and Wu, *Chinese Capitalism*, 168, 362–63; William Rowe, *Hankow: Commerce and Society in a Chinese City, 1796–1889* (Stanford: Stanford University Press, 1984), 61; Yong Xue, "A Fertilizer Revolution? A Critical Response to Pomeranz's Theory of Geographic Luck," *Modern China* 33, no. 2 (April 2007): 195–229; Christopher Isett, *State, Peasant, and Merchant in Qing Manchuria, 1644–1862* (Stanford: Stanford University Press), 223–28. The actual volume of bean cake transported to Shanghai is the subject of scholarly dispute.
12. Xue, "A Fertilizer Revolution?" 205; see also K. C. Liu, *China's Early Modernization and Reform Movement: Studies in Late Nineteenth-Century China and American-Chinese Relations* (Taipei: Institute of Modern History, Academia Sinica, 2009), 40.
13. On the general features of the Chinese economic structure that inform this assessment, see Xu and Wu, *Chinese Capitalism*, 380–82.
14. Xu and Wu, *Chinese Capitalism*, 368–69.
15. Xu and Wu, *Chinese Capitalism*, 370–71.

The main crops fertilized by bean cake were cotton, silk, sugar, and rice. Silk was the second largest item in China's international trade. Cotton was a key commodity used in domestic handicraft production, and cotton cloth was one of the empire's principal items of domestic circulation. Consequently, beans and their transport were part of an extended commodity chain that connected markets in northern and southern China as well as Europe, the United States, and Japan. Rice presents a somewhat more complex picture. While some rice became a commodity sold to feed urbanized, commodity-producing communities in Jiangsu, Zhejiang, Fujian, and Guangdong, other rice (along with grains such as millet, sorghum, and wheat)—as much as 466 million pounds a year—shipped to Beijing as a nonmonetized contribution to the imperial state, known as *cao yun* (漕運, tribute rice).[16]

Recent studies by Madeline Zelin and Meng Zhang have demonstrated how commercial fortunes in the salt and timber trades were often "derivative of hereditary privilege and political ties" as well as state procurement systems.[17] Through its ties with *cao yun*, the soy trade at mid century was another. Each year, the government commandeered the number of private ships it estimated were needed for the transport of tribute rice. In 1826, over 1,500 Shanghai-based *sha chuan* participated in *cao yun* and delivered between 285 million and 317 million pounds of rice to Tianjin, the entry point for such shipments. The government used the majority of *cao yun* to feed the large non-food-producing population of the capital city, and it periodically released the remainder at fixed prices to modulate Beijing's grain market. Food shortage, the dynasty understood, was a sensitive trigger for popular unrest, and "there was supposed to be no subsistence-related reason for the residents of Beijing to find fault with the government."[18] During the Qing dynasty merchants and shipowners became an important part of this political stability project, as they were the ones who procured the grain and transported it. In return, they received

---

16. Lillian Li and Alison Dray-Novey, "Guarding Beijing's Food Security in the Qing Dynasty: State, Market, and Police," *Journal of Asian Studies* 58, no. 4 (1999): 992–1032; Harold C. Hinton, *The Grain Tribute System of China (1845–1911)* (Cambridge, MA: Harvard University Chinese Economic and Political Studies, 1956), 7. Calculation based on Hinton's assessment that 3.5 million piculs of grain were expected in Beijing each year in the early nineteenth century. Grain tribute was a long-standing institution of imperial China. During the Ming dynasty it was transported through the Grand Canal using conscripted, often military labor. After 1684, the Qing experimented using merchant ships to transport tribute grain. During the Daoguang reign (1820–1850), the court began to use a coastal route; this route gained importance. During and after the Taiping Rebellion when inland transport was riskier and the Grand Canal suffered from structural problems.
17. Madeleine Zelin, *The Merchants of Zigong: Industrial Entrepreneurship in Early Modern China* (New York: Columbia University Press, 2005), 12; Meng Zhang, *Timber and Forestry in Qing China: Sustaining the Market* (Seattle: University of Washington Press, 2021).
18. Li and Dray-Novey, "Guarding Beijing's Food Security," 993. The same could be said for other regions. Up until 1749, the court had restricted the export of soybeans from the northeast for similar reasons.

compensation from the state. This included payments for freight charges, a repair allowance, and other voyage expenses, including crew meals, ballast, and gratuities. To favor the ships for their service, participants were granted duty-free entry of additional cargo at Tianjin (equal to up to one-fifth the rice cargo, later raised to 30 percent) as well as tax exemptions on cargoes of beans and bean cake shipped from Yingkou.[19]

For the first generation of post-war economic historians in China, large-scale merchant operations and merchant-capital accumulation like that exhibited in the soy trade presented an important question: were they evidence of a nascent, indigenous capitalism? For some, such as Fang Xing (方行), it was necessary to investigate further the specific details of merchant capital. "The production and expanded circulation of commodities are historical preconditions for the creation of capital," he wrote, "but not all kinds of circulation are conducive to the emergence of capitalism. *We need to know how the commodities in question are produced, how they are circulated, and in what kind of market.*"[20] In this view, only some forms of commodity circulation lend themselves to building a society in which capital is a dominant social form. As I understand it, the totality of the soybean–*cao yun* circuit points to how in the Qing Empire commodity production and circulation (i.e., for sale in the market) and other forms of production and circulation (i.e., for redistribution by the political center) were entangled. Soy commodities from Yingkou were transformed through agricultural processes in Jiangnan into noncommodity rice, a good that existed by virtue of state fiat and that, by feeding the political capital's population, reproduced the political order. The *sha chuan* that moved soy commodities and *cao yun* were, in turn, both a resource that sustained chains of commodity production *and* a resource that helped reproduce Qing political power. Aid to the state, moreover, helped to subsidize merchant capital because the government provided both a northbound cargo and tax exemptions. If the *sha chuan* were themselves a capitalist project, as scholars have concluded, they were also participants in a noncapitalist project of political order-making from which they benefited.

Struggle over Soy Market Access: Who Gets to Transport and Why?

Soon after Yingkou and a second northern port, Yantai (煙台), opened as treaty ports in 1861–1862, the soybean trade became the site of a protracted struggle

---

19. Harold Hinton, *The Grain Tribute System of China, 1845–1911* (Cambridge, MA: Harvard University Asia Center, 1956), 23–24, 76–78.
20. Fang Xing, "The Retarded Development of Capitalism," in *Chinese Capitalism*, 380; emphasis added.

between the Shanghai shipping community, foreign merchants, and their respective governments. As discussed in previous chapters, the Treaty of Tianjin did much to grow the geographic and commercial domains in which foreign firms could operate. It officially sanctioned foreign cabotage and gave foreign firms access to circuits of domestic commercial circulation including in restricted commodities, such as copper cash and grain. Yet despite opening Yingkou and Yantai to foreign ships, the treaty interdicted British participation in the largest commodity trade at the ports— that of soybeans and bean cake. Although the British merchant community pressed for access to the "immense" trade on the grounds that foreign ships sailing north with goods to sell at the new treaty ports would need to take on some form of return cargo, Qing negotiators countered that foreign participation would undermine the extant shipping communities in Zhejiang, Fujian, Jiangsu, and Shandong.[21] Qing treaty negotiators did bother to disclose that these four shipping communities were also the primary participants in *cao yun*.

Not even a year passed between the 1860 ratification of the Treaty of Tianjin and the next occasion when British diplomats pressed again for access to the soy trade. According to an early study by Britten Dean, trade in Yantai was based on barter, not silver, so the only way British importers could accept payment for their import cargoes was in beans.[22] The British consul at Yantai initiated a request to allow British traders to buy and sell soy, and in August 1861, the minister at the British Legation in Beijing, Frederick Bruce, tried to convince Qing authorities that foreign shipping would not hurt the Chinese commercial community. "The increase of a foreign trade at the port would not fail to open new channels of employment to native craft," he wrote to the Zongli yamen. He further noted that market mechanisms would both "sufficiently check any tendency to excessive exportations" as well as ensure plenty of grain imports from Southeast Asia in times of need.[23] An open market, Bruce argued, would self-regulate to ensure ample food supplies, and connections to global trade would grow economic opportunities.

The response sent by Zongli yamen to Bruce suggests officers of the yamen were far from persuaded. Foreign ships, they noted, were faster than Chinese craft and so offered lower freight rates. If given access to beans and beancake from Yingkou and Yantai, foreign shippers would inevitably reap large profits, while "the native vessel's freights will be high, and its cargo unsaleable." This would hurt multitudes who relied on the trade for their subsistence.

---

21. "The Supplement to the Treaties of Tien-tsin," *NCH*, November 20, 1858, 62; "Report in the Revision of Tariff, etc.," Inclosure in No. 213, *Correspondence Relative to the Earl of Elgin's Special Missions to China and Japan, 1857–1859* (1859) [2571], 403.
22. Dean, *China and Great Britain*, 81.
23. British Legation to Zongli Yamen, draft, 6 August 1861, TNA, FO 228/907.

The yamen concluded:

> The loss sustained by the native trader will set him smuggling, and his plea when caught will be that high freights made him smuggle. The Chinese Government in its administration earnestly seeks to be just, and a measure like this which would filch unseen the profits of the Chinese merchant, is not such as will keep the people contented.[24]

Alert to the costs associated with transportation time as well as interactions between costs and market prices, officers of the Zongli Yamen worried that the lopsided advantage foreign firms would hold in the market would lead to illicit commercial activity and social instability. In terms of a policy calculus, the yamen was not tempted by Bruce's offers of growing commercial activity and greater integration into regional commodity circuits. Rather, the Zongli yamen's response affirmed extant arrangements in the name of the stability they provided—both for the shipping community and for the state. As a concession, the Zongli yamen offered a compromise: if foreign merchants really wanted to trade in beans, they could do so by hiring junks to transport them.

Bruce was not satisfied. In February the following year, shortly before the soy season opened, he wrote again to the Zongli yamen, elaborating some of the implicit points of the political economy his letter the previous year had left unsaid. "It is well known," the letter began,

> that goods of small bulk and of value are generally despatched [sic] in steam-ships and other foreign vessels – the cause of this preference being their fast sailing, and the principle of insurance. . . . *These vessels* would bring up the cargo at a lower rate of freight, if they could obtain a return cargo from the Northern Ports. Goods would thus be sold at a cheaper price which would be very beneficial to the consumer and which would at the same time increase the Customs Revenue by leading to increased consumption. The merchant would be able to invest the proceeds of the sale of his goods in produce to the benefit of the people, and to the advantage of the Northern Provinces.[25]

In this elaboration of the British community's position, Bruce rejected the Zongli yamen's compromise that British merchants use Chinese junks. Junks, Bruce argued, were not what was wanted because they could not produce the transformative gains anticipated by the British merchant or his representative. What was wanted were faster-sailing, insured boats that would do much more than transport soy products. These boats would circulate goods more quickly, offer lower rates of freight, catalyze

---

24. Zongli Yamen to Beijing Legation, trans. Thomas Wade, 20 August 1861, TNA, FO 228/908.
25. Beijing Legation to Zongli Yamen, draft, 11 February 1862, TNA, FO 228/911.

cheaper prices, and consequently stimulate more consumption, production, and circulation.[26]

In essence, Bruce offered the Zongli yamen a political economy of capital expansion, which called upon the Qing government to trade in the reproduction of a concrete, particular social group for the growth of general processes of value creation. The goal of correct policy, Bruce's subtext argued, was not to move soy beans; the goal was to make available cargo—any cargo—that would put ships into motion moving goods. Return cargo in faster-moving ships would mean lower costs of transportation, and the capital saved or invested in goods turned over quickly would then be available to reinvest to stimulate further production and trade. In lieu of soybeans turning into rice, the circuit Bruce envisioned was money returning to its immediate point of departure more quickly so it could begin the cycle anew more often. Stated somewhat differently, in Bruce's vision the use value of soy beans was incidental to the value their carriage could produce. Also incidental was the existing class of boat owners who relied on the beans to make their living. They made no appearance in his vision of commerce, which called forth a generic merchant and an equally generic consumer, both of whom flexibly responded to prices and unspecified opportunities. Bruce, unlike his Chinese counterparts who had seen unemployed boatmen swell the ranks of anti-state protesters,[27] was not alarmed by the prospect that Chinese soy shippers might lose their livelihoods because other opportunities would inevitably emerge. Foreign ships carrying cheap cargoes to and from northern ports would enable Qing subjects to consume more and incentivize more production. More of what was not even a question.

Following Helen Dunstan's work on eighteenth-century Chinese political economy, it is possible to infer that much of Bruce's proposals was likely intelligible to Qing officials familiar with mid-eighteenth-century discussions about the "possibilities of an amoral conception of the market—one in which self-interest, refigured as the vehicle of market forces, was not to be naively thwarted in its normal paths."[28] At the same time, it was also likely that Bruce's invocation of an explosion of mass consumption would have been conceptually novel. According to Dunstan, no "market conscious" official of the 1740s conceived of such a scenario, and since 1800, necessities such as food and rent had consumed a greater percentage of declining peasant incomes. Large populations within the Qing Empire had grown more destitute at

---

26. Dean provides evidence that this scenario was communicated to the British Legation by Dent & Co. in October 1861; see *China and Great Britain*, 85.
27. Elizabeth Perry, *Challenging the Mandate of Heaven: Social Protest and State Power in China* (Armonk: M. E. Sharpe, 2002), chap. 2. Unemployed boatmen were a key constituency in the Small Sword Rebellion of 1853–1855. They would also form part of uprisings in Shandong in 1862–1863.
28. Helen Dunstan, *State or Merchant? Political Economy and Political Process in 1740s China* (Cambridge, MA: Harvard University Press, 2006), 143.

the same time import-export trade had boomed.[29] Dovetailing with this decline in popular well-being, beginning in 1800 Qing statecraft appears to have swung in the direction of an embrace of frugality and renewed emphasis on agricultural production at the expense of support for trade and nonessential consumption.[30]

It was not economic logic but security concerns that shifted Qing policy on the soy trade. Bruce ended his 1862 letter with an implicit offer of military assistance against the Taiping rebels in return for access to the soy trade. The move was shrewd. Since the previous fall, key Jiangnan cities, including Shanghai, Ningbo, Hangzhou, and Zhapu had all been captured or besieged by Taiping forces. In February 1862, supplies in Shanghai were dwindling, and government forces were fighting a multi-front battle against the rebels who threatened to move north toward Beijing in the spring. Knowing that local communities and territorial authorities in Ningbo and Shanghai had petitioned for foreign assistance and that foreign mobilization was a key part of Shanghai's defense, Bruce added to his petition the following lines:

> I may mention that the opening of this trade [at the northern ports] will prove beneficial to the cause of the order and government. For any port where foreign interests are large, foreign nations will not fail to prevent these places from becoming the theater of Civil War, and from consequent destruction.[31]

In other words, more British ships docked at Tianjin, Yingkou and Yantai, lessened the possibility that those quarters would become staging grounds for a rebel assault on Beijing.

This time, the Zongli yamen bit. The office's reply, issued only a few days later, took the British minister at his word: foreign participation in the trade would be small, what smuggling there was would stop, and the British would help protect the ports and the merchant communities in them. The yamen further acknowledged that the development of British commercial interests in the north would yield not only defense benefits but economic ones as well, making possible "the assembling of merchants in large numbers at every port along the coast, and to the prosperity of trade." Goods would continue to circulate amid the ongoing rebellion, the government reasoned, if Chinese merchants felt foreign countries would help protect their movement.[32]

---

29. Richard Von Glahn, *The Economic History of China: From Antiquity to the Nineteenth Century* (Cambridge: Cambridge University Press, 2016), 358–61, 370–72.
30. Margherita Zanasi, *Economic Thought in Modern China: Market and Consumption, c. 1500–1937* (Cambridge: Cambridge University Press, 2020), 109–24.
31. British Legation to Zongli Yamen, draft, 11 February 1862, TNA, FO 228/911; on progress of Taiping presence in Jiangnan, see Great Britain, *Papers Relating to the Rebellion in China and Trade on the Yang-tze-kiang River* (1862) [2976]; see also Dean, *Great Britain and China*, 90.
32. Zongli Yamen to British Legation, trans. Thomas Wade, 15 February 1862, TNA, FO 228/912. Already, foreign ships had offered protection to Chinese merchant vessels for several decades,

Foreign Participation Phase 1: Speed and Dislocation

Qing permission for foreign vessels to transport soy products was granted in time for the 1862 season, during which eighty-six foreign vessels visited the port. Exports of soy products in such vessels was modest but enough to have possibly displaced 230–260 junks out of an estimated population of several thousand ships that called at the port annually.[33] General market conditions, though, altered enough that by the end of the season in August, junk owners based in Shanghai had registered an official protest with the Chinese superintendent of the Shanghai Customs, Wu Xu, against foreign participation. The acting governor of Jiangsu, Li Hongzhang, forwarded the petition to the Zongli yamen, coupled with his own observations on the situation: For nearly two centuries coastal populations, he wrote, "have been wont to build junks and go to the sea, each man ... carrying and dealing in the produce for which his native place was remarkable." This "junk trade," moreover, Li observed, had contributed generously whenever "aid has been called for [by the state]," most particularly in the transport of tribute grain, which "devolves entirely upon the junk traders." This work, Li remarked, "is no slight help to the finances of the state, and the means of the people," and yet now they were threatened by foreign traders. If, Li argued, business at Yingkou and Yantai "are caught in the net as well, the junk trade of China will be ruined at once" and with it the livelihoods of coastal peoples, money for the army, and the means of transporting grain to Beijing.[34]

Several features of this complaint ask for our attention. The first is the importance of commercial actors to noncommercial projects. The junk owners, in their own eyes and in Li's, were not merely traders but collaborators in projects of imperial strength and stability: providing the food that fed the military and the million or so residents in Beijing. Second, echoing established statecraft discourse, the petitioners argued that their particular social role grew out of specialized production in their native places.[35] Contrary to the British minister's claim that foreign shipping

---

though on an ad hoc and unauthorized basis. Later commentary on the Qing government's 1862 decision suggests that Prince Yixin did not completely trust Bruce's offer given how unpredictable (*po ce* 叵測) the British could be, but they wanted the aid and to prevent British collusion with the Taiping; see CBYWSM (digital), TZ, juan 32, 19.2–21.2.

33. Great Britain, *China. No. 4* (1864), *Commercial Reports from Her Majesty's Consuls in China, for the Year 1862* (1864) [3302], 6–9. According to IMC figures, in the 1862 season foreign vessels exported soy products valued at 170,000 taels and weighing about 340,000 piculs (about 20,000 tons). To arrive at the possible number of displaced junks, I used an average of 1,000 shi junk capacity, which is on the low end of the possible scale.
34. Zongli Yamen to Beijing Legation, trans. Thomas Wade, 19 August 1862, TNA, FO 228/912.
35. For example, "Merchants bring scarceness and abundance into contact and assemble goods for the profit of the realm," Jin Fu 靳輔 (1633–1692), "生財裕餉第一疏" [On creating wealth and augmenting provisions, memorial one]," reprinted in He Changling and Wei Yuan, *Huangchao jingshi*

would broadly benefit Chinese traders, the junk merchants testified that entrance of foreign merchants into the soy trade frayed the tie between places of origin and commercial circulation, leaving unemployed junks without any social or economic function. Against Bruce's abstracted actors with their speed and unceasing movement, the petition forwarded by Li Hongzhang invoked, albeit obliquely, place-specific produce of discrete use values and incontrovertible employment also tied to place. The shipowners of Shanghai did not envision new lines of trade emerging for their vessels. Nor was this connection between place and occupation mere rhetoric or hyperbole. *Sha chuan* were well built to navigate the sandy shoals of the Shandong coast but would easily be overwhelmed by the rougher oceans to the south.[36]

The junk owners' petition had its desired effect. The superintendent of trade at Shanghai, who received the complaint, concurred in his remarks on the petition that "the largest [native] trade done at Shanghai has always been the trade in beans." If foreign shipping succeeded in arrogating this trade for itself, it would be "the ruin of the junk trade . . . [which] would seriously affect the question of war supplies and the transport of grain by the sea [to the capital]." In Beijing, the Zongli yamen received the petition with sympathy and agreed that "the case of the junk owners is fully deserving of commiseration." Its leaders reminded the British minister that he had assured the yamen that foreign interest in the soy trade would be minimal and British merchants would not "monopolize" it. Soon thereafter, the Zongli yamen informed the British Legation that it wished to interdict soy shipments in foreign vessels to Shanghai.[37] Four months later, the British minister unsurprisingly rejected the plan, arguing the petitioners surely could not be correct about the effects of foreign shipping on the Chinese bean trade. Foreign shipping, which in 1862 was already largely steam based, could not possibly find profit in an article of such large bulk and little value, he argued. He furthermore chastised the Zongli yamen for suggesting the interdict in light of all the military aid the British navy had recently provided. Had they not prevented Taiping naval expeditions out of Ningbo and Zhapu and lately rid Chusan of a piratical fleet of two hundred vessels?[38]

---

wenbian (1826), cited by Christine Moll-Murata, *State and Crafts in the Qing Dynasty (1644–1911)* (Amsterdam: Amsterdam University Press, 2018), 304.
36. Xue, "A Fertilizer Revolution?" 210.
37. Zongli Yamen to British Legation, trans. Thomas Wade, 19 August 1862, TNA, FO 228/912. Authorities in Guangzhou had also refused to land foreign-shipped beans, but it was not included in the yamen's proposed restriction. It was only in Shanghai where foreign shipping was having a negative impact on the local merchant community. IMC trade reports indicate additional large markets for soy products in Fuzhou, Shantou, and Xiamen. On Guangzhou, see Dean, *Great Britain and China*, 85.
38. British Legation to Zongli Yamen, draft, 20 December 1862, TNA, FO 228/911.

Foreign soy transport and the consequent erosion of junk traffic at Yingkou and Yantai continued through the 1863 and 1864 seasons. In the fall of 1864, Li Hongzhang in Shanghai began to agitate anew for some change in policy, and over the course of the next seven months, he sent several memorials on the subject to Beijing. The memorials were composed of further merchant petitions, reports from local officials, and Li's own observations, which all reiterated the line of argument against foreign participation laid out in the 1862 petition. In both the additional details they provide and the language they use, as well as the alternative solutions they propose, these communications demonstrate the extent to which Qing officials discerned the sum of differences between British commerce in China and Qing merchant activity.

What struck officials in Shanghai most strongly was the uniquely placeless and opportunistic quality of Euroamerican trading activity. In the words of the Shanghai Customs superintendent and local *lijin* bureau, as quoted by Li Hongzhang, "the steamers and foreign ships come and go in foreign oceans, conduct trade in the port of every country; profit and power is in their hands, there is no where they do not go, there is no good they do not carry." This activity, officials contrasted to that of the *sha chuan*: "the boats in Shanghai only go to the northern ocean, and in this trade strive for a ten percent profit." Whereas foreign traders inserted themselves into every possible trade, if Shanghai shippers were unable to carry a specific cargo from a particular region (i.e., soybeans), they became useless, anchored in port, and began to rot.

For Li in Shanghai, local economic and social stability were firmly linked to the availability of soy cargo. Its loss, Li argued, meant a long-term loss of resources. "Every day, [the junks'] potential [*shi* 勢] is necessarily wasted," he wrote. Such losses were both physical, in the form of the rotting ship, and less tangible—withering money reserves (*ben* 本) that could not be put to use to keep commerce moving (*jiaoyi liutong* 交易流通). The inevitable consequences of this wasted *shi*, Li anticipated, were the loss of merchant fortunes and hardships for those families, a diminished local tax base, as well as an out-of-work class of seafarers. This last possibility was in some ways the most alarming. The history of imperial rule offered plenty of evidence that displaced persons often turned to robbery and could potentially organize into larger, more dangerous collectives. Seafarers were persons of the lowest class who "have no other industry/occupation to preserve themselves," and Li expected that once out of work they would scatter into myriads of illegal activities—looting, robbing, and harming travelers.[39] Without useful employment for so many, further social damage was inevitable.[40]

---

39. CBYWSM (print), TZ, juan 28, 38.1–41.1.
40. Betty Peh-T'i Wen, *Ruan Yuan, 1764–1849: The Life and Work of a Major Scholar Official in Nineteenth Century China before the Opium War* (Hong Kong: Hong Kong University Press, 2006),

A second matter of concern was the way foreign shipping altered market dynamics in the soy trade. The influx of boats into Yingkou and Yantai raised the price of soy products there, and slower-moving junks, which returned to Shanghai later in the season, had to contend with "narrowed" channels of sale and lower prices in a crowded market.[41] Speed, pace Bruce, had not produced more profit to invest but, rather, more competition for cargo and more difficulty recouping investment. The actual sequence of events along the empire's coast demonstrated what Zongli yamen officials seem to have suspected in their resistance to opening the trade: speed-up was not an unqualified benefit to society. Rather, what happened in Shanghai demonstrated that speed (and these are my words, not theirs) recalibrated conditions of capital reproduction. These new conditions disadvantaged *sha chuan*, the declining state of which also destabilized the region's grain transport. Two years into foreign carriage, Li warned the court, purchases of tribute rice in Jiangsu fell short, as did the availability of boats to transport the rice. For officers of the Qing government, it was not obvious how *cao yun* could continue if foreign participation in the soy trade continued.[42]

Foreign Participation Phase 2: Local Mobilization

While Li struggled to realize a change of policy in Beijing, merchants in Shanghai took matters into their own hands. Sucheta Mazumdar shows in her study of Chinese sugar markets that merchant groups routinely deployed overt forms of coercion to achieve market control and protect their social and economic position.[43] It is precisely this extra-economic power that was brought to bear when foreign shipping endangered the *sha chuan*. In the summer of 1865 a group of junk owners and importers of northern produce launched a successful embargo against the import at Shanghai of soy products in foreign vessels. September 1864 was the last month foreign vessels discharged soy cargos at Shanghai until June 1867.[44] The merchants' at organizing meant that even though officials in Beijing, pressured by the British Legation, called for an end to the embargo, official proclamations had little effect. In the summer of 1866, for example, although the embargo was officially interdicted,

---

83–84, 87; Hsiao Kung-chuan, *A History of Chinese Political Thought*, Vol. 1, *From the Beginnings to the Six Century A.D.*, trans. F. W. Mote (Princeton: Princeton University Press, 1979), 355–60.
41. CBYWSM (print), TZ, juan 28, 38.1–41.1; Xue "A Fertilizer Revolution?" 210.
42. CBYWSM (digital), TZ, juan 32, 15.1–16.2.
43. Sucheta Mazumdar, *Sugar and Society: Peasants, Technology, and the World Market* (Cambridge, MA: Harvard University Asia Center, 1998), 316–18, 392–94, 396.
44. Great Britain, *Commercial Reports from Her Majesty's Consuls in China, Japan, and Siam, 1866–1868* (1867–1868), 2, 204.

two "test" boats—one British, one Prussian—chartered by Chinese merchants could not find buyers in Shanghai for their cargo.[45]

Local success enforcing the embargo put authorities in Beijing in a difficult position. Although the mobilization of extra-economic power to achieve market ambitions was a common gambit, treaty regulations gave foreign states standing to object to and to block the political alliance between *sha chuan* owners and local officials. When the fate of the two "test" boats became known at the British Legation, the new minister, Rutherford Alcock, determined to force more effective action by the Zongli yamen. Alcock had already spent more than a decade in China, previously as British consul at Fuzhou, Shanghai, and Canton. Like his predecessor, Frederick Bruce, Alcock was only somewhat diplomatic in his reminders to the Zongli yamen that local commercial governance was now an international affair. Chinese merchant actions in Shanghai, Alcock warned the yamen, undermined treaty rights. Not only had the government in 1862 granted Britain a specific (and apparently permanent!) privilege to ship soy, but the 1863 Qing treaty with Denmark had legalized the soy export trade from Yingkou and Yantai for all treaty signatories.[46] In the spring of 1867, with the onset of the soy trading season and the interdict still in effect, Alcock admonished Prince Yixin, "it would be a matter of great regret at this stage of our relations if a few monopolizing junk owners could be able to create such an unpleasantness . . . [that] compelled the foreign governments interested to seek some more effective remedy."[47]

The embargo did, in all events, end in the summer of 1867, owing to both pressure brought to bear by Alcock and internal policy adjustments. Frustrated by lack of effective action by officials in the capital, Alcock shifted the target of his diplomatic pressure and paid a personal visit to Zeng Guofan (曾國藩, 1811–1872), the senior and well-respected governor general with jurisdiction over Shanghai. Although available records do not divulge any lines of reasoning used by Alcock or Zeng during their conference, after the visit Zeng ordered another proclamation against the embargo. This one quickly resulted in the charter by Chinese merchants at Shanghai of northbound foreign vessels.[48] But changed conditions at Shanghai

---

45. Beijing Legation to Zongli Yamen, draft, No. 9, 27 March 1867, TNA FO 228/931; "The Bean Trade: British Consulate Shanghai General Chamber of Commerce," *NCHMR*, June 22, 1867, pp. 118–19.
46. The Sino-Danish treaty gave Danish vessels access to the open treaty ports without any cargo reservations and explicitly expunged from the tariff language that excluded these ports from Danish participation in the bean and pea trades. By virtue of most-favored nation clauses, all other treaty signatories were entitled to the same access.
47. Beijing Legation to Zongli Yamen, draft, No. 9, 27 March 1867, TNA, FO 228/931.
48. Zeng Guofan, Entry Book of Letters from Yamen, No. 36, likely 4 June 1867, trans. W. C. Hillier, TNA, FO 230/79; "The Bean Trade," *NCHMR*, 22 June 1867, 115; "The Bean Trade," *NCHMR*, 15 June 1867, 106; Great Britain, *Commercial Reports 1866–1868*, 204.

should not be credited to foreign pressure alone. By the time Zeng acted, Beijing had settled on solving the *sha chuan* dilemma by providing their owners with more business and revenue. A first measure, approved in 1865, lifted restrictions on the Fengtian grain trade to create more cargo for *sha chuan*.[49] Beijing also increased the rate of freight the government paid for *cao yun*. "By this means," Zeng Guofan explained to Alcock, "the Chinese merchants have a way out of their difficulties, and [the measure] will enable them, without fear of ruin, to desist from squabbling over the profits of the bean trade."[50]

Assessing Historical Significance

Qing Protectionism?

The situation at Shanghai was not a simple case of nationalist protectionism against foreign intrusion. Even at the height of the crisis, the majority of the buying and selling of soy was in the hands of Chinese firms, even if the shippers were not.[51] The situation, rather, was one of shifting terrain. The deterritorialization of the soy trade that followed from foreign participation in it reshaped the grounds of government decision-making. Previously, it had been possible for Qing statesmen to advocate unequivocally for a policy of *liutong* (流通)—that is, "commercial circulation of maximum volume and velocity."[52] Eighteenth-century governors including Chen Hongmou (陳宏謀, 1696–1771) and Wang Guodong (王國棟, 1692–1776), as well as the Qianlong emperor embraced profit-oriented commercial circulation as a creator of steady supplies of goods and stable prices. Market stability was further facilitated by paternalistic policies, such as state delineation of sales areas and overt controls on the pace of sales.[53] Under the newly deterritorialized trading conditions, however, *liutong* had become a problem; newly amplified velocities and volumes of trade, particularly in steamships, destabilized prices, both in the Shanghai soy

---

49. CBYWSM, TZ, juan 32, 15.1–16.2, 18.2, 21.2. It became possible to ship conjointly beans, millet, and "mixed grains" without a permit. Notably, the discussion of easing restrictions noted that foreign ships carrying grain escaped the licensing requirements applied to Chinese ships doing the same. The change helped equalize terms of trade for Chinese and foreign firms.
50. "The Bean Trade," *North China Herald and Market Report*, June 15, 1867, 106; see also Zeng Guofan, Entry Book of Letters from Yamen, No. 36, likely 4 June 1867, trans. W. C. Hillier, TNA, FO 230/79.
51. Great Britain, *Commercial Reports from H. M. Consuls in China and Japan 1865* (1866) [3740], 252; Great Britain, *Commercial Reports for H. M. Consuls in China 1864* (1866) [3587], 126.
52. William Rowe, *Saving the World: Chen Hongmou and Elite Consciousness in Eighteenth-Century China* (Stanford: Stanford University Press, 2001), 198.
53. Zelin, *Merchants of Zigong*, 6–7; Rowe, *Hankow*, 74. In Hankou, stone-carrying boats were assigned sequential numbers upon arrival and were "allowed to strike bargains only when all prior boats had completed their sales."

market and in the Yingkou textile market, which British firms flooded with unsalable goods.[54]

A second problem with the new form of commercial circulation was its destruction of existing mercantile wealth. When Li Hongzhang invoked the poignant image of junks rotting in their anchorages, his point of reference was not technological obsolescence. At no point during this era did any Qing official issue a eulogy for junks; as late as the 1940s, vessels of many different traditional builds remained integral to the movement of goods in China.[55] Rather, what Li and others worried about was the future of mercantile contributions to larger political projects. Recall that *sha chuan* were integral to a spatially-limited hybrid circuit of circulation. Designed for the sandy shoals of the Shandong coast, the boats transported Jiangnan tribute rice to Tianjin, which subsidized their transport of soy and bean cake back to Jiangnan, where the nitrogen-rich substances contributed to the cultivation of export commodities and more tribute rice. At least one strain of imperial political-economic thought cherished and supported the wealthy for the sake of their material contributions to the empire.[56] Here, officials acted to preserve contributions to the empire that were inconvertibly tied to the use values of *sha chuan*, soy, and rice.

Obviously, on both sides of the soy trade debate lay different economic interests. What is more interesting and less well understood are the modes of social reproduction those interests represented. While Qing officials acted to preserve contingent, concrete forms social reproduction took, for British merchants and their government the concrete features of the soy trade were ancillary to a more global and abstract project. British arguments for access to the northern soy markets emphasized that faster and higher volumes of transport would lower freight rates for northbound and southbound goods. Those lower freight rates would reduce the costs of those goods, which suggested increased rates of profit and wider markets for the goods. Future beneficiaries of such trade growth were not specific to any one place, but were potentially anywhere. By this logic, if selling goods at Yantai required taking on cargo of feather boas, that is what the British would have agitated to access. The commodity was incidental to the ultimate goal of growing circulation. As a last testament to this point, British participation in the soy trade was fleeting. After a disastrous 1868 season when soy demand in the south weakened, foreign shippers did not return north for beans.

---

54. Great Britain, *Commercial Report 1869*, 84, 87.
55. G.R.G Worcester, *Junks and Sampans of the Yangtze: A Study in Chinese Nautical Research* (Shanghai: Statistical Department of the Inspectorate General of Customs, 1947–1948).
56. Helen Dunstan, *Conflicting Counsels to Confuse the Age: A Documentary Study of Political Economy in Qing China, 1644–1840* (Ann Arbor: Center for Chinese Studies, University of Michigan, 1996), 128–31.

The British argument for foreign participation in the soy trade was ultimately grounded in faith in the self-regulating market as a machine of general social prosperity. With all participants free to make choices in their best self-interest, speed would bring cheapness and cheapness would bring growth. Qing resistance to foreign carriage of soy queried the wisdom of a wholesale embrace of circulation mediated by market forces alone. Even though it was not unheard of for imperial officials to embrace commerce in highly general terms, it was also the case that this embrace was firmly tied to the reproduction of local communities.[57] Put somewhat differently, authorities in the Qing Empire routinely deployed concrete metrics by which to evaluate the effects of commerce. Were merchants contributing to general wealth through the distribution of nature's resources?[58] Was the state enabling them to continue this work?[59] Qing leaders distinguished, say, between the positive effects of luxury consumption in wealthy Jiangnan, where thousands of people were employed by daily theatrical performances, and the need to encourage frugality in regions where resources were more scare.[60] In all these instances, key metrics for state policy were the specific livelihood conditions for the majority of the people in a socio-economically distinct area and the concrete effects of merchant activity in that area. Although commerce was valued as a means to stimulate employment and an optimal distribution of resources, evidence does not suggest that in the mid-nineteenth century Qing officials embraced the self-regulating market as an institution appropriate to all times, all places, and all commodities.

Recognition of the flexible approach Qing authorities took toward market operations and state intervention asks us to reframe the choice facing Qing officials in 1862–1867. From where Prince Yixin, Li Hongzhang, and others stood, the question was not so much one of economic principles, as suggested by Bruce, but a political one—what forces would order, disorder, or reorder social and economic life? The market or the government? In this light, the embargo at Shanghai was less a monopolistic protest against British treaty rights, as British observers branded it, and more accurately a competing form of coercion: the social-commercial power of the Shanghai *sha chuan* owners and against abstract coercion of the market. Foreign shipping companies counted on market mechanisms to grow their own position in the trade. The *sha chuan* owners mobilized market institutions and relationships as a way to insist persons, not market forces, would determine who prospered. In the soy trade debate, both sides accused the other of "monopolizing" the soy trade: the

---

57. See, for example, Wang Guodong in Dunstan, *Conflicting Counsels*, 309.
58. On nature as wealth, see Man-huong Lin, *China Upside Down: Currency, Society, and Ideologies, 1808–1856* (Cambridge, MA: Harvard University Press, 2007), 136–37, 191.
59. Zhang, *Timber and Forestry*, 143. The government was cautious not to ruin timber merchant's business through official purchases.
60. Zanasi, *Economic Thought*, 88–89, 117.

British because Chinese merchant groups exercised social power to the exclusion of British shippers, the Chinese because market forces privileged foreign firms.

A Marriage of Overt and Abstract Coercion

When the foreign community won participation in the soy trade, it was not on the basis of political-economic wisdom. Bruce succeeded in his campaign because the Qing were fighting a prolonged civil war and wanted aid in that war. Moreover, the empire's military forces had just lost a second war to the British in 1860, and the imperial court could not be sure the British would not start another one if their commercial demands were not met. In short, overt military coercion—the ability to wield it as well as the desire to avoid it—was a large, if background, element in the ability of the British to extract and secure their participation in the soy trade. That participation became a beachhead for introducing the more abstract coercion of capital which was felt when processes of speed-up recalibrated the conditions of capital accumulation in the trade. If we connect the dots between British diplomacy and its achievements, we see an instance in which the coercive state power was instrumental to the creation of the "free market," with destabilizing consequences.[61]

The specific forms destabilization took reflected the capacity of the Chinese commercial class and the capacity of the government to assimilate to the coercive terms of commerce and governance under the treaty regime. As Chinese firms worked to remain the dominant commercial agents in the Qing Empire, their practices shifted in response to tools and possibilities that foreign presence introduced. The desire to profit, at the firm level, worked to institutionalize new temporalities and conditions of trade as socially general, and in this process, Chinese merchants who consigned foreign steamships to ship their cargoes were agents of capitalism's advance as much as, if not more so than, foreign firms. By the turn of the century, Chinese traders had almost completely abandoned the junk as a mode of transportation in the soy trade.[62] The state, meanwhile was hamstringed in its efforts to preserve the junk community at Shanghai and thereby preserve its own commitments to imperial order. It is clear from the historical research of the past several decades that even while Qing leaders embraced market forces, they also embraced market stability in the name of social and political stability. "If people do not have a constant livelihood, they cannot have constant minds" was a tenet articulated by Mencius, recited by eighteenth-century governors, and on display in the central government's

---

61. The history of capitalism is rife with such instances. One that comes to mind here is the creation of the English labor market as discussed in Karl Polanyi's *The Great Transformation*.
62. Isett, *State, Peasant, and Merchant*, 230. Isett cites estimates that allocate 80 percent of the 1901 soybean export trade to foreign steamships.

measures to stabilize cargoes and profits for *sha chuan* owners. Little in the treaty-based regulatory apparatus, however, recognized constancy as an important element in social reproduction. The long-term logic of the treaty regime was to set free the coercive powers of market competition in the name of growth.

The State and Ceaseless Accumulation

Present in Fredrick Bruce's advice to Qing policymakers in February 1862 was an image of what we might call the "ceaseless accumulation of capital"—that is, an ongoing flux and reflux of ever-increasing commodities and money, moving ever more quickly to more places. His valorization of this process reflected, perhaps one-sidedly, his own nation's recent historical experience. Since the 1780s, Britain had become a society in which "revolutionary change became the norm," and waves of social dislocation were married with liberal faith that these were necessary consequences of constant progress toward a greater good: aggregate, overall growth.[63] From within this liberal tradition, Bruce overlooked and minimized the fears of social dislocation that animated Qing authorities in Shanghai and in the Zongli yamen.

Most commonly and consistently, imperial political economy practiced during the Qing dynasty valued commerce as a means to transfer surpluses of use values to areas where they were needed. For example, in Fujian, in the early part of the eighteenth century, the governor-general advised cultivating trade relations with Siam to bring rice to the land-poor coastal province. "What is produced locally is no longer sufficient to feed the people," he wrote. "The only way to resolve the problem is to open the ocean so that surpluses in trade can supplement insufficiency in farming, and both the rich and the poor will benefit from it."[64] To support commercial circulation more generally, territorial administrators advocated policies and practices that supported the bodies of merchants: roads for them to travel and inns for their sojourns, medical aid for those traveling and protection for the same from bandits. Policies also sought to preserve merchant resources: tax remissions issued to conserve and protect their "vigor."[65]

At the time of the soy trade debate, most commercial circulation in the Qing Empire was the result of regional specialization in goods of everyday use, and the limits of these markets were customary and demographic. Although wealthy Jiangnan communities provided elastic markets for luxury goods, growth in China's

---

63. Eric Hobsbawm, *The Age of Revolution 1789–1848* (New York: Vintage, 1996), 28.
64. Ng Chin-Keong, *Boundaries and Beyond: China's Maritime Southeast in Late Imperial Times* (Singapore: NUS Press, 2017), 92–94. Ng quotes from 大清實錄 SZ, 54:18.
65. Rowe, *Saving the World*, 198–200; Dunstan, *Conflicting Counsels*, 311–13.

long-distance trade was not driven, as it was for Europeans venturing abroad, by faster and higher volume commodity production and the need to find markets for goods.[66] The majority of this commercial circulation in the Qing Empire involved large volumes of grain and small quantities of other goods.[67] This difference is important for thinking about the role of commercial circulation in the reproduction of a given social order. In the capitalist mode of production up and running in Great Britain in the nineteenth century, faster production of more commodities and the circulation urgently needed to sustain this growth were the beating heart within the ceaseless accumulation of capital. Capital only exists in a constant process of growth, and that growth in the nineteenth century hinged on commodities reaching farther, moving more quickly, and moving more cheaply.[68] This modality of social reproduction is what Frederick Bruce wished upon China.

Through this lens, what is remarkable about the soybean episode is how clearly it illustrates how a commercial society is not coterminous with a capitalist society. In China in the mid-nineteenth century, wealthy merchants collected in places like Guangzhou and Shanghai, and these, like their European counterparts, engaged in practices that rationally allocated resources to grow their investments. But theoretically, as well as historically, there are circumstances in which merchants and the process of capital reproduction they engineer *link up with* the production of use values and circumstances in which the capital possessed and circulated by merchants are "absorbed" into the production process as a "mere moment." In the former, as Marx put it, "it is trade that shapes the products into commodities," and in the latter, it is "the produced commodities whose movement constitutes trade."[69] What Marx was getting at here, and in other places where he develops his analysis of commercial capital, is that the capitalist mode of production changes the relations between production and circulation.[70] In the absence of a capitalist mode of production, commercial capital is an independent sphere of operations, taking goods where it finds them with no necessary relation to the production process, though such a

---

66. Isett, "China," citing Philip Huang, Y. Ma, and I. D. de Jong; Xu and Wu, *Chinese Capitalism*, 380–82.
67. Isett, "China," 110–11, citing scholarship by C. Wu, X. Xu, S. Guo, Lillian Li, and Bernhofen et al. Even still, in the nineteenth century, the commodification of grain was more limited in China than elsewhere in the world. By some estimates, following a period of market disaggregation during Daoguang reign (1820–1850), only 12 percent of all grain produced in China was traded.
68. Karl Marx, *Capital: A Critique of Political Economy*, vol. 1, trans. Ben Fowkes (New York: Vintage Books, 1977), chap. 4; Eric Hobsbawm, *The Age of Capital 1848–1875* (New York: Vintage, 1996).
69. Karl Marx, *Capital: A Critique of Political Economy*, vol. 3, trans. David Fernbach (New York: Penguin, 1981), 445.
70. Marx, *Capital*, vol. 3: chaps. 16–18, 20; Karl Marx, *Capital: A Critique of Political Economy*, vol. 2, trans. David Fernbach (New York: Penguin, 1978), chaps. 14 and 15.

relation is possible, whether in the form of material or monetary advances.[71] The capitalist mode of production, strictly speaking, differs from production mediated in some fashion by commercial capital because within the fully developed capitalist mode of production, production and circulation form a unity mediated by value. In the relationship's simplest form, industry can only continue to produce if merchants have unloaded their previous purchases; merchants can only continue to sell if industry has produced more goods. Fundamental to the relation is the growth imperative inherent in capital, which puts both industrial capital and commercial capital on courses of expansion, with feedback loops between both spheres with regard to temporality and scale.[72] Expansion and acceleration are from a Marxian standpoint, necessary for the existence of a capitalist society given that the telos of capital is growth. It follows that the multiplication of human needs and multitudes of commodities to serve them is also necessary. In this fashion, particular use values and their movement become subordinate to the project of capital expansion. When the dominant form of social wealth is value, use values become contingent and ephemeral.[73]

Conclusion: A Concrete History of Abstract Coercion

The Marxian theory of capitalist specificity appears rather abstract until we examine something like the soybean episode. Whereas the British Legation pushed for policies that reproduced the social function of value circulation appropriate to a capitalist society, Qing authorities held firm that their policies would better support the reproduction of particular use-value movements as well as the material wealth of discrete communities. Neither side was "wrong"; they just spoke from historically specific standpoints that expressed the role of (abstract) value production in each polity.

Pace Charles Addis, Qing authorities could indeed see economic laws. They knew slower junks would lose to faster-sailing steamers. But the role of the state was to prevent such a thing from happening. Just as the role of the state was to ensure that rice circulated and that the poor might make their living from petty sales of food stuffs. It was the abdication of responsibility for these larger considerations

---

71. Jairus Banaji, *A Brief History of Commercial Capitalism* (Chicago: Haymarket Books, 2020); Marx, *Capital*, vol. 3, 448–49.
72. Both the geographic expansion of trade and its contraction can express the speed-up in production that produces larger volumes of goods and needs more material inputs. The former occurs when the goods are sold, the latter when there is "overproduction," which often causes a contraction or slowdown in production.
73. It is capitalism that has given us the Chia Pet, the Pet Rock, generations of obsolete workout equipment, and more recently, the escape room.

that lurked behind Li Hongzhang's wariness of British authorities, whom he found to be pragmatic to a fault. As we see Qing authorities practicing commercial governance in the episode described above, commercial governance involved political choices designed to respond to and balance the local effects of markets and forms of market integration, which acted unequally on participants. Addis invoked a "laissez-faire, laissez-aller" policy as necessary for good governance, but this position was not, contrary to how he saw it, a universal truth. The self-regulating market only began to yield general prosperity, even in England, according to some accounts, once royal paternalism ended and labor was set free from land, from customary occupations as well as from its geographic immobility.[74] "A self-regulating market demands nothing less than the institutional separation of society into an economic and a political sphere," observed anthropologist and economist Karl Polanyi.[75] From the Qing point of view, this separation was a poor standpoint for governance to take. Chinese officials instead would likely have agreed with the besieged Silesian handloom weavers who confronted similar forms of abstract coercion half a world away: "We should help [our neighbor] guard and increase his livelihood and property."[76]

---

74. Karl Polanyi, *The Great Transformation: The Political and Economic Origins of Our Time*, 2nd ed. (Boston: Beacon, 2001), esp. pt. 2, sec. 1.
75. Polanyi, *The Great Transformation*, 74.
76. Quoted in Hobsbawm, *The Age of Revolution*, 201. Original penned ca. 1844.

5
Boundary Struggles
Treaties, Taxation, and the Erasure of Difference

> It is hardly self-evident what constitutes a "problem" for law to solve. What is a problem for one society may simply not be a problem for another.[1]

A main argument in this study is that for a period of time, centered on the mid-nineteenth century, British agents in China attempted to import, alongside their Lancaster textiles, new ways of governing trade. Yet there already existed in China well-established ways of governing trade formed in dialogue with prevailing social, political, and economic arrangements. The foregoing chapters have laid out how, after 1861, that governance was disordered, disrupted, and spasmodically reconstituted. Central to these processes of deterritorialization and reterritorialization, I have argued, was global capital circulation across political boundaries.

Perhaps the fullest expression of this project's ambitions was a decades-long campaign, from the late 1860s into the 1880s, to change Qing domestic taxation. Taxation, of course, is a sovereign right, but the Euro-American community saw in Qing sovereignty over Chinese merchants existential threats to capital reproduction. Key practices of Qing statecraft, including local fiscal administrative autonomy, spatially responsive policy implementation, and extra-bureaucratic participation in state projects, all seemed to threaten the ability of foreign capital to expand and reproduce. Consequently, the British-led campaign against Qing domestic taxation was never only about lowering charges on trade; it was also a reterritorialization effort to entail new limits on state sovereignty and provincial autonomy, to redefine territory, and to reorient the minds of those who governed.

---

1. Teemu Ruskola, *Legal Orientalism: China, the United States and Modern Law* (Cambridge, MA: Harvard University Press, 2013), 33.

This chapter examines foreign discontent with Qing domestic commercial taxation. In these pages I develop critical context for the following chapter, wherein I discuss Qing experiments with new taxation strategies, which began in the 1880s and culminated in the New Policies (*xin zheng* 新政) era, ca. 1901–1911. Most accounts of the Qing "fiscal state" emergent in the last decades of the nineteenth century have not considered the noisy background of foreign diplomacy, which for several decades pressured Qing leaders to centralize fiscal power. Yet these efforts and their grounding in treaty privileges are inseparable from shifts by parts of the Qing government, visible after 1887, to consolidate revenue streams and centralize their collection. In this chapter I explain how capital and the treaties worked together to advance claims against Qing fiscal practices. I contrast these claims with steady resistance to fiscal consolidation and centralization visible in both the provinces and Beijing. The defense of *lijin* marshaled by agents of the Qing Empire is often either absent from histories of the Qing fiscal state or is understood as a power struggle between provincial authorities and the central government. Both accounts have missed how the treaty apparatus and capital circulation mediated this struggle in important ways.

Conventional diplomatic histories of the 1860s–1880s center on Qing-British treaty negotiations—namely, the effort in 1868–1869 to revise the Treaty of Tianjin and the creation of the Chefoo Convention (*Yantai tiaoyue* 煙台條約) negotiated in 1876 after a deadly assault in Yunnan on a British survey team. On both occasions, treaty negotiations produced a robust record of the British establishment's enduring ambitions and discontents as well as Qing counter-critiques of their activities in China. This chapter considers these events in the context of a broader official and unofficial documentary archive and thereby reframes treaty negotiations as moments that crystallized more diffuse and pervasive disagreements about proper commercial governance. My investigation provides new and necessary framing for the history of Qing experiments in taxation taken up in Chapter 6. Most studies of Qing government "reform," typically treat experiments in fiscal organization as exclusively internal affairs, but there are formal similarities as well as institutional links between late Qing fiscal reorganization and the fiscal administrative reorganization foreign governments lobbied for in the name of growing commercial profits. Together, this chapter and the next argue that fiscal centralization in the last decades of Qing rule should be understood in relationship to the viral growth of the treaty regime. Both the endogenous and exogenous factors that shaped Qing tax strategies at the turn of the century expressed the position of the Qing Empire within circuits of global capital circulation and the net of treaty obligations.

Pre-treaty Concerns about Commercial Taxation

Within the Qing Empire, discussions about how to best arrange commercial taxation did not, of course, begin in the treaty era. The relationship between state coffers and the people's prosperity was a question central to Qing fiscal policy, and for much of the dynasty, the government employed what Richard von Glahn calls a "providential" mode of fiscal governance.[2] "Store wealth with the people" was an often-cited mantra, famously endorsed by the Qianlong emperor (r. 1736–1795). He and his grandfather, the Kangxi emperor (r. 1662–1722), believed the basis of a rich state was a healthy, prosperous, and moral populace, supported by low agricultural taxes and minimal taxation of commerce, industry, and consumption.[3] This fiscal policy unfortunately contributed to the government's early nineteenth-century fiscal woes, when revenue shortfalls coincided with other long-term demographic and economic trends. These difficulties effectively structured the end of the Qing "prosperous age."[4] In the first decades of the nineteenth century, elites and administrators began to rethink multiple dimensions of imperial governance, including taxation.

During a period of economic decline some historians call the "Daoguang depression" (c. 1820–1850), a cadre of reform-minded elites focused attention on the paired issues of funding the state (*guoji* 國計) and providing for the people (*yangming/minsheng* 養命/民生). These scholars, some of whom became key actors within the later self-strengthening program, rejected the model of the frugal state promoted by the Qianlong emperor. Underfunded local offices, they argued, preyed on the people, and a frugal state could only engage in the most perfunctory administration of important matters such as flood control and defense.[5] Instead, foreshadowing the preoccupation with "wealth and power" (*fuqiang* 富強) characteristic of Qing official discourse from the 1860s onward, scholar-officials such as Bao Sichen (包世臣, 1775–1855) and Feng Guifen (馮桂芬, 1809–1874) placed growing the state's fiscal resources at the foundation of virtuous governance.[6] They prioritized well-managed finances (*licai* 理財) as central to the proper order of the state (*jingguo*

---

2. Richard Von Glahn, "Modalities of the Fiscal State in Imperial China," *Journal of Chinese History* 4, no. 1 (January 2020): 1–29, here 9–10.
3. Margherita Zanasi, *Economic Thought in Modern China: Market and Consumption c. 1500–1937* (Cambridge: Cambridge University Press, 2020), 22–23; Von Glahn, "Modalities," 22. The two largest sources of commercial tax were revenue from the salt monopoly and customs duties.
4. On tax shortfalls and public expenditures, see Man-houng Lin, *China Upside Down: Currency, Society, and Ideology, 1808–1856* (Cambridge, MA: Harvard University Press, 2007), 133–36.
5. Lin, *China Upside Down*, 136–37; William Rowe, *Speaking of Profit: Bao Shichen and Reform in Nineteenth Century China* (Cambridge, MA: Harvard University East Asian Research Center, 2018); Walter Montgomery, "The 'Remonstrance' of Feng Kuei-fen: A Confucian Search for Change in Nineteenth Century China" (PhD diss., Brown University, 1979), 120–22.
6. Rowe, *Speaking of Profit*, 18–19.

經國).⁷ It was impossible for a ruler to achieve the charisma, military force, virtue, or prowess necessary to rule, they argued, without sufficient economic resources distributed equitably between the people and the government.⁸

The Daoguang-era reformers hoped the state could renew its capacities to govern effectively through an expansion in productive activity and judicious taxation of commercial profits. Reformers endorsed increased commercial taxation, either through privatization of the lucrative salt trade or increased taxes on merchants' and artisans' profits.⁹ Bao Sichen's proposals, examined by William Rowe, called for taxing either salt merchants' profits or the accumulated wealth of merchants and craftsmen, pegged to their level of capitalization. At other times reformers called for expanded land use and crop cultivation to increase the supplies and surplus of the people and to expand the state's fiscal basis.¹⁰ For nearly a millennium, Chinese scholars had debated whether "the wealth of Heaven and Earth is fixed in amount" (Sima Guang, 1019–1086), or whether commerce and production could be stimulated to grow through targeted investment (e.g., Wang Anshi's [1021–1086] "New Policies").¹¹ After the 1850s, what Peter Lavelle calls "[a] new level of consciousness regarding the prospects for a more intensive and extensive exploitation of the natural world" manifested in statecraft projects. Governor General Zuo Zongtang (左宗棠, 1812–1885), in Gansu, for example, began in the 1870s a series of projects. to expand rice, cotton, and mulberry farming.¹²

Enter *Lijin*

When widespread commercial taxation did erupt in the Qing Empire after 1850, it was not an integrated solution to the dynasty's fiscal troubles but rather a patchwork of ad hoc measures responding to immediate exigencies.¹³ Moreover, the actual commercial revenues collected by the dynasty from the 1850s onwards—customs duties, transit taxes, producer levies, and other retail taxes—looked little like recommendations made only a relatively short time prior. Rather than taxing accumulated wealth, new levies intervened in processes of production and circulation

---

7. Rowe, *Speaking of Profit*, 186.
8. Rowe, *Speaking of Profit*, 49.
9. Rowe, *Speaking of Profit*, 65–66, 100–102; Lin, *China Upside Down*, 140.
10. Rowe, *Speaking of Profit*, 77–78; Montgomery, "Remonstrance," 161.
11. Zanasi, *Economic Thought*, 31–35.
12. Peter B. Lavelle, *The Profits of Nature: Colonial Development and the Quest for Resources in Nineteenth-Century China* (New York: Columbia University Press, 2020), 102–6.
13. The name *lijin* refers to a levy at the rate of 1/100th of a good's value. Euro-American contemporaries as well as many historians have used the term to identify a wide range of levies taken from commercial activity. Chinese-language historical documents use *lijin* in conjunction with more specialized terms.

that generated wealth. The new taxes were typically pegged to the value of the good and taken prior to the good's final sale.[14] Consequently, taxation became a sometimes critical factor in the making and unmaking of trade routes and markets; it compounded the uncertainty and speculation that naturally inhered in merchant operations.[15]

The vast array of commerce-based levies that produced state revenue after 1854 went by a number of different names but were gathered together into what, with Lydia Liu, we might call a "supersign"—*lijin* (釐金).[16] A supersign, according to Liu, is "not a word but a hetero-cultural signifying chain," the product of joining terms from different cultural and linguistic worlds. In this case, *lijin* (alt: lekin, leking, likin) emerged in English as a product of equivalence making between qualitatively different practices. Throughout this book, *lijin* has been a key part of the commercial landscape. But it may be helpful at this moment to recall its central features and administrative structure.

The levies collectively known as *lijin* began in 1853 without authorization from Beijing as local transit fees in northern Jiangsu Province, where they were collected to make up for shortfalls in land tax and regular customs duties (*chang shui* 常稅) in areas disturbed by the Taiping Rebellion.[17] *Lijin* was never an empire-wide practice but was most prevalent around the waterways and canal system in the lower Yangzi valley, which channeled much of the empire's commerce. Decades into its collection, 50 percent of *lijin* revenues pooled in four provinces—Jiangsu, Zhejiang, Fujian, and Guangdong.[18] The court's role in administering *lijin* was minimal. Although it did sanction the practice and incorporate it into the Board of Revenue's central auditing system, the central government did not manage details of tariffs or collection procedures. Prior to the twentieth century, once or twice a year provinces communicated total collection amounts, the number and location of collectorates, and the names of collecting officials.[19] Closer supervision arrived only in Guangxu 34 (1908), when as part of tax reform programs, the central government called for provinces to submit daily, quarterly, and annual *lijin* reports.[20] Within provinces, the contours of

---

14. My discussion does not take up brokerage taxes or salt taxes.
15. By 1890, 65 percent of government revenue came from commercial sources. See Lin, *China Upside Down*, 140–41.
16. Lydia He Liu, *The Clash of Empires: The Invention of China in Modern World Making* (Cambridge, MA: Harvard University Press, 2004), 13.
17. David Pong, "The Income and Military Expenditure of Kiangsi Province in the Last Years (1860–1864) of the Taiping Rebellion," *Journal of Asian Studies* 26, no. 1 (November 1966): 49–65.
18. Stephen Halsey, "Money, Power, and the State: The Origins of the Military-Fiscal State in Modern China," *Journal of the Economic and Social History of the Orient* 56, no. 3 (2013): 392–432.
19. He Wenkai, *Paths towards the Modern Fiscal State: England, Japan, and China* (Cambridge, MA: Harvard University Press, 2013), 155.
20. Halsey, "Money, Power, and the State," 413.

lijin administration varied; procedures, the spatial distribution of collection points, and even its bureaucratic structure changed not infrequently.[21] According to Luo Yudong's classic history of *lijin*, it was typical for provinces to manage *lijin* using a hierarchical bureaucracy staffed with gentry awaiting official posts, which collected taxes at barriers distributed along major thoroughfares and at the entrance to markets. However, it was also the case that officials often collaborated with merchant groups to organize collection in mutually advantageous ways.[22] Sometimes these agreements appointed merchant groups, including wholesalers, to administer *lijin* collection on the state's behalf.

Although commercial taxes had never before been collected on such a large scale for such an extended duration as they were between 1853 and 1911, *lijin* collection replicated some long-standing features of tax collection more generally. The Qing dynasty ran what Christopher Isett has called a "tax-office state" that "depended upon the administrative skills of degree-holding elites to collect the revenue that funded the costs of administration." Elites in this system customarily used office as a conduit for personal income, and office holders routinely collected surcharges, fines, and gifts and engaged in other forms of peculation to fund their offices and supplement their salaries.[23] Such practices also filtered down to lower-level office staff.[24] Within limits, this unofficial augmentation of income (which the Euro-American community referred to as "corruption" and "squeeze") was often accepted by the Qing court as a necessary, if not ideal, part of the costs of administration.[25] If, as Isett puts it, "the Qing state was thus an immense vehicle for facilitating private accumulation through office holding," *lijin* collections created a new frontier for such accumulation.[26] Wealthy families, large wholesalers, and merchant organizations all participated in *lijin* administration in order to protect profits and make profits. Reports of officials cashiered for underreporting *lijin* revenues indicate how far these efforts sometimes went.[27]

---

21. Pong, "Income and Military Expenditure," 57. For a full discussion of different collection methods, see Luo Yudong, 中國釐金史 [History of China's *lijin*], 2 vols. (Shanghai: Shang wu yin shu guan, 1936).
22. Luo, [History of China's *lijin*]; Susan Mann Jones, *Local Merchants and the Chinese Bureaucracy, 1750–1950* (Stanford: Stanford University Press, 1987); William Rowe, *Hankow: Commerce and Society in a Chinese City, 1796–1889* (Stanford: Stanford University Press, 1984).
23. Christopher Isett, "China: The Start of the Great Divergence," in *The Cambridge Economic History of the Modern World*, ed. Stephen Broadberry and Kyoji Fukao (Cambridge: Cambridge University Press, 2021), 1:97–122, here 101.
24. Bradley Reed, *Talons and Teeth: County Clerks and Runners in the Qing Dynasty* (Stanford: Stanford University Press, 2000).
25. Madeline Zelin, *The Magistrate's Tael: Rationalizing Fiscal Reform in Eighteenth Century Ch'ing China* (Berkeley: University of California Press, 1984).
26. Isett, "China," 101.
27. He, *Paths*, 166, 168.

These key features of *lijin*—widespread use, decentralized collection from goods prior to their sale, and integration into practices of personal accumulation—are precisely what made the Qing path toward greater state wealth a focus of foreign merchant ire. If in the post-Taiping era, the quantity of tax revenues, as R. Bin Wong has argued, were never a problem; how they were collected became an issue entangled with geopolitics and Euro-American commercial expansion.[28] What Qing authorities developed as separate revenue streams and pragmatic adaptations to local conditions, their foreign counterparts considered a single widespread threat to capital. First, there were the levies themselves, which British observers considered to be so numerous as to make for a "suicidal" system of state revenue.[29] Second, *lijin* revenues appeared to incentivize provincial officials to ignore or to reject treaty-based tax exemptions. British merchants lodged innumerable complaints with their treaty port consuls over incidents of "illegal" taxation—instances wherein local officials insisted on the collection of local taxes. It is impossible to know just how many of these incidents were in fact illegal taxation and how many were failed attempts at revenue fraud by merchants. What is clear in archival records is the extent to which British and Qing authorities fought over the boundaries that regulated Qing commercial taxation: boundaries between people, boundaries between places, and even boundaries between taxes themselves.

Boil, Then Simmer: A Brief Note on Sino-British Diplomatic Relations, 1860–1880

Before examining disagreements over the nature of Qing domestic taxation, it is helpful to first paint in broad brushstrokes the diplomatic terrain. After the Treaty of Tianjin, Sino-British diplomatic relations settled at a slow simmer. In practice, no one was really happy with the treaty regime. Qing officials suffered regulatory transgressions by foreign firms, disturbances in their revenue collection, and new limits on their administrative autonomy. British merchants routinely complained of violations of their treaty rights and pressed for further concessions. Disputes between the two sides were frequent at the local level and typically escalated to tense diplomatic exchanges between the Zongli yamen and British Legation.

A tone of exasperation pervades both sides of the diplomatic record produced in the imperial capital. The British minister, first Rutherford Alcock (tenure

---

28. R. Bin Wong, "Taxation and Good Governance in China, 1500–1914," in *The Rise of Fiscal States: A Global History, 1500–1914*, ed. Bartolome Yun-Casalilla and Patrick K. O'Brien, with Francisco Comin Comin (Cambridge: Cambridge University Press, 2012), 353–77.
29. Great Britain, Foreign Office, *Diplomatic and Consular Reports on Trade and Finance. China. Reports on the State of Trade at the Treaty Ports of China (1897)* [C.8277-127].

1865–1871) and then Thomas Wade (tenure 1871–1883), insisted that China's domestic taxation was ruining trade, that British merchants were owed compensation for market losses, and that the central government needed to rigorously discipline local officials. Key foreign affairs officials, imperial prince Yixin (奕訢, 1833–1898) and later Li Hongzhang (李鴻章, 1823–1901), countered with suspicions that British merchants abused their treaty privileges, repeatedly explained that extra-treaty commercial taxation was a provincial matter, and trusted that proclamations would settle outstanding issues.

During these decades of discontent, the Qing and British governments also negotiated two treaties. The first set of negotiations involved revising commercial provisions of the Treaty of Tianjin, and was led by Prince Yixin and Alcock. Discussion began in 1868 with a contentious airing of discontent by both sides but ended with an agreement (sometimes referred to in English as the Alcock Convention) that included limited taxation of foreign imports and all Chinese exports intended for markets abroad, regardless of who carried them. The convention, however, which Beijing was ready to implement, was rejected in London because it did not provide enough of what British merchants wanted to hazard what they would give up.[30] The second treaty was the Chefoo Convention, negotiated in 1876, by Alcock's successor, the irascible sinologue Thomas Wade, and the formidable territorial administrator Li Hongzhang, who as the governor-general of Zhili and commissioner of trade at the northern ports, was heavily involved in foreign affairs. In the wake of the dead Alcock Convention, Wade reinvigorated the campaign against Qing domestic taxation, deployed consular officials to systematically gather data on *lijin*, and when opportunity arose, sought to accomplish what Alcock had not.[31] The agreement Li and Wade negotiated initiated significant changes in opium taxation, discussed at length in the next chapter.

---

30. Key documents on the revision negotiations and positions taken by the British merchant community can be found in Great Britain, China. No. 5 (1871), *Correspondence respecting the Revision of the Treaty of Tien-tsin*, reprint (San Francisco: Chinese Materials Center, 1975), hereafter CRRTT. Supplementing this public record, first published in 1871, is Ian Nish, ed., *British Documents on Foreign Affairs: Reports and Papers from the Foreign Office Confidential Print*, pt. 1, series E, vol. 20 (University Publications of America, 1994), hereafter BDFA. The Qing official record of negotiations, including solicited memorials from the provinces, can be found in *Chouban yiwu shimo* (CBYWSM) (digital), TZ, juan 63.

31. Wade summarizes his conduct in Sir T. Wade to Earl of Derby, 14 July 1877, in Nish, BDFA, 22:8–66; For excerpts and summary of *lijin* intelligence gathered through consular network, see TNA, FO 233/83, folio 50–94; "Memorandum by Mr. Wade respecting the Revision of the Treaty of Tien-tsin," CRRTT, 429–67. For an account of Wade's conduct that draws attention to its colonial character, see James L. Hevia, *English Lessons: The Pedagogy of British Imperialism* (Durham, NC: Duke University Press), 150–52.

This chapter reframes these two episodes of treaty negotiation as moments when the looming issue of proper commercial governance crystallized into concrete proposals. I do so by situating these diplomatic negotiations within a larger chorus of voices—those of British consuls and merchants, treaty port newspapermen and courts, local Qing administrators, and ministers representing other treaty signatories—that contested and defended local commercial taxes in the 1860s, '70s, and '80s. Within the broader context these voices generate we more clearly see how capital's border-crossing circuits generated terms of Sino-British relations.

Boundaries between Persons: Sovereignty in the Age of Capital

As we saw in Chapter 3, no one involved in the creation of the first two Sino-British treaties, neither official nor merchant, anticipated the extent to which British trade in China would depend on the collaboration of Chinese persons. Treaty clauses that gave foreign persons permission to travel inland for the purposes of trade and gave them rights of residence at treaty ports created opportunities for direct contact between British firms and a wider network of Chinese buyers and producers. Chinese persons either as employees, partners, or independent middlemen were central to the movement of import and export goods. As these relations intensified (rather than loosened) in the 1860s, British traders quickly tuned into the great extent that British capital reproduction depended on the extra-treaty conditions under which Chinese businesses operated.

Partners in Peril and Canaries in the Coal Mine

In Susan Mann Jones's 1987 study of merchant communities in China, she tells a poignant story of Chinese firms in Ningbo (寧波) during the mid-1860s, whose fortunes soared when the Taiping Rebellion and US Civil War sent exports of silk, tea, and cotton streaming through the port's waterways, only to fall precipitously when those conflicts subsided.[32] These boom years, as Mann tells it, were also a boon for local authorities, who peppered local waterways and roads with *lijin* barriers. Then when the tides of global exports ebbed, the tax stations provoked a wave of complaints that Mann termed "Ningbo's *lijin* resistance movement." Merchants faced the "grim specter of local depression" and petitioned officials for relief.

From the petitions submitted by Ningbo merchants, Mann reconstructed principles of merchant-state relations in the late Qing. Unexpectedly, this affair in Ningbo is also an entry point into foreign complaints about Qing taxation and

---

32. Jones, *Local Merchants*, 138–44.

British efforts to incorporate Chinese persons into treaty-based commercial regulation. Mann found the merchant memorials in a volume of Japanese scholarship, but they are also part of the British Foreign Office archives, which preserved them, in Chinese and English, as enclosures sent by the Ningbo consul to the British minister in Beijing.[33] Within the Foreign Office archive, the papers sit alongside other correspondence, collected from consuls and concerned British merchants, documenting "onerous" local commercial taxes, which by threatening Chinese merchants also threatened British trade. In this archival frame, state-merchant relations in Ningbo also open a door into a years-long campaign to discredit local fiscal regimes and to appropriate Chinese experiences with domestic taxation as evidence that foreign trade was also imperiled. This story goes as follows.

In June 1866, the Ningbo consul, R. J. Forrest, alerted his superior in Beijing that local *lijin* levies had paralyzed trade at Ningbo and prompted disturbances at nearby Taizhou (台州). He learned of the problems through visits to the consulate by several of the area's Chinese merchant groups from whom he later obtained copies of petitions for tax relief presented to the local prefect. The petitions, Forrest summarized, documented excessive taxes in the area—"on goods for permission to enter a market, for leaving the same, and even on their sale in the market. There are import dues, boat taxes, licenses for employing boats, fees for revising tax certificates, and barriers where extortion is invariably practiced." Moreover, Forrest claimed, the levies were not a purely Chinese affair but also imperiled British importers. "That this system affects foreign merchants is sufficiently evident," Forrest wrote. "Some goods are unsalable, although in demand. . . . Foreign goods the moment they leave foreign protection are looked on as valuables from which it is impossible to extort too many contributions."[34]

Forrest's report received a sympathetic hearing in Beijing. British minister Rutherford Alcock wrote to the Zongli yamen on the subject, which in turn asked for reports from the governors in Zhejiang (Ma Xinyi 馬新貽) and Shandong (Yan Jingming 閻敬銘).[35] Although I have not been able to find the governors' reports, what Alcock thought about Forrest's communication from Ningbo comes to the surface a year later, in the fall of 1867, when the Legation incorporated the events at Ningbo into a more general picture of poor governance produced by "arbitrary exactions of the local Mandarins under the head of *lijin* taxes." In a letter to the

---

33. Mann's source is Sasaki Masya, "Ninpo shoninno rikin keigen seigan goshu" [Petitions of Ningbo merchants for lightening *lijin* taxes], *Toyo gakuho* 50, no. 1.
34. Ningbo Consulate to Beijing Legation, No. 17, 11 September 1866, TNA, FO 228/409.
35. Zongli Yamen to British Legation, No. 37, 12 July 1866, trans. Murray, TNA, FO 230/79; Zongli Yamen to British Legation, No. 41, 28 July 1866, trans. Murray, TNA, FO 230/79. Neither the *Chouban yiwu shimo* or the Zongli yamen archive in Taiwan hold copies of the governors' reports. COVID-19-era travel restrictions prevented me from investigating possible alternative repositories.

Zongli yamen, written shortly after Alcock returned from a tour of the treaty ports, the British minister confronted his diplomatic counterparts with claims that not only did British firms "complain their trade is paralyzed," but Chinese traders as well "declare everywhere how grievously their trade suffers under the heavily arbitrary varied burdens laid upon it."[36] The Chinese merchants, Alcock claimed, could not press their case for themselves but nonetheless suffered from the same poor fiscal strategies and "unscrupulous officials" that plagued the foreigner trader. In their suffering, Alcock suggested, Chinese traders and British traders were one and the same.

The British Legation built its case against local taxation from a steady stream of intelligence generated by British consular officials, who offered explicit connections between the fate of Chinese merchants and the fate of British capital. In one such report, written in November 1869, the Ningbo consulate forwarded testimony from two British firms, Rees & Co. and Hudson & Co., which had learned in great detail of the taxes paid by a Shaoxing wine merchant named Zhu Yuanxing.[37] Zhu was from the village of "Shangbeng" where his family had long manufactured wine. On May 30, Zhu left Shaoxing for Hankou with a shipment of three hundred cases of wine. His journey, as Rees and Hudson told it, was one of numerous delays and levies—eighteen in all, sometimes separated by only a few miles. The tale of the journey offered a warning: Zhu spent nearly six weeks in transit and paid so much in taxes that he lost 224 taels on the venture. In their letter to the consul, Rees and Hudson asked, was it "judicious and for the benefit of foreign trade to allow foreign goods, even after they have become property of Chinese, to pass under such exactions as these native goods?"[38] The threat was clear: if foreign trade depended on Chinese partners, the fate of foreign capital was in the hands of the Qing fiscal apparatus.

One striking feature of the concerns voiced at Ningbo in 1866 and again in 1869 is the disregard for jurisdictional distinctions between Chinese trade and foreign trade. The Chinese merchants who petitioned their prefect in Ningbo were not involved in foreign trade but domestic commodity trades: sugar, indigo, and medicines. Neither was Zhu, the wine merchant, a node in circuits of British capital reproduction. But commenting on the letter from Rees and Hudson, the Ningbo consul observed, "The moral I presume . . . is that if *native goods* in native hands are subjected to such ruinous imposts whilst in transit, *foreign goods* in native hands cannot be supposed to escape more easily."[39] Chinese protest and suffering were useful evidence to substantiate the truth and the depth of the problems faced by British commercial capital. Indeed, as Alcock prepared to renegotiate the Treaty

---

36. British Legation to Zongli Yamen, No. 28, 19 September 1867, draft, TNA 228/931.
37. Ningbo Consulate to Beijing Legation, No. 18, 15 November 1869, TNA, FO 228/469.
38. Ningbo Consulate to Beijing Legation, No. 18, 15 November 1869, TNA, FO 228/469, Enclosure no. 1.
39. Ningbo Consulate to Beijing Legation, No. 18, 15 November 1869, TNA, FO 228/469.

of Tianjin, he observed that British merchants across the treaty ports unanimously clamored against "the excessive taxation to which all the articles entering into their trade are subjected." According to intelligence the legation had gathered, "it is not only excessive in degree, becoming prohibitive in some cases, and capricious and unequal in its levy at different ports or places in the interior, *but illegal even in a Chinese point of view*."[40] Domestic circulation of China-made, Chinese-owned goods offered useful illustrations of a point that was becoming central to British diplomacy in China: the uncontrolled and rapacious nature of domestic taxation.

British commercial capital was also concerned about levies taken from Chinese merchants because the latter were key participants in the chain of buying and selling that generated British capital returns. This concern, Chapter 3 showed, surfaced early in the 1860s, most visibly in relation to treaty privileges and the tea trade. As the decade progressed and worries persisted, British consuls and British firms attempted to protect Chinese hands and British profits from local taxes. In Ningbo, the British consul appealed fines levied on Chinese dealers of "foreign manufactories."[41] In Dengzhou (登州, today's Penglai 蓬萊), a British opium dealer instructed the Chinese shop retailing his product to not pay the local *lijin* on account that the drugs originated with a British firm.[42] At Shanghai, foreign purchasers of silk transported there by Chinese firms asked for refunds of the *lijin* the Chinese firms had paid during transit.[43] These actions expressed the crux of the issue from the British point of view. Chinese persons, who sold imports and exports, were an integral part of British capital accumulation. The ultimate sale of imports came after the Chinese bearer of the goods had passed through his country's tax apparatus, and the cost of exports rose in proportion to inland taxes paid by Chinese firms. Thus, despite clear regulatory distinctions between foreign traders and Chinese merchants, Euro-American capital was very much interested in, indeed dependent on, what happened to Qing subjects. As the German minister in China put it sometime later, "It is a question of taxing the goods and not the person of the sender."[44]

---

40. Sir Rutherford Alcock to Lord Stanley, No. 33, 23 December 1867, CRRTT, 81.
41. "Copy of a circular of instructions upon a report by the superintendent of customs at Ningpo, of the punishment of the Chuan-ta and other dealers in foreign manufactories (lit. dealers in cloth), to the effect that the treaty is not to be broken for the sake of lijin," 23 April 1872, Legation translation, TNA, FO 233/83.
42. Consul Meadows to British Legation, No. 22, 17 September 1867, TNA, FO 228/913, Enclosure no. 5.
43. Zongli Yamen to British Legation, No. 3, 8 January (1864), trans. British Legation, TNA FO 228/936.
44. German Minister Von Brandt to the Zongli Yamen, 23 January 1886, Enclosure no. 1, also in Mr. O'Conor to the Marquis of Salisbury, No. 49, 4 February 1886, TNA, Confidential Print (Numerical Series), 881/5414, 27.

Commodities and Sovereign Borders: Exchange or Circulation?

As the date for revision of the Treaty of Tianjin approached, the accumulation of documentary evidence and sheer persistence of merchant complaints convinced the British Legation that Chinese power to levy taxes from Chinese persons "might destroy all foreign commerce with China at any given time by simply imposing at their pleasure prohibitive duties and exactions."[45] Yet the British establishment in China had very narrow grounds on which to push for changes in what was a domestic matter. Even the metropolitan center of British global commercial expansion—the London-based Board of Trade—acknowledged the sovereign right of the Qing Empire to tax its own subjects as it saw fit, even when foreign goods were involved.[46] British officials had to admit that only specifically granted treaty rights provided any possibility for limiting Qing domestic taxation, and it was a matter of dispute in China whether these rights applied to persons or goods.

On the other side of the episodes in Ningbo and Dengzhou mentioned above were Qing officials. They asserted that political sovereignty over Chinese persons meant the collection of *lijin* was completely outside the bounds of legitimate foreign interest or action (*yu yangshang haowu ganshe* 與洋商毫無干涉). "The trades are separate" (*zhongwai tongshang xiangxi fenbie* 中外通商向係分別), argued the Dengzhou *daotai* Chao Lubing (抄錄兵), pointing out that boundaries respecting this division were agreed on in the treaties between China and England.[47] Selling opium to a Chinese retailer, Chao argued, made the opium a "Chinese good" (*zhongguo huowu* 中國貨物)—that is to say, one coded by the political power (read: regulations) of the Qing state. Chao's colleague in Ningbo argued a similar case when cargoes of British imports were seized by officials at a tax barrier on the city's north side. When "British goods had passed into the hands of Chinese merchants, they ceased to have any protection from native charges," he informed the British consul.[48]

Several years later, in interviews with Li Hongzhang in 1874 and with members of the Zongli yamen in 1875, the British Legation heard echoes of the arguments offered at Ningbo and Dengzhou. In these conversations, British minister Thomas Wade and legation Chinese secretary William Mayers tried to erase the distinction between foreign goods in foreign hands and foreign goods in Chinese hands. No

---

45. British Legation to Zongli Yamen, No. 28, 19 September 1867, draft, TNA 228/931. Rees and Hudson used similar language. Treaties, they argued, existed so as to not "leave the power in the hands of the Chinese government to curtail, weaken, and eventually ruin all trade in foreign goods." See Ningbo Consulate to Beijing Legation, No. 18, 15 November 1869, TNA, FO 228/469, Enclosure no. 1.
46. Foreign Office to T. F. Wade, 23 September 1870, TNA, FO 228/488.
47. Consul Meadows to British Legation, No. 22, 17 September 1867, TNA, FO 228/913, Enclosure no. 5 (Chinese copy).
48. Ningbo Consulate to Beijing Legation, No. 12, 21 April 1869, TNA, FO 228/469.

matter the particular language of specific treaty provisions, they argued, the intent of the treaties had been to limit the amount of duty the Chinese government was entitled to take from British imports.[49] In response, Zongli yamen officials insisted on sovereignty over Qing subjects: "no amount of taxation imposed on British imports once these were in the hands of Chinese, could be regarded as a breach of treaty."[50] Even as the legation painted *lijin* as an "oppressive and irregular" levy, the yamen defended the tax on the grounds that it was *"levied only from Chinese subjects."*[51]

At stake in the question of whether taxation acted upon a good or a person was the relationship between political power and capital: did political power set the terms of capital accumulation or did capital accumulation set the terms for governance? For the British it was clearly the latter. The consular and merchant intelligence networks that busily decoded domestic taxation made all too visible a threat that Qing sovereignty posed, not to British merchants who were clearly protected by treaty, but rather to British capital and capital more generally. Merchants complaints, moreover, make clear for our purposes here, that whether the commodity was a cargo of Malwa opium for sale in a treaty port or a chest of tea transiting through Hankou, for the British establishment in China, the proper standpoint for governance was not whose "hands" carried the commodity but whose capital animated its movement.[52] Qing resistance, on the other hand, helps us better understand how, as a standpoint for commercial governance this ontological claim invoked a correlative erasure of political boundaries and sovereignty. Qing officials insisted that the empire's territorial boundaries coded and recoded goods. Exports began their movement as Chinese goods; imports ended their existence as British goods once they were sold to Qing subjects. Commercial governance that taxed goods not persons would have institutionalized global trade as an unbroken circulation of capital through time and across space. Qing authorities countered this deterritorializing/reterritorializing push with an effort to maintain institutions of exchange

---

49. "Journal of Transactions with the Governor General Li Respecting the Peruvian Treaty and Other Matters," 3 May 1874, TNA, FO 233/62; "Memorandum of Visit to G. Secy Li, 30 August 1875," TNA, FO 233/62.
50. British Legation, 3 February 1875, Record Book of Interviews with Chinese Authorities, TNA, FO 233/35, folio 70.
51. British Legation, 24 January 1875, Record Book of Interviews with Chinese Authorities, TNA, FO 233/35, folio 68; emphasis mine. Ministers in the Zongli yamen at the time included Mao Changxi (毛昶熙, 1817–1882), Dong Xun (董恂, 1810–1892), Shen Baozhen (沈葆楨, 1820–1879),and Chong Hou (崇厚, 1826–1893). By this time, Mao, Dong, and Chong had all spent time on the front line of treaty administration as the northern superintendent of trade (*beiyang dachen* 北洋大臣).
52. This standpoint expresses in naturalized form Marx's analysis of capital as subject. Karl Marx, *Capital: A Critique of Political Economy*, vol. 1, trans. Ben Fowkes (New York: Vintage Books, 1977), 254–57; Moishe Postone, *Time, Labor, and Social Domination: A Reinterpretation of Marx's Critical Theory* (Cambridge: Cambridge University Press, 1993), 269–70.

through which they would continue to exercise territorial and personal sovereignty. In lieu of governing circulating commodities, the state would continue to govern persons with particular political identities and obligations.

Boundaries within Space: Territorial Implications of Commodity Capital Flows

It was not just political jurisdiction over people that an expansive interpretation of the treaty regime threatened. Commodity capital flows under the treaty framework also recoded the boundaries that structured inland fiscal administration. Whereas Qing authorities used extant political institutions and jurisdictions to structure the movement of goods, the British establishment in China agitated for an inversion: political jurisdictions would disappear in the wake of the commodity's movement.

Provincial Deterritorialization, Imperial Reterritorialization

The treaty stipulation that offered the most radical reimagining of the Qing Empire was the transit pass. The privilege, initially envisioned in the Treaty of Nanjing and outlined in the Treaty of Tianjin, limited taxation on foreign imports and foreign-owned exports if they paid a specific charge (transit duty) that went to the customs account of the central government. The pass was popular with both foreign and Chinese merchants. At times, the latter even passed domestic commodities, such as sugar grown in Fujian, through Hong Kong in order to have the cargo recoded as foreign trade and thereby eligible for transit passes. According to Anglophone reports, transit passes were the savior of trade at Ningbo in the mid-1860s, the reason British textiles reached more distant inland markets in the 1870s, the impetus for the relocation of ginseng processing from Canton to Hong Kong, and testament to the enduring wrongness of the Qing fiscal system, which the foreign community felt delegated too much commercial tax authority to the provinces.

As it succeeded in lowering some circulation costs, the transit pass also generated its own controversial territoriality. The transit pass claimed for its cargo a unitary "free" transit zone, coterminous with the entire imperial domain, and within this domain, the pass "protected" extra-imperial circuits of capital accumulation from delay or additional cost. Yet occupying this very same physical space of empire were the multitudes of *lijin* collectorates, each an expression of delegated fiscal authority and the more composite territoriality engineered by the practice of "governing to accommodate local conditions" (*yindi zhiyi* 因地制宜).

The capacity of the transit pass to reterritorialize Qing territory was perhaps most clearly visible in the tea-growing regions proximate to the Yangzi River, where the provincial boundaries between Hubei, Anhui, and Jiangxi all converged near the treaty port of Jiujiang (九江). Jiujiang was administratively part of Jiangxi province, but it was also a closer mart for certain Hubei tea districts than the Hubei provincial treaty port of Hankou, farther upriver. In these relatively affluent provinces, which had also been the site of fighting between imperial forces and Taiping rebels, authorities had to balance the competing imperatives to remit collected revenue to other locations throughout the empire at Beijing's order and to maintain sufficient funds to meet extraordinary provincial expenditures, including local reconstruction projects. Tea was a large source of revenue for authorities in these provinces, and in the mid-1860s, each province issued regulations to channel leaves to provincial marts where *lijin* collectorates could first tax the tea before it left the province. Teas grown in Hubei, for instance, were required to transit through Hankou and pay tax there so that each province, in the words of the Hubei Lijin Committee, would "receive what is properly its own, without making more than one charge."[53] To further protect this important local revenue, authorities in Hubei and Jiangxi agreed that neither province would issue transit passes for goods purchased in the other province. Authorities at Ningbo in Zhejiang Province also declined to issue transit passes for tea districts in neighboring Anhui because they knew authorities in Anhui would not acknowledge the passes.[54]

These policies incited a torrent of British claims against Qing authorities for wrongful taxation and failure to respect the treaties. In Ningbo, the British consul estimated that in September 1866 alone, he had written nearly one hundred letters on the subject of transit passes.[55] When such reports made their way from the treaty ports to Beijing, treaty language allowed the British Legation to recode the local fiscal strategy as acts of "uncontrolled action" by provincial officials. In an angry communication to the Zongli yamen, the British minister Rutherford Alcock charged that refusal to grant interprovincial transit passes fell afoul the wording of treaty clauses. "It is nowhere laid down in the Treaty, or any subsequent Regulation based

---

53. Jiujiang Consulate to Beijing Legation, "Report on the Working of the Transit Certificate System at Jiujiang," 1 February 1864, TNA FO 228/371; Jiujiang Consulate to Beijing Legation, No. 7, 17 February 1864, TNA, FO 228/371; Beijing Legation to Zongli Yamen, No. 21, draft, 12 January 1867, TNA, FO 228/931.
54. Ningbo Consulate to Beijing Legation, No. 18, 29 September 1866, TNA, FO 228/409; Consul Gardner to Li Futai, No. 59, 12 October 1866, TNA, FO 670/97C; Ningbo Daotai to IMC Commissioner, No. 134, 4 September 1866, *China and the West: The Maritime Customs Service Archive from the Second Historical Archives of China, Nanjing*, ed. Robert A. Bickers and Hans van de Ven (Reading, UK: Primary Source Microfilm, 2004), microfilm reel 174, (hereafter CMC microfilm); Ningbo Daotai to IMC Commissioner, No. 189, 27 November 1866, CMC microfilm reel 174; Ningbo Daotai to IMC Commissioner, No. 205, 20 December 1866, CMC microfilm reel 174; Ningbo Daotai to IMC Commissioner, No. 1, 4 January 1867, CMC microfilm reel 174.
55. Ningbo Consulate to Beijing Legation, No. 18, 29 September 1866, TNA, FO 228/409.

Boundary Struggles 157

Figure 5.1: This map, centered on Anhui, shows the approximate borders of Anhui, Hubei, Jiangsu, Jiangxi and Zhejiang. Map amended to clarify provincial borders and show location of Jiujiang. This section of the Yangzi River forms the border between Hubei and Jiangxi. Source: China, Imperial Maritime Customs, *Decennial Report on Trade at the Treaty Ports of China, 1881–1891* (Shanghai: Statistical Department of the Inspectorate General, 1892).

thereon," he wrote to the Zongli yamen, "that any pass or passport taken out by a British subject at any open port shall not be valid at any place through the Empire, open to the visits of the Foreign merchant for purposes of trade."[56] Imperial authorities agreed. So although the Hubei government insisted that "the [British] merchant must of course conform to the regulations of the High Authorities of Hubei," offices more closely tied to treaty administration, such as the imperial commissioner of trade at Shanghai, countered that transit passes were valid and necessary for interprovincial commerce.[57]

By committing itself to its treaty obligations, imperial officers in Beijing became coauthors in the alternative territoriality institutionalized in the transit pass. In part, upholding these obligations was necessary to keep at bay British threats that "Her Majesty's Government" would not indefinitely "suffer" the Chinese system of taxation.[58] But authorities in Beijing were also committed to accruing treaty transit taxes as funds for the "*guojia*" (國家, state).[59] Following from these two commitments, the empire's new foreign affairs apparatus institutionalized against the spatiality of *yindi zhiyi*, the unitary spatial imaginary immanent within the transit pass. The result was two contending forms of territoriality practiced at different levels of the Qing government—that produced by the idiosyncratic management of local circumstances for local needs and that which subordinated local initiatives and priorities to international obligations. In an extreme example of international subordination, under the transit pass regime, even simple modifications of paperwork protocols had to be devised by imperial commissioners in conjunction with foreign consuls and submitted to the Zongli yamen and foreign ministers in Beijing for application at all ports.[60]

Although the priority given to central government revenues by authorities in Beijing was not out of the ordinary, the simultaneous operations of *lijin* and transit passes, in the same spaces and over the same activities, gave the exercise of any inland revenue prerogative an antagonistic bent. As He Wenkai has pointed out, Qing fiscal management depended on "assignment orders to allocate revenue from regions of collection" to meet spending needs elsewhere. This meant that what provinces did not collect in *lijin* was not available to meet their obligations as dictated by Beijing. Stated somewhat differently, to uphold its international obligations and to keep foreign aggression at bay, the central government undermined its own system of fiscal administration. Its quota-based fiscal operations and system of interprovincial

---

56. Beijing Legation to Zongli Yamen, No. 21, draft, 12 January 1867, TNA, FO 228/931.
57. Jiujiang Consulate to Beijing Legation, No. 7, 17 February 1864, TNA, FO 228/371; Daotai to IMC Commissioner, No. 195, 7 December 1866, CMC microfilm reel 174.
58. Beijing Legation to Zongli Yamen, No. 28, 19 September 1867, draft, TNA, FO 228/931.
59. CBYWSM Tongzhi chao, juan 63, 25.2.
60. British Legation to Zongli Yamen, draft, 31 December 1853, TNA, FO 228/914.

aid became increasingly dysfunctional during the treaty era.[61] Dysfunction, in turn, bred resistance. In 1870, several years after the imperial commissioner reprimanded Hubei authorities, the Imperial Maritime Customs (IMC) commissioner at Jiujiang reported that Jiangxi officials again refused to recognize transit passes issued at Hankou, and Hubei authorities again would not recognize passes issued at Jiujiang.[62] Continued resistance by provincial authorities to reterritorialization by the transit pass in turn fed a growing sense within the Euro-American community that the central government was either unwilling or unable to exercise its rightful prerogatives and that nothing short of full-scale fiscal overhaul would secure foreign trade.

Lijin in the Ports

A second front in the struggle to recode Qing territory to make it more amenable to capital reproduction were the treaty ports themselves. Qing authorities felt the ports were an ideal place to collect *lijin* because commerce collected within them. Yet, for precisely the same reason, the British community and others wanted to bar *lijin* from their limits. Unsurprisingly, a primary site of this contested reterritorialization effort was Shanghai, where high volumes of trading activity were mirrored by high incidence of *lijin* taxation. In the mid-1860s, levies included a 3 percent ad valorem tax on imported textiles and a 10 percent ad valorem tax on coal (used commercially to fire tea). Opium, prior to its transit inland, paid four taxes: one in the Foreign Settlement, one at its East Gate, one to a merchant group that managed much of the opium trade, and one for local defense funds.[63] Ten years later, according to some (histrionic) estimates, nearly every good that transferred from a foreign importer to a native firm paid at least a 2.5 percent ad valorem tax to the "tax collectors who stand at the very doors of [the] hongs."[64]

Although Shanghai may have been exemplary, it was not alone. In 1867, opium imported into Fuzhou (福州) paid ten different local fees and taxes.[65] In 1870, foreign imports at Xiamen (廈門) paid separate charges to the *lijin* office, the *lijin* bank, an in-door department and an out-door department (both associated with the *lijin* collectorate), an office halfway between the customs jetty and the *lijin* office, and at least one barrier.[66] Reports from Zhenjiang (鎮江) the same year described the operation of at least seven different *lijin* collectorates all "taking toll one after

---

61. He, *Paths*, 154–55.
62. IMC, *Trade Reports for 1870*, 131.
63. Great Britain, *Commercial Reports from Her Majesty's Consuls in China, 1866* (London: Harrison), 3.
64. "Lekin Levies in the Settlements," NCHSCG, 4 July 1874; "Local Squeezes," NCHSCG, 15 May 1875.
65. IMC, *Trade Reports for 1867*, 47.
66. IMC, *Trade Reports for 1870*, 97.

40   TRADE REPORT.

(Enclosure No. 1.)

Comparative Table of (approximate) Barrier Charges and Transit Duty.

N.B.—In "Barrier Charges" are included *li* (厘), *shui* (税), and *chuan* (捐), as paid by Native merchants.

The table is arranged alphabetically.

Description of Merchandize.	To or From what Place.	Classifier of Quantity.	Barrier Charges H. K. Tls	Transit Duty H. K. Tls	Barrier Charges are what % of value of Article.
Cotton Cloth, Native,	Hai-mên,	Pecul,	1.2.3.5	0.7.5.0	2.6
	T'ung-chow,		1.2.3.5	0.7.5.0	2.6
Cotton, Raw,	Hai-mên,	Pecul,	0.8.2.4	0.1.7.5	5.4
	T'ung-chow,		0.8.2.4	0.1.7.5	5.4
Glass,	Yang-chow,	100 Sq. feet,	0.1.7.6	0.0.7.5	4.6
Iron,	Chang-chow,	Pecul,	0.1.4.1	0.0.6.2	4.6
	Ju-kao,		0.2.3.8	0.0.6.2	7.9
	Liu-ho,		0.2.3.5	0.0.6.2	7.83
	Nanking,		0.2.3.5	0.0.6.2	7.83
	Ning-kuo-fu,		0.2.8.2	0.0.6.2	9.4
	Hsien-nü-miao,		0.2.5:2	0.0.6.2	8.4
	Ta-chiang,		0.1.5.7	0.0.6.2	5.23
	T'ai-chow,		0.2.7.5	0.0.6.2	9.16
	Tan-yang,		0.0.7.0	0.0.6.2	2.33
	Yang-chow,		0.1.1.1	0.0.6.2	3.7
	Yêu-ch'êng,		0.2.5.2	0.0.6.2	8.4
Sandalwood,	Lü-chow-fu,	Pecul,	1.0.3.9	0.2.0.0	26.4
	Hsien-nü-miao,		0.8.2.4	0.2.0.0	21.1
	Ta-chiang,		0.4.7.0	0.2.0.0	12
	Wu-hu,		1.0.0.0	0.2.0.0	25.9
	Yang-chow,		0.3.2.9	0.2.0.0	8.19
Shirtings, Grey,	Ch'ing-chiang-p'u,	Piece,	0.1.7.6	0.0.4.0	8
	Hsü-chow,		0.2.5.9	0.0.4.0	11.8
	Huai-an,		0.1.7.6	0.0.4.0	8
	Lü-chow,		0.2.4.7	0.0.4.0	11.2
	Nanking,		0.2.0.0	0.0.4.0	9.1
	Sha-kou,		0.1.7.6	0.0.4.0	8
	Shao-po,		0.2.2.3	0.0.4.0	10
	Hsien-nü-miao,		0.2.2.3	0.0.4.0	10
	Wu-hu,		0.2.4.7	0.0.4.0	11.2
	Yang-chow,		0.1.1.7	0.0.4.0	5.3
Shirtings, White,	Ch'ing-chiang-p'u,	Piece,	0.1.7.6	0.0.4.0	7.4
	Huai-an,		0.1.7.6	0.0.4.0	7.4
	Sha-kou,		0.1.7.6	0.0.4.0	7.4
	Shao-po,		0.2.2.3	0.0.4.0	9.9
	Hsien-nü-miao,		0.2.2.3	0.0.4.0	9.9
	Yang-chow,		0.1.1.7	0.0.4.0	5
Sugar, Brown,	Ch'ing-chiang-p'u,	Pecul,	0.4.0.5	0.0.6.0	13.5
	Nanking,		0.2.3.5	0.0.6.0	7.8
	Shao-po,		0.2.6.7	0.0.6.0	8.8
T-Cloths,	Ch'ing-chiang-p'u,	Piece,	0.1.1.7	0.0.4.0	5.3
	Lü-chow-fu,		0.2.4.7	0.0.4.0	11.2
	Hsien-nü-miao,		0.2.2.3	0.0.4.0	10
	Yang-chow,		0.1.7.6	0.0.4.0	8

Figure 5.2: Comparative table of barrier charges (*lijin*) and (treaty) transit duties on major articles of the British import trade, Zhenjiang, 1868. Source: China, Imperial Maritime Customs, *Reports on Trade at the Treaty Ports in China for the Year 1868* (Shanghai: Inspector General of Customs, 1869), 40.

96   TRADE REPORT.

TABLE showing the COST of INLAND CARRIAGE, TAXES, &c.; of some of the PRINCIPAL IMPORTS and EXPORTS.

Description of Goods.	From.	To.	Distance. Miles.	Charge of Carriage.	Taxes levied en route by Local Government.	Villages.	Total.
				Dollars.	Dollars.	Dollars.	Dollars.
INWARDS:—							
Opium, ... per Chest.	Swatow, ... 汕頭	An Poo, ... 巷埠	11	3.00	16.50	1.50	21.00
Cotton Yarn, ... ,, Bale.	,, ... ,,	,, ... ,,	11	0.40	...	...	0.40
Opium, ... ,, Chest.	,, ... ,,	Chaou Yang, ... 潮陽	11	3.00	16.50	1.50	21.00
Bean Cakes, per 100 Pieces = 50 Peculs.	,, ... ,,	,, ... 潮陽	11	3.00	..	...	3.00
Opium, ... per Chest.	,, ... ,,	Ne Yang. ...... 內洋	19	5.00	16.50	1.50	23.00
Cotton Yarn, ... ,, Bale.	,, ... ,,	,, ... ,,	19	0.40	..	...	0.40
Opium, ... ,, Chest.	,, ... ,,	Cheng Hae, ... 澄海	22	3.00	16.50	1.50	21.00
Ground Nut Cakes, ... ,, Pecul.	,, ... ,,	,, ... ,,	22	0.08	...	...	0.08
Opium, ... ,, Chest.	,, ... ,,	Chaou Chow-fu, 潮州府	33	7.00	16.50	1.50	25.00
Cotton Piece Goods, ... ,, Piece.	,, ... ,,	,, ... ,,	33	0.02	0.08	...	0.10
Woollen ,, ,, ... ,, ,,	,, ... ,,	,, ... ,,	33	0.04	0.28	...	0.32
Cotton Yarn, ... ,, Bale.	,, ... ,,	,, ... ,,	33	0.50	...	...	0.50
Ground Nut Cakes, ... ,, Pecul.	,, ... ,,	,, ... ,,	33	0.06	...	...	0.06
Opium, ... ,, Chest.	,, ... ,,	Hai Yang, ... 海陽	33	13.00	16.50	1.50	31.00
,, ... ,, ,,	,, ... ,,	Kea Ying Chow 嘉應州	163	13.00	16.50	1.50	31.00
,, ... ,, ,,	,, ... ,,	Kee Yang, ... 揭陽	44	4.00	16.50	1.50	22.00
Bean Cakes, per 100 Pieces = 50 Peculs.	,, ... ,,	,, ... ,,	44	4.00	...	...	4.00
Opium, ... per Chest.	,, ... ,,	Hwang Kang, 黃岡	45	3.00	16.50	1.50	21.00
OUTWARDS:—							
Paper, ... per Pecul.	Ting Chow-fu,. 汀州府	Chaou Chow-fu, 潮州府	274	0.33	...	...	0.33
China Ware, Coarse, ... ,, ,,	Kaou-peh, ... 高埠	,, ,,	52	0.04	0.10	...	0.14
,, ,, ,, ... ,, ,,	Chaou Chow-fu, 潮州府	Swatow, ... 汕頭	33	0.06	...	...	0.06
,, ,, ,, ... ,, ,,	Kaou Peh, ... 高埠	,, ... ,,	85	0.10	0.05	...	0.15
Sugar, Brown and White, . ,, 100 Bags.	Poo Ning, ... 普甯	,, ... ,,	59	15.00	3.30	...	18.30
,, ,, ,, ,, ,, ,, ,,	Kwang Kang, 黃岡	,, ... ,,	45	10.00	15.50	...	25.50
,, ,, ,, ,, ,, ,, ,,	Kee Yang, ... 揭陽	,, ... ,,	44	6.00	13.00	...	19.00
,, ,, ,, ,, ,, ,, ,,	Hai Yang, ... 海陽	,, ... ,,	33	10.00	3.30	...	13.30
Paper, ... ,, Pecul.	Chaou Chow-fu, 潮州府	,, ... ,,	33	0.06	0.04	...	0.10
Sugar, Brown and White,... ,, 100 Bags.	Chaou Yang, ... 潮陽	,, ... ,,	11	5.00	6.00	...	11.00

Figure 5.3: Table of *lijin* levies on imports and exports passing through Shantou, 1868. Source: China, Imperial Maritime Customs, *Reports on Trade at the Treaty Ports in China for the Year 1868* (Shanghai: Inspector General of Customs, 1869), 96.

another on the same bale of goods at the same station."[67] Around Hangzhou (杭州), the wine merchant Zhu Yuanxing, whose travels were detailed by Rees and Hudson, paid levies at inspection stations only miles apart from each other.[68]

These features of *lijin* collection—the multiple authorities and the multiple levies—expressed both its logic and its mode of administration. *Lijin* was a levy on goods and businesses, so from one point of view, it made good sense to collect it where goods and businesses collected. Ports, officials at the Zongli yamen argued, were the "most important preserve" of *lijin*, and if the tax was not collected in the ports, it would be impossible to collect it at all.[69] The multiplication of tax authorities, meanwhile, was the product of either the effort of a central *lijin* office to prevent smuggling (as in Xiamen) or the effect of organizing *lijin* collections according to trade. Furthermore, when political authorities delegated collection to merchant groups, it took on a fragmented character as each trade organized levies independently of others.

From the standpoint of total capital reproduction, these features of *lijin* collection were worrisome. Whereas a silk merchant might care only about taxes on silk, if one looked at commerce in toto, as the foreign community tended to do, the multiplicity of *lijin* levies made them appear pervasive. Rendered as a pervasive practice, the taxes were not merely a nuisance but a threat to the entire project of capital accumulation institutionalized in commercial treaties. As Alcock put it to Prince Yixin, "If taxes can be imposed by the local authorities upon staples of foreign trade at the ports without limit . . . any provincial authority without such limitation might make foreign trade impossible at his pleasure."[70]

As in other instances when the foreign community feared sovereign Qing prerogatives, Alcock and others to mobilize the language of treaty rights to limit the exercise of that sovereignty. In this case, however, treaties provided few grounds from which to protest municipal *lijin*. Treaties offered explicit provisions to protect goods "in transit" but did not stipulate where transit began. In light of this difficulty, the British diplomatic-commercial establishment advanced two arguments: The first was that treaties had re-created ports into a new kind of space freed from taxation.

---

67. W. G. Stronach, "Memorandum upon the Chinese Revenue System as related to the Transit Dues Commutation Scheme," 21 February 1870, *Chinese Secretary's Office, Volume 11, Transit Dues and Likin*, TNA, FO 233/83, folio 63–72.
68. Enclosure No. 1 in Consul Fittock No. 18, 15 November 1869, TNA, FO 228/469. The letter from Rees and Hudson enumerates individual barriers and levies paid at each.
69. Hugh Fraser, "Minute of a Meeting of the Commission of the Yamen," 19 June 1868, Inclosure 21 in No. 76, CRRTT, 209; Hugh Fraser, "Minute of a Meeting of the Mixed Commission at the British Legation, 27 June 1868," Inclosure 22 in No. 76, CRRTT, 209–10. Comments attributed to Zongli yamen officials.
70. Beijing Legation to Zongli Yamen, 5 July 1866, draft, TNA, FO 228/928.

The second was that foreign municipal administration in treaty ports created areas where Chinese persons came under foreign protection against domestic taxation.

One representative case of the Shanghai-based campaign against port *lijin* begins with a Portuguese businessman named Pedro Loureiro, resident in the city's Foreign Settlement, who contested a Qing seizure of opium he claimed belonged to him. The case, heard in 1874 by Shanghai's Mixed Court, was not unusual. A Chinese man transported several balls of opium within the limits of the settlement and was apprehended there by representatives of a group authorized by Qing territorial authorities to collect *lijin* from opium. Finding no evidence that the opium had paid *lijin*, the group charged the Chinese carrier with smuggling. In court, Loureiro claimed the opium was his property, the man was his employee, and the collection of the *lijin* tax was illegal.[71] In contesting the confiscation and the legality of the *lijin* tax, Loureiro raised two questions: what authority properly authorized detentions of Chinese persons in foreign employ, and was the *lijin* tax or any other tax by the Chinese territorial authorities recognized by the Shanghai Municipal Council (SMC)?[72]

Loureiro's questions were not his alone. For several years, Chinese authorities and the Anglo-American council running the Foreign Settlement (SMC) had wrangled over execution of Chinese legal jurisdiction within the limits of the Foreign Settlement, and at times, the SMC claimed that its practice of municipal administration assumed that China had yielded territorial jurisdiction.[73] To a large extent, this latter claim was legally dubious. Even the Foreign Office in London saw nothing in international law to support the council's position.[74] At the same time, however, if there were grounds on which it could be possible to practically limit the exercise of Qing sovereign jurisdiction, authorities in London and Shanghai agreed that

---

71. "Mixed Court," NCHSCG, 27 June 1874.
72. Pedro Loureiro to the Secretary of the Municipal Council, 20 June 1874, Shanghai Municipal Council Archives, Shanghai Municipal Archive, U1-2-260. Hereafter SMCA.
73. SMCA, U1-2-032-568. The Foreign Settlement and its structures of governance had gradually developed through diplomatic negotiations and regulatory revision, which took place without the substantive involvement of Qing authorities. See *The Shanghai Land Regulations: Origins and Purposes of the Present Code. Extracts from the Minutes of the Land-Renters' Meeting Held at Shanghai, 11th July, 1854* (Shanghai, 1854); "Law Reports," NCHSCG, 1 April 1875; Pär Kristoffer Cassel, *Grounds of Judgment: Extraterritoriality and Imperial Power in Nineteenth-Century China and Japan* (Oxford: Oxford University Press, 2012), 64–66.
74. A. M. Kotenev, *Shanghai: Its Mixed Court and Council* (Shanghai: North China Daily News & Herald, 1925), 14. In 1863, the Foreign Office instructed British minister Frederick Bruce that "the lands situated within the limits of the British Settlement are without a doubt Chinese territory, and it cannot reasonably be held that the fact of mere residence within those limits exempts Chinese subjects for fulfilling their natural obligations." Three years later, Minister Alcock again represented the government's view that "indisputable rights of jurisdiction on the part of the sovereign of China on Chinese soil over its own subjects." See "Letter by Sir Rutherford Alcock regarding Municipal Government in Shanghai," 16 July 1866, SMCA U1-2-032-576.

taxation was it. "Special exactions or acts of oppression" could warrant SMC efforts to better define the reach of foreign prerogatives.[75]

Lijin was a perfect fit for the occasion. The prevailing British interpretation of China's treaty obligations held that the Chinese government had consented to a contractual and commonsensical limit on their power to tax. Namely, because treaties explicitly levied customs duties and transit duties at specific rates, they also barred any further taxation on items of foreign trade. "Nothing can be clearer," Alcock explained to the Foreign Office during 1868 treaty revision negotiations, "as to right of [British] exemption from further charges."[76] To levy additional taxes once a foreign merchant sold the goods to a Chinese counterpart "was equivalent to that of a direct import duty in its action, and affected both the sale of the goods to the native dealer, and their consumption in the interior."[77] Interpreted in this way, the treaty recoded the collection of *lijin* within the Foreign Settlement, which was roughly coterminous with the port, as double taxation, which in the parlance of the day was "oppressive."

In the Loureiro case, the British Supreme Court of China and Japan opined that to allow the Chinese government to tax opium in the port under the cover that it maintained a right to tax it in the "interior" was "to strike a fatal blow at the root of all commercial treaties, because it gives another meaning to the infliction of 'import duties.'"[78] Other legal authorities in the port concurred. A young lawyer solicited by the SMC, W. V. Drummond, who was barely three years resident in Shanghai, argued that taxation of imported goods, after sale to a Chinese and before their movement to an "inland" region, made a mockery of the language of the treaty: "I can see nothing to justify our support of this argument which amounts to saying that immediately opium has left the possession of the foreign importer and passed into the possession of a Chinese, even though lying in a [warehouse] in Shanghai it is no longer at the port, and has passed into the interior!"[79] If, for Drummond, who went on to be one of the most respected (and richest) lawyers in Shanghai, the

---

75. "Letter by Sir Rutherford Alcock regarding Municipal Government in Shanghai," 16 July 1866, SMCA U1-2-032-576.
76. Sir R. Alcock to Lord Stanley, 22 January 1868, CRRTT, 100–102.
77. Hugh Fraser, "Minute of a Meeting of the Commission of the Yamen," 19 June 1868, Inclosure 21 in No. 76, CRRTT, 209; Rutherford Alcock, "Memorandum by Sir R. Alcock," Inclosure 23 in No. 76, CRRTT, 210–12.
78. "Walker v. Malcolm," *North China Herald and Supreme Court Gazette*, 1 May 1875.
79. Drummond to Shanghai Municipal Council, 9 June 1875, TNA, FO 233/83. On Drummond, see "Leading Residents of Shanghai," *Twentieth Century Impressions of Hong Kong, Shanghai, and Other Treaty Ports of China*, last edited August 31, 2018, https://en.wikisource.org/wiki/Page:Twentieth_Century_Impressions_of_Hongkong,_Shanghai,_and_other_Treaty_Ports_of_China.djvu/524. He also figures in Cassel's history of the Shanghai Mixed Court in *Grounds of Judgment*.

territoriality implied by the terms "port" and "interior" trumped the "natural obligations" of Chinese subjects to their sovereign, the logics of commerce and order demanded it so. To do otherwise, he wrote, would "admit the right of the Chinese to have tax gathers watching [warehouses] in the settlement, seizing goods, and levying taxes in our very midst."[80]

Concerned with the security of foreign property destined to become sold goods, the Euro-American community in Shanghai seized on "the terms on which the Foreign Settlements were formed" as grounds for limiting Qing-authorized taxation in port areas. The settlement, according to popular consensus, existed to create a secure space for foreign trade and a favorable environment for sales of goods, which is to say, the circulation and accumulation of capital. The intended use of the port as such by the Euro-American community recoded it as territory that should be emptied of commercial tax collection. Court opinions, like that in the Loureiro case, argued that even if treaties had failed to explicitly eliminate *lijin* from the ports, *lijin* was too onerous of a tax to be allowed. Claims of oppression expressed in political-legal terms what was more fundamentally an argument about the proper relationship between space, commerce, and governance. The foreign community did not overtly reject Qing territorial sovereignty in principle but did invoke commercial prosperity as a condition that might limit the exercise of that authority in a given place.

Counternarratives: Foreign Failures and Threats to Chinese Prosperity

It is hardly surprising that officials at all levels of Qing government defended *lijin* against British attempts to limit its collection. For authorities in the provinces, the revenue was an absolute necessity and a matter that involved only Chinese merchants and producers. For the Zongli yamen, nothing in the treaties limited the government's right to collect the tax. How it met its expenses was "a matter of Chinese autonomy."[81] Moreover, according to one interpretation of the treaties offered by the Zongli yamen, the documents entailed nothing to limit revenue collection at the treaty ports.[82] What is more noteworthy is that alongside this defense of fiscal autonomy, government officials mobilized counternarratives to explain prevailing risks to commerce and prosperity. These narratives queried the wisdom of foreign commercial expansion and foreign governance as they unfolded in Qing territory.

---

80. Drummond to Shanghai Municipal Council, 9 June 1875, TNA, FO 233/83.
81. CBYWSM (digital), TZ, juan 63, 25.1–25.2.
82. Robert Hart, "Proposals for the Better Regulation of Commercial Relations, Being a Memorandum Called for by the Zongli Yamen and Drawn Up by the Inspector-General of Customs, Beijing, January 23, 1876," Inclosure in No. 2, *China No. 3 (1877) Further Correspondence Respecting the Attack on the Indian Expedition to Western China, and the Murder of Mr. Margary* [C. 1832], 9. Hart mediated commerce-related discussions at the time of the Chefoo negotiations.

Against the claim that Euro-American capital was imperiled by *lijin*, Qing authorities suggested that commercial expansion itself explained the lack of spectacular foreign profits since 1861. Jiangxi governor Shen Baozhen (沈葆楨, 1820–1879), consulted during preparations for the treaty revision negotiations of 1868, observed, "When foreign trade was limited to Guangdong, profits were ten times, [but] then they moved on to five ports, moved on to the Yangzi River.... As the scope [of business] became more broad, expenses became greater, costs became greater, and profits became more minute."[83] This idea that more trade did not necessarily mean more profits found its way, sometime later, into an official reply from the Zongli yamen to the British Legation: "Recently, more ports have opened and the use of them has broadened. Foreign commerce is more crowded and sales routes more packed. Foreign merchants are scrambling."[84] While British merchants and the legation wanted to blame trading losses on the Qing fiscal system, Qing authorities countered that there was a broader economic context to consider. Competitive pressures meant that more opportunities for trade were not necessarily synonymous with greater profits. Moreover, the Zongli yamen noted, since opening the Yangzi River ports to Euro-Americans trade by Chinese merchants had also waned: "The people are many and the profits are meager."[85]

These declining fortunes were not an exclusively local phenomenon. In the year preceding these assessments (1866), a banking crisis erupted in London, which according to contemporary accounts reverberated into China's treaty ports. The IMC commissioner in Shanghai reported that even though commercial activity in China was growing, the London crisis meant "many respectable firms of long standing [in China] have succumbed ... and the Courts of Bankruptcy have investigated the accounts and wound up the affairs of too many foreigners trading in this empire."[86]

As to reputed problems with *lijin* administration, officials in the central government disagreed that these warranted the "reformation in the provincial administration in all matters connected to foreign trade," as called for by the British Legation.[87] Rather, the central government acknowledged that excessive taxation was a problem that could occur depending on who was the local authority in charge.[88] Preserved copies of *lijin* regulations indicate that as in other matters of governance, the moral orientation and integrity of the administrator were deemed critical. In Guangdong

---

83. CBYWSM (digital), TZ, juan 53, 6.1.
84. CBYWSM (digital), TZ, juan 63, 24.1.
85. CBYWSM (digital), TZ, juan 63, 24.1.
86. Great Britain, *Reports on Trade by the Foreign Commissioners at the Ports in China Open by Treaty to Foreign Trade for the Year 1866* (1867–1868) [3976] (London: Harrison, 1868), 1; see also 123–62.
87. Beijing Legation to Zongli Yamen, No. 28, 19 September 1867, draft, TNA, FO 228/931.
88. CBYWSM (digital), TZ, juan 53, 16.1; "Reply to the Several Propositions, Seriatim, of the British Minister, June 28, 1868," Inclosure No. 28 in No. 76, CRRTT, 215–17.

lijin officers were instructed to "administer their duties in a spirit of a pure life and to manage affairs earnestly" (*jieji fenggong, renzhen jingli* 潔己奉公，認真經理).[89] Yet at least one government censor pointed out that the amount of money generated at any given *lijin* collection point was enough to corrupt even "a man of habitual integrity." Virtuous administration was difficult when duty gave a man access to "extraordinary opportunities for profit." But rather than fault the delegation of fiscal power, Qing authorities sought to curb its excesses. The court called for the elimination of tax bureaus far away from centers of government, where bonds of kinship or friendship among gentry often "corrupted" collection, and it issued what it considered to be stringent proclamations with clear penalties for infractions of the treaties.[90]

At the same time Qing authorities constructed alternative interpretations of the *lijin* problem, they also discussed their own reasons for resisting changes to tax collection, particularly in the port areas. First, there was simply the fact that "a great proportion of the *lijin* and similar taxes imposed by the Provincial Governments is collected at the treaty ports, where trade is carried on to an extensive scale."[91] Removing collectorates from the port would necessitate the deployment of a much more robust collection apparatus lest commodities traveling out from the ports find routes to bypass tax stations. Second, imperial officials most familiar with foreign trading communities resident in China voiced concerns that creating *lijin*-free port areas would license foreign communities to further disrupt the well-being of Chinese residents in the area.

This latter concern requires some explanation. During negotiations at Chefoo in 1876 between Li Hongzhang and Thomas Wade, the two men discussed the possibility that if the Chinese government were to grant a *lijin*-free port area, it would be coterminous with "foreign concessions"—areas such as the Foreign Settlement at Shanghai, where foreign residents rented or owned land, lived under extraterritorial protection, and ran municipal affairs such as public works and police. For both sides, the proposal presented a reasonable compromise. The foreign community would

---

89. 廣東通省抽收釐金章程 [Regulations for the collection of *lijin* in Guangdong Province], Shanghai Library Ancient Documents, Record 522403.
90. Inclosure No. 2, "Supplement to a Memorial by Wu Ting Yüan, a Member of the Censorate, with Reference to the Abolition of the Leking Levy. Translation," British Minister Rutherford Alcock to Lord Stanley, No. 80, 15 January 1869, TNA, FO 881/1655, 289; 24 January 1875, "Interviews with Chinese Authorities," TNA, FO 233/35, folio 66–68. The central government periodically took steps to rein in *lijin* abuses. In 1868, the Board of Revenue suggested extending the rule of avoidance to *lijin* collection, and the Qing court called on provincial officials to retain principle offices but do away with "petty collectorates."
91. "Memorial by Li Hung-chang Reporting the Conduct and Issue of Negotiations at Chefoo, Dated September 14, 1876," TNA, FO 881/9301, 6; Li Hongzhang, "煙台議結滇案摺" [Chefoo discussions of the Yunnan case], *Li wenzhong gong quanji* (Taipei: Wenhai chubanshe, 1974–1983), 27:40.

get their *lijin*-free area. At the same time, most of these concessions were already centered on each port's wharf, so limiting the *lijin*-free "port" area to the concessions would confine the footprint of the *lijin*-free area to something smaller than the entire port city.

Yet, for Li and other key Qing decision-makers responsible for foreign affairs, following even this limited path entailed dangers. While the Euro-American community conceived of the *lijin*-free areas as simply a matter of eliminating additional burdens to commercial circulation, demarcating the areas would also give formal definition to spaces of non-Chinese municipal control. Up to this point, even in Shanghai, foreign governance had been legally unsettled enough that the Qing magistrate in the Loureiro case had suggested that the Foreign Settlement was best thought of as an area of overlapping jurisdictions, where both the SMC and *lijin* collectorates operated.[92] In 1877, with the signed Chefoo Convention calling for the demarcation of a lijin-free port area, Li Hongzhang and Shen Baozhen, now the commissioner of trade at the southern ports, anticipated that with settled boundaries in place, the SMC and other foreign-led councils would initiate new forms of taxation and land use that would disrupt the well-being of Chinese residents.[93]

Shanghai, again, was a paradigmatic site of concern. In his report on the negotiations at Chefoo, Shen noted that should plans for a *lijin*-free area move forward, the British consul at Shanghai wished to turn existing farmland into a boundary road to formally demarcate the settlement's borders. Although it was true, Shen admitted, that a few self-interested "traitors" (*jian min* 奸民) had in the past sold their land to foreign nationals, the general disposition of the people (*ren qing* 人情) was against increased foreign land ownership.[94] Li's report on the Chefoo negotiations concurred with the general tenor of Shen's assessment. He pointed out that further foreign territorial acquisition and governance was antithetical to political integrity (*zhongguo zhengti* 中國整體). The principled stand in these matters, he advised, was to "take a hold of the treaty to argue against the provision that foreign goods were exempt from *lijin*."[95]

For Shen in particular, the further reterritorialization of Chinese territory portended ill for the livelihood of Chinese port residents. The *lijin*-free area was sure to attract "cunning and sordid" merchants who "covet convenient and handy trade." These men would be complicit, Shen predicted, in the expansion of the SMC's own

---

92. Drummond to Shanghai Municipal Council, 9 June 1875, TNA, FO 233/83.
93. The sources for the following discussion are Li Hongzhang, "資報滇案議結" [Report on the Yunnan negotiations], Academia Sinica li shi dang an guan [Archives, Institute of Modern History, Academia Sinica], 01-21-032-01-005 (hereafter ASLSDAG); Shen Baozhen, "資報滇案議結" [Report on the Yunnan negotiations], ASLSDAG, 01-21-032-01-011.
94. Shen, [Report on the Yunnan negotiations], 25.
95. Li, [Report on the Yunnan negotiations], 12.

widespread, extortionate taxes. In a scathing counter-critique, Shen derided the municipal levies that the council took from Chinese residents to fund its police and streetlights. "House tax [*juan* 捐], lamp tax, cart tax, boat tax; all kinds of things, even dung and dirt are without exception, extorted and plundered, till there is practically nothing left."[96] No other country, Shen pointed out, allowed foreign nationals to collect municipal taxes, and although the Shanghai *daotai* had interdicted foreign levies from Chinese persons, the collections continued. To expand and settle the boundaries of the foreign concessions by setting *lijin*-free areas, Shen predicted, would only unleash foreign municipal committees to "run riot extorting the wealth of the Chinese people until they are full."[97]

Boundaries between Taxes: Quantitative Equivalence versus Qualitative Difference

Although both Qing and British authorities worried about the ill effects of poorly designed taxation, their concerns were fundamentally different. The taxes that bothered Shen collected revenue from concrete utilities residents needed, things immediate to life, like housing and sanitation, or to low-income employment, like carts. The Euro-American anti-*lijin* lobby worried more abstractly about burdens to capital accumulation. In their eyes, taxation subtracted from the surplus available for the merchant to realize when the good was finally sold. It was this abstract, quantitative lens that turned the Qing Empire's levies on different trades for different purposes into pervasive taxation on "commerce" that alarmed and mobilized the foreign community. And it was this abstract, quantitative lens that Qing authorities roundly rejected.

The question of whether all taxes were the same arose early in the operation of the treaty regime. As early as 1862–1863, British merchants with operations in Zhejiang and Jiangsu began to present to their consuls receipts, which, they claimed, proved their export produce had, despite the ostensible protection of the transit pass, paid other "exactions" en route.[98] The paperwork presented at Shanghai and Ningbo as proof of excess taxation, however, was not transit tax receipts but rather receipts for taxes levied on the goods prior to their transport—that is, the receipts recorded taxes levied on the Chinese growers, processors, and brokers.[99] Still, this

---

96. Shen, [Report on the Yunnan negotiations], 37–38. *Juan* is more accurately rendered as "public contribution," but I translate it here as "tax" for the sake of readability.
97. Shen, [Report on the Yunnan negotiations], 38.
98. See, for example, Zongli Yamen to British Legation, No. 3, 8 January 1869, TNA, FO 228/936; P. Hughes, "Report on the Working of the Transit Certificate System at Jiujiang," 1 February 1864, TNA, FO 228/371.
99. Zongli Yamen to British Legation, No. 3, 8 January 1869, TNA, FO 228/936.

qualitative distinction between transit taxes and levies from acts of production made no difference to British merchants or their consuls. They were, in the words of the Jiujiang consul, "arbitrary charges in the interior" that threatened foreign commerce.[100] Contributing to the sense of alarm was a recent British report on the transit pass system, which suspected that levies taken from growers, processors, and brokers were attempts by local authorities to circumvent the transit tax exemption offered by the treaty. If so, warned the consul at Jiujiang, there was no insurance these levies "may not be doubled or trebled next year, or next month."[101]

The British assessment of Qing taxes on producers and brokers was, at least in one important instance, off the mark. In the case of a recently introduced levy on tea growers in Jiangxi and Jiangsu, the provincial government introduced the tax for reasons very different from those suspected by British merchants and consuls. The change originated in 1863 with the Liangjiang governor-general Zeng Guofan (曾國藩, 1811–1872), who worried that collecting revenue from Chinese merchants by way of rewards had created a political problem. Zeng was an erudite scholar-official who read the classics daily and leaned toward works that championed morally transforming influences and ritual, both as a practice of personal propriety and of statecraft.[102] In the words of one profiler, Zeng "firmly believed in the importance of moral leadership for the creation of an exemplary center."[103] The problem Zeng identified with the reward system of raising local funds was that it weakened governance by offering office to those without the needed moral core.

For some years, the administrative offices in Zeng's jurisdiction had raised emergency revenue from the tea trade through the form of ad hoc but mandatory "contributions" (*juan* 捐) from merchants. These *juan* earned the contributor a reward of imperial distinction. Typically, purchased rank was expensive, sales were controlled in Beijing, and families only invested in it on behalf of an able son. But during the turbulent 1860s, rewards were increasingly tapped by provincial governments as a revenue stream, and prices plummeted. Rewards previously worth 100 taels could be bought for as little as 15 or 16 taels.[104] This heavy discount had made rank more available to more men, and a wider pool of persons eligible for lower-level

---

100. Hughes, "Report on the Working of the Transit Certificate System."
101. Hughes, "Report on the Working of the Transit Certificate System."
102. K. C. Liu, *China's Early Modernization and Reform Movement: Studies in Late Nineteenth-Century China and American-Chinese Relations* (Taipei: Institute of Modern History, Academia Sinica, 2009), 216.
103. Hao Chang, "The Intellectual Context of Reform," in *Reform in Nineteenth-Century China*, ed. Paul A. Cohen and John E. Schrecker (Cambridge, MA: Harvard University East Asian Research Center, 1976), 145–49, here 147.
104. Elizabeth Kaske, "Fund-Raising Wars: Office Selling and Interprovincial Finance in Nineteenth-Century China," *Harvard Journal of Asiatic Studies* 71, no. 1 (2011): 69–141. Zeng's tea trade problem seems to be related to but somewhat different from the problems Kaske describes.

civil service positions threatened, as Zeng saw it, to lower the quality of men in governance.[105] "Applications," the governor-general assessed, "are excessive and indiscriminate; this is not the prudent way to recruit talent."[106] Zeng ordered the practice discontinued, to be substituted with a local tax (*luodi shui* 落地稅) paid where tea was grown and prepared for marketing. Changing the source of state revenue from a merchant *juan*, convertible into rank, into a *luodi shui* from tea growers and brokers, he hoped, would decrease the number of receipts in circulation on the secondary market and cut off the otherwise inevitable path to political instability.

Zeng's orders did not strictly legislate who had to pay *luodi shui*, only that it be paid prior to transit. As it became organized, collection involved mixtures of growers, packers, brokers, and dealers, with the actual payee differing, depending on the commercial network. In some places, the tax was considered a levy on tea growers, in practice paid on their behalf by the packhouse owner, as a deduction from the purchase price. In other places, brokers of processed tea paid the tax and passed its cost along to purchasers. Whoever it was, the payee received a duty certificate (*shui dan* 稅單) that needed to accompany the tea as it continued its export journey. Tea without a *luodi shui* certificate would be detained at *lijin* barriers and the carrier fined.

The collection of *luodi shui* began in the summer of 1863. By October, British merchants had lodged formal protests over its collection. One early case involved a British merchant named Melliss, whose tea was stopped at a transit tax barrier in August.[107] The tea was not accompanied by any duty receipts, and when the officers asked the firm to pay the *luodi shui* in addition to the transit duty, it refused, and barrier officials confiscated the tea. Afraid the tea would deteriorate, the firm paid the duty. The protest Melliss lodged in Beijing was not only for compensation but one of principle: "British merchants cannot be made responsible for the previous payment of the natives of any impost whatever." His consul at Jiujiang, P. J. Hughes, agreed, arguing Melliss was only liable for transit duty. Not only was the *luodi shui* not his responsibility; insofar as the local duty increased the subtraction from Melliss's potential profit, Hughes thought, the *luodi shui* was a violation of treaty.

For local Qing authorities, British merchants had created their own problem by encroaching further into the tea network. Hughes's counterpart, the *daotai* at

---

105. Mary C. Wright, *The Last Stand of Chinese Conservatism: The T'ung-chih Restoration, 1862–1874* (Stanford: Stanford University Press, 1957), 85–87.
106. Chinese original in "Proclamation by Gov. General Tseng, July 22, 1863. Tax on Teas in Kiangsi," TNA, FO 233/83; English translation in "Proclamation by Tseng, Imperial Commissioner, Governor General of the Two Kiangs, etc.," TNA, FO 228/371. Translation mine from Chinese original.
107. Jiujiang Consulate to Beijing Legation, 21 October 1863, TNA, FO 228/352. It seems most likely, based on available records, that the person accompanying the tea was a Chinese agent of the firm.

Jiujiang, informed him that per the Board of Revenue in Beijing, *luodi shui* was not a tax on foreign merchants but taken from tea packhouses and brokers. These were responsible for delivery of a duty certificate proving payment was made. Melliss, however, circumvented the Chinese-owned packhouses and brokers. Rather, he (and he was not alone) bought his tea either direct from growers or in small parcels from petty dealers.[108] Melliss protested that such purchases made it hard to get receipts for *luodi shui*. But this protest begged the very point pressed by Qing authorities. Melliss, in his desire to cut out the Chinese middlemen, had appropriated a role typically taken by a Chinese merchant—that of gathering leaves from growers prior to their preparation and packing for export. By appropriating this role, did he then become subject to the same levies? The answer for the Jiujiang *daotai* was yes, namely because a local duty "cannot be looked on in the same light as the levy of *lijin* en route." The qualitative distinction between the two levies—one levied in the process of harvesting and processing the tea for export, the other levied when the tea took its journey as a finished product—had a substantive, practical consequence: since Melliss engaged in two separate activities, bringing the tea from the mountains into the market and then circulating it for export, he owed both the *luodi shui* and the transit duty.

In his rebuttal to the Jiujiang *daotai*, Consul Hughes did not deny that Melliss had engaged into two different stages of commodity production and circulation. Rather he argued that once Chinese produce was tied to foreign capital, it, like the merchant, fell under the jurisdiction of treaty, not provincial administration. The fact was, the consul argued, that much of tea processed in and around growing regions or found in Chinese-owned packhouses had already been bought with foreign advances. The advance of capital made "the teas undergoing preparation in these warehouses ... actually foreign property."[109] As foreign property intended for export, the teas, even when raw or in the process of being prepared, fell under treaty provisions that stated the payment of the treaty transit due "shall exempt the goods from all further inland charges whatsoever."[110] The logic of the consul's argument was one of deterritorialization: the Chinese produce, coming into contact with British capital, had ceased to be itself. The tea would continue to exist, but only as a form of British capital. And so, it should be governed as such.

This dispute over the transformative potential of capital investments was not resolved in 1863 or 1864, and protests against *luodi shui* reemerged in 1872, when

---

108. Jiujiang Daotai to Consul Hughes, 20 October 1863, consulate translation, TNA, 228/352.
109. P. J. Hughes, "Report on the Working of the Transit Certificate System at Jiujiang," 1 February 1864, TNA, FO 228/371.
110. Treaty of Tianjin, Article 28, in IMC, *Treaties, Conventions, Etc. between China and Foreign States*, 2 vols., vol. 1, 2nd ed., Miscellaneous Series No. 30 (Shanghai: Inspector General of Customs, 1917), 1:412–13.

a new complaint by a British merchant working out of Jiujiang prompted then–British minister Thomas Wade to call for an investigation into the tax. The event that precipitated the investigation was similar to the Melliss case. A firm, Anderson Brothers, was in the business of purchasing teas direct from growers and hired a Chinese establishment to fire and pack the teas. When the firm decided to take out transit passes for the teas, officials also charged *luodi shui*, which Anderson protested was in excess of the duties he was legally obligated to pay. Wade's investigation focused less on the fate of Mr. Anderson and more on outstanding suspicions that first, obstruction by provincial authorities had made transit passes an undesirable option for British merchants and second, that the *luodi shui* was, despite what Qing authorities said, "effected in order to obviate the loss of revenue through the action of transit passes."[111]

The legation's Chinese secretary, W. F. Mayers, headed Wade's investigation, which concluded in the autumn of 1873.[112] On the first charge of obstruction, Mayers found plenty of consular testimony that transit passes were not frequently used within tea country because merchants did not know "how the passes would answer." Through some areas, goods under transit pass traveled with less delay. Through others, however, *lijin* officials put goods under transit pass "at a disadvantage, by delaying the boats, opening every package, weighing a whole cargo, and exercising greater severity than would be done were the goods conveyed in the manner which best services their interests."[113] On the second charge that local officials created new taxes to circumvent the intent of the treaty pass, Mayers found from his informants that the "real reason" for the change issued by Zeng Guofan, was "the discovery that foreigners—as in the recorded cases of Dent & Co, Melliss & Co., and others at Jiujiang, had asserted the exemption of their teas from [*lijin*] . . . when transit passes were employed." His primary supporting evidence for this charge was simple quantitative equivalence: the amount of *luodi shui* was "identical" to the transit *lijin* in force prior to 1863. It must be the case, Mayers concluded, that Qing officials were engaged in a "trick" further of "bad faith." The trick proved that the power of the Chinese government to arrange domestic taxation easily exceeded the narrow bounds of the transit pass, and British officials cried foul. "No reason exists," Mayer speculated, "to restrain [the Qing government] from converting in a similar manner the *lijin* or barrier duty on silk, sugar, or other native staples into an equivalent 'grower's tax.'"[114]

---

111. Enclosure No. 1 in Mayers to Wade, 29 October 1873, TNA, FO 233/62.
112. For a summary of Mayer's findings, see Mayers to Wade, 29 October 1873, TNA, FO 233/62.
113. B. Brenan, "Memo on the Inland Transit Pass System," Inclosure No. 9 in Mayers, "Report."
114. Mayers to Wade, 29 October 1873, TNA, FO 233/62.

Through the 1870s, the continued existence of *lijin* and other domestic commercial taxes, including *luodi shui*, convinced most Euro-American treaty signatories that the Qing central government was failing to assert its proper authority and uphold its treaty obligations. Typically, treaty signatories brought such complaints to bear in bilateral negotiations. Then, in 1879, a series of memorandums authored by the ministers of Germany, the Netherlands, and Italy and circulated between the foreign legations in Beijing triggered the first ever multilateral trade negotiations in China. Termed the "Conference of Foreign Ministers" in British archives, throughout 1880, ministers and other high officials of the "treaty powers" met to discuss their shared grievances against the Qing government, foremost of which was "relief of foreign trade with China from undue taxation."[115]

The conference crystallized the Euro-American consensus that all taxes in China were similarly limited by treaty. Attendees reasoned that although "national" autonomy meant China had the right to levy additional taxes on foreign goods, China had voluntarily limited this right when it signed treaties that included provisions for foreign trade. These provisions did not merely grant rights and privileges to foreign nationals. Rather, the Italian minister wrote, the privileges were "inherent in foreign goods until they are thoroughly consumed."[116] The conference as a whole concurred. As one memorandum drafted in committee put it, "the object to be kept in view is the protection of the goods."[117] In short, from the viewpoint of goods, all taxes, whether customs duties at the border of empire or payments to brokers at an inland market, were all the same: threats. So, the reasoning went, if treaties existed to protect and extend foreign trade, they also existed to shield commodities from a Qing sovereign right.

The novelty and significance of the conference was not the content of its discussions, which largely tracked with decades of complaints. But the conference's form—formal, deliberative multinational coordination around a shared agenda of commercial regulation—signaled the extent to which global capital recognized Qing fiscal administration as a threat. Ministers from Austria, Belgium, Britain, Denmark, France, Germany, Italy, the Netherlands, Russia, Spain, and the United States eventually authored a joint communication to the Zongli yamen, which enumerated "Twenty Griefs" against Qing governance and requested a joint conference to discuss remedies, including the elimination of *lijin*.[118]

---

115. Inclosure 2 in No. 1, China No. 3 (1882), 2. Represented countries included Great Britain, German Empire, the United States, the Netherlands, Peru, Italy, Austria-Hungary, Denmark, Spain, France, and Belgium.
116. Ferdinand DeLuca, Minister of Italy, 25 September 1879, "Memorandum, Inland Taxation on Foreign Goods," Conference of Foreign Ministers, vol. 1, TNA, FO 233/51 (hereafter, CFM).
117. Untitled draft memo, CFM, folio 189.
118. Untitled draft memo, CFM, folio 188; Inclosure 4 in No. 1, *China No. 3* (1882); "Twenty Griefs," CFM.

Officials within the Qing government resisted the Euro-American campaign by calling into question the claim that quantitative equivalence between taxes made them "the same." Authorities both in the provinces and Beijing rejected the equivalence Euro-American authorities had created between imperial customs duties and provincial levies as well as *luodi shui* and transit *lijin*. *Luodi shui*, the *daotai* at Jiujiang insisted, was not a transit *lijin* because it was a tax payable by tea producers, unconnected with foreign trade and of no concern to tea purchasers.[119] In its response to the "Twenty Griefs," in the winter of 1880, the Zongli yamen rehearsed (yet again) how the transit pass system worked, and it reiterated that growers' taxes (*luodi shui*) "[have] been in existence for over two hundred years, and [have] nothing to do with the customs or transit duties; nor [are they] in any way connected with inland customs houses or *lijin* stations."[120] Indeed, in what social world does money paid by a farmer in the hills of Anhui become a liability for a merchant selling the said leaf in London?

Additionally, their arguments raise questions about grounds on which the Euro-American community generated equivalence between taxes. Zeng Guofan's switch to *luodi shui* originated in his worry over the qualitative effects of taxation on political and social order. The foreign community also worried about qualitative effects, but the qualitative effects they lost sleep over were generated by quantitative movements. In their world, transit tax and *luodi shui* were equivalent because taxing the merchant or taxing the grower produced the same increase in the quantity of money the tea needed to command in the market to realize surplus value, which was necessary to keep capital accumulation in motion. In this world, growers were no different from merchants insofar as both were different stages in the circuit of commodity capital.[121] That Qing authorities stood fast on the claim that they taxed discrete activities of growers, packers, and shippers should lead us not to wonder about their peculiarity so much as help us to grasp the peculiarity of the totality that is capital. Only in a capitalist society does social production and distribution entail the creation and mediation of a single substance—value.[122] Elsewhere, some people grow tea and others trade it.

---

119. "Note from Shiu [*sic*], Daotai of Jiujiang to W. F. Mayers," 14 October 1873, TNA, FO 233/62.
120. Inclosure 6 in No. 84, Zongli Yamen to Wade, 19 January 1880, Legation translation, TNA, FO 881/4530, 79.
121. In Marxian theory, value-producing societies are unique insofar as all social production produces the same thing—that is, value and all distribution is mediated by the value of labor. See Postone, *Time, Labor and Social Domination*, especially chap. 5.
122. For a discussion of the unique "total" character of capitalist society, see Postone, *Time, Labor and Social Domination*, 79–80.

Conclusion: Deterritorialization and Reterritorialization

There was no single moment when the foreign campaign against Qing taxation reached a climax or turning point. It was driven by a structural imperative and the inescapable anxieties this imperative generated in the context of Qing sovereignty. The social world created by capital, unlike one in which capitalist ventures are a mere element, operates under the pressures of a socially general rate of surplus value. This means that unlike the risks and pressures shaping premodern merchant adventures, which are episodic, the modern world of capital operates within a dynamic of growth under increasing pressure. One consequence of the relative fiscal-administrative autonomy practiced by Qing provinces was that this socially general dynamic had to find a way to work in more "places"—that is, geographically limited configurations of people, raw materials, currency, and regulatory regimes. Conditions of circulation were a particularly acute issue because British capital in China had very little control over the "abode of production," where the length of the working day or the employment of labor-saving technology otherwise shape and reshape the rate of surplus value. With their operations confined to the sphere of circulation, it was within this sphere that British firms had to find ways to realize the surplus value already produced.[123] Yet, when British merchants and their state representatives examined the state of British profit-making in China, they did not see the structural imperatives generated within their own form of social reproduction but rather found clear and present danger in Qing sovereignty and governance. Chinese personhood, forms of administrative autonomy, and revenue strategies chipped away at British profits.

---

123. Marx theorized that when a producer sells a commodity to a merchant, the surplus value divided into two parts—that taken by the producer, realized in the sale of the commodity to the merchant, and that taken by the merchant, to be realized as profit in the subsequent sale of the good. On the basis of this relationship, the average profit for commercial capital was the same as the general rate in other branches of production. Otherwise, he argued, the social composition of capital would change. Commercial capital, moreover, as part of a social division of capital contributed to the general rate of profit "according to the proportion it forms in the total capital." See Karl Marx, *Capital: A Critique of Political Economy*, vol. 2, trans. David Fernbach (New York: Penguin, 1978), chaps. 16 and 17. It should also be noted that within a Marxian framework transportation is a value-producing activity and can contribute to capital growth through accelerated turnover (*Capital*, vol. 2, chap. 3). Marx does not treat taxation as an element in his analysis of the rate of profit or commercial profit in *Capital*, but it seems likely that he would have classed commercial taxes, like commercial profit, as an additional division of surplus value. If we treat taxes (as certain as death) as an element of constant capital (overhead costs), it is clear that they lower the rate of profit. Thinking along these lines, what the spatial and temporal variation in Qing domestic taxation did was throw an extra-market wild card into the creation of a general rate of profit. Variations in commercial taxes created ill-defined subterritories with differing rates of profit, with an effect that which would not be dissimilar to that capricious rent increases or decreases might have on industrial capital.

As the Euro-American community campaigned, through the 1860s, 70s, and 80s, against Qing domestic taxation, the dynamics of commercial circulation structured by capital and the treaty apparatus led to fitful episodes of deterritorialization and reterritorialization. First, transit passes erased fiscal-administrative boundaries between provinces, if only for the limited set of foreign-owned cargoes eligible for the passes. Then in the 1870s Qing authorities began to expand the transit pass regime. Initially, various provincial authorities began, on their own account, to honor inward transit passes held by Chinese merchants.[124] Then, in 1874, the Zongli yamen granted foreign goods carried by Chinese-owned steamships access to the same transit tax exemptions available to foreign goods shipped in Euro-American vessels.[125] In 1880, the Zongli yamen formalized inward transit pass privileges to any Chinese merchant, and in 1896 it extended outward pass privileges to Chinese merchants.[126] By bringing Chinese merchants into the treaty regulatory apparatus, authorities hoped to strengthen Chinese firms against foreign counterparts. At the same time, the changes created the formal equivalence of persons vis-à-vis commodity capital that British authorities and merchants lobbied existed. In issuing the rule changes, the Zongli Yamen did not explicitly contradict its earlier reasoning about boundaries between Chinese and foreign trade, but the changes—issued in response to changed conditions for Chinese capital accumulation—did nonetheless institutionalize goods, not political subjects, as the standpoint for governance. Furthermore, because sub-imperial jurisdictional boundaries were meaningless under the transit pass regime, the rule changes reterritorialized Qing territory into a fiscal regulatory space episodically unified by commodity circulation. The further institutionalization of this space, through the consolidation of disparate domestic taxes, is the subject of the next chapter. In 1880, the Zongli yamen insisted on the qualitative difference between production and transportation taxes. By 1890, the quantitative dimensions of total revenue became a more compelling standpoint for fiscal administrative reorganization.

As reterritorialization brought down boundaries, it also created new ones. In particular, the extension of treaty privileges grew IMC jurisdiction and the boundaries it set around commercial governance. A few years after IMC operations began, Inspector General Robert Hart initiated efforts to remove the Chinese customs superintendent from involvement in day-to-day business, beginning with procedural changes that removed the superintendent's office from the production and circulation of knowledge about IMC collections and expenses.[127] By 1869, Hart

---

124. Chinese use of inward transit tax exemptions was honored as early as 1873 in Jiangxi Province. See Enclosure No. 7 in Mayers, 29 October 1873, TNA, FO 233/62.
125. IMC, *Circulars First*, no. 7, 24 March 1874.
126. IMC *Circulars Second*, no. 119, 4 November 1880, 232; no. 730 (1896); no. 735 (1896).
127. IMC, *Circulars First*, no. 4, 17 March 1864; no. 17, 10 November 1864.

advised customs commissioners that questions were not to be "prematurely" placed before the port's customs superintendent.[128] Then, in 1873, the Inspector General issued terse instructions to assert the independence of IMC offices from other parts of Qing administration. Commissioners, Hart instructed, were not to take the position of a subordinate to the Chinese superintendent at the port, and so long as they carefully abided by customs rules, IMC offices could "dispense with" consulting superintendents and cultivate their independence.[129] Rules governing the IMC's work were sanctioned not only by the emperor but the international community, and following them, Hart advised, a commissioner "need not make a mistake in the transaction of business."[130] The involvement of local officials in the management of treaty port trade was superfluous.

The IMC, as a functionally independent agency that served the empire and the world, subsequently took cognizance of more commercial activity and formerly discrete revenue streams. Increasingly, the IMC assumed jurisdiction over Chinese trade. In 1875, Hart set the precedent that even in cases where foreigners held a minority investment in a shipment, Chinese boats and Chinese-owned cargoes were subject to treaty rules and IMC jurisdiction.[131] Then, in 1887, owing to changes in opium taxation, the IMC began to manage the junk trade between Hong Kong, Macao, and Guangzhou. Soon thereafter, as loans became a feature of Qing finance, more of the junk trade and even *lijin* became part of the institution's portfolio of operations. Whereas historians have argued that regionalism was a powerful current in the post-Taiping era, the treaty apparatus offered a countervailing centripetal force.[132] Euro-American treaty signatories, recently made over into centralized nation-states, and treaty regulations, designed to create and administer a homogenous territory for the circulation of global capital, demanded from the Qing government coordinated policies and actions oriented toward international

---

128. IMC, *Circulars First*, no. 25, 1 November 1869. In the circular, Hart obliquely referred to the large number of customs-related cases that were accumulating, unresolved sometimes for years, on the desks of the foreign ministers and Zongli yamen.
129. IMC, *Circulars Second*, no. 13, 8 September 1873, 452.
130. IMC, *Circulars*, no. 24, 18 December 1873, 490.
131. Robert Hart, "Memorandum concerning Treatment of Foreign-Owned Goods in Native Bottoms at Chinese Treaty Ports," TNA, FO 233/80.
132. Franz Michael, *Regionalism in Nineteenth Century China* (Seattle: University of Washington Press, 1964); Stanley Spector, *Li Hung-chang and the Huai Army: A Study in Nineteenth Century Chinese Regionalism* (Seattle: University of Washington Press, 1964); Philip Kuhn, *Rebellion and Its Enemies in Late Imperial China: Militarization and Social Structure, 1796–1864* (Cambridge, MA: Harvard University Press, 1970); Frederic Wakeman Jr., "The Evolution of Local Control in Late Imperial China," in *Conflict and Control in Late Imperial China*, ed. Frederic Wakeman Jr. and Carolyn Grant (Berkeley: University of California Press, 1975), 1–25.

obligations. The IMC, which worked to detach itself from local intervention, more than any other agency in the empire, institutionalized this shift in orientation and the increasing importance of coordinated fiscal administration. Through the elimination of existing boundaries and the creation of new ones, throughout the 1860s into the 1880s, the treaty apparatus was becoming an expansive vector of the Qing Empire's reterritorialization into a territory whose governance expressed the logic and forms of capital.

6
Experiments for the Future

This report is only about money and ways to make even more. What do you really want? Don't forget that you are the father of your province. Even a loss would be acceptable—provided you taxed properly. You should feel ashamed for that.

—Qianlong Emperor (1744)[1]

Since at least the 1920s, economists and historians have argued that as it was in other parts of the world, China's participation in global trade during the nineteenth and twentieth centuries produced a widening geographic, economic, and social gulf between the prosperous and well connected and the poor and isolated.[2] In the Qing Empire, this "dual economy" had a fiscal regulatory dimension. International trade and steam shipping of high-value items, such as silk and opium, fed revenues through the Imperial Maritime Customs (IMC) to accounts controlled in Beijing. *Changguan* superintendents, however, struggled to meet their annual quotas with monies generated by the junk trade, which coastal and riverine steam carriage recorded as a lower capitalized sector that mostly trafficked cheap and bulky goods.[3] Provincial governments, meanwhile, leaned heavily on *lijin* revenues that were undercut by treaty privileges. These changing fiscal fortunes also expressed

---

1. Quoted in Yuping Ni, *Customs Duties in the Qing Dynasty, ca. 1644–1911* (Leiden: Brill, 2017), 18.
2. Man-houng Lin, "China's 'Dual Economy' in International Trade Relations, 1842–1949," in *Japan, China, and the Growth of the Asian International Economy, 1850–1949*, ed. Kaoru Sugihara (Oxford: Oxford University Press, 2005), 179–97, citing work by Simon Kuznets as well as Jeffrey G. Williamson, "Regional Inequality and the Process of National Development: A Description of Patterns," *Economic Development and Cultural Change* 13, no. 4, pt. 2 (1965): 3–47.
3. IMC, *Decennial Report for 1891*, 363; On silk: "Their high intrinsic value insures to the foreigner a practical monopoly due to the two requisites of safety and dispatch [*sic*]." See IMC, "Newchwang," *Trade Report for 1874*, 6.

changing geographies of commercial circulation. After 1860, the formerly prosperous commercial corridor along the Grand Canal became a poverty-stricken "hinterland" after coastal steam shipping altered market structures.[4] Elsewhere in the empire, "once important links to the world market" such Tainan, Shantou, Jiujiang, and Zhifu became second- or even third-tier markets, relative to treaty ports such as Taibei, Qingdao, and Shanghai.[5]

Without the copresence of multiple regulatory regimes, governments in China might have had more money. The ability of merchants, Chinese merchants in particular, to move between the treaty apparatus and the *changguan/lijin* regimes generated downward pressure on revenue. For example, when Guangdong provincial authorities issued new levies on kerosene, large consignments of the oil switched from junks to steamers, and the resulting losses to provincial revenue led officials to abandon the taxes.[6] Conversely, to maintain higher levels of traffic through the *changguan*, authorities in Formosa offered reduced duties to Chinese merchants using junks.[7] Governance both structured and responded to competitive processes of capital reproduction within China, and this interplay often undercut the total amount of revenue available to authorities within the empire.

In the context of this interplay between commerce and governance, a generation of officials and elites began to rethink the relationships between commerce and state wealth as well as strategies and tactics of domestic commercial taxation. The most prominent object of concern was *lijin*, and opium *lijin* in particular. Among historians of China, it is well known that *lijin* outlasted the dynasty and proliferated in the subsequent decades of fragmented political power and mounting military expenditures.[8] Perhaps for this reason, little has been written about plans and protocols, devised over several decades beginning in the 1880s, to replace *lijin* with systems of unified commercial taxation. Beginning with changes to imported opium taxation that commenced in 1887, interest in unifying domestic commercial taxes spread among officials and scholar elites. Bureaucrats hopeful to curb "corruption"

---

4. Kenneth Pomeranz, *The Making of a Hinterland: State, Society and Economy in Inland North China, 1853–1937* (Berkeley: University of California Press, 1993).
5. Lin, "China's 'Dual Economy.'"
6. IMC, *Decennial Report for 1891*, 559.
7. Great Britain, *Diplomatic and Consular Reports on Trade and Finance, China, Report for the Year 1887 on the Trade of Taiwan*, Foreign Office Annual Series, No. 332 (1888), 3. Subsequent consular reports (for 1891 and 1892) indicate the policy was likely the result of negotiation between the Chinese merchant community and officials. For a discussion of this relationship in nearby Lu-kang, see Donald R. DeGlopper, "Social Structure in a Nineteenth-Century Taiwanese Port City," in *The City in Late Imperial China*, ed. G. William Skinner (Stanford: Stanford University Press, 1977), 633–50.
8. For a contemporary account in the near postimperial period, see Stanley Wright, *Kiangsi Native Trade and Its Taxation* (Shanghai, n.p., 1920).

within *lijin* bureaus, provincial governments hungry for more revenue, and critics anxious to free China's economic growth from the fetters of *lijin* all found reasons to embrace more consolidated taxation.

These experiments in strategies and tactics of commercial taxation complicate existing narratives that point to fiscal competition between the capital and provinces. In established historiography, what Madeline Zelin calls "fiscal tug-of-war" between Beijing and the provinces appears to have been a constant from at least the Yongzheng reign (1722–1735) forward.[9] Accounts of the second half of the nineteenth century often emphasize an epidemic of surcharges on land, goods, commercial licenses, land transactions, alcohol, and gaming instituted by provincial governors to deal with the Taiping Rebellion. But these only added to the customary fees, surcharges, and "forced" contributions (*juan* 捐) that had reemerged in the Jiaqing reign (1796–1820) to cover ordinary costs of administration, which were often in arrears up through the Guangxu era (1874/75–1908). Many of the new levies from commerce were authorized in the imperial capital but not incorporated into the empire's statutes, meaning control of the revenue streams remained in the provinces.[10] Such local revenue prerogatives, past studies argue, were fiercely defended by provincial authorities, who during the course of the rebellion and in its aftermath built their jurisdictions into independent fiscal, military, and administrative entities.[11] According to these studies, any attempt by the Board of Revenue or other organs of the central government to modify or impinge on these revenue sources, "ran into very strong resistance on the part of the provincial governments."[12] Be this as it were, as was the case in earlier episodes of fiscal innovation (most notably the Yongzheng-era *huo hao* 火耗 reform) from the 1880s onwards officials in both the capital and the provinces also began to collaboratively experiment to answer the question of whether state revenue interests would be better served through significant institutional change.[13]

With an important difference. Unlike the *huo hao* reforms which institutionalized a separation of monies properly belonging to the provinces and were implemented autonomously at the provincial level, with reference to local needs and changing conditions (*yindi zhiyi* 因地制宜), experiments in the Guangxu era did much the opposite, seeking to undo the post-1854 apparatus built around a general

---

9. Madeline Zelin, *The Magistrate's Tael: Rationalizing Fiscal Reform in Eighteenth Century Ch'ing China* (Berkeley: University of California Press, 1984), 4. Zelin actually shows a much more complex relationship than her language suggests.
10. Marianne Bastid, "The Structure of Financial Institutions of the State in the Late Qing," in *The Scope of State Power in China*, ed. Stuart R. Schram (London: St. Martin's, 1985), 51–79, here 61–62.
11. Kent Deng, *China's Political Economy in Modern Times: Changes and Economic Consequences, 1800–2000* (London: Routledge, 2012), 67–70.
12. Bastid, "Structure of Financial Institutions," 62.
13. Zelin, *Magistrate's Tael*, 90–97.

principle of *yindi zhiyi*, geographic heterogeneity, fragmented fiscal authority, and "compromise with local constituencies."[14] The new strategy, which began to coalesce around 1890, was informed by a program to grow wealth and commerce and worked with market-driven commodity flows. The strategy consolidated provincial territory and transprovincial territory into undifferentiated regions of circulation, and tactics of revenue security that can be best described as noninterference shifted governance away from the cultivation and constraint of specific commodity movements. Rather, what had become known about commodity movements more generally was gradually assimilated into government procedures. I argue such efforts were experiments in the geographic and administrative organization of fiscal power that transcended the ostensible revenue competition between Beijing and the provinces. The "genealogy of technologies of power" visible in late Qing tax experiments points to an alternative schism within governance between schemas of heterogenous and homogenous territoriality.[15]

This chapter examines four distinct but related changes in imperial taxation typically discussed independently of one another: the creation in 1887 of an empire-wide zone of free circulation for imported opium; incomplete attempts in 1890 to make provincial opium *lijin* regimes more productive; the 1902 Sino-British Mackay Treaty, which eliminated all *lijin* in return for higher tariff rates; and the creation of an empire-wide zone of tax-free circulation for domestic opium in 1906. Whereas most histories of the period discuss the 1906 domestic opium regime as a step toward ending opium use, I trace the roots of the regime's design to concerns with fiscal management that gained urgency as Qing borrowing and debt increased. Beginning in the 1890s, elites inside and outside government began to critique *lijin* on practical grounds as well as political-economic ones. These arguments drew from a discourse of state-strengthening, as well as from evidence that the new tax regime for imported opium, which had eliminated opium *lijin* succeeded in generating higher revenue returns. The genealogy I provide here of how the strategies and tactics first used to tax a foreign import became generalized within currents of official political economy demonstrates how the project of wealth and power (*fuguo* 富國) appropriated strategies of commercial governance developed within the treaty port regime. Such appropriation intentionally and unintentionally reshaped the imperial polity into a more homogenous political administrative entity reliant on value circulation and capital growth for order and sovereignty.

---

14. Susan Mann Jones, *Local Merchants and the Chinese Bureaucracy, 1750–1950* (Stanford: Stanford University Press, 1987), 6.
15. Michel Foucault, *Security, Territory, Population: Lectures at the Collège de France, 1977–78*, ed. Michel Senellart, trans. Graham Bell (Basingstoke: Picador, 2009), 59. The phrase is Foucault's; the use in this context is mine.

The Opium Regime Change, 1887

Opium was one of the most frequently and highly taxed commodities in the Qing Empire. Treaty terms explicitly permitted the Qing government to tax and regulate the drug as it saw fit once importers sold it at port. Consequently, it was subject to the most variable levies devised by municipal and *lijin* authorities. According to an 1879 investigation by the IMC, the total revenue collected from a chest of foreign opium after import and prior to retail sale ranged from a low of 9 taels in Yichang (宜昌), Hubei to a high of 83 taels in Xiamen (廈門), Fujian.[16] In the matter of domestically grown opium, according to one official report, "no two provinces act alike."[17] The levies paid by a given cargo of foreign opium could have included treaty-based import duties, *tiexiang* (貼餉 a premium on silver currency, related to troop provisioning), *haifang* (海防 a levy for coastal defense), and *xiaohao* (銷號 a fee levied when silver ingot was melted down into smaller units).[18] According to other sources, it also could have contributed stamp taxes (*piaoshui* 票稅), military funds (*tuanlian jingfei* 團練經費 and *junxiang* 軍餉), luxury taxes (*huashui* 華稅), registration fees (*guahao* 掛號), and three classes of ad hoc levies (*bujuan* 補捐): additional (*jia* 加), acknowledged (*ren* 認), and warehouse (*zhan* 棧). Opium funded philanthropic projects and paid miscellaneous subsidies.[19] In keeping with the general devolution of bureaucratic responsibilities to local elites, characteristic of the period, these levies were often collected by groups of either merchants or local gentry.

In 1887, this heterogeneous, decentralized system of opium taxation came to a dramatic end. In that year, foreign opium began to enter the Qing Empire under the cognizance of a single regulatory regime, crafted consequent to 1876 negotiations at Chefoo between Li Hongzhang and Thomas Wade. Within Qing bureaucratic discourse the new strategy was referred to as "increase taxes and eliminate *lijin*" (*jia shui mian li* 加稅免釐) or alternately "joint collection" (*bing zheng* 並徵). The first name referred to the increased tariff duties that imported opium began to pay in 1887. The second name referred to the reason these duties were higher—new collection procedures that transmuted *lijin* into an 80 tael (per catty) duty taken by the IMC

---

16. IMC, *Opium*, Special Series No. 4 (Shanghai: Statistical Department of the Inspectorate General, 1881), 17, 46. IMC data suggest that opium tax rates and the frequency of taxation did not follow a set pattern. At the time of the report's publication, 10 taels equaled 3 pounds sterling.
17. IMC, *Native Opium, 1887*, Special Series No. 9 (Shanghai: Statistical Department of the Inspectorate General, 1888), 51.
18. IMC, *Opium*, 54.
19. He Lie, 釐金制度新談 [New investigations into the *lijin* system] (Taipei: Sili dongwu daxue, 1972), 189; W. S. K. Waung, *The Controversy: Opium and Sino-British Relations, 1858–1887* (Hong Kong: Lun Men Press, 1977), 199. The latter study also distinguishes between *xingli* (行厘 transit *lijin*) and *zuoli* (坐厘 *lijin* levied at landing).

at the time of import.[20] The reconfigured 110 tael charge was a boon for the central government's coffers, often remarked upon as a success story of Qing state-building. Yet, what the post-1887 opium taxation regime looked like and its reverberations through the imperial government have thus far been a lacuna in our picture of Qing opium policies. The regime shows in striking terms how regulatory tactics produced a specific configuration of Qing territoriality. As it was practiced, joint collection further elaborated the modalities of "mechanical correctness" already operating in IMC offices. As a substitute for *lijin*, it also expanded an alternative arts of governance defined by the exclusion of local conditions and local nonstate actors.

The post-1887 regime of opium taxation had multiple ground roots. During the British campaign to abolish all *lijin* from the treaty ports, Li Hongzhang warned that the proposal threatened a loss of revenue "so considerable that the plan could not possibly be carried into effect."[21] So during negotiations over the Chefoo Convention, British Minister Thomas Wade offered Li increased opium revenues. Cognizant that opium levies in the ports formed a considerable income to which Chinese authorities, by treaty, were "indisputably entitled," Wade counseled the Foreign Office, "I do think we are bound to assist the Chinese Government to protect itself against this loss [of opium revenue]."[22] But, he added, for the British government to support Qing collection of opium taxes, the current collection arrangements had to change. "The presence of the native executive employed to this end is, for many reasons, inconvenient," he wrote and suggested making "the presence of that executive unnecessary by transferring its functions to the foreign Customs Inspectorate."[23] To solve the problem of general *lijin* levies within port limits and to accommodate Qing revenue rights on opium Wade suggested all opium collections be vested in the IMC, which he felt was "an admirable organized service, whose proceedings would be as regular, as the action of the *lijin* collectorates' executive had proved itself, at Shanghai at all events, the most considerable of the open ports, to be fruitful of misunderstanding."[24]

Qing authorities had their own reasons to think that joint collection would be beneficial. By the 1880s, it was clear that ports such as Hankou, Wenzhou, Hangzhou,

---

20. IMC, *Opium*, 17, 46.
21. "Memorial by the Grand Secretary Li Hung-chang Reporting the Conduct and Issue of the Negotiations at Chefoo, Dated September 14, 1876," Legation translation, TNA, Confidential Print (Numerical Series), FO 881/3901; Li Hongzhang, "煙台議結滇案摺" [Yantai discussions of the Yunnan case], *Li wen zhong gong (Hongzhang) quan ji*, 27:40.
22. Wade to Lord Salisbury, No. 53, 10 May 1879, TNA, Confidential Print (Numerical Series), FO 881/4530.
23. Wade to Earl of Derby, 14 July 1877, TNA Confidential Print (Numerical Series), FO 881/3273, 52.
24. Wade to Lord Salisbury, No. 53, 10 May 1879, TNA, Confidential Print (Numerical Series), FO 881/4530.

and Ningbo and the countryside surrounding Chongqing (a key entrepot for the domestic trade) all engaged in competitive fiscal policy—offering discounts, low tax rates, or premiums to attract the opium trade.²⁵ In Fujian and Guangdong, the provincial governments fought what Peter Thilly describes as a "protracted trade war" over the trade.²⁶ The circulation of opium was not contained within or specific to any single province, so how local governments taxed it shaped routes of circulation and where opium revenues pooled. An increase in the *lijin* collected at Tianjin in 1881, for example, nearly halved the amount of opium sold in the port as merchants circumvented it to market the drug farther inland.²⁷ The losses to government revenue from path-changing opium flows were significant enough that two leading officials of the period, when asked by the central government for their opinions on the possibility of new arrangements for opium taxation, broke with conventional wisdom that supported *lijin*. In many respects, these two men, Li Hongzhang and Zuo Zongtang, were quite different. Whereas Zuo's governance was marked strongly by echoes of his education in the classics, Li's efforts to build "the dignity of the state" (*guoti* 國體) often strayed from the norms of Confucian statecraft.²⁸ But both argued for strategic and tactical changes to unify opium taxation: a single rate of *lijin* on imported opium to end competitive rate setting and stanch the flow of merchants to ports with lower levies.²⁹ Zuo further argued that tariff and *lijin* taxes on foreign opium could be combined into a single levy.³⁰

Finally, the opium import trade was a multifaceted regional and international affair. The regional political economy of opium, which also included British India and Hong Kong as well as Portuguese Macao meant that the new tax rate and

---

25. IMC, *Trade Reports for the Year 1868*, 62, 69, 70; IMC, *Decennial Report for 1891*, 88–104, 176, 396; IMC, *Decennial Report for 1901*, 1:153, 2:12, 54; Rowe, *Hankow*, 192; Yong Chen, "赫德與鴉片'稅厘並征'" [Robert Hart and joint collection of opium taxes and lijin], *Jinan xuebao* 4 (2006), 141. In some places, the discount could be as high as 80 percent. See Lin Man-Houng, "晚清的鴉片稅" [Late Qing opium taxation], *Si yu yan* 思語言 16, no. 5 (1979): 427–51, here 438.
26. Peter Thilly, *The Opium Business: A History of Crime and Capitalism in Maritime China* (Stanford: Stanford University Press, 2022), 107–12.
27. Li Hongzhang, "遵議鴉片厘稅事宜摺" [With respect to opium duties], in *Li Hongzhang quanji* (Hefei shi: Anhui jiaoyu chubanshe, 2008), 9:395.
28. Peter B. Lavelle, *The Profits of Nature: Colonial Development and the Quest for Resources in Nineteenth-Century China* (New York: Columbia University Press, 2020), 96; K. C. Liu, *China's Early Modernization and Reform Movement: Studies in Late Nineteenth-Century China and American-Chinese Relations* (Taipei: Institute of Modern History, Academia Sinica, 2009), 261–62, 276, 303, 331.
29. Li, [Opium duties], 395; Zuo Zongtang, "復陳增加洋藥土煙稅厘摺" [Reply with respect to increasing foreign and native opium taxes], GX 7.8.27, in *Zuo Zongtang quanji* [Collected works of Zuo Zongtang] (Changsha: Yuelu shu ban, 1986) 8:47.
30. Zuo Zongtang, "左宗棠奏嚴禁吸食鴉片先增洋藥土煙稅捐摺" [Zuo Zongtang's memorial on prohibiting opium smoking and growing by first increasing taxes on foreign and native opium], in *Li Hongzhang quanji*, 9:396–98, here 397; Zuo, [Opium taxes], 47.

collection procedures slowly evolved through multilateral negotiation. Macao and Hong Kong were large centers of smuggling activity, and recent history suggested to Qing administrators as well as British diplomats that new protocols would be needed to counteract the increased smuggling that a higher opium tariff would incentivize. In British India, meanwhile, the government was alarmed over what Wade's Chefoo Convention meant for opium firms and state finances. Last, for the new tariff to succeed, Wade needed to convince other treaty signatories to accept its terms. Different opium tariffs for different foreign nationals was not what Qing authorities had in mind.[31] Within the framework of the regional opium economy and treaty regime, numerous sovereignties had to agree about how the Qing Empire would govern opium. The one point of immediate agreement amongst these parties was that the IMC would administer the new regime.

Scholarship has generally glossed over what it meant to transfer opium *lijin* collection to the IMC. Many historians view the episode in light of the long arc of Qing anti-opium policies and suggest that opium tax reorganization was a strategy to more effectively police the trade and use higher taxes to drive down opium consumption.[32] Others have interpreted the transfer as part of Beijing's efforts to generate the central government's wealth and control, taking for granted that as an agency directly responsible to Beijing, the IMC was a natural institutional choice for centralized collection.[33] Recent Chinese scholarship has examined imported opium tax reform in the context of foreign efforts to eliminate *lijin*, but its emphasis on the IMC as a power-hungry, imperialist institution cuts short its consideration of the political economics and politico-spatial restructuring involved in creating unified collection.[34] To better understand the content and implications of imported opium

---

31. China: Further Correspondence: Chefoo Convention. Bound: China 12 (1887), Confidential Print (Numerical Series), TNA, FO 881/5632; Great Britain, *China No. 3 (1882) Correspondence respecting the Agreement between the Ministers Plenipotentiary of the Governments of Great Britain and China, Signed at Chefoo, September 13, 1876* [C. 3395]; Edward Hertslet, *Treaties, &C., between Great Britain and China; and between China and Foreign Powers; Orders in Council, Rules, Regulations, Acts of Parliament, Decrees, and Notifications Affecting British Interests in China, in Force on the 1st January, 1896* (London: Harrison, 1896), 1:78; Shên-tsu Wang, *The Margary Affair and the Chefoo Agreement* (London: Oxford University Press, 1940), 85, 118, 122; China: Further Correspondence: Chefoo Convention. Bound: China 12 (1885), Confidential Print (Numerical Series), TNA, FO 81/5227; Stanley Wright, *China's Struggle for Tariff Autonomy, 1843–1938* (Shanghai: Kelly & Walsh, 1938), 272–88.
32. Paul Wilson Howard, "Opium Supression in Qing China: Responses to a Social Problem" (PhD diss., University of Pennsylvania, 1998); Man-Houng Lin, "Late Qing Perceptions of Native Opium," *Harvard Journal of Asiatic Studies* 64, no. 1 (2004): 117–44.
33. Joyce Madancy, "Unearthing Popular Attitudes toward the Opium Trade and Opium Suppression in Late Qing and Early Republican Fujian," *Modern China* 27, no. 4 (2001): 436–83; R. Bin Wong, "Opium and Modern State Making," in *Opium Regimes: China, Britain, and Japan, 1839–1952*, ed. Timothy Brook and Bob Wakabayashi (Berkeley: University of California Press, 2000), 189–211.
34. Chen, [Hart].

tax reorganization, the next section examines the novel mechanisms the IMC engineered to supplant extant institutions and procedures for collecting revenue from opium commerce. Although the general contours of the reorganized collection quite readily lend themselves to narratives of state centralization, I argue that the shift contained transformations in the constitution of imperial authority that remain out of view in traditional analyses of late Qing power struggles between state and society, state and merchant, and the central government and provinces.

Central to the new tax regime was opium itself. Charged with holding opium in bond until all taxes were paid, the IMC developed elaborate protocols for registering, warehousing, and stamping all the opium balls, cakes, and chests its offices touched.[35] At the center of these procedures was a specialized "Opium Desk" that kept an "Opium Movement Book," in which each incoming shipment was enumerated and tracked until it was stamped for release. Office protocols also included duplicate registers that could be cross-checked and unique numbers issued to each parcel of the drug. At one point in the development of the opium procedures, Hart instructed four different kinds of customs employees to keep overlapping records of opium labels to "render the control over the labels much more effective."[36] This close supervision and individual labeling of opium balls while in bond facilitated their "free" circulation after they left IMC offices.

It is worth considering for a moment what this shift in tactics meant for strategies of imperial order, and in particular, what happened when the central government created a condition of "free circulation." Typically, as an economic concept, "free circulation" connotes removal, an unfettering, a liberation of trade from overt state control. Yet, when we compare the details of the IMC regime with what we know about earlier tactics of opium taxation in which opium circulation was mediated by merchant groups and local authorities, we see that the new strategy and tactics to secure opium did not so much secure conditions of commercial freedom for the trade as shift the fulcrum of control from a diffuse group of individuals to highly visible centers of collection.

This comparison is possible on the basis of a set of "Opium Compliance Registers," dated Xianfeng 10 (1860/1), and archived by the British Foreign Office as evidence of Qing tax practices. The provenance of the registers is not clear, but they were kept by private firms and outline merchant-based collection procedures.[37]

---

35. IMC, *Inspector General's Circulars, Second Series (Nos. 318–450) 1885–1889* (Shanghai: Statistical Department of the Inspector General of Customs, 1889), nos. 354 (4 January 1887), 356 (20 January 1887), 370 (25 April 1887), 371 (27 April 1887).
36. IMC, *Circulars Second*, no. 448 (30 March 1889).
37. "Opium Taxation: Books for Recording Transactions, Issued to Chinese Firms," TNA, FO 1080/96. It is not possible to tell from the documents or the archival filing system the geographic provenance of the registers.

These entailed the following: each opium firm's accounting department kept a register, which it received monthly from the regional Opium Tax and Contribution Bureau. When merchants (identified as being from Guangdong and Hunan) wanted to purchase opium from one of these firms, they first applied to the regional bureau for a certificate. At the time of purchase, the seller recorded the transaction as well as the imperial tax (*shui* 税) and local contribution (*juan* 捐) collected. Each month, the firms returned the registers to the bureau, which compared the entries with the certificates it had issued. The bureau's staff was composed of four appointees, selected from the accounting departments of firms currently in the trade. Consequently, the process of tax collection and auditing remained internal to the group of opium firms.

The Opium Compliance Registers index a governing strategy that recruited potentially obstructionist merchants into collaborators and paired merchant profit-seeking with service to the state. In return for self-governance, opium merchants pledged to collect revenues on the government's behalf and act as their own mechanism of compliance. Such delegation of state functions to extra-bureaucratic social groups, historians of modern China have argued, was a compensatory strategy for an empire that lacked a sufficiently large and robust bureaucracy.[38] Even so, it was also a strategy that instituted hierarchies of responsibility between the court and its subjects in an arrangement both sides found legitimate at least in part because it produced mutual benefits. The dynasty recruited merchant private interests into the service of the state and the people. Conversely, taking on these responsibilities put merchant communities in a position to negotiate with the state.

While this delegated collection offered a mechanism to align the social function and well-being of a specific social group with the more general well-being of the entire polity, IMC collection abandoned such ambitions. Hart chose instead to stamp opium balls with proof that tax was paid. He chose this tactic on the grounds that only by marking the individual commodity could he eliminate ambiguities generated in processes of marketing and distribution and thereby create for opium a zone of unfettered circulation.[39] Intact labels signaled to officials to let the opium pass without inspection or further charge. Broken or missing labels authoritatively identified smuggled opium. This tactic impressed merchant cargos into service as government informants. Whereas previously the merchant and the official had been able to manipulate records, the new labeling regime intended for the stamped commodity to keep their actions within legal bounds. Stated somewhat differently, whereas opium compliance registers called for a self-regulating merchant to

---

38. Jones, *Local Merchants*, 111–12, 29–32, 60–61; Bryna Goodman, *Native Place, City, and Nation in Regional Networks and Identities in Shanghai, 1853–1937* (Berkeley: University of California Press, 1995), 119, 129.
39. IMC, *Circulars Second*, no. 371.

produce himself as a mechanism for generating commercial and political order, the new tactics secured proper order quasi-independent of the merchant. The IMC's tactics eschewed managing the opium trade as a locally embedded affair conducted by numerous official functionaries and merchants and instead focused on engineering a flow of commodity capital through machinelike offices (see Chapter 2) that would transform opium balls into executors of fiscal-administrative order. In this role reversal, merchants were governed, not governing. Similarly, the moral quality of the official became less critical when the commodity could itself testify whether he acted in compliance with regulations or not.

"Rectify" Domestic Opium Taxes, 1891

The fiscal windfall produced by foreign opium *bing zheng* was substantial—between 5 and 6 million taels annually through 1894.[40] But with this increase in revenues came new dilemmas and disorders. In Xiamen (廈門), the closure of opium *lijin* bureaus cut off funds for the local examination hall, orphanage, and temples that provided alms to the poor.[41] Opium smugglers also found themselves without means of work. In Wuhu (蕪湖), several hundred displaced smugglers set to thieving and violence and attacked officers of a US steamship.[42] Meanwhile, the opium market began to shift. Although opium imports steadily declined after 1888, provincial leaders, deprived of foreign opium as a rich revenue source, intensified domestic opium cultivation and taxes on domestic circulation.[43]

After only a few years of the "joint collection" regime, it was clear to authorities in Beijing that something needed to be done about domestic opium taxation. It had been nearly a decade since memorials from Li Hongzhang and Zuo Zongtang had first outlined the difficulties provinces faced in taxing domestic opium circulation. Now official intelligence, very likely generated by Hart and the IMC, suggested that although opium cultivation was increasing throughout the empire, much of the domestic crop went from field to pipe untaxed or local officials siphoned off a

---

40. Tang Xianlong, ed., 中國近代海關稅收和分配統, 1861–1910 [Statistics on customs revenue collection and distribution in modern China 1861–1910] (Beijing: Zhonghua shuju, 1992), table 108.
41. Thilly, *Opium Business*, 114.
42. IMC, *Decennial Report for 1891*, 244–45.
43. According to tabulations by Tang Xianglong, import duties from opium peaked in 1888 at 2.5 million Kuping taels and declined thereafter. *Lijin* on foreign opium collected by the IMC likewise peaked at 6.5 million taels in 1888, a year after collection began. Although this income source likewise diminished in the succeeding years, it remained a substantial revenue stream—between 3 and 6 million taels a year. For the years 1888–1910, the central government controlled about three-quarters of the total customs revenues, the rest shared between provincial governments, customs operations, and other uses. See [Customs revenue] tables 107, 108.

large portion for personal enrichment.[44] Such revenue loss was not a new problem for Qing rulers. The Yongzheng emperor had faced a similar set of issues when he embarked on his program of fiscal institutional innovation. But unlike the Yongzheng court, which saw a problem of impoverished local administration and inadequately paid office holders, the Guangxu court saw an untapped growth opportunity.[45] The size of the opium trade suggested to authorities that earnestly managed opium taxation would add to military funds (*biyi xiangxu* 裨益餉需) and help restore economic sovereignty (*shouhui liquan* 收回利權). The question was how. Could the existing system of domestic opium *lijin* be fixed, or would revenues benefit more from "joint collection" on the same lines as imported opium?[46]

From all appearances, the current system of *lijin* collection was broke. There were competing explanations, however, as to what had broken it. One explanation, initially taken up by authorities in Beijing, was that there was a crisis in honest and earnest governance. In 1891, after provincial treasuries failed to have on hand money to send to famine-struck areas in Zhili, the Board of Revenue, Zongli yamen, and Grand Council (*Junjichu* 軍機處) called for "rectification" (*zheng dun* 整頓) of provincial domestic opium taxation.[47] Throughout the 1870s and 1880s, historian He Wenkai points out, many of the central government's regular assignment orders had gone unfilled owing to "delays, reductions, and arrears."[48] Yet leaders in Beijing could not be sure whether the problem was one of deliberate neglect or something else. The polity needed officials who would not merely collect taxes but also report the "full story" of what was collected where so the Board of Revenue could adequately monitor what revenue was available where.[49] The Guangxu court called for provincial governments to appoint "honest and talented" officials to investigate domestic opium accounts and clearly report back exact net receipts.[50] The rectifica-

---

44. *Da Qing shi lu* 大清實錄 [Veritable records of the Qing dynasty], Guangxu 光緒, Dezong jing huangdi shilu 德宗景皇帝實錄, Scripta Sinica (Taipei: Academica Sinica), GX16.4.15, juan 284, 783.1–785 (hereafter QSL). The record makes explicit reference to a report the yamen instructed Hart to make on which localities grew and sold Chinese opium as well as prevailing prices and taxes. It seems very likely the English version of this report is the 1887 IMC publication *Native Opium*.
45. Zelin, *Magistrate's Tael*, 4, 27–37, 96.
46. These discussions precede by nearly a decade the failed effort, launched in 1899 to "add taxes and abolish lijin." See Jones, *Local Merchants*, 151–52.
47. He Wenkai, *Paths towards the Modern Fiscal State: England, Japan, and China* (Cambridge, MA: Harvard University Press, 2013), 162. The funds should have been available in special provincial accounts for disaster relief mandated by the Board of Revenue in 1883.
48. He, *Paths*, 162–63.
49. QSL, juan 284, GX16.4.15, 785.1. The central government's concern with honest administration is strongly expressed in a follow-up communication a few months later in which the Junjichu is clearly frustrated that attempts to investigate embezzlement in Xuzhou has produced a useless investigation of corruption by an individual known himself to be corrupt. See juan 287, 829.2–830.2.
50. QSL, juan 284, GX16.4.15, 783.1–785.1. For an English-language précis of the concerns, see "Notes from the Native Press," NCHSCCG, 11 July 1890, 52.

tion campaign of 1891, like earlier initiatives to right the fiscal system, put better information and more honest governance at the beginning of the pursuit of strength and wealth.[51]

Some provincial authorities echoed Beijing's assessment that the actions of persons were undermining the system. Provincial audits routinely unearthed officials embezzling *lijin* revenues for personal gain.[52] In Hubei, a key transit province for Sichuan opium, Governor-General Zhang Zhidong (張之洞, 1837–1909) criticized unruly travelling merchants and fearful local collectors for lost revenues. Zhang was generally skeptical that absent of official regulation, merchants would perform their economically useful function.[53] In the context of the *zheng dun* campaign, he argued that merchants were bent on tax evasion and had been known to even swarm tax collection offices to evade levies. Local officials, Zhang postulated, in turn worried they would fall short of collection quotas and therefore offered discounts to attract trade but, in doing so, hurt overall collections.[54] A two-pronged solution, Zhang advised, required more stations and personnel on the main routes of opium traffic and no tolerance for discounts or "frivolous collections."[55]

Structural features of opium circulation and taxation offered a second explanation for the crisis. In their 1881 memorials, Zuo Zongtang and Li Hongzhang had noted that inland fiscal networks inspected and taxed opium at multiple points according to different rates depending on provenance and transit route. This network used paper receipts, issued to merchants, to identify opium shipments and testify to taxes paid. But paperwork in the hands of the traveling salesman did not easily pin down a uniform article of trade that could enter and exit circulation unnoticed. Merchants, Zuo and Li explained, sold opium on the move, breaking open chests as needed. This practice and the small size of opium packages meant merchants could mix balls of opium into other cargoes, hiding it from tax officials. Or merchants could pick up new supplies and claim the new cargo was the same opium that had already paid taxes. Most concerning, although opium crossed between provinces, each had their own regulations, which made cross-border policing almost

---

51. Zelin, *Magistrate's Tael*, 80–81, 271–72; GX16 4M; GX16 7M.
52. He, *Paths*, 168.
53. Peter Zarrow, *After Empire: The Conceptual Transformation of the Chinese State, 1885–1924* (Stanford: Stanford University Press, 2012), 124–25.
54. "Joint Proclamation by the Governor-General of the Hukwang and the Governor of Hupeh on the Taxation of Native Opium" [Chinese text], in IMC, *Decennial Report for 1891*, 123–25; Zhang Zhidong, "整頓土藥稅項籌議辦法" [Discussion of methods for the rectification of native opium taxes], in *Zhang Zhidong quanji di er ce zouyi* [Collected works of Zhang Zhidong volume 2 memorials], ed. Yuan Shuyi, Sun Huafeng, and Li Bingxin (Shijiazhuang: Hebei renmin chubanshe, 1998), juan 29, GX16.8M.24D, 768–72.
55. Zhang, [Rectification of native opium taxes].

impossible.⁵⁶ Zuo and Li each proposed that because differences in prices and taxes were the root of much illegal activity, a single tax rate should apply to all varieties of the domestic product.⁵⁷ Li further advised that native opium pay tax once and then circulate throughout the empire without further charge.⁵⁸

A key difference between the analysis offered by Zuo and Li and that given by the Zongli yamen and Zhang Zhidong was that whereas the former focused on the overall dynamics of commodity movements, the latter focused on locally specific conditions and persons. Opium, Zhang pointed out, took various routes through the Hubei countryside. It passed through many remote and secluded places, so if one was to tax it, one needed to catch it in hard to reach places. Some barriers successfully taxed opium; others did not. The problem, Zhang felt, was not the strategy of scattered taxation but its implementation, which required sufficient numbers of incorruptible staff. Akin to how the imperial bureaucracy classified administrative posts as troublesome (*fan* 煩), difficult (*nan* 難), wearisome (*pi* 疲), or a thoroughfare (*chong* 衝) to determine official appointments, Zhang recognized *lijin* collection points that were in "desolate and out of the way areas," along known smuggling routes, or on provincial frontiers, all of which he thought called for slightly different deployments of resources—a new bureau here, more examiners and patrol boats there, coordination with neighboring provincial authorities.⁵⁹ To unify taxes on domestic opium, which was the essence of the earlier proposals by Li and Zuo, Zhang submitted, reeked of "poor governance that would alienate the people."⁶⁰ Rather, the government should focus on recruiting enough quality personnel and putting in place a working system of rewards and punishments: "It is said that honest and enlightened government depends on the proper use of able persons; in financial matters even more so."⁶¹

Reports from other provinces, however, suggest that en masse commodity movements, particularly within the opium trade, were emerging as a possible standpoint for revised commercial governance. Reports sent to the Zongli yamen during the 1890–1891 *zheng dun* campaign indicated that unlike in the case of the tea trade thirty years earlier, when authorities in Hubei, Jiangxi, and Anhui had attempted to

---

56. Zuo, [Opium taxes], 47; Li, [Opium duties], 395.
57. Zuo, [Opium taxes], 47; Li, [Opium duties], 396.
58. Li, [Opium duties], 396.
59. R. Kent Guy, *Qing Governors and Their Provinces: The Evolution of Territorial Administration in China, 1644–1796* (Seattle: University of Washington Press, 2010), 57. Citing G. William Skinner, "Cities and the Hierarchy of Local Systems," in *The City in Late Imperial China* (Stanford: Stanford University Press, 1977).
60. Zhang, [Rectification of opium taxes].
61. Zhang Zhidong, "籌議整頓釐金辦法摺" [Consideration of methods for rectifying *lijin*], in *Zhang wenxiang gong quan ji zouyi*, ed. Shen Yulong 沈雲龍 Jindai zhongguo shiliao congkang di si shi liu ji (Taibei: Wenhai chubanshe, 1970), v. 456: 2974–2795.

constrain the movement of tea to feed provincial customs, emergent opium regimes responded to how opium traveled through and across provinces generating an apparatus that could, as Michel Foucault has put it, connect up "with the very reality of these fluctuations."[62] Whereas *lijin* was infamous for low tax rates at any given barrier but frequent incidences of levy and inspection, around the time of the *zheng dun* campaign tax regimes devised for domestic opium in Hunan, Hubei, and Jiangsu used a strategy of consolidated taxation and free circulation within the province.[63] In Fujian, Fengtian (Liaoning), and Yunnan, as well opium began in the 1890s to "circulate freely" within provincial boundaries after the payment of one or two taxes.[64]

Without further research, it is not clear whether the new regulations were dictated by Beijing, innovated by provincial authorities, or were the result of some compromise. What is clear is that these structural changes in opium *lijin*, designed as strategies to increase collected revenues, evolved in dialogue with the treaty taxation regime emanating out from IMC offices. Simultaneous with the *zheng dun* campaign, the IMC opened an office at Chongqing (重慶), a key port on the upper Yangzi River and a key entrepot for the busy opium traffic out of Yunnan and Sichuan. As foreign firms moved into the upper Yangzi area, they offered services as shipping agents for Chinese opium firms. This practice redirected Yunnan and Sichuan opium out of the *changguan* and *lijin* systems and into the IMC regime, which taxed cargoes twice (an export duty at Chongqing and a reentry duty at Yichang, Hubei) and then mandated the good's "free circulation."[65]

The IMC's regulations for domestic opium, issued by the Zongli yamen, used the force of imperial sovereignty to create a transprovincial circulation zone that stretched across the empire. As commentators would put it, it was "practically the Treaty system for the Foreign drug adapted for the Native."[66] At first, use of the system was moderate. Within a year of the IMC office opening at Chongqing, four of the ten Chinese opium firms active at a key entrepot of "Fou-chou" switched to shipping through foreign agencies in the new treaty port.[67] At the same time, as the introduction of treaty-based taxation had done for other commodities decades earlier, the IMC regime for domestic opium set a new framework for the operation of provincial tax regimes. IMC commissioners observed that after 1890, provincial

---

62. English language extracts of these reports appear in IMC, *Circulars Second*, no. 577, 13 June 1892, Enclosure 1; Foucault, *Security*, 59–60.
63. "Joint Proclamation"; IMC, *Decennial Report for 1891*, 327; He, *Paths*, 172. In Jiangsu, the shift followed the instruction of the central government.
64. See reports for Wenzhou, Fuzhou, Niuzhuang, Mengzi in IMC, *Decennial Report for 1891*.
65. On opening of Chongqing, see Imperial Maritime Customs, *Inspector General's Circulars*, vol. 5, Second Series (Shanghai: Inspectorate General of Customs, 1897), no. 541, 4 May 1891.
66. IMC, *Decennial Report for 1891*, 327.
67. IMC, *Decennial Report for 1891*, 94. The remaining six "larger" firms used the *chuangguan*.

domestic opium taxes were often kept below the rates charged by the IMC.[68] More significantly, many provincial regimes offered substantial weight discounts on their duties, finding that when they did not, opium firms quickly switched their business to IMC offices.[69] At the same time the structure of opium taxes converged around a principle that free circulation was a better source of profit (for the state), competition between the treaty regime and *lijin* continued.

Wealth and Taxes

The *zheng dun* campaign took place at a moment when many elites and scholars, often with ties to global commerce, also began to contemplate changes to domestic commercial taxation that would better accommodate programs of capital accumulation and growth. Unlike previous campaigns to rectify fiscal practice, which took shape around ideas of immutable needs and fixed wealth that needed to be carefully allocated, the anti-*lijin* campaign helped shape a vision of ever-increasing wealth and an expanding horizon of needs.[70] Throughout the "late Qing reform era" (conventionally, 1902–1911), Susan Mann Jones writes, "A changing ideology of tax collection and a new institutional structure attempted for the first time to combine two goals: to promote trade at national and local levels and to increase state revenue from commerce."[71] This, of course, had been the program of the IMC since it commenced operations; it was also the vision agitated for by at least two generations of foreign diplomats.

For Chinese critics of *lijin* outside the imperial bureaucracy, like Wang Tao (王韜, 1828–1897) and Zheng Guanying (鄭觀, 1842–1922), the tax was not simply a levy from trade but subtraction from total consumption and growth.[72] Zheng, who wrote extensively on matters of commerce and governance, warned in 1893 that *lijin* limited the extent of markets for local products "because tax rates drive costs up past the profit level" and because delays and multiple handlings at inspection barriers ruined the quality of goods.[73] Commerce and production could not grow

---

68. For rates, see native opium sections IMC, *Decennial 1891* and *Decennial 1901*. For an example of connected increases, see the Yichang 1901 report.
69. In 1901, the following treaty ports reported use of weight discounts by nearby *changguan* and *lijin* authorities: Mengzi (Yunnan), Ningbo (Zhejiang), Chongqing (Sichuan), and Shashi (Hubei). In 1897, authorities at Chongqing canceled the weight discount, only to reintroduce it after receipts fell off. IMC, *Decennial Report 1901*, 153.
70. On precedent, see Zelin, *Magistrate's Tael*, 267, 288.
71. Jones, *Local Merchants*, 145.
72. Paul A. Cohen, *Between Tradition and Modernity: Wang T'ao and Reform in Late Ch'ing China* (Cambridge, MA: Harvard University Press, 1974), 206, drawing from Wang's essay "Li juan bi lun."
73. Quoted in Jones, *Local Merchants*, 146.

in the shadow of *lijin*. "Without the removal of *lijin*, it will be difficult to invigorate commerce," Zheng warned his readers.[74] Concerned with overall levels of wealth, both within the merchant community and within China vis-à-vis the rest of the world, Wang and Zheng found fault with taxation strategies predicated on delegated authority and heterogenous conditions within China. Unlike previous critiques of excessive taxation, however, which focused on whether levies were consistent with Confucian governance, Zheng and Wang paid more attention to the structure of the levies. One solution favored by Wang and Zheng was that already tried in imported opium taxation: an increase in customs duties in return for the complete elimination of *lijin*.[75]

This critique of *lijin* became influential enough that the editors of *Huangchao jingshi wen xinbian* (皇朝經世文新編, 1898), which historian Andrea Janku has characterized as part of a new wave of statecraft manuals influenced by Chinese engagements with Western political economy, included several essays that took up the question of commercial taxation.[76] In this 1898 edition of the statecraft genre, a number of essays in newly organized sections on "Tariffs" (*shui ze* 稅則) and "Commerce and Governance" (*shang zheng* 商政) considered, often in numeric detail, the paths to wealth opened and foreclosed by foreign trade and different tax policies. Many of the essays were preoccupied with what some historians have called the "mercantilist" turn in governance. Nations like France, one essay pointed out, became wealthy through policies designed to grow their export trade. What low tax rates did not produce immediately, sales of goods ultimately did.[77] Another warned that taxes on domestic produce multiplied the burden on the people. This was a mistake, the essayist warned, as "the tax paid by the merchants is the capital [*zi* 資] of the people to buy things."[78] The earlier "Manchu paternalism" of the Yongzheng emperor had warned officials in the provinces, "The smallest grain of rice represents the blood and sweat of the people."[79] The emergent political economy of the 1890s thought first of the capacity of the people to generate demand for goods.

---

74. Zheng Guanying, "釐捐" [*Li* (*jin*) contributions], in *Shengshi weiyan* [Warning for a prosperous age], *Zheng Guanying ji* [Collected works of Zheng Guanying] (Beijing: Zhonghhua shu ju, 2013), 331.
75. Cohen, *Between Tradition*, 206; Zheng, [*Li*(*jin*) contributions].
76. Andrea Janku, "New Methods to Nourish the People: Late Qing Encyclopaedic Writings on Political Economy," in *Chinese Encyclopaedias of New Global Knowledge (1870–1930)*, ed. M. Dolezelov-Velingerova and R. G. Wagner (Berlin: Springer-Verlag, 2014), 329–65.
77. Ma Jianzhong, "論洋貨入內地免稅" [On foreign goods entering the interior tax-free], in *Huangchao jingshiwen xinbian* [21 juan] (hereafter HCJSWXB), ed. Mai Zhonghua (Shanghai: Yi shu ju, 1898), juan 12, 14–17.
78. Anonymous, "論稅則" [On tariffs], in HCJSWXB, juan 12, 4–6.
79. Quoted in Zelin, *Magistrate's Tael*, 81; on paternalism, see Zelin, *Magistrate's Tael*, 115.

Mercantilism aside, statecraft was becoming engaged in a more abstract project to grow commodity production and consumption.

As a whole, the newly included essays in *Huangchao jingshi xinbian* indicate that the question of tax-free commodity circulation had become central to statecraft and that this question incorporated into statecraft a broad, if sometimes novel, set of authorities, which ranged from reformer Xue Fucheng (薛福成, 1838–1894), to missionary and translator Reverend Timothy Richard (1845–1919), to British consuls who penned trade reports. Within this broad frame, answers to questions of enriching the people and not excessively burdening the people looked away from spatially and temporally specific governance. Even those who voiced skepticism about eliminating *lijin* in favor of increased customs duties, like Xue Fucheng, argued the object to be kept in view was the "general situation of all under heaven" (*tianxia daju* 天下大局) and not "one corner, one time, or one matter" (*yi yu yi shi yi shi* 一隅一時一事).[80]

In her work on late Qing knowledge production, Janku tracks the changing engagements and conceptual structures of Chinese scholars in the post-Taiping Qing Empire. She argues that new genres of scholarly texts and new organizational schemas within statecraft manuals indicate "a more activist state involvement with the economy at large," which I would add, moved between well-established concepts of the political domain writ large (e.g., *tianxia*) and more novel conceptualizations of statecraft. For example, Janku shows quite convincingly that the once central problem of famine relief "ceased to be a concern of the state," replaced by preoccupation with what could be gleaned from "the new science of political economy." Famine, for officials, was a spatially and temporally limited event that required a specific repertoire of preventative measures and preparation. The new political economy, by contrast, redirected scholar-officials' attention to an ongoing, limitless state project: growth.[81] As conceptualized in the new political economy, this growth was spatially and temporally unlimited and nonspecific. Pursuit of it projected an indefinite future, differentiated from the past in quantitative terms. Engineering this future was not a matter of limited measures but of wholesale reconsideration of governing strategies and tactics, including taxation.

It was nearly impossible for those engaged in the project of engineering aggregate growth to not think about the global context. Andrew Liu's recent study of the China tea trade shows how throughout the 1880s and 1890s global commercial competition produced a sense of "crisis" among elites and novel engagements with

---

80. Xue Fucheng, "洋貨加稅免厘議" [Comment on foreign goods (paying) increased duties for *lijin* exemption] in HCJSWXB, juan 12, 8–9.
81. Janku, "New Methods" 347.

questions of political economy.[82] One scholar-elite who connected this sense of crisis to China's domestic taxation was Ma Jianzhong, a Paris-educated official aligned with pro-merchant policies who outlined his "grand strategy for achieving wealth" in a seminal essay from the period, titled "On Enriching the People" (1890).[83] Ma felt that taxation was not just a local or domestic matter but one with geopolitical implications. *Lijin*, Ma argued, hurt both individual and collective wealth because it shaped the fate of China's commodities in a global market. "With both duties and *lijin* to pay, which in some cases together nearly amount to the selling price," global demand for China's produce had fallen, he wrote. "With light duties and reduced *lijin*, the selling price would be cheaper, hence facilitating an increase in exports which in turn will generate additional revenue." Ma acknowledged that initially, lower taxes might seem to pose a problem: "On a daily basis such revenue might not seem much," but over time, fueled by growth in production and trade, wealth would accumulate. "On a monthly basis there will be a surplus," he wrote.[84] High taxes, Ma reasoned, brought in more revenue from any given item but collectively produced only "short-term gain." Long-term wealth and strength followed if the state designed taxation strategy to grow China's share of global commerce.

The critique of *lijin* voiced by Ma and others invoked a broader and more abstract context for merchant activity and state practice than that previously entertained by leaders within the Qing government. The petitions for relief from *lijin* lodged in Ningbo in 1866 (Chapter 5) offered a litany of discrete injuries caused by economic downturn in the port: "6 of 10 mercantile assistants have been idle.... 5 out of 10 artisans and sailors have been wandering around without employment.... 7 out of 10 porters who walk the streets can no longer rely on the exercise of their strength for their livelihood."[85] These "critics" of *lijin* cited their own business difficulties and the negative effects of *lijin* prevailing in specific locations. That *lijin* was a problem in 1866 in Ningbo did not mean *lijin* was everywhere and always a problem. By contrast, Ma's object of concern that he wanted the imperial government to take seriously was aggregate economic activity and aggregate state revenue, which were regulated by globally scaled phenomenon and universal laws of the market.

---

82. Andrew Liu, *Tea War: A History of Capitalism in China and India* (New Haven: Yale University Press, 2020), especially chap. 5.
83. Ma Jianzhong, "On Enriching in the People (1890)," in *Strengthen the Country and Enrich the People: The Reform Writings of Ma Jianzhong*, ed. and trans. Paul Bailey (London: Routledge, 1998), 89.
84. Ma in Bailey, *Strengthen the Country*, 92–93.
85. Enclosure No. 1, TNA, FO 228/913.

Debt, Taxes, and Imperial Maritime Customs Expansion

At its top levels, the Qing government was increasingly interested in maximizing overall state revenue. Its interest in doing so had much to do with a qualitative shift in the nature of its fiscal obligations—namely, the growth of sovereign debt. Whereas from the early modern period onward, European states had consistently borrowed funds for state expenses, until the mid-nineteenth century the Qing Empire had not. Debt financing of state activity only entered imperial statecraft in piecemeal fashion during the mid-nineteenth century. The first instances of its use were during the Taiping Rebellion, when provincial authorities tasked with financing their own military expeditions, turned to foreign firms and eventually foreign banks, often securing loans on the local foreign customs revenues. Eventually, around £16 million transferred into and out of provincial treasuries in this way, prior to the conclusion of the Sino-Japanese War in 1895. After that war, the scale of government borrowing qualitatively and quantitatively shifted.[86] In 1895 alone, loan agreements negotiated by ministers in Beijing (through the Zongli yamen) led to the issuance of around $94 million in Chinese government bonds in European markets.[87] Some of this debt bought steamships and guns, but a lion's share paid indemnities owed to foreign governments and financed government operations, which now included paying down loan interest and principal.[88] When the Qing court abdicated political control, it transferred a debt of more than $526 million to its successor.[89]

Debt reshaped commercial governance, and the key vector of this reterritorialization was the IMC. During initial rounds of borrowing, lenders insisted on IMC revenues as security with the result that by 1897, 70 percent of IMC revenues were pledged to outstanding debt.[90] After this date, the Guangxu court began to unilaterally open new treaty ports to produce additional revenue and began to pledge alternative sources of revenue for repayment—first *lijin* and salt tax, then railway

---

86. Hans van de Ven, *Breaking with the Past: The Maritime Customs Service and the Global Origins of Modernity in China* (New York: Columbia University Press, 2014), 136–38; William N. Goetzmann, Andrey D. Ukhov, and Ning Zhu, "China and the World Financial Markets 1870–1939: Modern Lessons from Historical Globalization," *Economic History Review* 60, no. 2 (2007): 267–312.
87. Goetzmann, Ukhov, and Zhu, "China and the World Financial Markets," appendix 1. In Chinese money markets, the pound was worth roughly four times the dollar.
88. The Qing and Republican governments also floated domestic bonds and raised loans from domestic sources, but through the end of World War I, this was a smaller source of funds than foreign markets. See Huang Feng-Hua, *Public Debts in China* (New York: Columbia University, 1919), 13–17, 72–74.
89. Albert Feuerwerker, "Economic Trends, 1912–1919," in *The Cambridge History of China*, vol. 11, *Late Ch'ing, 1800–1911, Part 2*, ed. John King Fairbank and Kwang-Ching Liu (Cambridge: Cambridge University Press, 1983) 102.
90. Van de Ven, *Breaking with the Past*, 137, 141, 157.

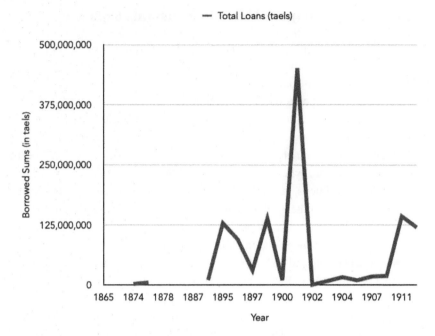

Figure 6.1: Government borrowing from domestic and international sources, 1865–1912. Source: Feng-Hua Huang, *Public Debts in China*, Studies in History, Economics, and Public Law, vol. 84, no. 2, no. 197 (New York: Columbia University, 1919).

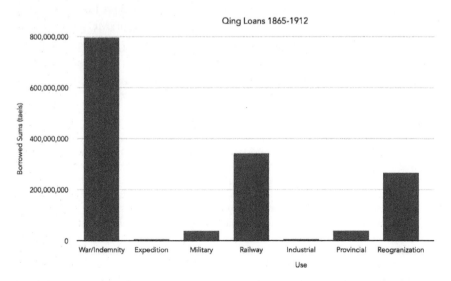

Figure 6.2: Purpose of government borrowing, 1865–1912. Source: Feng-Hua Huang, *Public Debts in China*, Studies in History, Economics, and Public Law, vol. 84, no. 2, no. 197 (New York: Columbia University, 1919).

revenues, and later opium revenues.[91] Per loan terms stipulated by lenders, pledging these revenues entailed transferring their collection oversight and administration from existing offices to the IMC. Consequent to these arrangements, Beijing's use of globally available capital to manage the empire's unequal integration into an aggressively imperialist geopolitical order, led to IMC jurisdiction over more imperial territory and commercial activity within that territory.

From the standpoint of European capital growth, the expansion of IMC management to additional Qing revenue streams was a resounding success. Qing government bonds offered remarkably stable yields for their holders, which "never moved outside of a narrow trading band between 5 1/2 and 6 per cent from 1899 to 1913."[92] Moreover, how the Qing government used much of the borrowed money also channeled capital returns to Europe, either to state treasuries as indemnity payments or to arms-makers and shipbuilders that sold hundreds of cannon and guns as well as many cruisers, battleships, and gunboats to Qing authorities.[93] The spurt of railway construction that began in China in 1895 often combined the two streams of income: many of the empire's initial railways were built by European financial syndicates whom the Qing repaid at 5–7 percent interest.[94]

But although distant banks and bondholders appreciated the rule-bound diligence of the IMC, the expansion of the agency's jurisdiction in the name of global obligations also generated local crises. For those engaged in the local implementation, IMC "takeovers" were not straightforward reassignments but perilous acquisitions. At Jiujiang, for example, IMC deputy commissioner Edmund Grimani warned that if the customs laid claim to as many *lijin* stations as adherence to "the strict letter of the agreement between the Chinese government and the banks" would warrant, they would "incur increased hostility from [local] officials and risk failure altogether."[95] Hostility did at times erupt, most famously at the Xiamen *changguan*, which came under IMC management in 1901. The newly installed IMC Commissioner fired two-thirds of the office staff, eliminated customary charges levied by customs clerks, and broke the precedent by which local merchant groups collected duties on behalf of the customs. In 1905, a riot erupted, fueled by the personal grievance

---

91. "Extracts from Canton Intelligence Report for June Quarter, 1898," *China No. 1 (1899), Correspondence respecting the Affairs of China* [C. 9131], 219; Goetzmann, Ukhov, and Zhu, "China and the World Financial Markets," appendix 1.
92. Goetzmann, Ukhov, and Zhu, "China and the World Financial Markets," 276–77.
93. Stephen Halsey, *Quest for Power: European Imperialism and the Making of Chinese Statecraft* (Cambridge, MA: Harvard University Press, 2015), table 5.1; Sau-yi Fong, "Guns, Boats and Diplomacy: Late Qing China and the World's Naval Technology" (PhD diss., Columbia University, 2022).
94. Huang, *Public Debts*, 30–43.
95. IMC, *Working of Likin Collectorates: Kiukiang, Soochow, and Hangchow*, Office Series, no. 88 (Shanghai: IMC Statistical Department, 1907), 4. Report written in 1898.

of a *changguan* clerk who had previously profited from his knowledge of tariffs and control of the registers and by the strict collection of long-standing fees, which was seen by the mercantile community as the levy of illegal exactions. Thirty rioters and three customs staff died.[96]

A Realm of Objective Necessities: Finance Capital and Commerce

Debt in the Qing Empire created new objective necessities that tied together circuits of commercial capital and circuits of financial capital. It was as a node in global commodity circulation that the empire could make itself into attractive territory for financial capital. For the government to access the capital necessary to modernize its military and build wealth-enhancing infrastructure, it first needed to generate revenue from trade. By the turn of the century, however, the ability of trade to generate revenue was undermined by another manifestation of global economic integration—the plummeting value of silver. Beginning in the 1870s, when France and Germany began to move toward the gold standard, the silver used in China as a primary currency began to lose value against gold. The loss in value lowered the effective tariff rates the state used to generate revenue and eventually increased the cost of servicing debts enumerated in foreign currencies.[97] To address these problems, in 1898 Beijing initiated a series of treaty revisions with various European countries.[98] Authorities in the capital wanted to raise duty rates to meet working expenses of the bureaucracy, to service international obligations and to continue capital-intensive programs of military modernization. The agreement authorities reached with Great Britain, four years later, went far beyond these modest goals to redesign all domestic commercial taxation.

The timing of negotiations with British counterparts ended up being critical to the final version of the new treaty. Initial conversations between the two sides began in December 1899, at the same time groups of hungry and anxious young men, calling themselves Boxers United in Righteousness, began to migrate from their homes in northwestern Shandong, further north, towards the capital,

---

96. For an account of this riot, see Weipin Tsai, "The Inspector General's Last Prize: The Chinese Native Customs Service, 1901–31," *Journal of Imperial and Commonwealth History* 36, no. 2 (2008): 243–58.
97. Until the 1870s, worldwide demand for silver kept its value afloat, which was important for keeping the value of a tael in China on a decent par with the value of silver on the London market. In 1871, as France and Germany prepared to convert to the gold standard, they began to sell their supplies of silver, and US silver-minted coins declined as a medium of exchange. The result was a plummet in the value of silver, which did not abate. For the effects in China, see Austin Dean, *China and the End of Global Silver, 1873–1937* (Ithaca: Cornell University Press, 2020).
98. Wright, *China's Struggle for Tariff Autonomy*, 344–45.

attracting adherents along the way. In a matter of months, the Boxer's movement, which targeted violence against Euro-American presence, culminated, in perhaps as many as 100,000 deaths and a march on Beijing by more than 19,000 troops from Great Britain, France, the United States, Russia, Japan, Germany, Italy and Austro-Hungry.[99] With troops inside the imperial capital, these foreign governments punished the Qing government in a series of moves James Hevia has characterized as the most far-reaching interference by Euro-American powers into the mechanisms of Qing rule. First, troops, diplomats, and foreign sojourners looted and polluted Qing sacred spaces.[100] After these "on the spot" punishments, hostilities concluded with yet another treaty known in English as the "Boxer Protocol" and in Chinese as *xinchou tiaoyue* (辛丑條約). Informed by orientalist notions about the inability of the Chinese government to understand anything other than overt domination, the protocol not only mandated the dynasty execute or exile its own officials—a move Hevia describes as "an extraordinary demand by any standard of international intercourse," but it also reorganized the institutional structures of the central government.[101]

On the one hand, the reorganization of Qing institutional structures set out in the protocol were the product of specific Euro-American demands.[102] At the same time, the protocol was formulated at a moment when the central government was prepared to make much more sweeping reforms. Only a few weeks after the Qing court agreed in December 1900 to foreign demands to elevate a newly formulated Ministry of Foreign Affairs (*waiwu bu* 外務部) to the highest rank among central government departments, it issued a sweeping edict initiating what are commonly referred to as the *xinzheng* (New Policy 新政) reforms. The New Policies edict, issued at the end of January 1901, invoked textual and historical tradition alongside

---

99. Paul A. Cohen, *History in Three Keys: The Boxers as Event, Experience and Myth* (New York: Columbia University Press, 1997), 14–56. The Boxers were local organizations of young men, concentrated in northern China, that engaged in collective boxing and religious rituals, including spirit possession. Inspired by ideas of invulnerability, in the winter of 1899–1900, the number of boxing groups grew, drawing adherents from a large population idled by a long drought. Feeling a sense of crisis, members attacked what they saw as the most immediate signs of social and economic disruption: Christianity. Boxer groups murdered missionaries, burned churches, looted the homes of Chinese converts, and occasionally killed them. By the summer of 1900, large coalitions of Boxers occupied both the northern port city of Tianjin and the imperial capital of Beijing. See also Joseph W. Esherick, *The Origins of the Boxer Uprising* (Berkeley: University of California Press, 1987); Xiang Lanxin, *The Origins of the Boxer War: A Multinational Study* (New York: RoutledgeCurzon, 2003).
100. James L. Hevia, *English Lessons: The Pedagogy of British Imperialism in China* (Durham, NC: Duke University Press, 2003), 197–201.
101. Hevia, *English Lessons*, 242–58.
102. Richard S. Horowitz, "Breaking the Bonds of Precedent: The 1905–06 Government Reform Commission and the Remaking of the Qing Central State," *Modern Asian Studies* 37, no. 4 (October 2003): 775–97.

the need for wealth and power (*fu qiang* 富強) to authorize a thorough overhaul (*zheng dun* 整頓) of governmental affairs (*zheng shi* 政事).[103] The agenda of ambitious transformation touched on methods of governance (*zhifa* 治法), laws and regulations, education, military organization, popular welfare (*minsheng* 民生), and financial administration.[104]

Amid the "scrutiny" and institutional changes called for by the Boxer Protocol and the reform edict, tariff negotiations restarted. Framing the negotiations was a new 455 million tael "gold debt" indemnity charged 4 percent interest, the largest ever levied on the Qing.[105] Consequently, internal discussions between lead negotiator Sheng Xuanhuai (盛宣懷, 1844–1916), the Zongli yamen, and IMC inspector general Robert Hart included a broad consideration of alternate imperial tax strategies, including an end to *lijin*. Hart had long pressed the central government to adopt a fiscal regime centered on customs revenues and policies that would grow commercial circulation. He presented these ideas to the Zongli yamen at various moments, including the 1868 British treaty revision and again in 1876, during the Chefoo negotiations. This time, lead negotiator Sheng Xuanhuai shared some of Hart's ideas. Sheng had been involved in matters of imperial governance since 1870 when Li Hongzhang recruited him as an aide. By the time he led the tariff negotiations, he had amassed an impressive résumé of activity in key areas of commerce, industrialization, and state-strengthening.[106]

In deliberations, Sheng drew from the empire's experience with imported opium taxation to lay out the possibility for a political economy and fiscal strategy centered on commercial growth.[107] It was less important, he felt, whether revenue accrued to the accounts of the court or the provinces. "Really the critical strength or weakness of the whole plan should be the total amounts collected for all under heaven," he wrote.[108] Pointing to recently innovated imported opium tax procedures, he noted, "In the years since [joint collection] began, smuggling has decreased and

---

103. Douglas Reynolds, *China, 1898–1912: The Xinzheng Revolution and Japan* (Cambridge, MA: Council on East Asian Studies, Harvard University, 1993), 201–4.
104. Reynolds, *China*, 203–4; Julia Strauss, "Creating 'Virtuous and Talented' Officials for the Twentieth Century: Discourse and Practice in Xinzheng China," *Modern Asian Studies* 37, no. 4 (October 2003): 831–50.
105. The original protocol appeared in French and Chinese. An English translation can be found in United States Commissioner to China and William Woodville Rockhill, *Report of William W. Rockhill, Late Commissioner to China, with Accompanying Documents* (Washington, DC: Government Printing Office, 1901), 312–18.
106. Albert Feuerwerker, *China's Early Industrialization: Sheng Hsuan-huai (1844–1916) and Mandarin Enterprise* (Cambridge, MA: Harvard University Press, 1970).
107. Sheng Xuanhai, "盛等籌議加稅辦法摺光緒二十六年" [Deliberations on methods to increase taxes from GX 26], Yuezhang cheng an hui lan yi bian [Compendium of treaties, regulations, and cases, part B], GX 31, Academica Sinica (hereafter YZCAH), juan 16, 1–8.
108. Sheng, [Deliberations on methods], 7.2–8.1.

revenues have greatly increased. This is truly the greatest benefit accrued to China since it opened to trade."[109] It seemed possible to Sheng that following the model for imported opium, one-time collection of duties from other select goods would sufficiently expand state income such that the central government could eliminate the increasingly discredited practice of *lijin*. But Sheng was less confident than Hart had been about the consequences of such a strategy. As prolific as the new imported opium regime was, Sheng was cautious about a strategy that relied on market operations. *Lijin* was flexible and ad hoc. It could always be altered when conditions required. Treaty-based taxes were static, so a successful switch from *lijin* to customs depended on growing trade. "For foreign goods and domestic goods to make up the revenue deficit," he observed, "each year the number passing through must increase. Whether the amount of the increase [in revenue] is ample or scant will depend on sales [*xiaolu* 銷路]."[110] Relying on customs revenues was risky, for Sheng, because it tied state fortunes to capricious, global markets. "It is hard to predict what the actual numbers will be," he admitted. Even so, the logic of market-based growth appealed to him: "The foreign merchants we asked all say that in general *lijin* creates difficulties; because it is numerous and confusing it creates market obstacles. If *lijin* were set at a definite rate and collected with the customs duty, such standardization would be simple and convenient and improve sales."[111]

To illustrate the new strategy and its risks, Sheng looked at China's tea exports. IMC reports showed declining exports against rising sales in China of Indian and Japanese alternatives. The problem, Sheng reported, was the lower tax burden the Indian and Japanese teas paid in their country of origin. China needed to follow suit: "Tea taxes are too heavy. We need to discuss decreasing them so tea will sell well." At the same time, though, Sheng warned, "if we lower the duty in tea, tea must sell well for revenue to increase." Hitching state revenue to global markets via a treaty tariff meant both the possibility of greater revenue and accepting the imperative to create the conditions of possibility for increased commodity sales.

When treaty revision negotiations with Great Britain concluded in 1902, the resulting agreement (En: Mackay Treaty; Ch: *zhong ying xuyi tongshang xingchuan tiaoyue* 中英續議通商行船條約) covered a wide range of commercial and financial matters. At the center of the agreement was a sixteen-part article governing taxation, both domestic and foreign. Prominent within this article was the explicit concession, long resisted by Qing authorities at all levels, "that the system of levying *lijin* and other dues on goods at the place of production, in transit, and at destination

---

109. Sheng, [Deliberations on methods], 2.2.
110. Sheng, [Deliberations on methods], 2.1. As a word connotating sales in a market, *xiao lu* especially invokes movement.
111. Sheng, [Deliberations on methods], 2.2.

impedes the free circulation of commodities and injures the interests of trade." It followed from this concession that China would now "discard completely those means of raising revenue." This included abolishing *lijin* barriers on "all roads, railways, and waterways," reporting to the British government the name and location of all remaining customhouses, equalizing duties between *changguan* and IMC offices, eliminating consumption taxes in foreign concessions and settlements, and converting *lijin* on interprovincially circulating domestic opium into border taxes paid in "one lump sum" at each province. To compensate for the loss of *lijin*, China would levy a limited surtax on foreign imports and exports as well as a "consumption tax" (*xiaochang shui* 銷場稅) on domestic produce not intended for export, collected at places of consumption. A network of IMC foreign staff would oversee the new arrangements, and British consuls were extended the codified "right" to demand prompt investigation and punishment of "illegal exactions or obstructions."[112]

The Mackay Treaty's tax provisions drew together different strands of deterritorialization and reterritorialization. On the one hand, the *lijin* concession offered victory to Alcock, Wade, and the generations of foreign merchants who had criticized *lijin* in very nearly the same terms as the new treaty. Like them, the treaty placed salability of goods at the center of state fiscal practice. Taxes such as *lijin* and other local levies (e.g., *luodi shui* or grower's taxes), previously defended Qing authorities on the grounds that they were gathered from different people in different places, were collectively abolished because they all had the same effect on the salability of goods. Salability, moreover, also authorized equivalent treatment of junk shippers and steam shippers, of Chinese firms and foreign firms. In practical terms, this new equivalence meant that local officials could not cultivate policies to privilege one group of commercial actors over another, as had been the case, nor could the empire make domestic tax policies to favor Chinese merchants. This last concession was a particularly important deterritorialization, if also a contradictory one. Although the treaty was crafted amid Chinese calls to invigorate Chinese capital against its foreign counterpart, treaty provisions precluded overt state support for Chinese merchants—contradicting the very project of "commercial warfare" (*shang zhan* 商戰) that in part inspired the critique of *lijin*.

A second process of deterritorialization and reterritorialization proceeded apace an ongoing erosion of internal autonomy for the sake of international financial entanglements. Monies from the new customs surtax would flow first to interest payments and to the sinking fund on extant foreign loans. To accomplish this transfer of revenue from China to Europe, the treaty shifted the work of revenue collection away

---

112. Article VIII, "Commercial Treaty, 1902" in China, Imperial Maritime Customs, *Treaties, Conventions, Etc. between China and Foreign States*. Miscellaneous Series, 2nd edition, vol. 1 (Shanghai: Statistical Department of the Inspectorate General of Customs, 1917), 547–55.

from local arrangements often penetrated by interpersonal negotiation to market forces and the mechanistic IMC. To end *lijin* in this way embraced technologies of power that mobilized abstract compulsions. By relying on the volume and value of international trade to fund the state, the new collection regime gave the power of revenue generation over to global commodity markets. Moreover, consolidation of domestic commercial taxation in the hands of the IMC signaled that henceforth, imperial wealth (commercial and state) would be the product of an empire-wide, engineered system, not the collective product of able administrators working within specific ecologies of economic activity and personalized power.

False Starts and Success on a Smaller Scale

For reasons both local and global, the Qing government never fully put into effect the *lijin*-free tax regime laid out in the Mackay Treaty. Within the halls of the capital, not everyone was confident in the new vision of imperial fiscal management. The Board of Revenue, also party to the Mackay deliberations, was more cautious than Sheng and the Zongli yamen in its approach to *lijin*. It was not possible, the board argued, to evaluate the negotiator's proposals in "general terms." It wanted authorities in the provinces to carefully evaluate local situations and assess the advantages and disadvantages of combining *lijin* with customs collections in the authorities' jurisdictions.[113] As pointed out by one official history of the plans, the diverse territory of the empire was still viewed as an impediment to a universal commercial tax regime. Geographically speaking, the empire's inland was considered to be "vast and expansive, with many branching streams that diverge."[114] Institutionally, critics of the plan pointed out, customhouses were nowhere near as extensive or numerous as *lijin* barriers. IMC stations might be capable of effectively taxing large-scale steamer-based trade, but small junks common in riverine transportation (*min chuan* 民船) would avoid taxation all together.[115] In short, the physical and social terrain of commerce suggested to important segments of the government that multiple inspection and collection points appeared more capable of catching more of the trade. Given these conditions, the Board of Revenue rejected the possibility that increased sales would drive revenue gains. *Lijin*, it pointed out, generated far more revenue from

---

113. "戶部等議復加稅免釐先事妥酌辦法摺" [The Board of Revenue's continued deliberations on initial implementation of tax increases and *lijin* exemption], YZCAH, GX29, juan 15, 1.2–4.2.
114. "加稅免厘及早實行議" [Early implementations of tax increases and *lijin* exemption], in *Qing dai shoushui wu dangan shiliao huibian* 清代稅收務檔案史料匯編 [A compendium of archival materials on tax revenue in the Qing dynasty], ed. Quanguo tushuguan wenxian suo wei fuzhi zhongxin [National Center for Microfilm Reproduction of Library Documents], 國家圖書館藏歷史檔案文獻叢刊 [National Library Historical Archives Series], vol. 26, 12675–82.
115. [Board of Revenue continued deliberations], assessment originally offered by Hubei and Hunan Governor General Zhang Zhidong.

foreign imports than could be compensated for by changes in customs collections. The many and various, they felt, could be much more prolific than the centralized and standard. A switch to joint collection was not to be taken up without serious deliberation.[116]

After negotiations with the British concluded, the probable success of the consolidated regime was not any clearer. To fully compensate for the loss of *lijin*, the new treaty authorized a consumption tax on domestic goods.[117] Yet Robert Hart, tasked with its implementation, worried that the tax taken at "places of consumption" looked a lot like the now-abolished *luodi shui*. Treaty language called for the government to "discard completely" the levy of "*lijin* and other dues on goods at the place of production, in transit, and at destination."[118] How would the consumption tax differ? Moreover, whose hands would pay it—the shopkeeper or the transporting merchant? Where would it be paid? Per treaty, the government could not set up any new tax offices, but merchants would likely not travel far to pay the tax. The rate of the "consumption tax" also posed difficulties. Hart struggled to find figures on actual *lijin* collections so he could create adequate compensatory rates for uniform application across the empire.[119]

Other important authorities doubted the wisdom of a uniform tariff. Zhang Zhidong, also consulted on the treaty's implementation, argued the consumption tax rate needed to be province specific, set according to thorough understanding of each province's salable goods, commodity prices, and marketing routes. But even if this was done, Zhang suggested, it was hard to say how the tax would actually produce revenue. If set any higher than 5 percent on items of everyday use, the poor might suffer (*pin min shou kun* 貧民受困). But with only luxury goods to fund the state, there would be revenue shortfalls. The Board of Revenue, already skeptical about the possibility of engineering a uniform tax system, agreed with Zhang.[120]

---

116. "戶部等會議加稅事宜摺光緒二十六年" [Joint discussions on the matter of tax increases, Guangxu 26 (1901)], YZCAH, juan 16, 8.1–14.2, here 13.1.
117. IMC, *Treaties, Conventions, Etc. between China and Foreign States*. Miscellaneous Series, No. 30 (Shanghai: Inspector General of Customs) 1:562–64.
118. As was typical, there was slippage between the English language "consumption tax," which implies a tax paid by the final user of a good and the Chinese-language *xiao chang* (銷場) tax, which implies a marketplace. The former would have been familiar to the British, as excise tax was a main engine of state revenue in the United Kingdom. The latter would look a lot more like China's broker-level taxes, which had long been a point of contention.
119. "總稅務司申覆預籌免釐加稅辦法文光緒二十九年" [Replies from the inspector general on preliminary preparations for methods of *lijin* exemption and tax increases, Guangxu 29 (1904)], YZCAH, juan 15, 10.1–14.1; "總稅務司申請續籌免釐加稅辦法文光緒二十九年" [Application from the inspector general to continue preparing methods of tax increase, Guangxu 29 (1904)], YZCAH, juan 15, 14.1–16.1.
120. "戶部等議復加稅免釐先事妥酌辦法摺光緒二十九年" [Board of Revenue continued deliberations], 1.2–4.2.

While these discussions went on, the Qing government began to implement certain provisions of the new treaty but unexpectedly struggled to secure the multinational cooperation needed to eliminate *lijin*.[121] The terms of the new Qing-British treaty only applied to trade in British-flagged vessels. Yet the Qing government was (reasonably) unprepared to do away with *lijin* for the British and keep it in place for everyone else. Fifteen other treaty signatories needed to assent to the new taxation regime. Only three—the United States, Japan, and Portugal—ever did. Germany and Italy entered into negotiations but walked away. The others, including Russia, Germany, and France, demurred entirely from entering into negotiations.[122] British records of these negotiations suggest that other signatories, like Great Britain, saw any treaty negotiation as an opportunity to press for long-sought concessions. According to British observers, it was impasse over these unrelated provisions, rather than any strong position in favor of *lijin*, that undermined designs for a changed system of domestic tax collection. Not that the British were all that more compromising. When in 1909 the Qing government called for a multinational commission to secure uniform consent to the import and export surtaxes stipulated in the Mackay Treaty, Great Britain refused its support, complaining that the Chinese government had not yet done enough to implement other treaty provisions—namely, currency reform and the creation of mining regulations friendly to foreign investment.[123]

Tax unification

Despite the impasse over the Mackay Treaty, after 1902 the logic of taxation it attempted to institutionalize nonetheless remained attractive to many. The last time Qing rulers had substantially and programmatically overhauled taxation, efforts focused on designing a system that would produce upright officiating. As explained by Madeline Zelin, the Yongzheng fiscal reforms were a meaningful rationalization of fiscal administration, at the heart of which was a monetization of *yang lien* (養廉), a project to nourish the virtue of officials by providing them adequate income.[124] This project solved the problem of adequate fiscal resources at the scale of the

---

121. E. Swatow, "Memorandum Showing the Steps Taken by China to Carry Out the Provisions of the Commercial Treaty of September 5 1902," in *British Documents on Foreign Affairs: Reports and Papers from the Foreign Office*, Series E, vol. 13, ed. Ian Nish, Kenneth Bourne, and D. Cameron Watt (Silver Spring, MD: University Publications of America, 1994), 430.
122. C.S.C., 31 December 1907, "Memorandum Showing the Steps Taken by China to Carry Out the Provisions of the Commercial Treaty of September 5 1902," in *British Documents on Foreign Affairs*, vol. 13, 528–30.
123. J. Jordon, "Annual Report," in *British Documents on Foreign Affairs: Reports and Papers from the Foreign Office*, Series E, vol. 14, ed. Ian Nish, Kenneth Bourne, and D. Cameron Watt (Silver Spring, MD: University Publications of America, 1994), 121.
124. Zelin, *Magistrate's Tael*, 96.

individual. The scale of the solution pursued after 1902 was ultimately the empire writ large.

It should be kept in mind that in the structure of Qing government, provincial governors and governors-general held equal rank with the Board of Revenue and were capable of implementing their own commercial tax plans.[125] After 1901, in some provinces, such as Jiangxi and Gansu, provincial leaders began to consolidate different ad hoc levies (*juan* 捐) into a single charge. Commenting on efforts by Jiangxi governor Ke Fengshi (柯逢時, 1845–1912), the Board of Revenue noted in 1903 that consolidated collection (*tong juan* 統捐) in Jiangxi appeared to be more convenient for merchants and to help stanch peculation.[126] In Gansu two years later, officials consolidated levies on one of the largest items of commerce: cloth. Citing indemnity obligations and military expenses, the governor-general, in conversation with the eight largest cloth trading firms, equalized the tax rate on all kinds of cloth, erasing previous distinctions between colored and white cloth, place of origin, and intended destination. After the initial experiment increased tax yields from cloth, Gansu authorities extended the strategy to Mongolian salt, everyday goods, and timber. According to a chronicle of the period penned by local official Wang Shuzhuan, the change was admirable for how it "unified the power of the numerous; and used simplicity to harness the many. Collections now had the propensity to become more flourishing with each passing day."[127] Indeed, research estimates that Gansu commercial tax collections tripled over the next nine years.[128]

Authorities also revisited domestic opium taxes. In 1903, Manchu bannerman and Hubei governor Duanfang (端方, 1861–1911) memorialized to Beijing on plans to unite the levies on opium moving through Hubei and Hunan.[129] Two years later, officials in Hubei and Hunan began joint management of imperial and local levies on processed and unprocessed domestic opium (*tu shui gao juan* 土稅膏捐). This arrangement soon expanded into a "four-province cooperative unified tax" (*si sheng he ban tong juan* 四省合辦統捐) with the participation of Jiangxi and Anhui and operations centered in Yichang, a treaty port on the Yangzi River.[130] Observers

---

125. Sun E-Tu Zen, "The Board of Revenue in 19th Century China," *Harvard Journal of Asiatic Studies* 24 (1962–1963): 175–228.
126. Chen Guanghui, "論清末甘肅統捐者開辦" [On the opening of unified taxation in Gansu in the late Qing], *Journal of Neijiang Normal University* 29, no. 1 (2014): 83–87, here 83.
127. Chen, [On the opening of unified taxation], 84.
128. Chen, [On the opening of unified taxation], 86, drawing from Luo Yudong, 中國釐金史 [A history of *lijin* in China].
129. Ho Honwai, "清季中央與各省財政關係的反思" [Reflections on the financial relationship between the central government and provinces in the Qing dynasty], *Zhongyang yanjiuyuan, Lishiyuyansuo jikan* 72, no. 3 (September 2001): 597–696, here 638.
130. Huang Hongxun, ed., 永綏廳志30卷 [30 volumes of Yongsui Hall Records], Zhongguo dizhi ku, Erudition, juan 14, 4–5.

in the Junjichu were impressed by the increased revenue yielded by this cooperative collection, which also allowed opium to transit freely between the provinces after paying a single tax. If collection in Guangdong, Guangxi, Jiangsu, and Fujian were added to create an eight-province zone, they reasoned, "the collections would be even more considerable." Collecting tax in one place appeared to "reduce strain on merchants and add to [state] funds." The inner council also contemplated direct imperial oversight over the eight-province zone. If earnestly managed by the Finance Ministry and Board of Revenue in Beijing, the inner council reasoned, provincial revenue quotas would not only be met but exceeded.[131]

Soon after these deliberations, eight-province unified collection began under the cognizance of the Board of Revenue, which appointed Ke Fengshi to manage it. Ke lauded the strategy's "innate benefits." "Gathering together many streams into one origin changes many little drops into an ocean.... [This] does not go so far as to increase burdens on the financial resources of the people, and yet has a great benefit for the national revenue [*guo ke* 國課]."[132] Then, after ten months on the job, Ke recommended the empire-wide expansion of the system with direct supervision by a special official in Beijing.[133] By May 1906, officials in Beijing were ready to move forward with his recommendation.

In its final form, the unified system of domestic opium taxation included a single tax, referred to as the "consolidated tax on domestic opium" (*tu yao tong shui* 土藥統稅), which once paid, exempted the opium from all further taxation in the eighteen-province zone. Local rebates, which had previously concentrated opium traffic through particular provinces, were explicitly prohibited.[134] Revenue was shared between provincial accounts and those of the new Finance Ministry (*caizheng ju* 財政局), with a quota allocated to the former and surplus reserved for the latter. The system also created a transprovincial structure of supervision that reported directly to Beijing. At the head of the collection apparatus was an imperial central office (*zong ju* 總局) stationed at Wuchang (武昌), which reported actual income and expenditure on a quarterly basis.[135] Below it, nine regional suboffices (*fen ju* 分局) were staffed by *daotai*-level officials to collect remittances and distribute monies to the provinces (recall that *daotai* were imperially appointed to supplement and

---

131. QSL, juan 537, Guangxu 31 M12D10, 149.1–149.2. These deliberations likely drew from reports generated by Manchu bannerman Tie Liang (鐵良, 1863–1938), a minister in the Ministry of War, who completed a tour of Jiangsu in 1905. See Ho, [Reflections on the financial relationship], 638–39.
132. Enclosure No. 2 in IMC, *Circulars Second*, vol. 9, no. 1314, 16 January 1906.
133. QSL, juan 557, Guangxu 32 M03D07, 379.1–379.2.
134. IMC, *Circulars Second*, vol. 9, no. 1343, 26 May 1906. The English-language circular consists of several Chinese enclosures, including Chinese versions of the new regulations and copies of instructions issued by the Finance Ministry and Board of Revenue.
135. Ho, [Reflections on the financial relationship], 639.

supervise the provincial bureaucracy). Both the central office and suboffices were authorized to communicate directly with the Finance Ministry in Beijing. At a third level of administration, the task of collecting the levies fell on the IMC and an apparatus of "bureaus and barriers." A clerk appointed by each *fen ju* attended domestic opium business at each IMC office.[136] For the first time since the drug's appearance, all domestic opium shipments, no matter their origin and no matter their destination, were gathered under one regulatory regime.

The final arrangements for domestic opium created a new cascade of responsibility that treated its taxation as single, distinct revenue stream rather than a territorially diffused one. This consolidation corresponded to organizational changes within the new Finance Ministry, which in 1906 was in the process of creating functionally specific divisions. Whereas the Board of Revenue's internal organization corresponded to the structure of territorial organization and local products, the Finance Ministry divided responsibility for commercial taxes between a Bureau of Duties and a Bureau of Excise.[137] In day-to-day operations, work performed by the IMC merged with the work done by other Qing collection offices. Executing its domestic opium collection duties, the IMC officially acted on "behalf" of the imperial Domestic Opium Office (*zong ju* 總局) to whom it reported monthly and from which it received the critical stamps and forms that marked opium shipments as tax-paid. This formal bureaucratic subordination was a novelty for an agency that had designed much of its own paperwork and went so far as to ship in its stationery and stamps from London. Conversely, it was the IMC's own inspection and collection procedures, first instituted at Yichang in the 1890s, that provided the model for managing transborder flows of domestic opium.[138] Measures such as these equalized the regulatory conditions under which domestic opium circulated and deauthorized the kinds of overt personal or political intervention to shape opium markets.

As with imported opium, the fulcrum of the new regime was paperwork that documented and marked opium shipments. Of these, the *lan zhi zhao* (藍執照) tells us the most about the new governing tactics. The *lan zhi zhao*, aka "blue receipt," was issued by the first non-IMC office or barrier encountered by an opium shipment. Here, the opium paid the unified tax and in return received the blue receipt. When the opium passed into an IMC office to transship to a steamship, the office collected

---

136. IMC, *Circulars Second*, no. 1343, 26 May 1906.
137. Ch'üan-shih Li, *Central and Local Finance in China: A Study of the Fiscal Relations between the Central, the Provincial, and the Local Governments* (New York: Columbia University, 1922), 18–26.
138. IMC, *Circulars Second*, vol. 9, no. 1343, 26 May 1906. Yong Chen attributes the model put in place to IMC inspector general Robert Hart. Indeed, Hart had for some time lobbied to unify *lijin* and customs duties on native opium, but it is not clear that he is the sole source of the final rate or the protocols. See "赫德与鸦片税厘并征" [Robert Hart and joint collection of opium taxes and *lijin*], *Jinan xuebao* 4 (2006): 141–47.

the blue receipt, stamped it, retained it, and enclosed it with a monthly report sent to the Imperial Branch Office. Once in the hands of the Central (Opium) Office, the collections reported in the blue receipts formed the basis for the provincial quota of opium revenue.[139]

Certainly, the operations themselves are fairly standard for the era, but they also express two ways in which the interaction between commerce and governance had changed. Recall that in the past, the Qing central government had little supervision over barrier operations and did not enforce any kind of regular reporting of receipts. When faced with reports of misdeeds they considered how to produce greater moral rectitude. The new arrangements deemphasized the importance of the moral official. Instead, they harnessed the speed-up of commercial circulation, manifest in the use of steam shipping, to produce interagency supervision. That is, when most (if not all) opium shipped via steamers because of the time/distances steam carriage shrunk, "blue receipts" ensured that the IMC would routinely collect nearly complete records of provincial levies. This paperwork trail, in turn, allowed the central government to abstractly "discipline" local collection offices as a matter of course: provincial governments could only receive what they properly recorded.

Much work went into creating the system of unified opium taxation, but this did not mean that all authorities were thoroughly won over by the new strategy. According to historian Ho Honwai, unified collection in Sichuan and Yunnan closed down shortly after it commenced, and operations ceased in Guizhou two years later. All three provinces were important opium-growing regions, and the consolidated tax system interfered with "local sales."[140] Ho does not explain these difficulties, but the lack of evidence that Beijing objected to the change suggests that that imperial authorities were not committed to centralized fiscal power for its own sake; local particularity remained a compelling standpoint for governance when it produced maximum revenue.

Conclusion: Abstract Territoriality

Several common threads run through the various experiments with domestic commercial taxation that coalesced between 1887 and 1906. One is the homogenization of imperial territory. Despite whatever very concrete differences existed within the empire, regulatory regimes emerged that treated all spaces and places as formally equivalent. In his study of rural Shandong during roughly the same period covered here, Kenneth Pomeranz argues that local officials held a "profoundly localistic" economic orientation. "Both the provincial government and many county governments

---

139. IMC, *Circulars Second*, no. 1343, 26 May 1906.
140. Ho, [Reflections on the financial relationship], 639.

tried to make their jurisdictions economically meaningful units in which they could control matters such as currency without interference from broader markets."[141] Other governing projects, such as the effort to effectively tax transborder commodity movements or to generate greater wealth for the polity in a competitive global environment shifted the "economically meaningful unit" shifted upward to "China" as a whole. Provincial governance, in particular, seems to have been caught between the localist orientation identified by Pomeranz and its role as a constituent part of the empire writ large, which was being re-institutionalized through changing practices of fiscal management. Established statecraft orthodoxy mobilized local authorities to evaluate local specifics and craft local policies; emergent political economy, which relied on aggregate data about commodity volumes and values in the treaty ports, first imagined the effects commerce could produce and designed a system to produce these effects.

While homogenous territoriality projected a means to increase wealth and power, the technologies of power deployed to generate this space advanced the alternative schema of governance that had originated in the treaty ports. Opium taxes, because of the decisive ways in which they changed in a relatively short time, offer a pithy illustration of these changes. First, the transborder circulation of opium within the empire had long stymied efforts to effectively police or maximize state revenue. By contrast, the consolidated tax regimes, initiated in 1887 and 1903, took the contours of commodity circulation as their object and logical starting point. In this sense the opium regimes descended from treaty-based commercial facilities such as the transit passes, drawbacks, and exemption certificates, which came before them. Second, circulating opium, like other commodities passing through the treaty apparatus, came to be governed by bureaucratic operations that used the depersonalized coercion of paperwork trails and reporting protocols to keep the actions of men within proper bounds. The art of governing men with men, which still seemed possible in 1890, by 1906 apparently offered fewer advantages than following the model of abstract coercion institutionalized in the treaty regime. Uniform tax collection controlled by paperwork protocols rather than personal negotiations shifted the fulcrum of compliance from the person (whether official or merchant) to the good. Institutionally, the emulation and personal mortality important in neo-Confucian governance became beside the point.

The novel arrangements for domestic opium taxation were an experiment to harness a widely circulating commodity to the collective's benefit. In this sense, opium was one of several commodities that performed such a role during Qing rule. Imperial officials, for example, had long organized annual grain shipments to fill reserve granaries and feed Beijing's population. But in comparison with grain,

---

141. Pomeranz, *Making of a Hinterland*, 65–66.

it was opium's value, not its use value, that benefited the people and the polity. And it was opium's value-mediated movements from places of production to places of consumption that the state eventually assimilated into its strategies and tactics of governance. The "free" circulation of domestic opium was a fiscal strategy that both territorialized a whole, internally undifferentiated "state" and expanded the scope of the value-mediated polity beyond its previous limits inscribed by the treaty regime.

The ascendance within governance of the commodity's value dimension over its use-value dimension made it possible for Qing leaders and reformist elites to champion the power of the unified over the power of the numerous. In one important classical model of governance, "state regulation must be based on detailed knowledge of the real conditions," such as market prices, population, natural resources, skills, seasonal changes, and regional peculiarities.[142] The art of governance explicated by texts such as the *Guanzi* was an art of precise, tactical intervention, wherein authorities addressed themselves to the dispositions of the varied and numerous, even if those were known to follow regular patterns. By contrast, the art of fiscal consolidation was an art of designing a system in which particularities were subordinate to more abstract equivalences. The former art changed the rate of tax on Anhui tea because of crop fluctuations; the latter figured out the appropriate level of value-based tax on all Chinese teas so they could compete globally against Indian teas.

As this example suggests, global capital was inseparable from the changing scale at which Qing governance acted. Whereas at the start of the treaty area, Li Hongzhang in Jiangsu and Prince Yixin at the Zongli yamen had worried about how to keep the pulse shippers in business, forty years later, Sheng Xuanhuai at the Board of Works speculated about macroeconomic impact of tax policy. Sheng did not echo earlier concrete visions of rotting ships and roving seamen-cum-bandits, but instead tried to predict how more abstract and aggregate social forms—sales and markets—would interact with taxes. Importantly, the abstract and aggregate was not merely a framework for thinking about the varied and numerous but the real social form Sheng intended to state to govern. The combination of state debt and globally competitive capital accumulation, both of which constituted problems at the scale of the geopolitically embedded sovereign polity, made plausible the general social form of "Chinese capital." The emergence of this social form, evident in the Chinese critique of *lijin*, I argue, extended the changing strategies and tactics of commercial governance, initially developed in China to grow foreign capital, to its internal commerce as well. In its last few years of rule, Qing governance, previously the target of foreign-led reterritorialization efforts, became itself a vector of reterritorialization by capital.

---

142. Pomeranz, *Making of a Hinterland*, 250.

Conclusion

This book has discussed many topics not typically gathered into one study. In order of the chapters, these include Qing interdomainial relations and international law, the Imperial Maritime Customs (IMC) and bureaucratic innovation, Qing strategies and techniques of trade management, Sino-British commercial competition and cooperation, *lijin* and extra-bureaucratic participation in local administration, opium management, and "New Policy" era changes in fiscal management. My work on each of these topics is indebted to the specialist studies cited throughout, and yet also suggests that each of these fields of historical activity and historical change became connected histories through their incorporation into capital's reproductive process.

In the viral metaphor I introduced at the beginning of the book, I argued that capital, like a virus, appropriates existing institutions and practices and incorporates them into its own reproductive process. If this book has at all succeeded, I have shown, for each of the topic areas listed above, how capital "infected" Qing governance, taking what it needed from its host. The viral metaphor has its limits, though. Strictly speaking, a virus kills its host cells. My claims are more measured. At each site of infection, capital encountered resistance from Qing authorities, and at the end of Qing rule, while capital's advance was significant, it was also limited. For instance, imperial cosmology remained important even as enthusiasm grew for technocratic governance of the sort modeled by the IMC. Kang Youwei, a leader of the 1898 reform movement, advocated wholesale reorganization of the central government's bureaucracy, at the same time he called upon the transformative power of the sage-king. Imperial rites and the imperial calendar were not discontinued until 1924.[1] The emperorship endured throughout the treaty era, but operated within new limits. During the period covered in this book, even Qing relations with Choson Korea,

---

1. Richard Horowitz, "Breaking the Bonds of Precedent: The 1906 Government Reform Commission and the Remaking of the Qing Central State," *Modern Asian Studies* vol. 37 no. 4 (October 2003): 775–97, here: 782; Peter Zarrow, *After Empire: The Conceptual Transformation of the Chinese State, 1885–1924* (Stanford: Stanford University Press, 2012), 35–36, 261–62.

which long affirmed Qing suzerainty, shifted away from universal rulership to the norms of international law.[2] With regard to commercial activity, my claims have less to do with the course of China's economic history or the making or unmaking of merchant operations and more to do with how commercial activity and regulatory frameworks interacted. In these interactions, I observe how regulatory frameworks catalyzed forms of multinational capital, and I point out how established strategies and tactics to police and tax this behavior became in many cases less workable, less lucrative, and contributed to the court's ongoing problems with foreign diplomatic pressure.

The gravity well pulling at merchants and administrators was the regulatory regime administered by the IMC, which I argue was an alien institution not because it was run, at its highest levels, by Europeans and Americans but because it introduced a program of maximum revenue growth, fueled by accelerated value circulation and bureaucratic protocols designed to promote trade. In this context, it was not only highly visible novel technologies such as steamships that changed time and cost distances, but also the less visible pieces of paper that traveled with the cargo—transit passes, drawbacks, and exemption certificates—that advanced capital's paradigmatic "space-time compression."

The IMC did not kill off its counterparts, the *changguan* and *lijin* collectorates. When, in the final two decades of the dynasty, the IMC began to assimilate *lijin* and *changguan* into its own mass, it was because circuits of commercial capital within the Qing Empire had become integral to the government's participation in global circuits of finance capital and because Qing leaders had internalized the idea that a regulatory apparatus designed to work *with* the movement of goods would yield greater returns for the state. Michel Foucault, in his work on eighteenth-century France, has described this shift in statecraft as one from discipline to security.[3] With some adaptation, Foucault's description seems apt here as well, particularly with reference to opium taxation. Into the early 1890s, to fix problems within commercial tax collection, Qing authorities focused on methods to cultivate the discipline of merchants and officials. But by the end of the decade, new and rearranged apparatuses increasingly incorporated what was known of patterns in opium movement. The reality of opium in the empire, rather than ideals of moral behavior, became the starting point for securing a larger revenue from the drug.

---

2. Seonmin Kim, *Ginseng and Borderland: Territorial Boundaries and Political Relations between Qing China and Choson Korea, 1636–1912* (Berkeley: University of California Press, 2017).
3. Michel Foucault, *Security, Territory, Population: Lectures at the Collège de France, 1977–78*, ed. Michel Senellart, trans. Graham Burchell (Basingstoke: Picador, 2009).

Elites and the End of the Qing

The strategic shift from discipline to security in the Qing Empire had at least one effect, the full repercussions of which intersected with what we already know about the end of Qing rule. Throughout the nineteenth century, elite participation in new spheres of government responsibility expanded significantly. Gentry and wealthy merchants became formal components of local tax police and tax collection, organizers of militia and the sea transport of grain; they led post-rebellion reconstruction and compiled local gazetteers, creating narratives of their locality and their place within in it.[4] *Lijin* collection was part of this expanded field of activity. Even where taxes were not farmed to merchant groups ("undertaking tax authority"/*renjuan*/ 認捐), *lijin* bureaus were often staffed with local gentry recruited outside normal bureaucratic channels. Gentry performance of these duties, historians have argued, was part of a Chinese "liturgical tradition."[5] When run on the strength of elites' interpersonal relations, *lijin* bureaus at times resisted efforts by provincial authorities to standardize and regulate their operations.[6] It is this elite participation in policing and taxing commerce that the treaty-based regime of commercial governance rejected and proscribed. Whether in the form of empire-wide trade facilities, limits on local taxation, or bureaucratic "mechanical correctness," the treaty regime offered an alternative modality of organizing commerce and governance.

What can this finding tell us about the end of Qing rule? A generation ago, pathbreaking scholarship looked to local elites to explain how dynastic rule lost its legitimacy. Using newly available local archives, historians examined elite political activism, changes in state-society relations, and long-term trends of commercialization and urbanization.[7] Collectively, these studies make the case that the imperial court was unable to keep up with or satisfy local demands for change. Agitated by calls for constitutional self-government, the empire was, in the words of Susan Naquin, "fast disintegrating" with few resources available to shore

---

4. Philip Yuen-sang Leung, "Crisis Management and Institutional Reform: The Expectant Officials in the Late Qing," in *Dragons, Tigers, and Dogs: Qing Crisis Management and the Boundaries of State Power in Late Imperial China*, ed. Robert J. Antony and Jane Kate Leonard (Ithaca: Cornell East Asia Program, 2002), 66–67, 73.
5. Susan Mann Jones, *Local Merchants and the Chinese Bureaucracy, 1750–1950* (Stanford: Stanford University Press, 1987), 95.
6. Philip Kuhn, *Rebellion and Its Enemies in Late Imperial China: Militarization and Social Structure, 1796–1864* (Cambridge, MA: Harvard University Press, 1970), 161–62.
7. Mary Backus Rankin, *Elite Activism and Political Transformation in China: Zhejiang Province, 1865–1911* (Stanford: Stanford University Press, 1986); R. Keith Schoppa, *Chinese Elites and Political Change: Zhejiang Province in the Early Twentieth Century* (Cambridge, MA: Harvard University Press, 1982). Research in this vein also includes work by Zhang Pengyuan, Zhang Yufa, John Fincher, Joseph Esherick, and Edward Rhoads.

it up.[8] More recently, historians have re-emphasized the significance of administrative and legal reforms in Beijing after 1906, arguing that while Qing-era constitutional reforms were "depressingly short lived", administrative innovations such as the creation of a ministerial system of government left in place important building blocks for the postimperial order.[9] Neither approach has completely resolved the question of why the Qing dynasty so quickly dissolved in 1911, and in important ways, these studies speak past one another. But reading across them leaves one with the sense that there was a deep disconnect between the efforts of local activists to build a better future and Beijing's work to reinvigorate state structures.

For the most part, the history told here figures peripherally in previous scholarship's attempts to explain what happened in 1911. Yet, the treaty regime, authorized in Beijing and operative wherever "foreign" goods traveled, cut across Qing governance at all scales: local, provincial, and central. The regime fostered an alternative arts of governance that by the first decade of the twentieth century both barred local participation in certain domains of governance previously open to it and rejected the principles of local autonomy and local suitability that were important political considerations before but especially during the constitutional debates of the "New Policies" era.[10] Even before delegations sent by the Guangxu court to investigate political institutions in Europe and America brought back recommendations for a constitutional system, the empire's governing processes had been reshaped by capital circulation and Euro-American political economy. If the Qing Empire, as many historians have argued, was ultimately torn apart by the opposing forces of centralization and decentralization, the treaty regime was a significant factor in aggravating that tension and giving it forms of expression around issues of local rule-making and commercial taxation.[11]

---

8. Susan Naquin, *Peking: Temples and City Life, 1400–1900* (Berkeley: University of California Press, 2001), 685.
9. Horowitz, "Breaking the Bonds of Precedent," 797; see also contributions by Roger Thompson, Luca Gabbiani, Julia Strauss, and Jerome Bourgon in *Modern Asian Studies* 37, no. 4 (2003): 769–73, 799–862.
10. William Rowe, *Hankow: Commerce and Society in a Chinese City* (Stanford: Stanford University Press), 185. Rowe notes merchants in Hankou specifically complained about "the progressively smaller voice allowed merchant representatives in the making [of *lijin*] collection policy." Philip Kuhn, *Origins of the Modern Chinese State* (Stanford: Stanford University Press, 2002), chap. 2; John E. Schrecker, *The Chinese Revolution in Historical Perspective* (New York: Greenwood, 1991), 128–35; Tu-ki Min, *Men and Ideas in Modern Chinese History* (Seoul: Seoul National University Press, 1997), 152–53; Frederic Wakeman Jr., *Telling Chinese History: A Selection of Essays*, ed. Lea H. Wakeman (Berkeley: University of California Press, 2009), 380.
11. For a review of the state-society approach dominant in the 1980s, see Mary B. Rankin, John K. Fairbank, and Albert Feuerwerker, "Introduction: Perspectives on Modern China's History," in *The Cambridge History of China*, vol. 13, *Republican China, 1912–1949, Part 2*, ed. John K. Fairbank and Albert Feuerwerker (Cambridge: Cambridge University Press, 1986), 1–73, esp. 49–63.

One place where we can see the extent to which the schisms shaped by the treaty regime animated an emergent arts of governance are the fiscal plans that immediately followed the revolution of 1911. Many studies now argue that a deeper story of state building bridges the imperial and Republican periods. A look at taxation supports this periodization, at the same time it points to the treaty regime as a key pillar of this bridge. A full story of the Republic of China's first budgets exceeds the space and purposes here. What is of interest are proposals put forth in 1912 and 1913 by the Ministry of Finance to codify differences between "local" and "national" administration, with specific reference to revenue streams and responsibilities. The proposals show that while the republic engaged with the question of how to best reorganize local governance, its engagement with the world continued on terms inherited from the Qing.[12]

The national allocations recommended by the ministry proposed to codify what had de facto evolved out of existing precedent during the treaty port era. These revenue allocations drew heavily from commerce and included customs duties, which were now under the exclusive control the IMC; the salt gabelle, which was "reformed" after 1911 by another British bureaucratic innovator—Sir Richard Dane; and consumption-based taxes on the model outlined in the 1902 Mackay Treaty.[13] The funds, in turn, were to continue to be allocated to the new nation-state's geopolitical survival and geoeconomic obligations: indemnity payments, foreign loans servicing, and military expenses. From the standpoint of fiscal management, the Republic of China was a unit inscribed by capital circulation and geopolitical competition. Alternatively, the ministry's proposals recoded revenue from land— previously the court's largest source of revenue—as a source of provincial and local revenue. Taxes on land as well as business operations were tapped to fund a wide range of projects whose effects would be immediately felt at the local level: education, police, public works, and public industry among them. In departure from imperial practice, the costs of each level of administration would be borne separately. The new government discontinued the "common purse" and interprovincial transfers of revenue that created problems in the treaty era.

A History of Capital

Although it is possible to place a history of the treaty regime within the framework of late-Qing tension between imperial and local authority, it is also the case that

---

12. Ch'üan-shih Li, *Central and Local Finance in China: A Study of the Fiscal Relations between the Central, the Provincial, and the Local Governments* (New York: Columbia University, 1922), 73–79.
13. On salt, see S. A. M. Adshead, *The Modernization of the Chinese Salt Administration, 1900–1929* (Cambridge, MA: Harvard University Press, 1970).

the history of the treaty regime, as a history of capital, exceeds the categories and narrative boundaries that framework provides. Treaties were a technology of commercial governance that multiplied the ways in which capital was present in the Qing Empire. After 1842, foreign trade did not remain the same. As written, Qing commercial treaties permitted foreign firms to be in more places with fewer restrictions on their movement and their dealings with Chinese firms. In practice, the expanded circulation of Euro-American ships, their flags, and their nationals mixed Euro-American capital with a wider array of Chinese goods, persons, and resources. These collaborations manifest as changing patterns of commercial activity as well as administrative problems. "Smuggling" and revenue fraud proliferated under a regulatory framework predicated on the separation of Chinese and foreign trade. I have argued that these administrative difficulties were more than just trouble for Sino-British relations; they also expressed the deterritorializing and reterritorializing processes of capital.

Treaties were a technology of commercial governance that reconditioned how territorial officials governed trade. Euro-American capital in China was, fundamentally, capital that was vulnerable to Qing sovereignty. Beginning with the creation of the treaties themselves, which recoded active, moral officials as servants of prescribed scripts, treaty administration demobilized a range of strategies used by the Qing state to generate order and prosperity and narrowed Qing commercial governance to forms of instrumental reason. Obligated by treaty to admit Euro-American consuls and ministers as collaborators in trade administration, the Qing government endured repeated consul that good governance meant allowing capital reproduction to govern government action. From within its own customs office, Qing employee inspector general Robert Hart sought to reformulate fiscal practice around capital growth and to hive off commercial administration from the larger set of concerns that typically centered governance, including the specific utility of goods as well as temporally specific local circumstances.

The paradigm shift in Qing commercial governance was indeed most starkly visible in the offices and operations of its new maritime customs agency, the IMC. Here, a cadre of foreign employees of the court cultivated paperwork, procedures, and reporting protocols that modeled disinterested administration and the "mechanical" application of ends-means reasoning. Aside from the important work the IMC did to combat smuggling and to develop the empire's harbor infrastructure, a core project pursued by the customs was the twinned growth of trade and revenue—a purely quantitative rather than qualitative concern. The tax structures administered by the IMC deterritorialized and reterritorialized ports into nodes of coordinated bureaucratic action connected by paths of capital circulation. Under the direction of Hart, moreover, IMC commissioners sidelined the participation of territorial officials in the agency's day-to-day operations, lest their local and political priorities interfere with the self-mediating sphere of capital growth Hart was working to engineer. Although the economic significance of this administrative network remains a question for researchers, what is clear is that the IMC advanced two significant changes in Qing governance: the institutionalization of a calculus for governance that was primarily quantitative and mediated by value and a paradigm shift away from locally specific action informed by moral education to administrative unity and uniformity enforced through disinterest and protocol.

Treaty regulations and their effects on commercial activity directed the empire to govern a different reality, both present and projected. The same tax exemptions that shaped IMC operations also institutionalized as an object of governance a limitless flow of goods, which were less important for their concrete utilities and more important for their abstract, quantifiable value. This was the same object that British authorities in China pressed the Zongli yamen to privilege as a social good instead of the soy transport junks and the same object the Euro-American community feared was imperiled by Qing sovereignty. Indeed, much of the consistency in the processes of deterritorialization and reterritorialization traced here resulted from the singularity of the dominant social form that energized the viral growth of the treaty regime. The extension of treaty-based tax exemptions to Chinese merchants, beginning in the 1870s, simultaneously institutionalized Chinese merchants as conduits of capital circulation and limited their political-fiscal obligations to the empire. Stated somewhat differently, when provincial authorities and the Zongli yamen equalized the commercial playing field between Euro-American and Chinese merchants, they also admitted capital as a social form capable of mediating sovereign-subject relations. Similarly, the active deconstruction of provincial boundaries through the creation of consolidated taxation introduced the mediation of capital circuits into the creation of administrative territory. *Daqing* (大清) and *tianxia* (天下), two categories through which Qing rulers conceptualized their domain, had the capacity to encompass and incorporate difference. During the treaty era, experiments with commercial taxation engineered a dissimilar and more mundane form of spatially extensive undifferentiated territoriality mediated by value, what I have called territorial homogeneity. Territorial form followed function.

(Re)theorizing the End of the Qing

A state, in an important sense, is the effect of a set of institutions and practices. The Qing state was one in which persons and practices to constitute relations between persons mattered. This was true at the apex of the government where the emperor had a personal duty to perform ritual offerings to the ancestors and in the many government offices throughout the empire where county magistrates cultivated relations with city gods. Trade with "men from afar" likewise, until the treaty era, had been ordered through ritual enactments of imperial grace, expressed in duty structures and measuring ceremonies, as well as through the cultivation of dependency between foreign firms and their Chinese partners who were needed to land goods, pay duties, and refurbish their ships. Throughout the treaty era, the regulatory apparatus evacuated persons, their moral qualities and their discretion from commercial governance. In their place, it put rule-bound action and instrumental reason in pursuit of endless growth. The Qing state that built plans to end *lijin* was, practically speaking, not the same one that authorized *lijin* fifty years earlier.

We can also observe historical disjuncture when we look at the ends pursued in the formation and execution of commercial governance. When the treaty regime began, what mattered to Qing authorities was the amount of rice in Ningbo, whether *sha-chuan* owners would continue to sail north for soybeans, and who truly "owned" the bale of imported cotton shirting confiscated on an inland waterway. These were concerns about concrete utilities, about the fate of persons and their resources for livelihood, and about the application of political jurisdiction. Such concerns put locally specific conditions of socioeconomic reproduction at the center of official praxis. The projects put in motion under the treaty apparatus, by contrast, concerned growing value across political jurisdictions with the assumption that its faster movement and quantitative augmentation would improve the lives of all as well as the wealth and strength of the state. Much of the work of Euro-American diplomacy, merchant activism, and treaty-based institutional activity during the treaty era involved recoding political jurisdictions and limiting the exercise of administrative power so as to not interfere with this project. One effect of this regulatory regime was the reimagining of imperial territoriality. In the 1860s when the coasting trade disordered imperial finance, "China" was not the salient unit for commercial-fiscal administration. After 1887, it was. Shaping this territorial imaginary and its institutional expressions was a political economy of growth, counseled by the Euro-American community, urged on by reform-minded elites as necessary to the empire's future fortunes, and immediately necessary at court in order to service international debt obligations.

In this light, the end of Qing rule is the triumph of a new national modernity mediated by capital growth and international competition. It is almost too easy to invoke a contrast between the letter Emperor Qianlong sent King George III in 1793 in which he informed the lesser lord "our Celestial Empire possesses all things in prolific abundance and lack no product within its own borders" and a 1915 complaint by the Republic of China's minister of commerce, industry, and agriculture that China, in recent decades, had "been unable to capture the foreign markets" in tea, that its silk industry was still in "an infant stage," and that "it has been impossible to place out present products in any large quantities on the foreign market."[14] Despite whatever economic self-sufficiency China retained in 1915, global demand and the global production of value mediated its levels of "wealth and power."

Commerce, Capital, and Coercion

The shift in governance that took place in China during the second-half of the nineteenth century raises questions about alterity and global economic integration. Half a century ago, historians used the metaphor of "waking" to describe fin de siècle political change in China and "modernization" to explain changes to its political institutions. More recently scholarship has preferred to discuss the "pragmatism" of Qing state-builders. While this more recent argument sheds the Eurocentrism of the earlier discursive paradigm that characterized China as a backwards and somnambulant, its implicit reliance on instrumental reason to explain historical change nonetheless creates an explanatory vacuum and in some respects is itself ahistorical. Certainly, there were many capable administrators in the Qing government who managed an unenviable portfolio of foreign aggression, unruly merchants, and desperate finances. Some, like Li Hongzhang, did come to wear their classical training lightly. But even so, the emergence of pragmatism as a grounds for decision-making is more productively engaged as a phenomenon to be queried by the historian rather than as an at-hand explanation for courses of action. The historically specific conceptual resources and moral orientations with which Qing officials, whether in Beijing or in a magistrate's office, comprehended their tasks and resisted the vortex of the treaty regime are an important part of the governing landscape. They tell us what was different about the Qing Empire, and there is much we can learn from that difference.

A key lesson of Qing alterity, I have argued, is the historical specificity of capital. The ways in which key features of capitalist modernity struck smart, educated, thoughtful men as odd or undesirable holds important lessons for understanding what is different about capitalist society. This critique is especially needed given that capitalist society's own forms of thought tend to universalize or naturalize its historical specificity. Prince Yixin could see what Rutherford Alcock could not. One message the Qing viewpoint teaches concerns boundaries. Territorial boundaries were and continue to remain salient to the geopolitical order, but the movement

---

14. "The Resources of China," *The Far Eastern Review* 12, no. 2 (1915): 53–56, here 55. In fact, China did not produce "all" that it needed. Silver gained from foreign trade was crucial to the function of the Chinese economy. See Ho-fung Hung, "Imperial China and Capitalist Europe in the Eighteenth-Century Global Economy," *Review* (Fernand Braudel Center) 24, no. 4 (2001): 473–513. In my reading, Qianlong was likely not blind to this fact but referenced the ability of Chinese producers to provide all the concrete useful items central to everyday life.

of capital across those boundaries can also recode their significance, in order that capital may appropriate the resources it needs to grow. In China, capital circulating under the treaty regime recoded boundaries between persons as well as those between discrete political territories, inscribing novel limits around Qing personal and territorial sovereignty. When, where, and how Qing officials could act upon Chinese merchants, boats, and cargoes came to depend on the latter's relationship to foreign capital.

A second lesson concerns the different forms of coercion entailed in deterritorialization and reterritorialization. The overt military coercion and political domination characteristic of Euro-American imperialism elsewhere in the world was only ever momentarily present in China: cannon shot in the Pearl River, the looting and destruction of the Summer Palace (Yuanming Yuan), the multinational military parade to the center of the Forbidden City. Yet Euro-American presence in China, no less than in formal colonies, decoded and recoded alien territory into space where global circuits of capital could circulate and reproduce. If China at the end of the nineteenth century looked different from Egypt or West Africa where property and labor regimes had been reconfigured, it was because commercial circulation—shipping, buying, and selling—was the object at the center of Euro-American coercion in China. Treaties performed the work of transforming the regulatory environment so as to expand and protect new capital circuits; the IMC worked to sideline from commercial governance personalized power and political considerations; tax facilities altered time and cost distances to ease accumulation.

In traditional Marxist theory, capital is coercive because capitalists exploit laborers. This is not that story. I have argued that the treaty regime was coercive in the sense that it imposed "objective" determinations on Qing strategies and tactics of governance and that these objective determinations expressed the historically specific, quasi-objective needs of nineteenth-century capital seeking a "spatial fix." This conceptualization has more in common with what Ellen Meiksins Wood has called the "detachment of economic power," which does not so much sever domination from the state but extend political domination "far beyond the limits of direct political domination."[15] Unlike Wood and others, including classical theorists such as Vladimir Lenin and Rosa Luxemburg, as well as Giovanni Arrighi (*The Long Twentieth Century*) and Michael Hardt and Antonio Negri (*Empire*), I am less interested using capital as a lens through which to reconceptualize the exercise of political power and more interested in how the "abstract coercion" of capital becomes institutionalized in new settings. The more "abstract" coercion taking place in China resonated with colonialism elsewhere insofar as local political self-determination was radically disrupted by capital, which circulated through the Qing Empire as

---

15. Ellen Meiksins Wood, *Empire of Capital* (New York: Verso, 2003), 9–13.

cargoes of goods and as an evaluative, regulative standpoint for governance. In this vein, perhaps the most concrete form of this abstract coercion was state debt. Loan terms extracted from Qing government included front-end obligations to expand IMC management and to transform other parts of state administration. Of course, the debt itself also exercised a coercive force, intensifying the need to grow commerce and state revenue together.

When the Qing Empire ended, the program of growth continued. The new government actively solicited influxes of foreign capital, using them to dredge harbors and extend railways. The Republican government initiated collaborations with American experts and industrial firms to explore and exploit its coal and oil deposits; officials in the Department of Agriculture and Commerce evaluated the potential to grow fishery output.[16] In 1915, to make it clear that the Republic of China was open for business, the central government created a Commercial and Industrial Commission tasked with organizing industrial and commercial experiments, collecting and distributing data about economic conditions and economic opportunities in China and developing exhibits of Chinese produce and manufactures.[17]

The history told here might seem to suggest that these arts of governance were shaped in crucial ways by Qing experiences with commercial treaties, which gradually persuaded authorities of the need for nationally coordinated economic policy, for a central budget, for a political economy of growth. But this is not a story of continuity. How authorities from Prince Yixin to Shen Baozhen to unnamed prefects struggled against capital's appropriation of governance points out ways in which the social and political-economic logics of capital were a historical disturbance. Alternatively, the ease and determination with which Nationalist China naturalized the logics and practices of liberal capitalism as simply good, modern governance suggests that the new regime broke with its imperial predecessor in matters other than constitutional governance. As a praxis, imperial governance integrated heaven and earth using range of instruments, including the personal discernment of moral officials, to identify what should be done in any temporally and spatially limited situation. The program of economic growth, by contrast, was much more straightforward and narrow. Both the goal and the means were capital.

---

16. Such projects are covered in detail by the Shanghai-based *Far Eastern Review*, years 1912–1916.
17. "The Resources of China," *Far Eastern Review* 12, no. 2 (1915): 53–56.

Appendix

Although the term "treaty port" is commonplace, by the end of the Qing dynasty, the sites of trade that came under the cognizance of the Imperial Maritime Customs (IMC) exceeded those "opened" to foreign trade by way of bilateral treaties. It may be more accurate to understand them as places where the treaty-based regulatory regime operated. The following list of such ports is based on the IMC's *Decennial Reports on Trade at China's Treaty Ports, 1902–1911*. The first ten entries are the ports that commonly appear in the text. Afterwards, the list follows the north-south, west-east schema employed by IMC reports.

Historical Name	Present-Day Name	Chinese-Character Name	Latitude	Longitude
Canton	Guangzhou	廣州	23.12911	113.264381
Amoy	Xiamen	廈門	24.451941	118.078072
Fuchow	Fuzhou	福州	26.074301	119.296539
Ningpo	Ningbo	寧波	29.87491	121.537498
Chinkiang	Zhenjiang	鎮江	32.195	119.447
Kiukiang	Jiujiang	九江	29.66135	115.96345
Hankow	Hankou	漢口	30.558045	114.30697
Newchuang	Yingkou	牛裝營口	40.65419	122.22637
Chefoo	Yantai	煙台	37.552026	121.377639
Tien-tsin	Tianjin	天津	39.09945	117.23513
Harbin	Harbin	哈爾濱	45.75282	126.65133
Kirin	Jilin	吉林	43.8381	126.5497
Hunchun	Hunchun	琿春	42.862821	130.366036
Lungchingtsun	Longjing	龍井	42.7713889	129.4233333
Antung	Dandong	丹東	40.1211	124.3943
Tatungkow	Dadonggou	大東夠	39.8775	124.147

Appendix

Historical Name	Present-Day Name	Chinese-Character Name	Latitude	Longitude
Dairen	Dalian	大連	38.9	121.6
Chinwangtao	Qinhuangdao	秦皇島	39.8882	119.5202
Kiaochow	Jiaozhou	膠州	36.2647	120.0334
Chungking	Chongqing	重慶	29.5637	106.5504
Ichang	Yichang	宜昌	30.692	111.287
Shasi	Jingzhou	荊州	30.3363	112.2414
Changsha	Changsha	長沙	28.228	112.939
Yochow	Yuezhou	嶽州	29.3564	113.1289
Wuhu	Wuhu	蕪湖	31.3526	118.4331
Nanking	Nanjing	南京	32.060833	118.77889
Hangchow	Hangzhou	杭州	30.267	120.153
Wenchow	Wenzhou	溫州	27.9938	120.6993
Soochow	Suzhou	蘇州	31.3	120.619444
Santuao	Sandu'ao	三都澳	26.620552	119.702373
Swatow	Shantou	汕頭	23.354	116.682
Kowloon	Jiulong	九龍	22.316667	114.183333
Lappa	Wanzai	灣仔	22.1	113.516667
Kongmoon	Jiangmen	江門	22.5789	113.0815
Samshui	Sanshui	三水	23.155833	112.896667
Wuchow	Wuzhou	梧州	23.4767	111.279
Nanning	Nanning	南寧	22.8167	108.3275
Kiungchow	Qiongzhou	瓊州	20.0032	110.354
Pakhoi	Beihai	北海	21.481	109.12
Lungchow	Longzhou	龍州鎮	22.345	106.854167
Mengtse	Mengzi	蒙自	23.3961	103.3649
Szemao	Pu'er City	普洱	22.7868	100.9771
Tengyueh	Tengchong	騰沖	25.016667	98.483333

Bibliography

Archives

Academia Sinica jinshi suo danganguan 中研究院近史所檔案館 [Archives, Institute of Modern History, Academia Sinica], Taipei, Taiwan (ASLSDAG)
Ancient Documents, Shanghai Library, Shanghai, China
School of Oriental and African Studies Archives, University of London, London, England (SOAS)
Shanghai Municipal Council Archives, Shanghai Municipal Archives, Shanghai, China (SMCA)
The National Archives, Kew Gardens, London, England (TNA), Series: Foreign Office (FO)

Published Historical Materials

Abbass, S. H. *Manual of Customs' Practice at Shanghai under the Various Treaties Entered into between China and the Foreign Powers. Supplemented with the Tariff, Treaty Port Regulations on the Opening of the Treaty Ports in China for Commerce with Great Britain, Etc.* [In English.] Shanghai: Kelly & Walsh, 1894.
"ART. I. Present Condition of the Chinese Empire, Considered with regard Both to Its Domestic and Foreign Relations, Especially as Affected by the Late War and Treaty." *Chinese Repository* 12, no. 1 (January 1843): 1–8.
Auber, Peter. *China. An Outline of Its Government, Laws, and Policy: And of the British and Foreign Embassies to, and Intercourse with, That Empire.* London: Parbury, Allen, 1834.
Barton, J. *Observations on the Circumstances which Influence the Condition of the Labouring Classes of Society.* London: n.p., 1817.
Bickers, Robert, and Hans van de Ven, eds. *China and the West: The Maritime Customs Service Archive from the Second Historical Archives of China, Nanjing.* Reading, UK: Primary Source Microfilm, 2004.
Cayley, E. S. *On Commercial Economy in Six Essays.* London: J. Ridgway, 1830.
China. Imperial Maritime Customs. *Decennial Report on Trade at the Treaty Ports of China, 1881–1891.* Shanghai: Statistical Department of the Inspectorate General of Customs, 1892.

China. Imperial Maritime Customs. *Decennial Report on Trade at the Treaty Ports of China, 1892–1901*. Shanghai: Statistical Department of the Inspectorate General of Customs, 1902.

China. Imperial Maritime Customs. *Decennial Report on Trade at the Treaty Ports of China, 1902–1911*. Shanghai: Statistical Department of the Inspectorate General of Customs, 1913.

China. Imperial Maritime Customs. *Inspector General's Circulars. First Series 1861–1875*. Service Series No. 7. Shanghai: Statistical Department of the Inspectorate General of Customs, 1879.

China. Imperial Maritime Customs. *Inspector General's Circulars. Second Series (Nos. 318–450) 1885–89*. Service Series No. 13. Shanghai: Statistical Department of the Inspectorate General of Customs, 1889.

China. Imperial Maritime Customs. *Inspector General's Circulars. Second Series*. Vol. 5. Shanghai: Inspectorate General of Customs, 1897.

China. Imperial Maritime Customs. *Native Opium, 1887*. Special Series No. 9. Shanghai: Statistical Department of the Inspectorate General, 1888.

China. Imperial Maritime Customs. *Opium*. Special Series No. 4. Shanghai: Statistical Department of the Inspectorate General of Customs, 1881.

China. Imperial Maritime Customs. *Report on the Working of Amoy Native Customs*. Office Series No. 85. Shanghai: Statistical Department of the Inspectorate General of Customs, 1906.

China. Imperial Maritime Customs. *Reports on Trade at the Treaty Ports in China for the Year 1867*. Shanghai: Inspector General of Customs, 1868.

China. Imperial Maritime Customs. *Reports on Trade at the Treaty Ports in China for the Year 1868*. Shanghai: Inspector General of Customs, 1869.

China. Imperial Maritime Customs. *Reports on Trade at the Treaty Ports in China for the Year 1869*. Shanghai: Inspector General of Customs, 1870.

China. Imperial Maritime Customs. *Reports on Trade at the Treaty Ports in China for the Year 1870*. Shanghai: Inspector General of Customs, 1871.

China. Imperial Maritime Customs. *Reports on Trade at the Treaty Ports in China for the Year 1874*. Shanghai: Inspector General of Customs, 1875.

China. Imperial Maritime Customs. *The Soya Bean of Manchuria*. Special Series No. 31. Shanghai: Statistical Department of the Inspectorate General of Customs, 1911.

China. Imperial Maritime Customs. *Treaties, Conventions, Etc. between China and Foreign States*. Miscellaneous Series No. 30. 2 vols. Shanghai: Statistical Department of the Inspectorate General of Customs, 1908.

China. Imperial Maritime Customs. *Working of Likin Collectorates: Kiukiang, Soochow, and Hangchow*. Office Series No. 88. Shanghai: Statistical Department of the Inspectorate General of Customs, 1907.

Da Qing shi lu 大清實錄 [Veritable records of the Qing dynasty]. Guangxu 光緒. Dezong jing huangdi shilu 德宗景皇帝實錄, 1927. Scripta Sinica 漢籍電子文獻.

Dalrymple, Alexander. *Oriental Repertory*. 2 vols. London: W. Ballintine, 1808.

Dick, Thomas. *Regulations of the Chinese Maritime Customs.* Edited by Shanghai Office of Maritime Customs. Shanghai: A. H. De Carvalho, 1864.

Dixon, George. *A Voyage round the World.* London: George Goulding, 1789.

Great Britain. (1865). Commercial Reports from Her Majesty's Consuls in China, 1862–1864. [3489]

Great Britain. (1866). Commercial Reports from H. M. Consuls in China and Japan for the Year 1865. [3740]

Great Britain. (1867–1868). Commercial Reports from H. M. Consuls in China, Japan, and Siam, 1866–1868. [4079]

Great Britain. (1840). Correspondence relating to China. [223][224][230][234]

Great Britain. (1857). Correspondence relative to Entrance into Canton, 1850–1855. [2173]

Great Britain. (1859). Correspondence relative to the Earl of Elgin's Special Missions to China and Japan, 1857–1859. [2571]

Great Britain. (1888). Diplomatic and Consular Reports on Trade and Finance, China, Report for the Year 1887 on the Trade of Taiwan. Foreign Office Annual Series, No. 332.

Great Britain. (1830). First Report from the Select Committee on the Affairs of the East India Company: China Trade. Sessional Paper No. 644.

Great Britain. (1862). Papers relating to the Rebellion in China and Trade on the Yang-tze-kiang River. [2976]

Great Britain. (1867–1868). Reports from the Foreign Commissioners at Ports in China Open by Treaty to Foreign Trade for the Year 1866. [3976]

Great Britain. (1867). Reports from the Foreign Commissioners at the Various Ports in China, for the Year 1865. [3823]

Great Britain. China. (1866). Commercial Reports from Her Majesty's Consuls in China for the Year 1864. [3587]

Great Britain. China. (1861). Treaties between Her Majesty and the Emperor of China. With Rules for Trade and Tariff of Duties. [2755]

Great Britain. China. (1844). Treaty between Her Majesty and the Emperor of China, Signed, in the English and Chinese Languages, at Nanking, August 29, 1842. With Other Documents Relating Thereto. [521]

Great Britain. *China. No. 1* (1865). Foreign Customs Establishment in China. [3509]

Great Britain. *China. No. 1* (1899). Correspondence respecting the Affairs of China. [C. 9131]

Great Britain. *China. No. 1* (1902). Correspondence respecting the Affairs of China. [Cd. 1005]

Great Britain. *China. No. 3* (1864). Papers relating to the Affairs of China. [3295]

Great Britain. *China. No. 3* (1877). Further Correspondence respecting the Attack on the Indian Expedition to Western China, and the Murder of Mr. Margary. [C. 1832]

Great Britain. *China. No. 3* (1882). Correspondence respecting the Agreement between the Ministers Plenipotentiary of the Governments of Great Britain and China, Signed at Chefoo, September 13, 1876. [C. 3395]

Great Britain. *China. No. 4* (1864). Commercial Reports from Her Majesty's Consuls in China, for the Year 1862. [3302]

Great Britain. *China. No. 5* (1871). Correspondence respecting the Revision of the Treaty of Tien-Tsin. [C. 389]

Great Britain. *China. No. 5* (1885). Correspondence respecting the Duties on Opium in China. [C. 4448]

Great Britain. *China. No. 7* (1870). Commercial Reports from Her Majesty's Consuls in China and Siam. [C. 84]

Great Britain. Foreign Office. (1897). Diplomatic and Consular Reports on Trade and Finance. China. Reports on the State of Trade at the Treaty Ports of China. [C.8277–127]

Hertslet, Edward. *Treaties, &C., between Great Britain and China; and between China and Foreign Powers; Orders in Council, Rules, Regulations, Acts of Parliament, Decrees, and Notifications Affecting British Interests in China, in Force on the 1st January, 1896.* London: Harrison, 1896.

Huang Hongxun 黃鴻勳, ed. *Yong sui ting zhi* 永綏廳志 30 juan [30 volumes of Yongsui Hall records], n.p., 1908. Zhongguo dizhi ku 中國地志庫. Beijing ai ru sheng shuzihua ji shu yanjiu 北京愛如生數字化技術研究中心.

Jiang Tingfu 蔣廷黻, ed. *Chouban yiwu shimo buyi* 籌辦夷務始末補遺 [Complete record of foreign affairs addendum]. *Minguojian chaoben* 民國間抄本 ed., 1936. Scripta Sinica 漢籍電子文獻

Krausse, Alexis. *China in Decay: The Story of a Disappearing Empire.* London: G. Bell, 1900.

Li Hongzhang 李鴻. *Li Hongzhang quan ji* 李鴻章全集 [The collected works of Li Hongzhang]. Edited by Gu Tinglong 顧廷龍 and Dai Yi 戴逸. 39 vols. Hefei shi 合肥市: Anhui jiao yu chu ban she 安徽教育出版社, 2008.

Li Hongzhang 李鴻章. *Li wen zhong gong quan ji* 李文忠公全集 [Collected memorials of Li Hongzhang]. Jindai Zhongguo shiliao congkan xu bian 近代中國史料叢刊續編, edited by Shen Yunlong 沈雲龍. Taibeixian Yonghezhen 臺北縣永和鎮: Wen hai chubanshe 文海出版社, 1974–1983.

Lin Zexu. "Art. I Letter to the Queen of England from the High Commissioner Lin, and His Colleagues." [Translation.] *Chinese Repository* 8, no. 10 (February 1840): 497–503.

Lockyer, Charles. *An Account of the Trade in India.* London: Samuel Crouch, 1711.

Mai Zhonghua 麥仲華, ed. *Huangchao jingshiwen xinbian* 皇朝經世文新編 [A new compilation of statecraft texts of the imperial dynasty]. 21 juan. Shanghai 上海: Shanghai shuju 上海書局, 1898.

Matheson, James. *The Present Position and Prospects of the British Trade with China Together with an Outline of Some Leading Occurences in Its Past History.* London: Smith, Elder, 1836.

Nish, Ian, ed. *British Documents on Foreign Affairs: Reports and Papers from the Foreign Office Confidential Prints Part I, from the Mid-Nineteenth Century to the First World War. Series E. Vol. 13. China Miscellaneous, 1894–1910.* Silver Spring, MD: University Publications, 1994.

Nish, Ian, ed. *British Documents on Foreign Affairs: Reports and Papers from the Foreign Office Confidential Prints Part I, from the Mid-Nineteenth Century to the First World War. Series E. Vol. 14. Annual Reports on China, 1906–1913.* Silver Spring, MD: University Publications, 1994.

Nish, Ian, ed. *British Documents on Foreign Affairs: Reports and Papers from the Foreign Office Confidential Prints Part I, from the Mid-Nineteenth Century to the First World War. Series E.* Vol. 20. *China's Rehabilitation and Treaty Revision, 1866–1869*. Silver Spring, MD: University Publications, 1994.

Phipps, John. *A Practical Treatise on the China and Eastern Trade Comprising the Commerce of Great Britain and India Particularly Bengal and Singapore with China and the Eastern Islands*. London: William H. Allen, 1836.

Quanguo tushuguan wenxian suo wei fuzhi zhongxin, 全國圖書館文獻縮微複製中心 [National Center for Microfilm Reproduction of Library Documents], ed. *Qing dai shoushui wu dangan shiliao huibian* 清代稅收檔案史料匯編 [A compendium of archival materials on tax revenue in the Qing dynasty]. 國家圖書館藏歷史檔案文獻叢刊 [National Library Historical Archives Series] vol. 26.

Read, Sheridan P. "The Chinese as Business Men." *The Century Illustrated Monthly Magazine*, n.s., 38 (May–October 1900): 864–68.

San kou tongshang dachen zhi Tianhaiguan shuiwusi zhawen xuanbian 三口通商大臣至天海關稅務司札文選編 [Selected correspondence between the imperial commissioner of trade at the three ports and the Tianjin customs commissioner]. Tianjin 天津: Tianjinshi danganguan 天津市檔案館, 1989.

Shanghai (China: International Settlement). Municipal Council. *Gongbuju Dongshihui Huiyilu* 工部局董事會會議錄 [The minutes of the Shanghai Municipal Council]. Shanghaishi Danganguan Bian 上海市檔案館編. Shanghai: Shanghai guji chubanshe 上海古籍出版社, 2001.

Six Essays on the Trade of Shanghai: Reprinted from the "Celestial Empire." Shanghai: Printed at the "Gazette" Office, 1874.

The Shanghai Land Regulations: Origins and Purposes of the Present Code. Extracts from the Minutes of the Land-Renters' Meeting Held at Shanghai, 11th July, 1854. Shanghai, 1854.

Townend, Edward. *Tables Shewing the Cost of Tea, with All Charges, as Bought in Hankow by the Pecul of 133 1/3 Pounds Avoirdupois for Taels of Sycee, and Sold in London by the Pound Avoirdupois, at the Several Exchanges*. London: Smith Elder, 1863.

"Treaty of Nanking." *Chinese Repository* 13 (1844).

United States Commissioner to China and William Woodville Rockhill. *Report of William W. Rockhill, Late Commissioner to China, with Accompanying Documents*. Washington, DC: Government Printing Office, 1901. https://www.loc.gov/item/tmp96022434/.

Wenqing 文慶, ed. *Chouban yiwu shimo* 籌辦夷務始末 [Complete record of foreign affairs]. *Qing neifu chaoben* 清內府抄本 ed. Beijing: Gugong bowuguan 故宮博物館, 1929–1931.

Wenqing 文慶, ed. *Chouban yiwu shimo* 籌辦夷務始末 [Complete record of foreign affairs]. *Qing neifu chaoben* 清內府抄本 ed., 1930. Scripta Sinica 漢籍電子文獻.

Williams, S. Wells. *The Chinese Commercial Guide*. 5th ed. Hong Kong: A. Shortrede, 1863.

Yuezhang cheng an hui lan yi bian 約章成案匯覽乙篇 [Compendium of treaties, regulations, and cases, part B]. Qing Guangxu 31 dian shi zhai shiyin ben 清光緒三十一年點石齋石印本 ed. Scripta Sinica 漢籍電子文獻. Taipei 臺北: Academica Sinica 中央研究院.

Zhang Zhidong 張之洞. *Zhang wenxiang gong quan ji zouyi* 張文襄公全集 奏議 [The complete works of Zhang Zhidong, memorials]. Edited by Wang Shunan 王樹枏. 26 vols. Taibeixian Yonghezhen 臺北縣永和鎮: Wenhai chubanshe 文海出版社, 1970.

Zhang Zhidong 張之洞. *Zhang Zhidong quan ji di er ce zouyi* 張之洞全集 第二冊 奏議 [Complete works of Zhang Zhidong volume 2 memorials]. Edited by Yuan Shuyi 苑書義, Sun Huafeng 孫華峰, and Li Bingxin 李秉新. Shijiazhuang 石家莊: Hebei renmin chubanshe 河北人民出版社, 1998.

Zheng Guanying 鄭觀應. *Shengshi weiyan* 盛世危言 [Warning for a prosperous age]. In *Zheng Guanying ji* 鄭觀應集 [Collected works of Zheng Guanying], edited by Xia Dongyuan 夏東元. Beijing: Zhonghhua shu ju 中華書局, 2013.

Zheng Zhenduo 鄭振鐸, ed. *Wanqing wenxuan* 晚清文選 [Selected writings from the late Qing]. Zhongguo zhexue dianzihua jihua 中國哲學書電子化計劃 [Chinese Philosophical Text Digitization Project]. https://ctext.org.

Zuo Zongtang 左宗棠. *Zuo Zongtang quanji* 左宗棠全集 [Collected works of Zuo Zongtang]. 15 vols. Changsha 長沙市: Yuelu shu she 岳麓書社, 1986.

Periodicals

Far Eastern Review (Shanghai)
North China Daily News (Shanghai)
North China Daily News and Market Report (1867–1869) (Shanghai)
North China Herald (1860–1867) (Shanghai)
North China Herald and Supreme Court & Consular Gazette (1870–1941) (Shanghai)

Articles, Books, and Chapters

Adorno, Theodor. "On the Fetish Character in Music and Regression of Listening." In *The Essential Frankfurt School Reader*, ed. Andrew Arato and Eike Gebhardt. New York: The Continuum Publishing Co., 1982 [1938].

Adshead, S. A. M. *The Modernization of the Chinese Salt Administration, 1900–1929*. Cambridge, MA: Harvard University Press, 1970.

Andreini, Attilio. "The Meaning of *Qing* in Texts from Guodian Tomb No. 1." In *Love, Hatred, and Other Passions: Questions and Themes on Emotions in Chinese Civilization*, edited by Paolo Santangelo and Donatella Guida, 149–65. Leiden: Brill, 2006.

Antony, Robert J., and Jane Kate Leonard, eds. *Dragons, Tigers, and Dogs: Qing Crisis Management and the Boundaries of State Power in Late Imperial China*. Ithaca: Cornell East Asia Program, 2002.

Arrighi, Giovanni. *The Long Twentieth Century: Money, Power, and the Origins of Our Times*. New York: Verso, 1994.

Arrighi, Giovanni, Takeshi Hamashita, and Mark Selden, eds. *The Resurgence of East Asia: 500, 150, and 50 Year Perspectives*. New York: Routledge, 2003.

Aylmer, G. E. "Bureaucracy." In *The Companion Volume to the New Cambridge Modern History*, vol. 13, edited by Peter Burke, 164–200. Cambridge: Cambridge University Press, 1979.

Bailey, Paul, ed. and trans. *Strengthen the Country and Enrich the People: The Reform Writings of Ma Jianzhong*. London: Routledge, 1998.
Banaji, Jairus. *A Brief History of Commercial Capitalism*. Chicago: Haymarket Books, 2020.
Banno, Masataka. *China and the West, 1858–1861: The Origins of the Tsungli Yamen*. Cambridge, MA: Harvard University Asia Center, 1964.
Barish, Daniel. *Learning to Rule: Court Education and the Remaking of the Qing State, 1861–1912*. New York: Columbia University Press, 2022.
Barlow, Tani E. "Colonialism's Career in Post-war China Studies." In *Formations of Colonial Modernity in East Asia*, ed. Tani E. Barlow, 373–412. Durham, NC: Duke University Press, 1997.
Bastid, Marianne. "The Structure of the Financial Institutions of the State in the Late Qing." In *The Scope of State Power in China*, edited by Stuart R. Schram, 51–79. London: St. Martin's, 1985.
Beal, Edward, Jr. *The Origin of Likin, 1853–64*. Cambridge, MA: Chinese Economic and Political Studies, Harvard University, 1958.
Berg, Maxine. *The Machinery Question and the Making of Political Economy, 1815–1848*. Cambridge: Cambridge University Press, 1980.
Bergère, Marie-Claire. *Shanghai: China's Gateway to Modernity*. Stanford: Stanford University Press, 2009.
Bickers, Robert. "'Good Work for China in Every Possible Direction': The Foreign Inspectorate of the Chinese Maritime Customs, 1854–1950." In *Twentieth-Century Colonialism and China: Localities, the Everyday, and the World*, edited by Bryna Goodman and David Goodman, 25–36. London: Routledge, 2021.
Boecking, Felix. *No Great Wall: Trade, Tariffs, and Nationalism in Republican China, 1927–1945*. Cambridge, MA: Harvard University Asia Center, 2017.
Borchard, Edwin. "Relations between International Law and Municipal Law." *Virginia Law Review* 127 no. 2 (December 1940): 137–48.
Borokh, Olga. "Rethinking Traditional Attitudes towards Consumption in the Process of Formation of Chinese Economics (Late Qing and Republican Periods)." In *European and Chinese Histories of Economic Thought: Theories and Images of Good Governance*, edited by Iwo Amelung and Bertram Schefold, 233–45. London: Routledge, 2021.
Bowen, H. V. *The Business of Empire: The East India Company and Imperial Britain, 1756–1833*. Cambridge: Cambridge University Press, 2006.
Brandt, Loren. "Reflections on China's Late 19th and Early 20th Century Economy." *China Quarterly* 150 (1997): 282–308.
Brenner, Robert. "The Agrarian Roots of European Capitalism." In *The Brenner Debate: Agrarian Class Structure and Economic Development in Pre-industrial Europe*, edited by T. H. Ashton and C. H. E. Philpin, 213–328. Cambridge: Cambridge University Press, 1985.
Brown, Shannon R. "Cakes and Oil: Technology Transfer and Chinese Soybean Processing, 1860–1895." *Comparative Studies in Society and History* 23, no. 3 (1981): 449–63.
Brown, Shannon R. "The Partially Opened Door: Limitations on Economic Change in China in the 1860s." *Modern Asian Studies* 12, no. 2 (1978): 177–92.

Bruner, Katherine F., John K. Fairbank, and Richard J. Smith, eds. *Entering China's Service: Robert Hart's Journals, 1854–1863*. Cambridge, MA: Council on East Asian Studies, Harvard University, 1986.

Brunero, Donna. *Britain's Imperial Cornerstone in China: The Chinese Maritime Customs Service, 1854–1949*. London: Routledge, 2006.

Cao Ying 曹英. *Bu pingdeng tiaoyue yu wan Qing Zhong Ying maoyi chongtu* 不平等條約與晚清中影貿易衝突 [Unequal treaties and Qing-British trade conflict]. Changsha 長沙: Hunan renmin chubanshe 湖南人民出版社, 2010.

Cassel, Pär Kristoffer. "Extraterritoriality in China: What We Know and What We Don't Know." In *Treaty Ports in Modern China: Land, Law, and Power*, edited by Robert Bickers and Isabella Jackson, 23–42. London: Routledge, 2016.

Cassel, Pär Kristoffer. *Grounds of Judgment: Extraterritoriality and Imperial Power in Nineteenth-Century China and Japan*. Oxford: Oxford University Press, 2012.

Chang, Chihyun. *Government, Imperialism and Nationalism in China: The Maritime Customs Service and Its Chinese Staff*. New York: Routledge, 2013.

Chang, Hao. "The Intellectual Context of Reform." In *Reform in Nineteenth-Century China*, edited by Paul A. Cohen and John E. Schrecker, 145–49. Cambridge, MA: Harvard University East Asian Research Center, 1976.

Chang, Hsin-pao. *Commissioner Lin and the Opium War*. Cambridge, MA: Harvard University Press, 1964.

Chen Guanghui 陳光輝. "Lun Qing mo Gansu tongjuan zhe kaiban 論清末甘肅統捐者開辦" [On the opening of unified taxation in Gansu in the late Qing]. *Journal of Neijiang Normal University* 內江師範學院報 29, no. 1 (2014): 83–87.

Chen, Li. *Chinese Law in Imperial Eyes: Sovereignty, Justice, and Transcultural Politics*. New York: Columbia University Press, 2016.

Chen Yong 陳勇. "Hede yu yapian shuili bingzheng 赫德與鴉片"稅厘並征"" [Robert Hart and joint collection of opium taxes and *lijin*]. *Journal of Jinan University* 暨南學報, no. 4 (2006): 140–47.

Cheong, W. E. *The Hong Merchants of Canton: Chinese Merchants in Sino-Western Trade*. Richmond, UK: Curzon, 1997.

Chesneaux, Jean. *Peasant Revolts in China, 1840–1949*. London: Norton, 1973.

Chu Chin. *The Tariff Problem in China*. Studies in History, Economics and Public Law 72, no. 2. New York: Columbia University, 1916.

Chu, Raymond W., and William G. Saywell. *Career Patterns in the Ch'ing Dynasty: The Office of Governor General*. Ann Arbor: University of Michigan Center for Chinese Studies, 1984.

Cohen, Emmeline. *The Growth of the British Civil Service, 1780–1939*. Hamden, CT: Archon Books, 1965.

Cohen, Paul A. *Between Tradition and Modernity: Wang T'ao and Reform in Late Ch'ing China*. Cambridge, MA: Harvard University Press, 1974.

Cohen, Paul A. *Discovering History in China: American Historical Writing on the Recent Chinese Past*. New York: Columbia University Press, 1984.

Cohen, Paul A. *History in Three Keys: The Boxers as Event, Experience, and Myth*. New York: Columbia University Press, 1997.

Cohen, Paul A. "The New Coastal Reformers." In *Reform in Nineteenth-Century China*, edited by Paul A. Cohen and John E. Schrecker, 255–64. Cambridge, MA: Harvard University East Asian Research Center, 1976.
Cohen, Paul A., and John E. Schrecker, eds. *Reform in Nineteenth-Century China*. Cambridge, MA: Harvard University East Asian Research Center, 1976.
Collis, Maurice. *Foreign Mud, Being an Account of the Opium Imbroglio at Canton in the 1830's & the Anglo-Chinese War That Followed*. New York: Knopf, 1947.
Comaroff, John, and Jean Comaroff. *Ethnicity, Inc.* Chicago: University of Chicago Press, 2009.
Coyle, Diane. *GDP: A Brief but Affectionate History*. Princeton: Princeton University Press, 2014.
Crafts, Nicholas. *Forging Ahead, Falling Behind, and Fighting Back: British Economic Growth from the Industrial Revolution to the Financial Crisis*. Cambridge: Cambridge University Press, 2018.
Crossley, Pamela Kyle. "The Rulerships of China." *American Historical Review* 97, no. 5 (1992): 1468–83.
Crossley, Pamela Kyle. *Wobbling Pivot, China since 1800: An Interpretative History*. Oxford: Wiley Blackwell, 2010.
Cua, Antonio S. "*Xin* (Mind/Heart) and Moral Failure: Notes on an Aspect of Mencius's Moral Psychology." In *Human Nature, Ritual and History: Studies in Xunzi and Chinese Philosophy*, 348–70. Washington, DC: Catholic University of America Press, 2005.
de Bary, Wm. Theodore. *The Message of the Mind in Neo-Confucianism*. New York: Columbia University Press, 1989.
Dean, Austin. *China and the End of Global Silver, 1873–1937*. Ithaca: Cornell University Press, 2020.
Dean, Britten. *China and Great Britain: The Diplomacy of Commercial Relations, 1860–1864*. Cambridge, MA: East Asian Research Center, Harvard University, 1974.
DeGlopper, Donald R. "Social Structure in a Nineteenth-Century Taiwanese Port City." In *The City in Late Imperial China*, edited by G. William Skinner, 633–50. Stanford: Stanford University Press, 1977.
Deleuze, Gilles, and Félix Guattari. *A Thousand Plateaus: Capitalism and Schizophrenia*. Translated by Brian Massumi. Minneapolis: University of Minnesota Press, 1987.
Deleuze, Gilles, and Félix Guattari. *Anti-Oedipus: Capitalism and Schizophrenia*. Translated by Robert Hurley, Mark Seem, and Helen R. Lane. Minneapolis: University of Minnesota Press, 1983.
Deng, Kent. *China's Political Economy in Modern Times: Changes and Economic Consequences, 1800–2000*. London: Routledge, 2012.
Dimsdale, Nicholas, and Ryland Thomas. *UK Business and Financial Cycles since 1660, Volume 1: A Narrative Overview*. London: Palgrave Macmillan, 2019.
Dirlik, Arif. "Chinese Historians and the Marxist Concept of Capitalism: A Critical Examination." *Modern China* 8, no. 1 (January 1982): 105–32.
Duara, Prasenjit. *Culture, Power, and the State: Rural North China, 1900–1942*. Stanford: Stanford University Press, 1988.

Dunnell, Ruth W., Mark C. Elliot, Phillippe Foret, and James A. Millward, eds. *New Qing Imperial History: The Making of Inner Asian Empire at Qing Chengde*. Abingdon, UK: Taylor & Francis, 2004.

Dunstan, Helen. *Conflicting Counsels to Confuse the Age: A Documentary Study of Political Economy in Qing China, 1644–1840*. Ann Arbor: Center for Chinese Studies, University of Michigan, 1996.

Dunstan, Helen. *State or Merchant: Political Economy and the Political Process in 1740s China*. Cambridge, MA: Harvard University Press, 2006.

Eberhard-Bréard, Andrea. "Robert Hart and China's Statistical Revolution." *Modern Asian Studies* 40, no. 3 (2006): 605–29.

Elman, Benjamin. *A Cultural History of Civil Examinations in Late Imperial China*. Berkeley: University of California Press, 2000.

Elman, Benjamin. *Civil Examinations and Meritocracy in Late Imperial China*. Cambridge, MA: Harvard University Press, 2013.

Elvin, Mark. Introduction to *The Chinese City between Two Worlds*, edited by Mark Elvin and G. William Skinner, 1–16. Stanford: Stanford University Press, 1974.

Esherick, Joseph. "Harvard on China: The Apologetics of Imperialism." *Bulletin of Concerned Asian Scholars* 4, no. 4 (1972): 9–16.

Esherick, Joseph. *The Origins of the Boxer Uprising*. Berkeley: University of California Press, 1987.

Fairbank, John King. "Creation of the Treaty System." In *Cambridge History of China*, edited by John Fairbank, 213–63. Cambridge: Cambridge University Press, 1978.

Fairbank, John King. "Synarchy under the Treaties." In *Chinese Thought and Institutions*, edited by John King Fairbank, with contributions by T'ung-tsu Ch'u, 204–31. Chicago: University of Chicago Press, 1957.

Fairbank, John King. *Trade and Diplomacy on the China Coast: The Opening of the Treaty Ports, 1842–1854*. Cambridge, MA: Harvard University Press, 1953.

Fairbank, John King, Katherine Frost Bruner, Elizabeth MacLeod Matheson, and James Duncan Campbell. *The I. G. in Peking Letters of Robert Hart, Chinese Maritime Customs, 1868–1907*. Cambridge, MA: Belknap Press, 1975.

Fang Xing. "The Retarded Development of Capitalism." In *Chinese Capitalism, 1522–1840*, edited by Xu Dixin and Wu Chengming, translated by Li Zhengde, Liang Miaoru, and Li Siping, 375–401. New York: St. Martin's, 2000.

Farquhar, Judith B., and James L. Hevia. "Culture and Postwar American Historiography of China." *positions* 1, no. 2 (1993): 486–525.

Fay, Peter Ward. *The Opium War, 1840–1842: Barbarians in the Celestial Empire in the Early Part of the Nineteenth Century and the War by which They Forced Her Gates Ajar*. Chapel Hill: University of North Carolina Press, 1975.

Feng Tianyu 縫天瑜. *Zhang Zhidong pingzhuan* 張之洞評傳 [An annotated biography of Zhang Zhidong]. Nanjing 南京: Nanjing daxue chubanshe 南京大學出版社, 1991.

Feuerwerker, Albert. *China's Early Industrialization: Sheng Hsuan-Huai (1844–1916) and Mandarin Enterprise*. Cambridge, MA: Harvard University Press, 1970.

Feuerwerker, Albert. "Economic Trends, 1912–1919." In *The Cambridge History of China*. Vol. 12, *Republican China, 1912–1949, Part 1*, edited by John King Fairbank, 28–127. Cambridge: Cambridge University Press, 1983.

Feuerwerker, Albert. "Economic Trends in the Late Ch'ing Empire, 1870–1911." In *The Cambridge History of China*. Vol. 11, *Late Ch'ing, 1800–1911, Part 2*, edited by John King Fairbank and Kwang-Ching Liu, 1–69. Cambridge: Cambridge University Press, 1980.

Feuerwerker, Albert. *The Chinese Economy, ca. 1870–1911*. Ann Arbor: Center for Chinese Studies, University of Michigan, 1969.

Findlay, Ronald, and Kevin H. O'Rourke. *Power and Plenty: Trade, War and the World Economy in the Second Millennium*. Princeton: Princeton University Press, 2007.

Fong, Sau-yi. "Guns, Boats and Diplomacy: Late Qing China and the World's Naval Technology." PhD diss., Columbia University, 2022.

Foster, John Bellamy, Brett Clark, and Richard York. *The Ecological Rift: Capitalism's War on the Earth*. New York: New York University Press, 2010.

Foucault, Michel. *Security, Territory, Population: Lectures at the Collège de France, 1977–78*. Edited by Michel Senellart. Translated by Graham Burchell. Basingstoke: Picador, 2009.

Furuta, Kazuko. "Kobe as Seen as Part of the Shanghai Trading Network: The Role of Chinese Merchants in the Re-export of Cotton Manufactures to Japan." In *Japan, China, and the Growth of the Asian International Economy, 1850–1949*, edited by Kaoru Sugihara, 23–48. Oxford: Oxford University Press, 2005.

Gardella, Robert. *Harvesting Mountains: Fujian and the China Tea Trade, 1757–1937*. Berkeley: University of California Press, 1994.

Gardella, Robert. "Reform and the Tea Industry and Trade in Late Ch-ing China: The Fukien Case." In *Reform in Nineteenth-Century China*, edited by Paul A. Cohen and John E. Schrecker, 71–79. Cambridge, MA: Harvard University East Asian Research Center, 1976.

Gardner, Daniel K. *The Four Books: The Basic Teachings of the Later Confucian Tradition*. Indianapolis: Hackett, 2007.

Geaney, Jane. *On the Epistemology of the Senses in Early Chinese Thought*. Honolulu: University of Hawai'i Press, 2002.

Giersch, C. Patterson. *Corporate Conquests: Business, the State and the Origins of Ethnic Inequality in Southwest China*. Stanford: Stanford University Press, 2020.

Goetzmann, William N., Andrey D. Ukhov, and Ning Zhu. "China and the World Financial Markets 1870–1939: Modern Lessons from Historical Globalization." *Economic History Review* 60, no. 2 (2007): 267–312.

Goldin, Paul. "Economic Cycles and Price Theory in Early Chinese Texts." In *Between Command and Market: Economic Thought and Practice in Early China*, edited by Elisa Sabattini and Christian Schwermann, 43–77. Leiden: Brill, 2022.

Goodman, Bryna. *Native Place, City, and Nation: Regional Networks and Identities in Shanghai, 1853–1937*. Berkeley: University of California Press, 1995.

Goodman, Bryna, and David S. G. Goodman. *Twentieth-Century Colonialism and China: Localities, the Everyday and the World*. New York: Routledge, 2012.

Greenberg, Michael. *British Trade and the Opening of China, 1800–42.* Cambridge: Cambridge University Press, 1951.

Grewe, Wilhelm Georg. *The Epochs of International Law.* Berlin: Walter de Gruyter, 2000.

Guy, R. Kent. *China's Political Economy in Modern Times: Changes and Economic Consequences, 1800–2000.* London: Routledge, 2012.

Guy, R. Kent. *Qing Governors and Their Provinces: The Evolution of Territorial Administration in China, 1644–1796.* Seattle: University of Washington Press, 2010.

Halsey, Stephen. "Money, Power, and the State: The Origins of the Military-Fiscal State in Modern China." *Journal of the Economic and Social History of the Orient* 56, no. 3 (2013): 392–432.

Halsey, Stephen. *Quest for Power: European Imperialism and the Making of Chinese Statecraft.* Cambridge, MA: Harvard University Press, 2015.

Hamashita, Takeshi. "Despotism and Decentralization in Chinese Governance: Taxation, Tribute, and Emigration." In *China, East Asia, and the Global Economy,* edited by Takeshi Hamashita, Linda Grove, and Mark Selden, 27–38. London: Routledge, 2008.

Hamilton, Gary, Chang Wei-an, and Chi-kong Lai. "The Importance of Commerce in the Organization of China's Late Imperial Economy." In *The Resurgence of East Asia: 500, 150, and 50 Year Perspectives,* edited by Giovanni Arrighi, Takeshi Hamashita, and Mark Selden, 173–213. London: Routledge, 2003.

Hao, Yen-p'ing. *The Commercial Revolution in Nineteenth-Century China: The Rise of Sino-Western Mercantile Capitalism.* Berkeley: University of California Press, 1986.

Hardt, Michael, and Antonio Negri. *Empire.* Cambridge, MA: Harvard University Press, 2001.

Harley, C. Knick. "British and European Industrialization." In *The Cambridge History of Capitalism.* Vol. 1, *The Rise of Capitalism: From Ancient Origins to 1848,* edited by Larry Neal and Jeffrey Williamson, 491–532. Cambridge: Cambridge University Press, 2014.

Harley, C. Knick. "Trade: Discovery, Mercantilism and Technology." In *The Cambridge Economic History of Modern Britain,* edited by Roderick Floud and Paul Johnson, 175–203. Cambridge: Cambridge University Press, 2004.

Hart, Jennifer. "Sir Charles Trevelyan at the Treasury." *English Historical Review* 70, no. 294 (January 1960): 92–110.

Harvey, David. *Limits to Capital.* Rev. ed. New York: Verso, 2006.

Harvey, David. *The Condition of Postmodernity: An Enquiry into the Origins of Cultural Change.* Oxford: Blackwell, 1989.

Hay, Jonathan. "The Kangxi Emperor's Brush Traces: Calligraphy, Writing, and the Art of Imperial Authority." In *Body and Face in Chinese Visual Culture,* edited by Wu Hung and Katherine R. Tsiang, 311–34. Cambridge, MA: Harvard University Asia Center, 2005.

He Lie 何烈. *Lijin zhidu xintan* 厘金制度新探 [New investigations into the *lijin* system]. Taipei 臺北: Sili dongwu daxue, Taiwan shangwu yinshu guan zong jingxiao 私立東吳大學,臺灣商務印書館總經銷, 1972.

He, Wenkai. *Paths towards the Modern Fiscal State: England, Japan, and China.* Cambridge, MA: Harvard University Press, 2013.

Hevia, James L. *Cherishing Men from Afar: Qing Guest Ritual and the Macartney Embassy of 1793*. Durham, NC: Duke University Press, 1995.

Hevia, James L. *English Lessons: The Pedagogy of Imperialism in Nineteenth-Century China*. Durham, NC: Duke University Press, 2003.

Hevia, James L. *The Imperial Security State: British Colonial Knowledge and Empire-Building in Asia*. Cambridge: Cambridge University Press, 2012.

Hinton, Harold. *The Grain Tribute System of China, 1845–1911*. Cambridge, MA: Harvard University Asia Center, 1956.

Hirschman, Albert O. *The Passions and the Interests: Political Arguments for Capitalism before Its Triumph*. Princeton: Princeton University Press, 1997.

Ho Honwai 何漢威. "Qingji zhongyang yu gesheng caizheng guanxi de fansi 清季中央與各省財政關係的反思" [Reflections on the financial relationship between the central government and provinces in the Qing dynasty]. *Zhongyang yanjiuyuan, Lishi yuyan yanjiusuo jikan* 中央研究院歷史語言研究所集刊 [Bulletin of the Institute of History and Language Academia Sinica] 72, no. 3 (September 2001): 597–696.

Hobsbawm, Eric. *Industry and Empire: The Birth of the Industrial Revolution*. New York: New Press, 1999.

Hobsbawm, Eric. *The Age of Capital 1848–1875*. New York: Vintage, 1996.

Hobsbawm, Eric. *The Age of Revolution 1789–1848*. New York: Vintage, 1996.

Horowitz, Richard S. "Breaking the Bonds of Precedent: The 1905–06 Government Reform Commission and the Remaking of the Qing Central State." *Modern Asian Studies* 37, no. 4 (October 2003): 775–97.

Horowitz, Richard S. "Politics, Power and the Chinese Maritime Customs: The Qing Restoration and the Ascent of Robert Hart." *Modern Asian Studies* 40, no. 3 (2006): 549–81.

Howard, Paul Wilson. "Opium Suppression in Qing China: Responses to a Social Problem, 1729–1906." PhD diss., University of Pennsylvania, 1998.

Howe, Anthony. "Britain and the World Economy." In *A Companion to Nineteenth-Century Britain*, edited by Chris Williams, 7–33. Malden, MA: Blackwell, 2004.

Hsiao Kung-chuan. *A History of Chinese Political Thought*. Vol. 1, *From the Beginnings to the Six Century A.D.* Translated by F. W. Mote. Princeton: Princeton University Press, 1979.

Hsü, Immanuel C. Y. *China's Entrance into the Family of Nations: The Diplomatic Phase, 1858–1880*. Cambridge, MA: Harvard University Press, 1960.

Hsü, Immanuel C. Y. "Late Ch'ing Foreign Relations, 1866–1905." In *The Cambridge History of China*. Vol. 11, *Late Ch'ing, 1800–1911, Part 2*, edited by John King Fairbank and Kwang-Ching Liu, 70–141. Cambridge: Cambridge University Press, 1980.

Hu Jichuang. *A Concise History of Chinese Economic Thought*. Beijing: Foreign Languages Press, 1988.

Huang Feng-Hua. *Public Debts in China*. New York: Columbia University, 1919.

Huang Liu-Hung. *A Complete Book concerning Happiness and Benevolence: A Manual for Local Magistrates in Seventeenth-Century China*. Translated and edited by Chu Djang. Tucson: University of Arizona Press, 1984.

Huenemann, Ralph. *The Dragon and the Iron Horse: The Economics of Railroads in China, 1876–1937*. Cambridge, MA: Council on East Asian Studies, Harvard University, 1984.

Hughes, Edward, and H. O'Brien. "Sir Charles Trevelyan and Civil Service Reform, 1853–5." *English Historical Review* 64, no. 250 (January 1949): 53–88.

Hummel, Arthur W., ed. *Eminent Chinese of the Ch'ing Period (1644–1912)*. Washington, DC: Government Printing Office, 1943–1944.

Hung, Ho-fung. "Imperial China and Capitalist Europe in the Eighteenth-Century Global Economy." *Review* (Fernand Braudel Center) 24, no. 4 (2001): 473–513.

Isett, Christopher. "China: The Start of the Great Divergence." In *The Cambridge Economic History of the Modern World*, 2 vols., edited by Stephen Broadberry and Kyoji Fukao, 1:97–122. Cambridge: Cambridge University Press, 2021.

Isett, Christopher. *State, Peasant, and Merchant in Qing Manchuria, 1644–1862*. Stanford: Stanford University Press, 2007.

Jackson, Isabella. *Shaping Modern Shanghai: Colonialism in China's Global City*. Cambridge: Cambridge University Press, 2019.

Janku, Andrea. "New Methods to Nourish the People: Late Qing Encyclopaedic Writings on Political Economy." In *Chinese Encyclopaedias of New Global Knowledge (1870–1930)*, edited by M. Dolezelov-Velingerova and R. G. Wagner, 329–65. Berlin: Springer-Verlag, 2014.

Ji, Zhaojin. *A History of Modern Shanghai Banking: The Rise and Decline of China's Finance Capitalism*. Armonk: M. E. Sharpe, 2003.

Jian Bozan 翦伯贊. *Zhongguo li gangyao* 中國歷綱要 [Outline of Chinese history]. Beijing: n.p, 1962.

Johnson, Linda Cooke. *Shanghai: From Market Town to Treaty Port, 1074–1858*. Stanford: Stanford University Press, 1995.

Jones, Susan Mann. *Local Merchants and the Chinese Bureaucracy, 1750–1950*. Stanford: Stanford University Press, 1987.

Jones, Susan Mann. "Merchant Investment, Commercialization, and Social Change in the Ningpo Area." In *Reform in Nineteenth-Century China*, edited by Paul A. Cohen and John E. Schrecker, 41–48. Cambridge, MA: Harvard University East Asian Research Center, 1976.

Jullien, François. *The Propensity of Things: Toward a History of Efficacy in China*. Trans. Janet Lloyd. New York: Zone Books, 1995.

Kaske, Elisabeth. "Fund-Raising Wars: Office Selling and Interprovincial Finance in Nineteenth-Century China." *Harvard Journal of Asiatic Studies* 71, no. 1 (2011): 69–141.

Keenan, Barry C. *Neo-Confucian Self-Cultivation*. Honolulu: University of Hawai'i Press, 2011.

Keene, Edward. "The Treaty-Making Revolution of the Nineteenth Century." *International History Review* 34, no. 3 (2012): 475–500.

Keller, Wolfgang, Ben Li, and Carol Shuie. "Shanghai's Trade, China's Growth: Continuity, Recovery, and Change since the Opium War." NBER Working Paper Series 17754, National Bureau of Economic Research, Cambridge, MA, January 2012. http://www.nber.org/papers/w17754.pdf.

Keller, Wolfgang, Ben Li, and Carol Shuie. "The Evolution of Domestic Trade Flows When Foreign Trade Is Liberalized: Evidence from the CMCS." In *Institutions and Comparative Economic Development*, edited by Masahiko Aoki, Timur Kuran, and Gerard Roland, 152–72. New York: Palgrave Macmillan, 2012.

Keller, Wolfgang, Javier Santiago, and Carol Shuie. "China's Domestic Trade during the Treaty Era." *Explorations in Economic History* 63 (2017): 26–43.

Kiernan, V. G. *British Diplomacy in China, 1880 to 1885*. New York: Octagon Books, 1970.

Kim, Seonmin. *Ginseng and Borderland: Territorial Boundaries and Political Relations between Qing China and Choson Korea, 1636–1912*. Berkeley: University of California Press, 2017.

Kishlansky, Mark A., ed. *Sources of World History*. Vol. 2. New York: HarperCollins, 1995.

Koll, Elizabeth. *Railroads and the Transformation of China*. Cambridge, MA: Harvard University Press, 2019.

Kose, Hajime. "Chinese Merchants and Chinese Inter-port Trade." In *Japanese Industrialization and the Asian Economy*, edited by A. J. H. Lathan and Heita Kawakatsu, 129–44. London: Routledge, 1994.

Kotenev, A. M. *Shanghai: Its Mixed Court and Council*. Shanghai: North China Daily News & Herald, 1925.

Kuhn, Philip. *Origins of the Modern Chinese State*. Stanford: Stanford University Press, 2002.

Kuhn, Philip. *Rebellion and Its Enemies in Late Imperial China: Militarization and Social Structure, 1796–1864*. Cambridge, MA: Harvard University Press, 1970.

Ladds, Catherine. *Empire Careers: Working for the Chinese Customs Service, 1854–1949*. Manchester: Manchester University Press, 2013.

Lam, Tong. *A Passion for Facts: Social Surveys and the Construction of the Chinese Nation-State, 1900–1949*. Berkeley: University of California Press, 2011.

Lanning, George, and Samuel Couling. *The History of Shanghai*. 2 vols. Shanghai: Kelly & Walsh, 1921.

Lavelle, Peter B. *The Profits of Nature : Colonial Development and the Quest for Resources in Nineteenth-Century China*. New York: Columbia University Press, 2020.

Lee, Leo Ou-fan. *Shanghai Modern: The Flowering of a New Urban Culture in China, 1930–1945*. Cambridge, MA: Harvard University Press, 1999.

LeFevour, Edward. *Western Enterprise in Late Ch'ing China: A Selective Survey of Jardine, Matheson & Company's Operations, 1842–1895*. Cambridge, MA: Harvard University Asia Center, 1968.

Leung, Philip Yuen-sang. "Crisis Management and Institutional Reform: The Expectant Officials in the Late Qing." In *Dragons, Tigers, and Dogs: Qing Crisis Management and the Boundaries of State Power in Late Imperial China*, edited by Robert J. Antony and Jane Kate Leonard, 61–78. Ithaca: Cornell East Asia Program, 2002.

Leung, Yuen-sang. *The Shanghai Taotai: Linkage Man in a Changing Society, 1843–90*. Honolulu: University of Hawai'i Press, 1990.

Levy, Jonathan. "Capital as Process and the History of Capitalism." *Business History Review* 91 (2017): 483–510.

Li, Ch'üan-shih. *Central and Local Finance in China: A Study of the Fiscal Relations between the Central, the Provincial, and the Local Governments*. New York: Columbia University, 1922.

Li, Lillian, and Alison Dray-Novey. "Guarding Beijing's Food Security in the Qing Dynasty: State, Market, and Police." *Journal of Asian Studies* 58, no. 4 (1999): 992–1032.

Li, Yi. *Chinese Bureaucratic Culture and Its Influence on the 19th-Century Steamship Operation, 1864–1885: The Bureau for Recruiting Merchants*. Lewiston, NY: Edwin Mellen, 2001.

Liang, Samuel Y. *Mapping Modernity in Shanghai: Space, Gender, and Visual Culture in the Sojourners' City, 1853–98*. New York: Routledge, 2010.

Lin, Man-Houng. *China Upside Down: Currency, Society, and Ideologies, 1808–1856*. Cambridge, MA: Harvard University Press, 2007.

Lin, Man-Houng. "China's 'Dual Economy' in International Trade Relations, 1842–1949." In *Japan, China, and the Growth of the Asian International Economy, 1850–1949*, edited by Kaoru Sugihara, 179–97. Oxford: Oxford University Press, 2005.

Lin, Man-Houng. "Late Qing Perceptions of Native Opium." *Harvard Journal of Asiatic Studies* 64, no. 1 (2004): 117–44.

Lin, Man-Houng. "Wan Qing de yapian shui 晚清的鴉片稅 [Late Qing opium taxation]." *Si yu yan* 思語言 16, no. 5 (1979): 427–51.

Liu, Andrew. "Production, Circulation, and Accumulation: The Historiographies of Capitalism in China and South Asia." *Journal of Asian Studies* 78, no. 4 (2019): 767–88.

Liu, Andrew. *Tea War: A History of Capitalism in China and India*. New Haven: Yale University Press, 2020.

Liu, K. C. *China's Early Modernization and Reform Movement: Studies in Late Nineteenth-Century China and American-Chinese Relations*. Taipei: Institute of Modern History, Academia Sinica, 2009.

Liu, Lydia He. *The Clash of Empires: The Invention of China in Modern World Making*. Cambridge, MA: Harvard University Press, 2004.

Liu, Lydia He. *Translingual Practice: Literature, National Culture, and Translated Modernity—China, 1900–1937*. Stanford: Stanford University Press, 1995.

Liu, William Guanglin. *The Chinese Market Economy, 1000–1500*. Albany: State University of New York Press, 2015.

Liu Zeng-He 劉增合. "Qingmo jin yan shiqi de yapian tongshui jiufen 清末禁煙時期的鴉片統稅糾紛 [Opium tax disputes during the period of late Qing opium-smoking prohibition]." *Jindai shi yanjiusuo jikan* 近代史研究所集刊 [Bulletin of the Institute of Modern History Academia Sinica] (2004): 53–104.

Lufrano, Richard. "Maintaining the Equilibrium: Balancing Interests of Commerce and Local Government." In *Dragons, Tigers, and Dogs: Qing Crisis Management and the Boundaries of State Power in Late Imperial China*, edited by Robert J. Antony and Jane Kate Leonard, 79–109. Ithaca: Cornell East Asia Program, 2002.

Luo Yudong 羅玉東. *Zhongguo lijin shi* 中國釐金史 [History of China's *lijin*]. 2 vols. Shanghai 上海: Shang wu yinshu guan 商務印書館, 1936.

Lutz, Catherine A. *Unnatural Emotions: Everyday Sentiments on a Micronesian Atoll and Their Challenge to Western Theory*. Chicago: University of Chicago Press, 1988.

Madancy, Joyce. "Unearthing Popular Attitudes toward the Opium Trade and Opium Suppression in Late Qing and Early Republican Fujian." *Modern China* 27, no. 4 (2001): 436–83.
Marx, Karl. *Capital: A Critique of Political Economy*. Vol. 1. Translated by Ben Fowkes. New York: Vintage Books, 1977.
Marx, Karl. *Capital: A Critique of Political Economy*. Vol. 2. Translated by David Fernbach. New York: Penguin, 1978.
Marx, Karl. *Capital: A Critique of Political Economy*. Vol. 3. Translated by David Fernbach. New York: Penguin, 1981.
Masya, Sasaki. "Ninpo shoninno rikin keigen seigan goshu [Petitions of Ningbo merchants for lightening *lijin* taxes]." *Toyo gakuho* 50, no. 1.
Mazumdar, Sucheta. *Sugar and Society: Peasants, Technology, and the World Market*. Cambridge, MA: Harvard University Asia Center, 1998.
Melancon, Glenn. *Britain's China Policy and the Opium Crisis: Balancing Drugs, Violence and National Honour, 1833–1840*. Burlington, VT: Ashgate, 2003.
Mêng, S. M. *The Tsungli Yamen: Its Organization and Functions*. Cambridge, MA: Harvard University, 1962.
Metzger, Thomas A. *The Internal Organization of Ch'ing Bureaucracy: Legal, Normative, and Communication Aspects*. Cambridge, MA: Harvard University Press, 1973.
Michael, Franz. *Regionalism in Nineteenth Century China*. Seattle: University of Washington Press, 1964.
Min, Tu-ki. *Men and Ideas in Modern Chinese History*. Seoul: Seoul National University Press, 1997.
Mokyr, Joel. "Accounting for the Industrial Revolution." In *The Cambridge Economic History of Modern Britain*, 2 vols., edited by Roderick Floud and Paul Johnson, 1:1–27. Cambridge: Cambridge University Press, 2004.
Moll-Murata, Christine. *State and Crafts in the Qing Dynasty (1644–1911)*. Amsterdam: Amsterdam University Press, 2018.
Montgomery, Walter. "The 'Remonstrance' of Feng Kuei-fen: A Confucian Search for Change in Nineteenth Century China." PhD diss., Brown University, 1979.
Morse, Hosea Ballou. *The Chronicles of the East India Company, Trading to China 1635–1834*. 5 vols. Oxford: Clarendon Press, 1926–1929.
Mote, Frederick. *Intellectual Foundations of China*. 2nd ed. New York: McGraw Hill, 1989.
Motono, Eiichi. *Conflict and Cooperation in Sino-British Business, 1860–1911: The Impact of the Pro-British Commercial Network in Shanghai*. New York: St. Martin's, 2000.
Motono, Eiichi. "'The Traffic Revolution': Remaking the Export Sales System in China, 1866–1875." *Modern China* 12, no. 1 (January 1986): 75–102.
Murphey, Rhoads. "The Treaty Ports and China's Modernization." In *The Chinese City between Two Worlds*, edited by Mark Elvin and G. William Skinner, 18–71. Stanford: Stanford University Press, 1974.
Naquin, Susan. *Peking: Temples and City Life, 1400–1900*. Berkeley: University of California Press, 2001.

Nathan, Andrew. "Imperialism's Effects on China." *Bulletin of Concerned Asian Scholars* 4, no. 4 (1972): 3–8.

Ng Chin-Keong. *Boundaries and Beyond: China's Maritime Southeast in Late Imperial Times*. Singapore: NUS Press, 2017.

Ng Chin-Keong. *Trade and Society: The Amoy Network on the China Coast, 1683–1735*. Singapore: Singapore University Press, 1983.

Ni, Yuping. *Customs Duties in the Qing Dynasty, ca. 1644–1911*. Leiden: Brill, 2017.

Nylan, Michael. *The Five "Confucian" Classics*. New Haven: Yale University Press, 2001.

Ocko, Jonathan K. *Bureaucratic Reform in Provincial China: Ting Jih-Ch'ang in Restoration Kiangsu, 1867–1870*. Cambridge, MA: Harvard University Press, 1983.

O'Leary, Richard. "Robert Hart in China: The Significance of His Irish Roots." *Modern Asian Studies* 40, no. 3 (July 2006): 583–604.

Osterhammel, Jürgen. "Semi-colonialism and Informal Empire in Twentieth Century China: Towards a Framework of Analysis." In *Imperialism and After: Continuities and Discontinuities*, edited by Wolfgang J. Mommsen and Jürgen Osterhammel, 290–314. London: Allen & Unwin, 1986.

Osterhammel, Jürgen. *The Transformation of the World: A Global History of the Nineteenth Century*. Princeton: Princeton University Press, 2014.

Parker, Jason H. "The Rise and Decline of I-Hsin, Prince Kung, 1858–1865: A Study of the Interaction of Politics and Ideology in Late Imperial China." PhD diss., Princeton University, 1979.

Parry, Clive, ed. *The Consolidated Treaty Series*. 243 vols. Dobbs Ferry, NY: Oceana Publications, 1969–1980.

Pashukanis, Evgeniĭ. *The General Theory of Law & Marxism*. New Brunswick, NJ: Transaction, 2002.

Peck, James. "The Roots of Rhetoric: Professional Ideology of America's China Watchers." *Bulletin of Concerned Asian Scholars* 2, no. 1 (October 1969): 59–69.

Pelcovits, Nathan. *Old China Hands and the Foreign Office*. New York: American Institute of Pacific Relations, 1948.

Perdue, Peter C. "Boundaries and Trade in the Early Modern World: Negotiations at Nerchinsk and Beijing." *Eighteenth-Century Studies* 43, no. 3 (2010): 341–56.

Perry, Elizabeth. *Challenging the Mandate of Heaven: Social Protest and State Power in China*. Armonk: M. E. Sharpe, 2002.

Pines, Yuri. Introduction to *Ideology of Power and Power of Ideology in Early China*, edited by Yuri Pines, Paul Goldin, and Martin Kern, 1–29. Leiden: Brill, 2015.

Plaks, Andrew. "*Xin* as the Seat of the Emotions in Confucian Self-Cultivation." In *Love, Hatred, and Other Passions: Questions and Themes on Emotions in Chinese Civilization*, edited by Paolo Santangelo and Donatella Guida, 113–25. Leiden: Brill, 2006.

Polanyi, Karl. *The Great Transformation: The Political and Economic Origins of Our Time*. 2nd ed. Boston: Beacon, 2001.

Pomeranz, Kenneth. *The Making of a Hinterland: State, Society, and Economy in Inland North China, 1853–1937*. Berkeley: University of California Press, 1993.

Pong, David. "The Income and Military Expenditure of Kiangsi Province in the Last Years (1860–1864) of the Taiping Rebellion." *Journal of Asian Studies* 26, no. 1 (November 1966): 49–65.

Poovey, Mary. *A History of the Modern Fact: Problems of Knowledge in the Sciences of Wealth and Society*. Chicago: University of Chicago Press, 1998.

Postone, Moishe. *Time, Labor, and Social Domination: A Reinterpretation of Marx's Critical Theory*. Cambridge: Cambridge University Press, 1993.

Prazniak, Roxann. "Tax Protest at Laiyang, Shandong, 1910: Commoner Organization versus the County Political Elite." *Modern China* 6, no. 1 (January 1980): 41–71.

Qi Meiqin 祁美琴. *Qingdai queguan zhidu yanjiu* 清代榷關制度研究 [Research on the Qing customs system]. Hohot 呼和浩市: Nemenggu daxue chubanshe 內蒙古大學出版社, 2004.

Qiao, George. "The Rise of Shanxi Merchants: Empire, Institutions, and Social Change in Qing China, 1688–1850." PhD diss., Stanford University, 2017.

Rankin, Mary B. *Elite Activism and Political Transformation in China: Zhejiang Province, 1865–1911*. Stanford: Stanford University Press, 1986.

Rankin, Mary B., John K. Fairbank, and Albert Feuerwerker. "Introduction: Perspectives on Modern China's History." In *The Cambridge History of China*. Vol. 13, *Republican China, 1912–1949, Part 2*, edited by John K. Fairbank and Albert Feuerwerker, 1–73. Cambridge: Cambridge University Press, 1986.

Rawski, Thomas G. "Chinese Dominance of Treaty Port Commerce and Its Implications, 1860–1875." *Explorations in Economic History* 7, no. 1–2 (Autumn 1969): 451–73.

Reed, Bradley. *Talons and Teeth: County Clerks and Runners in the Qing Dynasty*. Stanford: Stanford University Press, 2000.

Reinhardt, Anne. *Navigating Semi-colonialism: Shipping, Sovereignty, and Nation-Building in China, 1860–1937*. Cambridge, MA: Harvard University Asia Center, 2018.

Reinhardt, Anne. "Treaty Ports as Shipping Infrastructure." In *Treaty Ports in Modern China: Land, Law, and Power*, edited by Robert Bickers and Isabella Jackson, 101–20. London: Routledge, 2016.

Reynolds, Douglas. *China, 1898–1912: The Xinzheng Revolution and Japan*. Cambridge, MA: Council on East Asian Studies, Harvard University, 1993.

Rockefeller, Stuart. "Flow." *Current Anthropology* 52, no. 4 (August 2011): 557–78.

Rogaski, Ruth. *Hygienic Modernity: Meanings of Health and Disease in Treaty-Port China*. Berkeley: University of California Press, 2004.

Rowe, William. *Hankow: Commerce and Society in a Chinese City, 1796–1889*. Stanford: Stanford University Press, 1984.

Rowe, William. *Saving the World: Chen Hongmou and Elite Consciousness in Eighteenth-Century China*. Stanford: Stanford University Press, 2001.

Rowe, William. *Speaking of Profit: Bao Shichen and Reform in Nineteenth Century China*. Cambridge, MA: Harvard University East Asian Research Center, 2018.

Rudolph, Jennifer M. *Negotiated Power in Late Imperial China: The Zongli Yamen and the Politics of Reform*. Ithaca: East Asia Program, Cornell University, 2008.

Ruskola, Teemu. *Legal Orientalism: China, the United States, and Modern Law*. Cambridge, MA: Harvard University Press, 2013.

Salzinger, Leslie. *Genders in Production: Making Workers in Mexico's Global Factories*. Berkeley: University of California Press, 2003.

Sartori, Andrew. *Bengal in Global Concept History: Culturalism in the Age of Capital*. Chicago: University of Chicago Press, 2008.

Sassen, Saskia. *Territory, Authority, Rights: From Medieval to Global Assemblages*. Princeton: Princeton University Press, 2006.

Schecter, Darrow. *The Critique of Instrumental Reason from Weber to Habermas*. New York: Continuum, 2010.

Schoppa, R. Keith. *Chinese Elites and Political Change: Zhejiang Province in the Early Twentieth Century*. Cambridge, MA: Harvard University Press, 1982.

Schrecker, John E. *The Chinese Revolution in Historical Perspective*. New York: Greenwood, 1991.

Scully, Eileen. *Bargaining with the State from Afar: American Citizenship in Treaty Port China, 1844–1942*. New York: Columbia University Press, 2001.

Seok, Bongrae. *Embodied Moral Psychology and Confucian Philosophy*. Lanham, MD: Lexington Books, 2013.

Sewell, William H., Jr. *Capitalism and the Emergence of Civic Equality in Eighteenth Century France*. Chicago: University of Chicago Press, 2021.

Sewell, William H., Jr. "Connecting Capitalism to the French Revolution." *Critical Historical Studies* 1, no. 1 (2014): 5–46.

Sewell, William H., Jr. "The Capitalist Epoch." *Social Science History* 38 (Spring 2014): 1–11.

Skinner, G. William. "Cities and the Hierarchy of Local Systems." In *The City in Late Imperial China*, 273–351. Stanford: Stanford University Press, 1977.

Spector, Stanley. *Li Hung-chang and the Huai Army: A Study in Nineteenth Century Chinese Regionalism*. Seattle: University of Washington Press, 1964.

Strauss, Julia. "Creating 'Virtuous and Talented' Officials for the Twentieth Century: Discourse and Practice in Xinzheng China." *Modern Asian Studies* 37, no. 4 (October 2003): 831–50.

Sun E-Tu Zen. "The Board of Revenue in 19th Century China." *Harvard Journal of Asiatic Studies* 24 (1962–1963): 175–228.

Sun Zuji 孫祖基. *Bupingdeng tiaoyue taolun dagang* 不平等條約討論大綱 [Discussion of the unequal treaties]. Beijing 北京: Beijing zhongxian tuofang keji fazhan youxian gongsi 北京中獻拓方科技發展有限公司, 2012.

Tang Xianlong 湯象龍, ed. *Zhongguo jindai haiguan shuishou he fen tongji, 1861–1910* 中國近代海關稅收和分配統, 1861–1910 [Statistics on customs revenue collection and distribution in modern China, 1861–1910]. Beijing 北京: Zhonghua shuju 中華書局, 1992.

Teng, Ssuyu, and John Fairbank. *China's Response to the West*. Cambridge, MA: Harvard University Press, 1954.

Thai, Philip. *China's War on Smuggling: Law, Economic Life, and the Making of the Modern State, 1842–1965*. New York: Columbia University Press, 2018.

Thilly, Peter. *The Opium Business: A History of Crime and Capitalism in Maritime China*. Stanford: Stanford University Press, 2022.
Thompson, E. P. *The Making of the English Working Class*. New York: Vintage Books, 1963.
Topik, Steven C., and Allen Wells. "Commodity Chains in a Global Economy." In *A World Connecting, 1870–1945*, edited by Emily S. Rosenberg, 593–812. Cambridge, MA: Harvard University Press, 2012.
Torbert, Preston M. *The Ch'ing Imperial Household Department: A Study of Its Organization and Principal Functions, 1662–1796*. Cambridge, MA: Harvard University Council on East Asian Studies, 1977.
Tribe, Keith. "'Industrialisation' as a Historical Category." In *Genealogies of Capitalism*, 101–20. Atlantic Highlands, NJ: Humanities Press, 1981.
Trocki, Carl A. *Opium, Empire, and the Global Political Economy: A Study of the Asian Opium Trade, 1750–1950*. London: Routledge, 1999.
Tsai, Weipin. "The Inspector General's Last Prize: The Chinese Native Customs Service, 1901–31." *Journal of Imperial and Commonwealth History* 36, no. 2 (2008): 243–58.
Tsin, Michael. *Nation, Governance, and Modernity in China: Canton, 1900–1927*. Stanford: Stanford University Press, 1999.
Tu Wei-ming. *Confucian Thought: Selfhood as Creative Transformation*. Albany: State University of New York Press, 1985.
Tucker, Robert C., ed. *The Marx-Engels Reader*. 2nd ed. New York: Norton, 1978.
Van de Ven, Hans. *Breaking with the Past: The Maritime Customs Service and the Global Origins of Modernity in China*. New York: Columbia University Press, 2014.
Van Dyke, Paul A. *Merchants of Canton and Macao: Politics and Strategies in Eighteenth-Century Chinese Trade*. Hong Kong: Hong Kong University Press, 2011.
Van Dyke, Paul A. *The Canton Trade: Life and Enterprise on the China Coast, 1700–1845*. Hong Kong: Hong Kong University Press, 2005.
Von Glahn, Richard. "Modalities of the Fiscal State in Imperial China." *Journal of Chinese History* 4 no. 1 (January 2020): 1–29.
Von Glahn, Richard. *The Economic History of China: From Antiquity to the Nineteenth Century*. Cambridge: Cambridge University Press, 2016.
Wakeman, Frederic, Jr. *Telling Chinese History: A Selection of Essays*. Edited by Lea H. Wakeman. Berkeley: University of California Press, 2009.
Wakeman, Frederic, Jr. "The Evolution of Local Control in Late Imperial China." In *Conflict and Control in Late Imperial China*, edited by Frederic Wakeman Jr. and Carolyn Grant, 1–25. Berkeley: University of California Press, 1975.
Wakeman, Frederic, Jr. *The Fall of Imperial China*. New York: Free Press, 1975.
Walker, Kathy Le Mons. *Chinese Modernity and the Peasant Path: Semicolonialism in the Northern Yangzi Delta*. Stanford: Stanford University Press, 1999.
Wallerstein, Immanuel. *The Modern World System III: The Second Era of the Great Expansion of the Capitalist World Economy, 1730–1840s*. London: Academic Press, 1989.
Wang, Dong. *China's Unequal Treaties: Narrating National History*. Lanham, MD: Lexington Books, 2005.

Wang, Hui. "From Empire to State: Kang Youwei, Confucian Universalism, and Unity." In *Chinese Visions of World Order: Tianxia, Culture, and World Politics*, edited and translated by Ban Wang, 49–64. Durham, NC: Duke University Press, 2017.

Wang, Shên-tsu. *The Margary Affair and the Chefoo Agreement*. London: Oxford University Press, 1940.

Wang Tieya 王鐵崖, ed. *Zhong wai jiu yuezhang huibian* 中外舊約章彙編 [Collection of China's historical international treaties]. 3 vols. Beijing 北京: Shenghuo, dushu, xinzhi san lian shudian, 生活，讀書，新知三聯書店, 1982.

Watt, John. *The District Magistrate in Late Imperial China*. New York: Columbia University Press, 1972.

Waung, W. S. K. *The Controversy: Opium and Sino-British Relations, 1858–1887*. Hong Kong: Lun Men Press, 1977.

Weber, Isabella M. "China's Ancient Principles of Price Regulation through Market Participation: The *Guanzi* from a Comparative Perspective." In *European and Chinese Histories of Economic Thought: Theories and Images of Good Governance*, edited by Iwo Amelung and Bertram Schefold, 246–58. London: Routledge, 2021.

Webster, Anthony. *The Twilight of the East India Company: The Evolution of Anglo-Asian Commerce and Politics, 1790–1860*. Martlesham, UK: Boydell & Brewer, 2009.

Wells, Richard Evan. "The Manchurian Bean: How the Soybean Shaped the Modern History of China's Northeast, 1862–1945." PhD diss., University of Wisconsin–Madison, 2018.

Wen, Betty Peh-T'i. *Ruan Yuan, 1764–1849: The Life and Work of a Major Scholar Official in Nineteenth Century China before the Opium War*. Hong Kong: Hong Kong University Press, 2006.

Will, Pierre-Etienne, and R. Bin Wong. *Nourish the People: The State Civilian Granary System in China, 1650–1850*. Ann Arbor: University of Michigan Press, 1991.

Williamson, Jeffrey G. "Regional Inequality and the Process of National Development: A Description of Patterns." *Economic Development and Cultural Change* 13, no. 4, pt. 2 (1965): 3–47.

Wise, Norton, and Crosbie Smith. "Work and Waste: Political Economy and Natural Philosophy in Nineteenth Century Britain (1)." *History of Science* 27, no. 3 (1989): 263–301.

Wise, Norton, and Crosbie Smith. "Work and Waste: Political Economy and Natural Philosophy in Nineteenth Century Britain (2)." *History of Science* 27, no. 4 (1989): 391–449.

Wise, Norton, and Crosbie Smith. "Work and Waste: Political Economy and Natural Philosophy in Nineteenth Century Britain (3)." *History of Science* 28, no. 3 (1990): 221–61.

Wong, John D. *Global Trade in the Nineteenth Century: The House of Houqua and the Canton System*. Cambridge: Cambridge University Press, 2016.

Wong, J. Y. *Deadly Dreams: Opium and the Arrow War (1856–1860) in China*. Cambridge: Cambridge University Press, 1998.

Wong, R. Bin. "Coping with Poverty and Famine: Material Welfare, Public Goods, and Chinese Approaches to Governance." In *Public Goods Provision in the Early Modern*

Economy: Comparative Perspectives from Japan, China, and Europe, edited by Masayuki Tanimoto and R. Bin Wong, 130–46. Berkeley: University of California Press, 2019.

Wong, R. Bin. "Opium and Modern State Making." In *Opium Regimes: China, Britain, and Japan, 1839–1952*, edited by Timothy Brook and Bob Wakabayashi, 189–211. Berkeley: University of California Press, 2000.

Wong, R. Bin. "Taxation and Good Governance in China, 1500–1914." In *The Global Rise of Fiscal States: A Global History, 1500–1914*, edited by Bartolomé Yun-Casalilla and Patrick K. O'Brien, with Francisco Comin Comin, 353–77. Cambridge: Cambridge University Press, 2012.

Wood, Ellen Meiksins. *Empire of Capital*. New York: Verso, 2003.

Worcester, G. R. G. *The Junks and Sampans of the Yangtze*. Annapolis: Naval Institute Press, 1971.

Wright, Mary C. *The Last Stand of Chinese Conservatism: The T'ung-chih Restoration, 1862–1874*. Stanford: Stanford University Press, 1957.

Wright, Stanley. *China's Struggle for Tariff Autonomy, 1843–1938*. Shanghai: Kelly & Walsh, 1938.

Wright, Stanley. *Hart and the Chinese Customs*. Belfast: W. Mullan, 1950.

Wright, Stanley. *Kiangsi Native Trade and Its Taxation*. Shanghai: n.p., 1920.

Wu, James T. K. "The Impact of the Taiping Rebellion upon the Manchu Fiscal System." *Pacific Historical Review* 19, no. 3 (1950): 265–75.

Wu, Shellen Xiao. *Empires of Coal: Fueling China's Entry into the Modern World Order, 1860–1920*. Stanford: Stanford University Press, 2015.

Xiang Lanxin. *The Origins of the Boxer War: A Multinational Study*. New York: RoutledgeCurzon, 2003.

Xu Dixin and Wu Chengming. *Chinese Capitalism, 1522–1840*. Translated by Li Zhengde, Liang Miaoru, and Li Siping. New York: St. Martin's, 2000.

Xue, Yong. "A Fertilizer Revolution? A Critical Response to Pomeranz's Theory of Geographic Luck." *Modern China* 33, no. 2 (April 2007): 195–229.

Yeh, Wen-Hsin. *Shanghai Splendor: Economic Sentiments and the Making of Modern China, 1843–1949*. Berkeley: University of California Press, 2008.

Yue, Meng. *Shanghai and the Edges of Empire*. Minneapolis: University of Minnesota Press, 2006.

Zanasi, Margherita. *Economic Thought in Modern China: Market and Consumption c. 1500–1937*. Cambridge: Cambridge University Press, 2020.

Zarrow, Peter. *After Empire: The Conceptual Transformation of the Chinese State, 1885–1924*. Stanford: Stanford University Press, 2012.

Zelin, Madeline. *The Magistrate's Tael: Rationalizing Fiscal Reform in Eighteenth Century Ch'ing China*. Berkeley: University of California Press, 1984.

Zelin, Madeline. *The Merchants of Zigong: Industrial Entrepreneurship in Early Modern China*. New York: Columbia University Press, 2005.

Zhang, Lawrence. *Power for a Price: The Purchase of Official Appointments in Qing China*. Cambridge, MA: Harvard University Press, 2022.

Zhang, Meng. *Timber and Forestry in Qing China: Sustaining the Market*. Seattle: University of Washington Press, 2021.

Zhao, Gang. *The Qing Opening to the Ocean: Chinese Maritime Policies, 1684–1757*. Honolulu: University of Hawai'i Press, 2013.

Zheng Beijun 鄭備軍. *Zhongguo jindai lijin zhidu yanjiu* 中國近代厘金制度研究 [Research on China's modern *lijin* system]. Beijing 北京: Zhongguo caizheng jingji chubanshe 中國財政經濟出版社, 2004.

Zhongguo zibenzhuyi mengya wenti taolun ji 中國資本主義萌芽問題討論集 [Collected essays on the question of the sprouts of capitalism in China]. Beijing 北京: Xinhua shudian 新華書店, 1957.

Zhou Jiming and Lei Ping, "*Qingdai jingshi sichao yanjiu shuping*" 清代經世思潮研究述評 [Critique of Studies on Qing Dynasty Jingshi Thought]. *Hanxue yanjiu tongxun* 漢學研究通訊 25 (2006): 1–10.

Zito, A. R. "City Gods, Filiality, and Hegemony in Late Imperial China." *Modern China* 13, no. 3 (1987): 333–71.

Index

Page numbers in bold refer to figures and tables.

abstract domination, 11–12; treaties and, 28–29
Addis, Charles, 117
Alcock Convention, 148
Alcock, Rutherford, 132–33, 147, 150–51, 156, 164
Arrighi, Giovanni (*The Long Twentieth Century*), 225
Arrow War (1856–1860), 15

Bao Sichen, 143–44
bing zheng (joint collection), 184, 185–86, 190, 204
Black Tea Hong. See *Xie Xing Gong*
Board of Revenue (*Hubu*), 65, 73, 182, 191, 207, 208, 212
Board of Trade (London), 153
Boat Inspection Guild (Ningbo), 103
Boecking, Felix, 58
boundaries, 113, 147, 177, 179; between foreign trade and Chinese trade, 151, 152, 153; between taxes, 169–70, 173–75; jurisdictional within ports, 163, 164–65, 167–68; territorial, 154, 155, 158, 224–25
Boxer Protocol, 203, 204
Boxer Rebellion, 202–3
British Legation (Beijing), 75, 78, 110–11, 115, 124, 129, 131–32, 139, 147, 156
Bruce, Frederick, 124–26, 137
Buchanan, W.M., 61–62

bureaucratic reform: in Europe, 62–63

"Canton system," 31, 46–48, 223; British criticism of, 32; paperwork and, 76–77, port charges, 47, **48**. See also *Yuehaiguan*
cao yun (tribute rice), 122, 123, 128, 134
Capital (Marx), 11
capital: bureaucratic process and, 83, 86, 87; ceaseless accumulation, 137, 139, 176; coercion and, 11, 136, 225; as dominant social form, 21, 118–19, 138, 222; essence of, 11; global circuits, 89–90; growth in China, 115, 125–26, 166; growth in Great Britain, 30, 137, 166; merchant, 3, 117, 118, 119, 123, 134; mode of production and, 138; multinational, 71, 110, 112, 114, 217; political subjecthood and, 112, 115; Sino-foreign, 87, 221; sovereignty and, 165, 176, 215, 222, 225; taxation and, 169, 172–74, 220; territory and, 222; as virus, 9–10, 20, 216, 222
capitalism: historiography, 12–13
changguan (regular customs), 69–70, 73, 80, 85, 92–93, 96, 110, 112, 180, 201, 217
Chefoo Convention, 142, 148, 168, 184, 185, 187
Chen Hongmou, 133

Chinese Maritime Customs. *See* Imperial Maritime Customs
Cixi (Empress Dowager), 14, 113
coercion: abstract, 135, 137, 207, 214, 225–26; law and, 29; modernization paradigm and, 7; overt, 28, 131, 135, 136, 203, 225; treaties and, 28, 29, 103, 136, 225. *See also* abstract domination
commercial revolution: in China, 3, 6
commodity circulation: accelerated, 118, 125–26, 131, 133; in China, 87, 90, 91; embraced by Qing authorities, 133, 137; and emergence of capitalism, 123; geographies of, 181; as object of governance, 214, 217, 222; political jurisdiction and, 155; purpose of, 118, 124–25, 128–29, 130, 134–35, 137, 223; shaped by capital, 138–39, 176; tax-free, 197, 206, 211
commodity form, 11
Conference of Foreign Ministers, 174–75
consular mediation (British), 24, 47, 78, 99, 100, 102–6, 110, 115, 116, 124, 150–52, 153, 156, 158, 171–72
costs of circulation, 27, 69, 217
culturalist paradigm: critique of, 7, 15, 16
customs protocols, 49. *See also* Imperial Maritime Customs, *Yuehaiguan*

daotai (circuit intendents), 15, 211–12; at Dengzhou, 153; at Hankou, 104, 106; at Jiujiang, 171–72, 175; at Ningbo, 24, 64–65, 85, 109, 112; at Shanghai, 169
debt (sovereign), 199, 202, 204, 217, 223, 226; Imperial Maritime Customs, and, 199, 201, 207
Deleuze, Gilles, 19
deterritorialization: abstract domination and, 29; of Chinese produce trade, 91, 99, 103–4, 133, 172; resistance to, 102–4; reterritorialization and, 19–20, 119, 154, 206–7, 221; treaties and, 27–28, 54, 89, 177. *See also* reterritorialization
drawbacks, 74–76, 78, 217
Drew, Edward B. (IMC Commissioner), 55
Drummond, W. V., 164
"dual economy," 181
Duanfang, 210
Dunstan, Helen, 126

East India Company (British), 31, 32
economic integration: within China, 3, 119, 126, 137–38; drawbacks and, 74; exemption certificates and, 71; global, 51, 122, 198, 202, 224; treaties and, 26–27, 54, 88
economic thought: in China, 21–22, 144
Elman, Benjamin, 37
emperorship: Guangxu, 191, 199, 219; Yongzheng, 14, 182, 191, 196, 209; Qianlong, 15, 60, 133, 143, 180, 223; Tongzhi, 113
en (imperial grace), 41–42
engine science, 61, 67–68, 79, 80, 81, 83, 84, 85
exemption certificate, 69, 70–72, 78, 217
extraterritoriality, 88, 91, 99, 113; British property and, 99–100, 115

Fairbank, John King, 6–7, 15, 53, 57
Fang Xing, 123
Feng Guifen, 143
Finance Ministry (*caizheng ju*), 211, 212, 220
"fiscal state," 142
flag: as basis for regulatory jurisdiction, 108, 109, 110, 209
Foreign Office (British), 163–64, 185, 188
Forrest, R. J. (consul), 150
Foucault, Michel, 183n15, 194, 217
fuguo (enrich the state), 183
fuqiang (wealth and power), 143, 204

Gingell, Raymond (consul), 102–3, 105–6

governance, commercial: abstract equivalence in, 215–16; depersonalization of, 45–48, 50, 54, 62, 80, 188, 189, 207, 213, 214, 223; ends of, 223; local specificity, 14, 25, 32, 72, 94, 100, 102–3, 223; new model for, 85, 178, 185, 214, 215, 218, 223; political choices and, 140; use values and, 223; value and, 139, 223
governance, local: 88, 103, 220, 222–23
governance, Qing: capital and, 226; conceptual shifts, 16–17; diversity within, 13–14, 80n102, 215; economic laws and, 139; embodied, 37, 39; emperorship, 14, 42–43, 216, 223; fiscal strategy, 142, 143–44, 158, 177, 213; flexibility within, 25, 215; frugality, 127, 143; growth and, 197, 198, 205, 223; institutional reorganization, 203–4; limited by treaty, 50, 88, 103, 112, 154, 162, 164, 219; shifts within, 16–17, 85–86, 177–78, 183, 189–90, 195, 197, 206–7, 212, 213–14, 217, 221–22, 226; subjectivity and, 17, 39–40, 50, 54, 191–92, 193, 209, 214; threat to foreign capital, 141, 151, 153–54, 162, 165, 176; textual tradition and, 18, 36–37, 39–40, 215
Grand Council (*Junjichu*), 191, 211
Guan Wen, 98
Guattari, Felix, 19
Guiliang, 96

Halsey, Stephen, 16
Hankou, 4, 5, 24–25, 100, 102–7, 111, 159
Hardt, Michael (*Empire*), 225
Hart, Roger, 59–60, 116, 177–78, 190, 204, 208, 221; critique of Qing customs management, 59. *See also* Imperial Maritime Customs
Hevia, James L., 19–20, 58, 203
Hong Kong, 8, 74, 96, 155, 178, 186–87
Horkheimer, Max, 55

Horowitz, Richard, 16
Hughes, P. J. (consul), 171–72

Imperial Maritime Customs (IMC): as alien, 217; collection costs, 60, 62, 63–64, 67; collection and expenditure reports, 65, **66**; domestic commodity circulation and, 95; early accounts of, 57; growth and, 56–86, 95, 217, 221; imperialism and, 57; institutional design, 59, 62, 67, 79–84; instrumental reason and, 85, 221; jurisdiction, 177–78, 185, 201, 206, 217, 220; "mechanical correctness," 60–61, 67, 83, 185; modernity and, 57–58; opium taxation and, 187–90, 194, 212; paperwork, 77–79, 188, 212–13; sovereign debt and, 199, 201, 207; time and, 81–82; trade reports, 58
instrumental reason, 55, 85, 221, 224
Isett, Christopher, 146

Janku, Andrea, 16–17, 196, 197
Jardine, William, 31
jia shui mian li (increase taxes and eliminate lijin), 184
jingshi, 18. *See also* statecraft thought
Jiujiang, 70, 93, 107, 109, 110–11, 112, 156, 157, 159, 170, 171–73, 201
Jones, Susan Mann, 149–50, 195
juan (tax/contribution), 170, 182; consolidation of, 210
junks, 125, 180, 181

Kang Youwei, 216
Ke Fengshi, 210, 211

Lam, Tong, 16
lan zhi zhao (blue receipt), 212–13
Lavelle, Peter, 144
Lenin, Vladimir, 225
Levenson, Joseph, 15
Liao River, 119

Li Hongzhang, 14, 116–17, 128, 130, 148, 153, 168, 185, 186, 192, 204, 216, 224
lijin, 93–94, 144–46, **160**, **161**, 180, 181, 205, 217; abolition of, 205–6; Chinese merchant protests against, 149–50; Chinese critique of, 183, 195–96, 198; collection of, 74, 105, 156, 159–62, 218; consolidation of, 194, 210, 211; corruption and, 146, 166–67, 191; defense of, 165–67, 207–8; Euroamerican protests against, 141, 147, 148, 150–52, 153, 156–57, 159, 162–64, 171, 174, 176, 205; rectification (*zheng dun*), 191–92; related arrests, 24, 163–64; as supersign, 145; transit passes and, 24, 102, 155–56, 173
Lin Zexu, 34; letter to Queen Victoria, 34–35
Liu, Andrew, 16, 17, 117, 197
Liu, Lydia, 44, 145
Liu Qiyu (magistrate), 102
liutong (circulation), 130, 133
loans (Qing government), **200**, 201
lorcha, 111–12
Loureiro, Pedro, 163
luodi shui ("grower's tax"), 171, 172–73, 175, 208
Lutz, Catherine, 40
Luxemburg, Rosa, 225

Ma Jianzhong, 198
Macao, 76–77, 178, 186–87
Manchester Chamber of Commerce, 31
Mao Hongbin, 98, 99
market: self-regulating, 29, 135, 140, 189
Marx, Karl, 10n28, 21, 100, 138, 139, 154n52, 176n123; *Capital*, 11
Mayers, W. F. (William) (Chinese secretary), 153, 173
Mazumdar, Sucheta, 12, 131
mercantilism, 196

mian shui dan. *See* exemption certificate
Ministry of Foreign Affairs (*waiwu bu*), 203
Mixed Court, 163
modernization paradigm: critique of, 7–8
"most-favored nation," 43–44

Naquin, Susan, 218
Negri, Antonio (*Empire*), 225
New Policies (*xin zheng*), 142, 203, 219

objectification: in treaty language, 42–43
opium, 4; merchant taxation of, 188–89; taxes, 148, 159, 184–85, 194; tax unification, 210, 211–13, 217; trade at Chongqing, 194. *See also bing zheng*
Opium War (1839–1842), 8, 50

Polanyi, Karl, 140
political economy: in Great Britain, 30, 61–62; in China, 17, 20, 60, 116, 137, 196, 197, 214
Pomeranz, Kenneth, 213–14
Postone, Moishe, 11–12, 29
Poyang Lake, 110–11
pragmatism, 224

qing (nature and mind), 38; commercial governance and, 35, 36, 38
Qing Empire: end of, 218–19, 223, 226
Qiying, 35

regulatory apparatus (treaty-based), 9–10, 56; ambiguity, 88, 91, 96, 107, 114–15; asymmetrical, 91, 94; disorder and, 114; plurality, 91, 92, 95–96, 112, 181
Reinhardt, Anne, 9
Republic of China: fiscal proposals, 220; global capital and, 226
reterritorialization: of Chinese merchants, 91, 112, 222, 225; of Chinese ships, 111, 225; exemption certificates and, 71–72; Imperial Maritime Customs

and, 59; of ports, 221; resistance to, 115, 159; transit pass and, 159, 177; of territory, 177, 179; vectors of, 215. *See also* deterritorialization
revenue: customs, 60, 180–81, 205, 220; evasion, 192; fraud, 78, 88, 94, 96, 109, 147; losses, 72, 181, 186, 191
Richard, Timothy, 197
"rights": in treaty language, 43–44
Rowe, William, 5, 105, 144
Rudolph, Jennifer, 15, 16

sampan, 103–4
san lian dan. See transit pass
Sassen, Saskia, 13
scale, 72–73, 198, 209–10, 214, 215, 219
sha chuan, 118, 119, 121, 122, 123, 130, 131, 134, 137
shang zhan (commercial warfare), 206
Shanghai, 70, 117, 121, 128–29, 131–32, 159–60; Bean Cake Association, 121; Municipal Council (SMC), 163, 168, 169
Shen Baozhen, 93, 154, 166, 168–69
Sheng Xuanhuai, 204–5, 216
shi (disposition), 35, 37, 98, 130
ship: as basis for regulatory jurisdiction, 108, 109, 111, 112
shipping: competition, 118, 124–25, 128
silver: value of, 202
Smith, Crosbie, 67
smuggling, 88, 98, 125, 163, 192, 221. *See also* revenue fraud
social reproduction, 117, 134–35, 138, 139, 176
sovereignty, 89, 91, 113, 115, 155, 163, 165, 174, 221, 225
soy trade, 117, 119, 121, 123–25, 127; embargo at Shanghai, 131–33
space-time compression, 83, 217
spatial fix: capital and, 30–31, 50–51, 114; China and, 20, 52–53, 225
state: building, 224; strengthening, 16

statecraft thought (*jingshi*), 17–18, 128n35, 196–97; *Huangchao jingshi xinbian*, 196–97
Superintendent of Customs, 24, 47, 49, 64, 77, 84–85, 110, 128, 130, 177–78
Supreme Court of China and Japan, 164

Taiping Rebellion, 113, 127, 129, 156, 182, 199
tax exemptions (non-treaty), 123
taxation (commercial): proposals to change, 144, 148, 181–82, 186, 193, 195–96, 198, 202, 204–5, 206, 208; by provincial governments, 167, 182; treaty limits on, 24–25, 153. See also *lijin*
tea trade, 4, 104–6, 156, 171–73, 205
territoriality, 183, 185, 222, 223; homogenization of, 183, 213–14, 222
Thai, Philip, 16, 88
Thilly, Peter, 186
"tipping point," 13
Traeger, 100
transit duty (*ban shui*), 94
transit pass, 1–2, 24, 69, 73–74, 102, 104–5, 155–56, 169, 173, 177, 217; territorial boundaries and, 155–56, 158, 159. See also *lijin*
treaties: abstract domination and, 28–29; as mechanism of control, 54; sovereignty and, 28; spatial fix and, 52–53, 221
treaty: Danish, 132; interpretation, 24, 91–92, 96, 99–100, 102–3, 105–7, 110–12, 153–54, 165, 168; making as global phenomenon, 26–28; obligations in China, 25, 50, 89
Treaty: of Hoomun Chai, 41; Mackay, 183, 205–6, 220; of Nanjing, 8, 35, 46, 48; of Tianjin, 8, 45; of Whampoa (French), 43; of Wang-Hea (U.S.), 44; revision, 142, 148, 202
treaty language: ambiguous, 107; interpellation and, 45, 50, 54;

non-correspondence between English and Chinese, 41–43, 108
"treaty port system," 56, 71
Trevelyan, Charles, 62
tribute rice. See *cao yun*

use values: circulation of, 118, 119, 214; relationship to value, 139

value: mediation, 11, 29, 118–19, 139, 175; role in governance, 215; sovereignty and, 183, 224; as wealth, 11, 139
van de Ven, Hans, 16, 58, 59
van Dyke, Paul, 48, 77, 90

wealth: different definitions of, 117–18, 139
Wade, Thomas, 147–48, 153, 167, 173, 185
Wallerstein, Immanuel, 54
Wang Guodong, 133
Wang Tao, 195–96
Wenxiang, 24, 96
Whewell, William, 67
Williams, S. Wells, 47
Wise, Norton, 67
Wong, R. Bin, 147
Wood, Ellen Meiksins, 225
Wright, Mary, 15
Wright, Stanley, 57
Wu Chengming, 12

Xie Xing Gong (Black Tea Hong), 105–6
xin (heart-mind), 39; commercial governance and, 34, 36, 38; governance and, 40
xing (original nature), 38; commercial governance and, 35, 36, 38
Xu Dixin, 12
Xue Fucheng, 197

Yangzi River, 70, 74–75, 93, 96, 113, **157**, 166, 184
Yantai, xi, 123–24, 128, 130–31
Yichang, 210
Yi-li-bu, 35
yindi zhiyi, 155, 158, 182–83
Yingkou, xi, 72, 119, 121, 123, 128, 130–32, 134
Yixin (Imperial Prince), 24, 39, 55–56, 71, 96, 128n32, 132, 148, 216
Yuehaiguan, 76–77, 95

Zarrow, Peter, 18, 41
Zelin, Madeline, 122, 182, 209
Zeng Guofan, 14, 39, 109, 132–33, 170–71
Zhang Meng, 122
Zhang Zhidong, 18, 192, 193, 208
Zheng Guanying, 195–96
Zongli geguo shiwu yamen (Zongli yamen), 24–25, 55–56, 65, 71–73, 79, 95–96, 109–10, 115, 117, 124–25, 127, 129, 132–33, 147, 150–51, 154, 158, 165–66, 175, 177, 191, 194, 204
Zuo Zongtang, 93, 144, 186, 192